Islands of Hope

Indigenous Resource Management
in a Changing Pacific

Islands of Hope

Indigenous Resource Management
in a Changing Pacific

**Edited by Paul D'Arcy and
Daya Dakasi Da-Wei Kuan**

Australian
National
University

ANU PRESS

PACIFIC SERIES

In memory of Papa Mape and his lifetime of marine conservation and guardianship of traditional learning.
19 May 1932 – 30 October 2013

Australian
National
University

ANU PRESS

Published by ANU Press
The Australian National University
Canberra ACT 2600, Australia
Email: anupress@anu.edu.au

Available to download for free at press.anu.edu.au

ISBN (print): 9781760465612
ISBN (online): 9781760465629

WorldCat (print): 1366227944
WorldCat (online): 1362406486

DOI: 10.22459/IH.2023

Printed by Lightning Source
ingramcontent.com/publishers-page/environmental-responsibility

Cover design and layout by ANU Press. Cover photograph: Papa Mape by Poema Duprel.

This book is published under the aegis of the Pacific editorial board of ANU Press.

Contents

Section Two: Reviving the land and the sea

Section Three: Local Responses to Climate Change

Section Four: Pacific Lessons for Humanity

Abbreviations

ADP	Ad Hoc Working Group on the Durban Platform for Enhanced Action
AOSIS	Alliance of Small Island States
COP	Conference of the Parties
CROP	Council of Regional Organisations in the Pacific
CSIRO	Commonwealth Scientific and Industrial Research Organisation
EEZ	exclusive economic zone
FSM	Federated States of Micronesia
GHG	greenhouse gas
GIS	geographic information system
HLSM	High-Level Support Mechanism
IEK	Indigenous ecological knowledge
IMF	International Monetary Fund
IPA	Indigenous protected area
IPPC	Intergovernmental Panel on Climate Change
IUCN	International Union for Conservation of Nature
LDC	Least-Developed Countries
MAFA	Micronesian & Australian Friends Association
MIO	Mandated Iwi Organisation
MLC	Māori Land Court
MPA	marine protected area
MPI	Ministry for Primary Industries
MPS	Micronesian Presidents' Summit

NGO	nongovernmental organisation
NRM	natural resource management
NSW	New South Wales
PCCR	Pacific Climate Change Roundtable
PIDF	Pacific Islands Development Forum
PIF	Pacific Islands Forum
PIFACC	Pacific Islands Framework for Action on Climate Change
PLG	Polynesian Leaders Group
PNG	Papua New Guinea
PSGE	post-settlement governance entity
SIS	Smaller Island States
SK	sumak kawsay
SPC	Secretariat of the Pacific Community
SPREP	Secretariat of the Pacific Regional Environment Programme
SRPIP	Specific Regional Plan for Indigenous Peoples
TTWMA	*Te Ture Whenua Māori Act 1993*
UN	United Nations
UNFCCC	United Nations Framework Convention on Climate Change
US	United States

List of figures

List of maps

List of plates

List of tables

Contributors

Tamatoa Bambridge is director of research at the French National Centre for Scientific Research, Centre for Island Research and Environmental Observatory (CRIOBE), Papetōʻai, Moʻorea, French Polynesia.

Stuart Bedford is a fellow at The Australian National University and associate at the Max Planck Institute for the Science of Human History in Leipzig, Germany. He has been involved in archaeological research in Vanuatu since 1995. He has been privileged to undertake research on most of the islands of the archipelago and has helped transform the understanding of its 3,000-year human history.

Associate Professor Jenny Bryant-Tokalau recently retired after a long career in the Pacific, including at the University of Papua New Guinea and the University of the South Pacific, as well as Monash University in Australia. Most recently, she taught in Te Tumu, the School of Māori, Pacific and Indigenous Studies at the University of Otago, New Zealand, and she remains in adjunct positions in the School of Geography, University of Otago and at the University of the South Pacific.

Salā George Carter is a research fellow in geopolitics and regionalism in the Department of Pacific Affairs at The Australian National University.

Lynette Carter (Kāi Tahu, Kāti Mamoe, Waitaha) recently retired as senior lecturer at Te Tumu, School of Māori, Pacific and Indigenous Studies, University of Otago. Lyn was also principal investigator for the Bio Heritage National Science Challenge project exploring the use of Indigenous knowledge in climate change adaptation for mahika kai (resources) in her own hapū (subtribe) region.

Yin-An Chen is an assistant research fellow at the Taiwan Society for the Commons Governance.

Paul D'Arcy is associate professor of pacific studies in the Department of Pacific Affairs, Coral Bell School of Asia and Pacific Affairs, The Australian National University.

Pauline Fabre recently gained her doctorate on effective lagoon ecosystems from the Centre for Island Research and Environmental Observatory in Mo`orea.

José Guerrero Vela is an Ecuadorian anthropologist, environmental conservationist and photographer who worked in the Ecuadorian Amazon before moving to the Galápagos Islands to take up his current position as a Galápagos National Park naturalist. He graduated with a master of science and environment and a graduate diploma in governance from The Australian National University.

Nicholas Halter is an Australian historian who has lived and worked in Micronesia and Fiji. Born in Sydney, he studied history at the University of Wollongong and The Australian National University. Since 2016, he has lectured in pacific history and historiography at the University of the South Pacific in Fiji. He has published two books with ANU Press: *Australian Travellers in the South Seas* (2021) and *Suva Stories: A History of the Capital of Fiji* (2022).

Jer-Ming Hu is associate professor in the Institute of Ecology and Evolutionary Biology at National Taiwan University, Taipei, Taiwan.

Phil Journeaux is an agricultural scientist with an MBA who currently works for AgFirst Waikato in Aotearoa New Zealand.

Myjolynne (Mymy) Kim is from Chuuk in the Federated States of Micronesia and is currently finishing her doctorate in the Department of Pacific Affairs at The Australian National University.

Tanira Kingi (Ngāti Whakaue, Ngāti Rangitihi, Te Arawa nui tonu, Ngāti Awa) has a PhD in agricultural economics and development from The Australian National University. Tanira recently retired after a long career in Aotearoa New Zealand's agricultural, forestry and horticultural industries. He sits on several Te Arawa entities and has extensive iwi (tribe) and hapū networks around the country and has worked with many Māori economic authorities and post-settlement entities on land-based economic development. He remains a research advisor and emeritus scientist with Scion Research and is currently a commissioner on the New Zealand Climate Change Commission Board.

Daya Dakasi Da-Wei Kuan comes from the Tayal indigenous group in Taiwan. Daya is associate professor in the Department of Ethnology at National Chengchi University, Taipei, Taiwan.

Vincent Lebot is a root and tuber crop breeder employed by the French Agricultural Research Centre for International Development (www.cirad.fr). He obtained his PhD in 1988 and has been working on root and tuber crops for the past 40 years. He was the scientific coordinator of the Taro Network for South East Asia and Oceania and coordinated the International Network for Edible Aroids. He is now investing his efforts in the development of agroforestry systems, aiming to strengthen smallholders' capacity to adapt to climate change.

Su-Mei Lo is assistant professor in the Department of Anthropology at National Taiwan University, Taipei, Taiwan.

Regina Macalandag is an empathy and governance scholar who gained her doctorate in public policy and governance at The Australian National University. Her research projects include governance, gender equity, social inclusion, sustainable development and state–Indigenous relations in the Philippines. Her current research interest is ethnographies of governance employing feminist theory and decolonising research methodologies.

Chels A. Marshall is an Indigenous ecologist from Gumbaynggirr country in northern New South Wales and graduated with her doctorate from The Australian National University in 2021. Chels is a First Nations cultural systems ecologist and a research fellow at Deakin University's National Indigenous Knowledges Education Research Innovation Institute.

Roannie Ng Shiu is a senior research fellow with the Faculty of Medical and Health Sciences at the University of Auckland and is also co-director of Te Poutoko Ora a Kiwa, the University of Auckland Research Centre for Pacific and Global Health.

**Jonathan Kay Kamakawiwo`ole Osorio** is dean of Hawai`inuiākea School of Hawaiian Knowledge. Dr Osorio received his doctorate in history from the University of Hawai`i at Mānoa.

Takarua Parent is completing a master's degree in Languages, Cultures and Societies in Oceania at the University of French Polynesia in Tahiti.

Gonzaga (Zag) Puas holds a bachelor of arts/diploma of education, bachelor of law, master of political science and a doctorate in Micronesian history. Born and raised in Chuuk State on the island of Lukunor, Federated States of Micronesia, and from the Sor clan, he is director of the Micronesian Institute for Research and Development and professor and Micronesian outreach coordinator at the Pacific Islands University, Guam. His ANU doctorate was published in 2021 by ANU Press as *Federated States of Micronesia's Engagement with the Outside World: Control, Self-preservation and Continuity*.

Patrick Rochette is a farmer and fisherman on the Taiarapu Peninsula in Tahiti. He has been a member of the Teahupo'o Rāhui Management Committee for 10 years and active promoter of this form of integrated society–ecosystem management across Tahiti.

Marguerite Taiarui was born and raised in Tahiti and has always been passionate about the marine environment. She studied marine sciences in New Zealand and Australia from 2012 to 2016, obtaining a Diploma in Marine Sciences, a BSc in Applied Biological Sciences, and a MSc in Fisheries Biology and Management. Her MSc research made her realise the complexity and importance of small-scale fisheries in French Polynesia and left her committed to the better understanding and management of Tahitian lagoon fisheries. She worked for the Direction of Marine Resources of French Polynesia from 2019 to 2021, helping to put in place restricted fishing areas with local communities' participation. Marguerite is currently completing a PhD on better fisheries management in French Polynesia and in the Pacific.

Melody Tay is a marine biologist and performance artist who recently graduated from Yale/NUS College at the National University of Singapore. Melody is interested in how art can be both a witness and an intervention to the present reality of climate change and the human stories that are intertwined in that problem. In her work, she explores wonder and the relationship between the experience of nature and the divine.

Teurumereariki Hinano Teavai-Murphy is associate director of the UC Berkeley Gump Station on Mo'orea, which promotes research, education and public service in sustainable development.

Anita Togolo gained her doctorate in the Department of Pacific Affairs at The Australian National University, focused on indigenous entrepreneurship and landowner businesses in Papua New Guinea's mining sector. She continues to work towards sustainable socio-economic outcomes for landowners impacted by resource development projects.

Steve Wakelin is an environmental microbiologist specialising in forest genomics and ecosystem functions at Scion (formerly the NZ Forest Research Institute).

Graham West is the director of Graham West Land Use Solutions Limited. He has worked in a variety of roles at Scion (formerly the NZ Forest Research Institute) for more than 40 years.

Emma Woodward is a senior research scientist with CSIRO based in Perth, Western Australia. A leader in co-design, she partners with Indigenous leaders to codevelop methods, tools, protocols and guidelines, facilitating the interweaving of multiple knowledges, values and interests, to build understanding and deliver collaborative solutions to land and sea management at regional and national scales.

Ai-Ching Yen is a part-time professor with the Department of Land Economics, National Chengchi University, Taiwan.

Papa Mape: A tribute

Teurumereariki Hinano Teavai-Murphy

Yves Teihotaata, known as Papa Mape, was born on 19 May 1932 in Papetō`ai, Mo`orea. He married Anita Johnston Christine, born on 15 May 1929, in Orofara-Mahina, Tahiti. Together they raised two children, Heiata Teihotaata, born on 22 March 1970, and Heimata Wilfred, born on 7 April 1973.

Papa Mape was a quiet and humble man, but passionate about his culture. His formal education in the French school system was limited; however, he acquired a remarkable education from his elders and further developed a profound expertise from his endless curiosity about the natural world. He often noted that his school was the ocean. In traditional times, Papa Mape would have been recognised as an a tahu`a tautai (expert in the marine world) and tahu`a ra`au (expert in traditional medicine).

Papa Mape witnessed the rapid and often disconcerting change of the mid- and late-twentieth-century world. Populations on Mo`orea and across French Polynesia rose, tourism and urban centres developed, traditions were lost and fisheries diminished. He said that when he was young, he could start an uru (breadfruit) cooking on the fire, then go out and get a fish to eat with it and be back before the uru was cooked. In later years, he lamented, the uru would be charcoal before he was able to find a fish. Because of these changes, he realised that he, too, had to embrace change and he experienced an unexpected but, perhaps, always latent calling to become a teacher. This meant going against traditions in which knowledge was passed down through the family in one-to-one interactions. But for Papa Mape, this concession was necessary given the urgency of the situation: traditional knowledge and the Mā`ohi (Indigenous Tahitian) philosophical frameworks of perception and conception in which that knowledge was and is embedded needed to be taught before they were lost. So, he taught. He taught about the ocean and about fish. He taught about plants and agriculture and medicine. He taught groups of Mā`ohi students, French schoolteachers, Western scientists and anyone who took the time to sit with him. His patience and humour served him well in this, and his words carried the weight of his deep knowledge of the natural world.

Often sought out in his later years to address the ecological and environmental media, Papa Mape embraced an integrated vision of island worlds and our relationships to them. As one journalist recorded him saying: 'Whatever you do on the land, the ocean suffers. Whatever you do in the ocean, the land suffers' (Eichenseher 2011). He was, with another knowledge steward from his village, the primary cultural expert to help restore and revitalise our lunar calendar, reporting on sustainable fishing and farming practices. He was the co-founder and president of honour of Te Pu `Atiti`a, a community-based organisation on Mo`orea dedicated to documenting, promoting and preserving biocultural heritage, marine and terrestrial biodiversity and traditional ecological knowledge, and which collaborates with the University of California at Berkeley's Gump Research Center to run the Atitia Center, 'which aims to inspire, teach, and reconnect Polynesian youth with their biocultural heritage'.

Yves Teihotaata passed away on 30 October 2013 in his beloved village of Papetō`ai. As the honorific he was known by, Papa Mape, suggests, he was a founding figure and a father to the Mo`orea community's efforts to navigate a path from ancestral wisdom and traditional ecological expertise towards a future of island sustainability. He remains for each of us the guardian of the ocean and a guiding star for all our island projects.

Plate 1: Papa Mape.
Source: Photo by Poema Duprel.

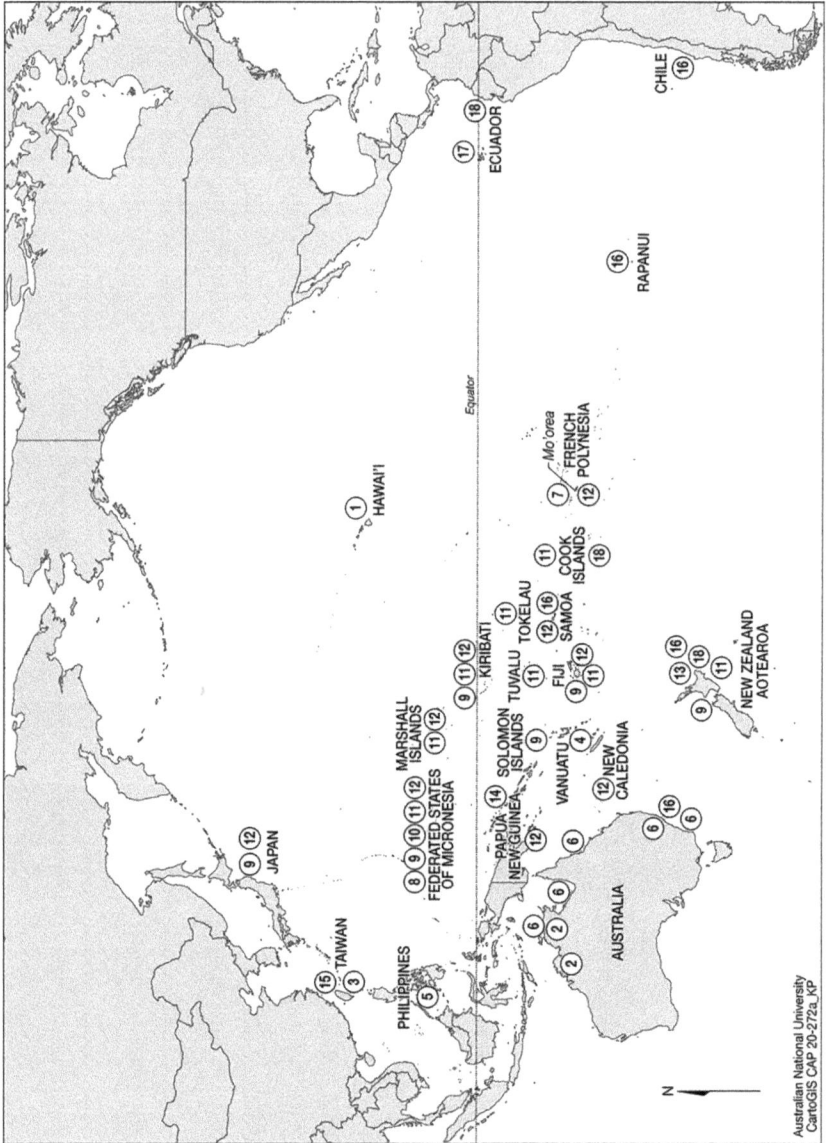

Map 1: The Asia-Pacific region, showing chapter locations.
Source: CartoGIS CAP 20-272a_KP, The Australian National University.

Introduction: Local practice and global interactions in the Pacific—Making the global local

Paul D'Arcy and Daya Dakasi Da-Wei Kuan

We live in a time of monumental upheaval and transition. Debates over the best ways to enhance human progress and development have been overtaken by overwhelming evidence that the unprecedented growth of the modern world economy poses an existential threat to humanity because of associated global environmental degradation. The overuse of carbon-producing energy sources heavily pollutes the atmosphere, raising global temperatures beyond the tolerance of many plant and animal species. The term 'Anthropocene' has been coined for this new era because human activity is, for the first time, changing Earth's ecosystems and climate on a global scale. The overwhelming scientific consensus is that these detrimental processes will soon be irreversible. The Asia-Pacific region is emerging as a key battleground for many of the most pressing environmental issues facing humanity. This edited collection highlights several local community actions across the Pacific, from Taiwan to Chile, which have successfully retained and enhanced local knowledge and autonomy. This has often had a positive impact on climate change mitigation by drawing on the lessons of these communities' past and their adaptation of external contemporary innovations.

Only a handful of developed nations now deny the extent of human damage to the environment. Pro-globalisation advocates have begun calling for greater consideration of sustainable environments in economic policy, while still arguing that expanded production and trade benefit humanity. They argue the past century of globalisation has led to unprecedented growth in the world economy that has lifted many out of absolute poverty. World Bank figures show the number of people living in extreme poverty has been cut in half since 1990, to just less than 1 billion people (Ortiz-Ospina and Beltekian 2014; Bartley et al. 2015). However, while the absolute size of the world economy has mushroomed, the inequality within it has also accelerated (Madeley 2003; Wright 2004; Klein 2014; Bregman 2017).

Local Pacific contexts

Indigenous peoples across the Pacific face many similar resource management issues relating to political marginalisation and territorial dislocation within the nation-states created by interlopers. In so-called settler societies, introduced Eurasian diseases combined with colonial-era mass immigration to make Indigenous peoples minorities in their own lands. In South-West Pacific communities where there was more limited European or Japanese migration after military coercion, the colonial legacy was by and large one of deeply fragmented, culturally diverse nation-states that operated on a scale far removed from the more intimate and organic relationships with land, sea and each other that communities had developed over many generations. Smaller, more coherent postcolonial nation-states in the central and eastern Pacific faced problems of economic viability in an ever-increasing global economy dependent on economies of scale, on the one hand, and distance from large markets with disposable income, on the other (Firth 1989; Bertram 2006; D'Arcy 2012).

Most of the Indigenous communities covered in this book live in either independent Pacific Island nations or as minorities in economically developed parliamentary democracies. In global terms, most Pacific Island nations are generally stable, accommodating social diversity. Their problems are more economic and environmental than political. The larger, resource-rich nations of the South-West Pacific export most of their resources unprocessed through multinational companies. In such relations, much of the profit goes offshore rather than benefiting locals. For example, income from fees paid by foreign fleets for the right to fish Pacific waters rarely equate to more than 3–10 per cent of the resale value of the catch (Bertram 1999, 2006; D'Arcy 2009, 2012, 2014). Once ocean territory is considered, there are no small Pacific Island nations, only large Pacific Ocean nations, as former Cook Islands prime minister Henry Puna noted (SPREP 2017b). The final category of Indigenous peoples covered in this collection are the original inhabitants who became minorities in settler-society nations based on pastoralism and mining (Aotearoa New Zealand, Australia and Chile) or intensive agriculture and associated deforestation (Taiwan, the Philippines and, to a lesser extent, Ecuador). All suffered social dislocation from massive loss of land and political and economic marginalisation. All have benefited from legal and political protections in the current generation.

Most recently established Pacific Island nations were forced to accommodate the neoliberal economic agenda of minimising government spending and maximising private-sector initiatives that prevailed from the early 1990s as part of the so-called Washington Consensus. They did so reluctantly as the process of nation-building was ongoing given their late independence and legacies of poor colonial infrastructure. Most of their donors were Western nations that embraced the neoliberal agenda, as did World Bank and International Monetary Fund (IMF) lending conditions. With small domestic private sectors and most multinational ventures in Pacific Island nations creating few local flow-on industries, foreign companies benefited, with taxes and duties collected by island governments dwarfed by company profits. Industries created by multinational enterprises generally created low-wage economies for locals such as tourism and the garment industry, which remained dependent on the economic and trade entry conditions in the purchasing nations on the Pacific Rim over which they had little influence (Firth 2000, 2006; Bertram 2006).

Mining, timber and fishing industries dominated by multinationals have inflicted considerable environmental devastation on the Pacific Islands region. At the same time, global capitalism's expanding consumption of natural resources and fossil fuel-based energy for industrial production has inflicted an even more devastating impact on the global environment. Pacific Island nations are key areas for local climate change damage, where global overuse of carbon-based energy sources heavily pollutes the atmosphere, raising temperatures beyond the tolerance of many species and sea levels beyond the capacity of island-building processes for low-lying atolls (Bell et al. 2016: especially pp. 11–16). Climate change is already making the occurrence of natural disasters more frequent and often more intense. Typhoons, drought, flooding and El Niño–La Niña climatic cycles cause severe damage whenever they hit Pacific communities. Climate change is also causing a rise in sea levels and changes to nearshore artisanal fisheries. Any one of these natural disasters can overwhelm the resources of a small nation. When Cyclone Ofa hit Tuvalu in March 2015, nearly half the population of approximately 9,500 was displaced by the flooding, which washed away houses and crops. Kiribati and Vanuatu were also hit by Ofa. The rapid provision of external aid was essential to recover from such damage (RNZ 2015). Given these changed circumstances, it is not surprising that Pacific Island nations have become increasingly assertive on the world stage and at international forums in condemning large carbon-emitting nations, including seeking diverse donors and political partners beyond their usual ones (Beck 2020; Craney and Hudson 2020; Smith and Wesley-Smith 2021; Kabutaulaka 2021). There has been no shortage of interested parties (Firth 2013; Fry and Tarte 2016).

This book argues that solutions to issues of Indigenous political empowerment and economic viability will only be economically, socially and ecologically sustainable if they take account of distinct local contexts and cultures and empower local resource guardianship, both of which can be enhanced by looking at how other local groups deal with broadly similar issues. We adopt a comparative framework by discussing a series of local resource management issues across the Pacific, which broadly demonstrate the dynamics of communities from local to regional scales navigating the challenge of asserting agency over their home (is)lands' environmental futures (Mawyer and Jacka 2018). In tacking between general principles of conservation, consultation and community empowerment and specifics of place, identity and cultural values, we will also indirectly explore how Indigenous groups might best interact with each other and with larger non-Indigenous populations for more effective resource management.

The collection draws together a diverse array of contributors working on Indigenous peoples' empowerment, from Australia and Taiwan in the west to Ecuador and Chile in the east. It arose from conference panels organised by the editors at the Pacific History Association Biennial Conference in Taiwan in December 2014 to explore common issues between Taiwanese Indigenous peoples and their distant cousins across the entire breadth of the Pacific. The conference was probably the most inspiring of our careers and even before it had concluded we had agreed that our panels should and must be published to reinforce the links and common experiences and interests that emerged between the communities discussed in the panels.

Two years earlier, Taiwan had hosted the International Austronesian Conference 'Weaving Waves' Writings: Memories, Stories and Spiritual Resonance in Oceania', in November 2012. One of the highlights of this conference was the honouring of two guardians of community knowledge from opposite ends of the Austronesian diaspora with Life Sustainability

Awards: Papa Mape from Mo`orea in French Polynesia and Lifok 'Oteng from Taiwan. These international awards, conveyed by the Taiwanese Government, 'celebrate individuals' actions and passions for nurturing and protecting cultural, spiritual and environmental sustainability' (D'Arcy 2014a).

Lifok 'Oteng is an 'Amis writer, historian and musician from the Yiwan peoples near Taidong. Papa Mape was the first non-Taiwanese to receive the award (D'Arcy 2014a). The conference was also his first trip outside French Polynesia and we still recall two special moments involving this humble man on his first trip to the island of his original ancestors. One was Papa Mape and Lifok 'Oteng being treated like rock stars by our predominantly young audience after the award presentation, with requests for selfie photos and more information about their work, which fills us with hope for the future from this new generation of extraordinary young Pacific peoples. This theme recurs throughout this book and rests on tangible examples rather than wishful thinking. The other was a long moment of silent reflection by Papa Mape as we stood facing a vast wall map of the Austronesian world in the Taiwan Indigenous Peoples Culture Park in the southernmost county of Pingtung, from the shores of which his ancestors originally began their journey, and pointing to where his home island of Mo`orea lay more than 10,000 kilometres to the south-east. Sadly, Papa Mape died the following year. The editors and contributors unanimously agreed to dedicate the book to Papa Mape. We hope our work sufficiently honours his message and actions despite a lengthy delay in publication for which we are profoundly sorry. We editors are so grateful to our contributors for staying with us to honour our collective promise, as well as to all staff at ANU Press for their incredible production and editing work, and the cartographic staff of ANU's CartoGIS for their truly world class, made-to-order maps which illuminate this work. The book's organisational flow owes much to the wonderful advice of Associate Professor Alex Mawyer at the University of Hawai'i at Mānoa. We are especially grateful to Professor Nicole Haley for her academic integrity in ensuring this project was able to proceed.

Indigenous voices from across the Pacific

The question of how Pacific Island peoples have dealt with colonial rule and post-independence global economic forces still divides Pacific studies between those arguing Pacific peoples were more active agents than passive victims and those arguing they were more active victims (Chappell 1995; Gonschor 2019). Global works on Indigenous and minority empowerment and the threat of climate change citing Pacific examples still largely characterise Pacific Islanders as victims. Several global leaders of environmental advocacy who highlight the contribution of Indigenous peoples to environmental conservation, such as Canadian David Suzuki (Suzuki and Knudtson 1997; Suzuki with McConnell and Mason 2007; Klein 2014), mention some Pacific peoples' remarkable achievements in cultural empowerment and environmental rehabilitation. However, Pacific Island communities are rarely a central focus. Many, if not most, of the community initiatives featured in this collection are relatively little known beyond our region or even within our region.

This idea of the importance and efficacy of local Indigenous resource management practices occurs throughout this collection. Most contributors argue that such local knowledge and practice can also enhance other management regimes in national and regional contexts. For this to occur, however, local peoples must be engaged as partners in decision-making and practice rather than merely consulted as 'stakeholders' affected by, but not part of, government-appointed decision-making and monitoring bodies. There has been an increasing acceptance in developed nations of the efficacy of Indigenous resource management and local community empowerment and participation in conservation, which has gathered momentum since Suzuki and others began to emphasise the benefits of this in the 1990s (Berkes 2007; Garnett et al. 2018; Jones et al. 2018). A feature that sets the Pacific apart from other parts of the world is the generally high level of state recognition of customary tenure and the large number of nation-states where Indigenous peoples form the majority of the population and government representatives.

Whether change will come about fast enough to create political pressure to reduce carbon emissions and sequester enough of the carbon already in the atmosphere is uncertain. The evidence in this collection fills we editors with great hope and optimism. This collection chronicles numerous practical and successful steps of climate change mitigation and adaptation, as well as environmental rehabilitation, that are being implemented by numerous Indigenous communities across our region. These local community actions are accumulating to gather momentum, while Australia's 2019–20 'Black Summer' of bushfires and the ongoing and near universal pleas from the world's scientific community force those advocating no change into increasingly shrill and untenable positions with voters. In celebrating the life and objectives of Papa Mape, *Islands of Hope* seeks to centre a periphery in public discourse and, in so doing, play a small part in celebrating the considerable but often unheralded achievements of our region's peoples and offer hope for those beyond our shores who are willing to see. In this context, we have opted to capitalise the term 'Indigenous' throughout and to not differentiate local language terms in italics unless contributors specifically requested so, reflecting the status of local knowledge as at home on the pages of this volume, hence not marked as 'foreign' terminology. All contributors especially draw hope from the next generation across the globe, who have demonstrated far greater general environmental awareness and respect than most powerbrokers of older generations in both the public and the private spheres.

Redefining progress in the Anthropocene

All the communities discussed in this collection have seen their political autonomy and economic resources diminished under, first, colonial rule and then global capitalism. However, they have also exhibited a great deal of continuity in retaining core elements of their territorial affiliation and cultural attitudes to resource management, sustainable development and social inclusiveness. Each of the contributors demonstrates that, in this regard, the communities they discuss are 'Islands of Hope' for all Indigenous communities and other global communities marginalised by the juggernaut of global capitalism or the increasingly frequent environmental consequences of climate change. The fossil fuel–driven conversion of resources into consumer items underpinning global capitalism is now unsustainable and poses an existential threat to humankind, and many fear governments have left it too late to reduce emissions sufficiently to avoid the global tipping point in atmospheric temperature rise. Globalisation lifted millions out of poverty but also increased the gap between financially prosperous societies and others, and has proven environmentally unsustainable in its current forms.

The Pacific peoples covered in this collection have always been active agents of history (Chappell 1995, 2015) whose lifeways played out across the vast land and seascapes of Oceania (D'Arcy 2009; Matsuda 2012). Documenting and arguing for the predominance of ongoing active agency and cultural continuity in the face of colonial and capitalist forces have been the predominant themes of Pacific history from its inception.

The same can probably be argued for anthropology, geography and, to a lesser extent, archaeology. Where the Pacific Islands played a notable role in wider archaeological and especially anthropological disciplinary theory—for instance, in the historical anthropological studies of the late Marshall Sahlins on the relationship between new processes, items and ideas and existing local, social, economic and ideological beliefs during the early decades of European contact with Hawaii, which he termed the 'structure of the conjuncture' (Sahlins 1981, 1983, 1985)—it is only recently that the ecosocial and human dimensions of this region's ecological and environmental dynamics have come into significant broad discussion across diverse domains (West 2006; Teaiwa 2014; Lauer 2017; Sterling et al. 2020).

In documenting the ongoing efficacy of Indigenous environmental guardianship linked to longstanding ancestral affinity with, and understanding of, local ecosystems and their flora and fauna, this collection argues for the resilience of cultural structures and beliefs to absorb and withstand external forces. However, the most important methodological contribution of this collection perhaps lies in advocating for enhanced roles for Indigenous and place-based ontologies in environmental and conservation sciences and practices (Berkes 2009; Dacks et al. 2019). Because making choices about environmental and ecological futures always hinges on the question 'who has the right to choose' (West 2006; Mawyer and Jacka 2018), local to regional scale governance and policymaking are fundamentally hinged on questions of the sovereignty of local and regional peoples, implicating regional environmental scholarship in all its current disciplines and forms in foundational political questions.

As the articles gathered in this collection demonstrate, past and present Indigenous active agency is now beyond dispute. This means the primary area of contestation must now be converting recognition of enduring and effective agency into present and future decision-making power. In diverse ways, explicitly and implicitly, assertively and subtly, all the pieces collected here summon into view the political dynamics and historical and contemporary sociopolitical contexts of environmental and ecological thinking and actions within and between their various communities. In the latter case, we particularly note the relevance of the concept of Oceanian sovereignty (Bambridge et al. 2021). As Bambridge and colleagues note, the idea of an Oceanian sovereignty transcending state territorial and legal definitions and rights to encompass both a shared identity linked to the connecting ocean and local affiliations based on regular, enacted affinity and care for all elements of landscapes and seascapes of self-identity emerged from the vision of the late Tongan scholar Epeli Hau`ofa (2005: 36). Such sovereignty complements that of the nation-state and can enhance local support for government and scientific initiatives. All such initiatives ultimately thrive or atrophy based on the degree of sustained local support, advocacy and participation they attract. However, such collaborations must be enduring partnerships to share and combine the environmental solutions of local, national and/or international partners rather than merely local community enactments of government or scientist-designed programs. This alternative form of development, the authors mentioned here seem to suggest, better matches the environmental and social needs of the Anthropocene.

Islands of Hope is organised into several thematic sections. Section One details the incredible diversity of crops and the flexibility of Indigenous food production systems, which rest on deep, intimate associations with the land and sea, as especially noted by Jon Osorio in the opening chapter on the poetics of Hawaiian senses of place. Such diversity enables flexibility in the face of environmental and climatic instability and enhances local water and nutrient cycles. In Chapter 2, Emma Woodward reveals the wealth of knowledge and diversity of management techniques and resources retained and effectively deployed in Aboriginal watershed management in northern Australia. Chapter 3, by Su-Mei Lo and Jer-Ming Hu, demonstrates similar diversity and knowledge in ʻAmis gardens in peri-urban contexts in Taiwan. In the case of Vanuatu, in Chapter 4, Vincent Lebot and Stuart Bedford demonstrate that local systems are far more productive than modern chemically assisted plantation cropping, with its restricted range of crops, as well as environmentally beneficial and self-sustaining. Enhanced local food production based on growing a variety of nutritional ground crops among tree crops, supplemented by harvesting forest foods, can create more income for local communities than the sale of logging rights and conversion of forest to oil-palm plantations, including by generating carbon credits for preserved forests. This diversity of production and preserved species also increases communities' climate change resilience. It allows communities the choice of devoting a smaller percentage of their land to cash crops in response to fluctuating global market demands if the opportunity arises (La Franchi and Greenpeace Pacific 1999; Madeley 2002, 2003; Bell et al. 2016; Suzuki and Hanington 2017: 152–61; Brown et al. 2018; Liu et al. 2019). Greater use of agroforestry also significantly increases the land's carbon sequestration potential.

All chapters demonstrate that, rather than passively wait for international agreements on carbon emission reductions, Pacific Islanders are acting locally now to preserve and enhance what we have and climate proof it as much as possible through replanting with appropriate species, water conservation and other measures. This collection argues that solutions to issues of political empowerment and economic viability will only be economically and ecologically sustainable and socially enduring if they take account of distinct local contexts and cultures. This and the need to empower local resource guardianship can be enhanced through looking at how other groups deal with broadly similar issues and contexts. This collection demonstrates that numerous local Indigenous systems are not only green and sustainable, but also much more productive than is usually claimed by advocates of industrial monocropping for global supply. Conservation is also best done at a local level and, in this, Indigenous peoples have a major role and a positive impact that are underrepresented in the literature.

Papa Mape's legacy relates to Section Two's theme that reviving and sustaining resource use involve guardianship rather than ownership. They also require a different concept of natural ecosystems as living entities with legal rights like all other legal entities—as in the legislation now granted in Ecuador and Aotearoa New Zealand—rather than being seen merely as natural resources for humans to use for their own advancement.

Section Four's first three chapters demonstrate that the nature of local Indigenous communities in Aotearoa New Zealand (Tanira Kingi, Steve Wakelin, Phil Journeaux and Graham West), Bougainville (Anita Togolo) and Taiwan (Ai-Ching Yen and Yin-An Chen) makes them well suited to selectively adopt outside ideas when they suit their needs while drawing on existing beliefs and practices to minimise disruption from transition. The last three chapters of this final section—Chapter 16 by Roannie Ng Shiu and Paul D'Arcy on Pacific Islanders and Chile, Chapter 17 by José Guerrero Vela on the Galápagos Islands and Chapter 18 by Melody Tai on South America and the Pacific—suggest the empowerment of nature and an emphasis on cultural and community stability have lessons for other Indigenous communities as well as the wider global community.

The havoc caused to global communication modes by the Covid-19 pandemic reinforces the need to increase local self-sufficiency, especially in drought, heat and salt-resistant crop variants, as we now increasingly live with the detrimental consequences of the Anthropocene. While we argue against withdrawing from global commodity trade, the evidence outlined in this collection demonstrates that Indigenous Pacific communities can and should become less dependent on global food exchanges. Indeed, all sections demonstrate that Indigenous food production is often more efficient than conventional export-focused monocropping, as well as producing much fewer harmful carbon dioxide emissions, the consequences of which are being most severely felt in some of the localities covered in this collection. This collection outlines various Pacific peoples' proactive responses to the more destructive aspects on the environment of industrial capitalism, in Section Two on reviving ecosystems and Section Three on climate change specifically. As the destructive consequences of progress measured by productive growth based on consuming more resources are now increasingly apparent, we conclude by suggesting that Pacific Indigenous values and practices challenge the notions of progress and economic efficiency that underlie the harmful processes just noted. They also point the way towards more sustainable development that embraces and directly benefits a larger proportion of the world's population than is currently the case. Such development can occur in a manner that is both sustainable and beneficial for ecological restoration of Earth's ecosystems.

Section Two's focus on reviving ecosystems switches from land to sea but also makes the case for a much greater role for traditional systems of resource management or, more correctly, resource guardianship, in land and sea restoration. Regina Macalandag and Chels Marshall (Chapters 5 and 6, respectively) point out the negative consequences of minimising Indigenous sea peoples' decision-making powers in marine management and the enormous benefits that could accrue from true partnerships in resource management, like those often already in place in land-based conservation and management. The best results in the restoration of degraded marine ecosystems occur when local coastal communities are empowered to work alongside marine scientists as partners and given legal recognition as such. This has been successfully demonstrated in the case of the Teahupo`o Marine Protected Area in Tahiti, outlined in Chapter 7 by Tamatoa Bambridge, Patrick Rochette, Takurua Parent and Pauline Fabre. In all cases, mobilising and inspiring local youth are vital for the transmission of knowledge and community coherence of purpose, to ensure successful, ongoing guardianship. The example of Kuchawa in Chuuk, discussed by Myjolynne Kim, Zag Puas and Nic Halter in Chapter 8, demonstrates that such mobilisation works to correct damage caused by global mass consumption such as pollution from excessive nonbiodegradable packaging, as well as to establish sustainable harvesting methods. All chapters emphasise that community coherence promotes sustainable harvesting by more inclusive distribution of harvests and catches. This chapter also links Section Two to Section Three, which is about reaching out to others to advocate for local solutions by focusing on the mobilisation of youth as the next generation of environmental guardians. The chapter looks back to learn from past practice while facing circumstances not seen in living memory.

Despite increasing evidence of the rising existential threat of climate change—such as the unprecedented forest fires in Australia in late 2019 and early 2020 and record high temperatures in Antarctica—mitigation still faces competing government priorities in the form of economic growth and global trade, accentuated by the economic devastation of the Covid-19 pandemic that began in early 2020. A rapid transition to renewable energy technologies while maintaining or expanding production and trade remains the preferred course of action for climate change mitigation for most large economies. The political will to meet scientific targets for necessary carbon emission reductions remains elusive, prompting the more assertive foreign policy stances of Pacific nations noted by Lynette Carter (Chapter 11) and George Carter (Chapter 12) in Section Three. In Section Four, Melody Tai (Chapter 18) suggests that local Pacific solutions, especially the legal empowerment of nature, may find willing ears among global youth and others deeply concerned about the inaction of world governments and the policy influence of the fossil fuel lobby.

Section Three's first two chapters note that Pacific peoples are finding that older solutions to Anthropocene issues such as the impact of climatic variation on crops and sea inundation are cheaper, more effective and locally sustainable. In Chapter 9, Jenny Bryant-Tokalau surveys the planning of artificial islands and other relocation strategies against the background of similar past practices. New ideas should be tested for effectiveness, as Zag Puas demonstrates in Chapter 10 by comparing the radically different effectiveness of two modern forms of seawall. He argues for older seawall forms used in combination with pre-existing solutions such as planting mangroves and pandanus as shoreline buffers, which also trap sand and act as nurseries for numerous fish species.

The positive social, economic and environmental impacts of the Teahupo`o rāhui-based Marine Protected Area discussed in Chapter 7 were partly ameliorated by an episode of coral bleaching in 2018–19. Tropical coastal communities around the Pacific now face a rising wave of coral bleaching as the Anthropocene takes hold. The overwhelming scientific consensus is that the human-induced global forces driving this rise in atmospheric and ocean temperatures pose an existential threat to humanity and a myriad ecosystem tipping points around the world. Yet, these harmful processes continue amid various levels of political denial within financially prosperous nations that have benefited from global capitalism built on fossil fuels. Climate mitigation action from the larger of these prosperous polluters is essential to ameliorating the damage being caused. This disturbing reality does not undermine any of the actions being advocated and implemented in this collection by Indigenous communities across our region. Any form of local empowerment and increased or regenerated local capacity enhances communities' capacity to deal with increasingly unstable climatic conditions and disruptions to global exchanges. Such measures as outlined throughout this collection will enhance local environmental sustainability until the global action required to ameliorate these destructive global processes is adopted on a meaningful scale. As teachers who work closely with young Indigenous scholars in Taiwan, the Pacific Islands and Australia, we editors are heartened by the depth of commitment and enthusiasm for environmental guardianship we see across the broad expanse covered in this collection. The legacy of Papa Mape lives on and flourishes.

Section One: Pacific Indigenous sustainable development

Introduction: Knowledge retained — Pacific Indigenous sustainable development

Daya Dakasi Da-Wei Kuan and Paul D'Arcy

This opening section outlines how Indigenous values and practices endure across the Pacific in ways that benefit the land and the sea. They also provide strength and comfort to those who follow these cultural understandings of the importance of identity, belonging and intimacy with our communities and our surroundings. The fact these cultures have endured and flourished through generations of ostensible domination by haole (the Indigenous local term for outsiders) speaks to the strength and benefits of these values and practices for those immersed in and shaped by them. Jonathan Osorio opens the collection with an all-encompassing reflection on what it means to be Kānaka Maoli (Indigenous Hawaiians), centred on the theme of intimacies in which land, sea, kin, community and ancestors interact and interweave to shape a profound sense of belonging through nurturing. All chapters in this section display a similar cultural intimacy with the local environment that challenges the society–nature nexus in Western thought. Intimate observation and a culture of nurturing characterise each chapter, with the degree of Indigenous control of ancestral lands a key component in the health and vibrancy of the land and sea, and of the local communities involved. When ancestors are seen to shape and live on in the land and the sea, objective scientific use of the environment for the greater good is not as rational as espoused. In far too many cases, the greater good usually means the good of someone not directly or intimately connected to the land in question, and not affected by the negative consequences of the purpose espoused.

Consistent Kānaka Maoli opposition to the construction of more and more observatories on the upper slopes of sacred Mauna Kea to take advantage of optimal space-viewing conditions have escalated in recent months and drawn support from Indigenous peoples across the Pacific. At the time of writing, these protests seem set to end plans to construct further observatories on the sacred mountain (Hawaii News Now 2020; ABC News 2019). This chapter also reminds us that there are different ways of telling history and stories—in song, chants and action. While the dispute over Mauna Kea may be perceived as a clash between modernity and tradition, this is a questionable binary. Modernity is often linked to the idea of linear progress, while tradition is portrayed as a vestige of outdated and quaint local ways that stifle progress and material benefits. This section demonstrates the high level of self-sufficiency and diversity of locally controlled ecosystems, emphasising sustainable food production for local use. Various chapters demonstrate the flexibility and fluidity of Indigenous social and economic organisation, including the willingness and ability to adapt external practices and precepts for community benefit.

In Chapter 2, research scientist Emma Woodward, from the Commonwealth Scientific and Industrial Research Organisation (CSIRO), discusses the effectiveness of two Aboriginal land management systems in tropical northern Australia, which is distinguished by distinct wet and dry seasons. Their systems require precise knowledge of natural harbingers and processes, and variations involved with seasonal transitions, as well as diverse and interrelated potential food sources at any time of the year. This science is built on precise observation and cultural interpretation, bonding people to the land as guardians. This knowledge is collated and communicated through seasonal resource management calendars. Drawing on the seasonal calendars of the Gooniyandi and Ngan'gi language groups, the author demonstrates that local traditional knowledge systems underlying resource management are diverse, complex and frequently unique. However, all share a strong emphasis on the observation of nature and their own practice. This approach continues to be enacted and tested according to changing circumstances and conditions, the spiritual and metaphysical belief systems that underpin much resource management practice and the unique phenological basis of resource management that is intimately woven within a detailed understanding of biology, hydrology and meteorology. Woodward notes that Aboriginal people have interacted with and managed their landscapes, seascapes and resources over 65,000 years of changing circumstances. The chapter ends by arguing for the efficacy of such seasonal 'calendars' derived from Indigenous-led resource management as tools for knowledge-sharing and more effective resource management. Woodward notes that such knowledge-sharing is best achieved by means of networks that can facilitate sharing and interaction around these tools/objects, both across cultures and between generations.

In Chapter 3, Taiwanese scholars Su-Mei Lo and Jer-Ming Hu detail the extensive local knowledge of wild edible plants among the 'Amis of 'Etolan village in south-east Taiwan. Many of these plants are cultivated in 'Amis gardens and their culinary and health benefits passed between generations, significantly extending their potential food supply in times of need such as are now being experienced across the Pacific because of climate change. As coastal-dwellers, many 'Amis draw sustenance from fish and seaweed and trade with mountain-dwelling communities such as the Tayal, who are the subject of Chapter 15. Local vegetable gardens preserve locality-specific food plant diversity, reduce household food purchasing costs and extend national food-crop diversity in case of plant disease or climatic hardship. Just as Zag Puas notes in discussing atoll diets in Chapter 10, these wild plants often serve as famine foods when other, more water-dependent crops wither. Trade and exchange with other tribes spread stock geographically, enhancing resistance to localised climate stress and pathogen outbreaks such as the devastating Samoan taro leaf blight of 1993 (Hunter et al. 1998; Lebot 2013). As Lo and Hu note, outmigration to urban areas in search of work and the social structure of 'Amis village life and economic roles mean that much of this botanical knowledge is largely held by women aged over 50 years. As Anita Togolo argues in Chapter 14 in the context of her native Papua New Guinea, matrilineal traditional economic organisation can be highly successful in both cash-crop and subsistence-crop production. While Lo and Hu note concern about a break in intergenerational botanical knowledge among the 'Amis, Myjolynne Kim, Zag Puas and Nic Halter outline in Chapter 8 how young villagers in the Micronesian state of Chuuk are not necessarily averse to learning and applying the biological knowledge of their elders. Young Chuukese are deeply concerned about and committed to environmental sustainability when they are suitably included and empowered in decision-making.

In the final chapter of this first section, long-time Vanuatu residents and scholars Vincent Lebot and Stuart Bedford outline the contemporary relevance and efficacy of traditional food production systems. While the previous two chapters detail the diversity of plant and other foods known and utilised in the gardens of the 'Amis and the seasonal foods known to

Gooniyandi and Ngan'gi speakers, Lebot and Bedford note a widespread concern across the Pacific Islands about the decline of traditional gardening production and knowledge and rising consumption of less-nutritious imported food. This imported food also dramatically increases the rate of noncommunicable diseases in the population, especially diabetes and heart disease. The imported food's chemically dependent mass production pollutes production areas while its transport to distant markets gives it a high carbon-emission load. Lebot and Bedford demonstrate that the redevelopment of local food cropping systems in Vanuatu 'will not only improve food security, but also increase the country's ability to sequester carbon and thus enhance their credibility in the international debate'. They demonstrate that the revival of certain traditional food cropping practices, which they label 'agrobiodiversity', could increase food production above the levels of commercial agribusiness systems, while at the same time broadening and improving dietary intake and health. Traditional agroforestry, growing a diverse range of crops on multiple tiered systems within partially cleared forest settings, also sequesters carbon rather than releasing it, unlike modern, export-focused commercial agriculture. Traditional forest gardens are also more climate change–proof and moisture retaining than modern cash-cropping systems. Revivals of traditional foods for enhanced food security and health benefits are also under way in Micronesia, as noted by Zag Puas in Chapter 10.

1

Intimacies: Poetics of a land beloved

Jonathan Kay Kamakawiwoʻole Osorio

This is a story, a moʻolelo. As a moʻolelo, it is not really my story, but it involves me, sometimes as the subject, sometimes as an unwitting object, sometimes as an unwilling participant. A moʻolelo that does not involve the teller is almost worthless—just about as worthless as a story that is only about the teller. This moʻolelo also involves you and there are a lot of you, because I have recounted this to several audiences since 2012 and now some of you will be reading this.

As an essay, this presentation is going to be complicated by the fact that it is meant to be sung. There are a half-dozen mele in this work—some that I have composed. Mele are songs and our people have been composing them as a record of our lives and as phrases of wonder and joy, lust and loneliness; they are expressions of awe for our world and the beings that share it with us. We have—and I will make this point clearer later—created intimacies among ourselves with mele and moʻolelo. Whenever I have given this presentation, it has been my aim to create that intimacy with an audience, regardless of who they are. I do not know whether that is possible in this medium, but I am going to try.

You will need to do some of the work yourselves and I will not be looking to see if you are. You will need to imagine these verses sung. You will need to imagine me lifting my voice, framing images with my hands, occasionally tearing up, because this is how I tell this moʻolelo.

This is about memory and how we commemorate the many lives that matter to us in mele and mo'olelo, and we should begin by remembering what the Protect Kaho'olawe 'ohana[1] taught us almost 40 years ago, that the 'āina (the land) is a life that matters to us, that as an ancestor or elder sibling, Hawai'i Pae'āina has been inscribing stories on the millions of lives that have been blessed enough to call her mother. The Reverend Lorenzo Lyons was infused with this aloha for Hawai'i, enabling him to write a song that is arguably the most recognisable mele among contemporary Hawaiians of any that have been composed. I think he could not help himself, having come to love the people whom he tended in such horrific times and at the same time comforted by the matchless beauty of Waimea.

Hawai'i Aloha

E Hawai'i e ku'u one hanau e
Ku'u home kulaiwi nei
Oli no au i na pono lani ou
E Hawai'i aloha e
E hau'oli e nā 'ōpio Hawai'i nei
Oli e, ole e
Mai nā aheahe makani e pā mai nei
Mau kealoha no Hawai'i[2]

I have come to the tentative conclusion that each human, though our experiences and relationships with one another allow us to carry and remember countless mo'olelo, is the purveyor of a single mo'olelo—one story that we seek and define and perfect in the course of our lives. Of course, I could merely be speaking as a historian who has a profound respect for stories and the people who remember and tell them. The action of remembering and revealing stories is significant, though no more so than other things we do as humans. I have never given birth, never survived personal combat, never navigated a canoe and crew into the wild sea, never lost or won a close election. By most measures, I have lived a distinctly uneventful life. And yet, what a life it has been.

---

1   The Protect Kaho'olawe 'Ohana was originally an organisation of young men and women who opposed the US Navy and Army's destruction of Kaho'olawe Island in the 1970s by going on to the island, risking imprisonment and death, between 1976 and 1978. See Osorio (2014).

2   *Hawai'i Aloha* is a hymn composed by the missionary Reverend Lorenzo Lyons in about 1865. Lyons came with the fifth company of American Board of Commissioners of Foreign Missions missionaries, teaching and preaching in Waimea, Hawai'i; he was a loyal subject of the kingdom and died in 1890.

Kahea i ke Aloha ʻĀina
Our mothers birthed this mighty land
and for our children yearned
Our kindred spirits call to us
To the ʻāina we return
Aloha ʻāina, kauoha nā kūpuna
This land was left for you
Na kākou kūkulu i ke ea
We send this song to you. (Osorio 2013)

The chain that links our living and conscious ʻāina, fenua and each generation of Kānaka before us and all those who come after us is both genealogy and memory. And I am going to reassure you that the story that you—all of you—are weaving for yourselves comes from your lands and your families and they will be added to all those voices speaking to your millions of descendants. That is the thing about stories; some of them are immortal though none of them is immutable.

Hawaiian Spirits Live Again
Cast your eyes down the mountainside
Out from the surf into the valley
Restlessly waiting through the years
Solemn and silent souls have gathered here
Waipiʻo
Where the old ways like the sea
Seem to flow unceasingly
And a thousand voices speak to me
Where the wave rushes on
And the mist rolls in
And Hawaiian spirits live again. (Osorio 1984)

I wrote this song for my grandmother Eliza Kamakawiwoʻole Osorio, who grew up in a society that was busy disparaging almost everything about Hawaiians, from our language, religion and history to our family relationships and ease with one another, and our emotions, which always seem so close to the surface. She bore that disparagement with an almost indignant disregard and behaved as though her personal conduct was more than enough evidence of our value as a people. She taught us that mana (power) comes not from having authority over others, but from having authority over yourself, being fully accountable for your own being.

I believe Eliza Osorio, who came from an ancient line of Ali`i (chiefs, nobles), understood something elemental about family and about life's essential transcendence. A committed Christian in the same denomination as Reverend Lyons, my grandmother worshiped the Christian God and would not allow a whisper of another deity's name in her presence. But fluent in `ōlelo Hawai`i, she sang, composed and dreamed in our language and seemed most at home when surrounded by the sound of it. Yet, in her own home, she mothered babies to whom she would not speak that language. Did she ever fear that her own children, grandchildren and great-grandchildren would seem like aliens to her?

She did teach us to sing in our language. Perhaps that reassured her. Once she told me of a chiefly ancestor, `Umialiloa,[3] and that is a story I have cultivated and retold perhaps a hundred times. I learned to think of the Ali`i as real, not mythical, beings, not just from my grandmother's story, but also through her impeccable modelling of them. She was a graceful and serious person whose elegance was never more on display than when she worked in her gardens or arranged the flowers in my father's hotel. When I ignored his advice to seek a career in law and became a singer/songwriter, I think my father was secretly pleased. My grandmother was never secretive about it, especially when I sang the mele of her youth.

Eliza was 20 years old when Lili`uokalani died and, in the hundreds of memorial services held for the Queen, I am certain, even without substantial written evidence, the Queen's best-known songs were sung in every Hawaiian church and gathering for months from the autumn of 1917. No more appropriate song could be chosen to say farewell than Lili`u's *Aloha `Oe*— already world famous and uniquely positioned to represent the Queen, her subjects and a haole imagination of a final and permanent passing of the kingdom and its claims to legitimacy.

Adria Imada's 2012 book, *Aloha America*, considers the tremendous popularity of the Queen's composition in the United States as coupled to an American colonial ethos: 'An "imagined intimacy" of empire was summoned through this song—an imagined relationship in which Hawai`i and the United States, figured as heterosexual lovers, were inseparable' (Imada 2012: 11, 154). But even colonials could recognise that, for Kānaka,

---

3   This is a particularly well-known mo`olelo and was written down by Samuel Kamakau, Abraham Fornander, David Malo, Kepelino and other nineteenth-century historians.

these mele had other, quite substantial meetings. In her 2013 article on *Aloha `Oe*, Imada describes the remembrances of a powerful and influential haole of the song's impact:

> Albert Pierce Taylor, an American who served as a secretary for the Hawaii Annexation Commission in the late 1890s, became an influential journalist, amateur ethnologist, and chief archivist in the territory. In his ethnographic account of Hawai`i published in 1922, *Under Hawaiian Skies*, Taylor associates 'Aloha `Oe' with the passing of the romantic kingdom. He witnesses the song at the funerals of two ali`i, the former Queen Lili`uokalani and her nephew Prince Jonah Kūhiō Kalaniana`ole. These 'semi-barbaric' funerals are occasions to mourn the loss of old, 'picturesque' Hawai`i: 'Never have Hawaiian voices blended more sweetly, with sobs in every note, as they have over their alii.' (Imada 2013: 40)

Consider the intimacies of those gatherings to mourn and honour the last of the great Ali`i and one can understand the nature of the fierce Kānaka Maoli resistance to the myriad cultural appropriations which by the twentieth century became, for Americans, an almost effortless undertaking. Even as Imada documents the extraordinary popularity of the Queen's song and its relentless commercialisation, she also recognises how closely bound are the song, the Queen, the overthrow and the American theft of our country in the framing of the contemporary native identity in Hawai`i.

That these two very different realities could coexist is not difficult to understand. But to label the ubiquitous commercialisation of *Aloha `Oe* simply as an appropriation understates the violence done to the song itself, as well as the culture from which it was taken. Consider a typical twenty-first-century appropriation in the Disney cartoon movie *Lilo and Stitch*.[4] A presumably Hawaiian older sister, having just lost her job, sings *Aloha `Oe* to Lilo while Stitch, a true alien, looks on, seemingly puzzled by this display of human filial devotion. The mele and its meaning have little to do with the drama of the moment. Disney wants this iconic song to be associated with this story, this mo`olelo, and it is a simple enough thing to accomplish.

The problem is not that it is appropriation. Several musicologists have caught Lili`u's borrowing of the tune in both the verse and the chorus of two different nineteenth-century European compositions. The tune of

----

4   See: www.youtube.com/watch?v=m0BYbPjlujc.

the verse resembles *The Rock Beside the Sea*, composed by Charles Crozat Converse and published in Philadelphia in 1857. The melody of the chorus resembles the chorus of George Frederick Root's composition *There's Music in the Air*, also published in 1857. I can tell you the history of nineteenth-, twentieth- and twenty-first-century Hawaiian music is one of appropriation in every form of mostly American music.

Appropriation works both ways, as does commercialisation. We Kānaka Maoli have taken your Frank Sinatra and your Elvis and your Beatles and made them into songs that people think we composed. The problem with appropriation in general and *Lilo and Stitch* in particular is that the movie is just so much of nothing and the song it appropriated was and is so powerful. *Lilo and Stitch* settles for romanticising this sibling relationship, which trivialises it. To romanticise something is not necessarily to trivialise, but in this case, the message of love for a younger sibling, the understanding of incipient separation or the erotic love of a couple are only tiny fragments of the love this song expresses.

Aloha ʻOe
Haʻaheo i ka ua i nā pali
Ke nihi aʻela I ka nāhele
E hahai ana paha i ka liko
Pua ʻāhihi lehua o uka

Liliʻuokalani and her party have been enjoying the refreshing hospitality of the Boyd family—friends who live in the uplands of Maunawili. The woman who is taking a farewell kiss from a cavalry officer is probably none other than her younger sister, Miriam Likelike. The Princess Likelike is married to a haole sugar planter, has a daughter barely three years old and is, like her sister, a devoted churchgoer and pillar of the society. But she is not simply some mocked-up reduction of Victorian womanhood; she has affairs and is quite open about them.[5]

She is Aliʻi. Both Liliʻu and Likelike are remnants, really, of a social and political class that once numbered in the tens of thousands, wielded tremendous authority and commanded such respect and that is now essentially disappearing—the result of a century of disease and horrific depopulation. Liliʻu is saying farewell to those lovers but also to this beautiful place where she and her family could simply take in the beauty of

---

5   Likelike is the composer of *Kuʻu Ipo i ka Heʻe Puʻe One*, a song that remembers an intense lovemaking with a surf-rider in the tall grass alongside a stream. Elbert and Māhoe (1978).

the land, the kindness of their friends and the comfort of being with others, and now must return to the responsibilities and respectabilities of leadership in Honolulu.

She is also saying aloha to that larger family of chiefs, utterly diminished and on the cusp of oblivion. Ha`aheo means 'proud', 'haughty', 'regal'. Her language describes both the chiefess and the mist that shrouds and nourishes the forest. She is acknowledging a way of life, a gracefulness of being, an ease of leadership and chiefly prerogative to love as one wishes. This is not nostalgia; this is mourning, and it foreshadows the sobbing ceremonies that will grieve for the monarchy and mourn the American takeover and Lili`u's own passing.

The rich layers of this mele provide continual inspiration for Kānaka, which Imada notes. Even fragments of the song, such as when Gabby Pahinui adds a suffix to his 1972 recording of the classic *Hi`ilawe*—a lavish steel-guitar rendering of *Aloha `Oe*—are, I think, a recognition of our continued devotion to this extraordinary wahine (woman) and to the Ali`i she so ably embodied (Imada 2013: 46). So, what does it mean that a song that can be so trivialised by a powerful, rich and numerous people is deeply, extravagantly experienced by our impoverished remnant of a nation struggling for our very lives?

> *Hawaiian Soul*
> I can recall the way your voice would fill the room
> And we would all be stilled by your melody
> And now your voice is gone and to the sea belongs
> All of the graceful songs that you had harbored
>
> They say before you left to seek your destiny
> That older voices called and drowned your laughter
> But I believe you knew what you would always be
> A beacon in the storm to guide us after
>
> Hawaiian Soul, how could you leave us
> You've not been lost at sea,
> You're only wandering
> Hawaiian soul, we sing your melodies
> And send them out to sea,
> You know the harmony. (Osorio and Borden 1979)

This is a love song for the Kānaka Maoli activists George Helm and Kimo Mitchell, who gave their lives in the struggle to rescue Kaho`olawe Island from the US military in 1977 (Osorio 2014). But the songwriter was young, callow, superficial and almost completely ignorant about his culture, with no ability to use his own language poetically. And, if this song portrays more than the writer knew, which I know it does, the kind of poetry that expresses such wholeness can only be unconscious.

It is not my purpose to engage the older scholars among us who wrote something brilliant as young men and women and have been telling variations of the same story ever since. I stated earlier that most of us have only one mo'olelo and we tell it with different variations over the years, but that is not what I mean here. I mean that when an event and your surroundings and your own readiness converge, it is possible to create something larger than yourself and when that happens you should simply be grateful, certainly not arrogant for the fact that you were chosen to deliver something beautiful and, for whatever time it possesses, meaningful.[6]

The Beauty of Mauna Kea
My friends and I would sometimes roam
The trails of Mauna Kea
And in the evening we'd come home
To see her standing there
The moon moves around her when she sleeps
The clouds stand beside her when she weeps
And I could be forgotten and a thousand miles away
And still I would recall the beauty of Mauna Kea.

And I live in the city now
And I see different things
In the nights when I'm alone
She's in my dreams
The wind spins around her when she wakes
The sun spreads his warmth across her face
And I could be forgotten and a thousand miles away
And still I would recall the beauty of Mauna Kea

Now to any land you go, she will be with you
If you love her like I do
Mauna Kea. (Beamer 1972)

---

6   *Hawaiian Soul* has been recorded six times that I know of, and I am sure I have sung this in front of audiences more than 2,000 times since Randy Borden and I composed it in 1977. I have told many audiences that the song was a gift, that it came through and not from us, and I tend to think about most of my 'creations' that way. But if the song was a gift to anyone, it was a gift to me. Every time I sing it, it affects the people who are gathered and I take refuge in that connection to my people.

Mauna Kea, or Mauna ʻo Wākea, dominates one's view-planes if you are from Hilo, Hāmākua or Waimea. It is not just its size; its greatness is in the way you can see the colours, vegetation and weather; how everything is defined by that mountain. The mountain, even below the timberline and up to the summit is wao akua (a place of gods). It is, or was, a wild and sensitive place, where humans did not live but would come for ceremony and to take and shape stone, to gather particular unique lāʻau (plants), to glimpse the land, sea and heavens from that extraordinary high place. They came to commune with its greatness and with the gods.

When Keola Beamer, a native of Waimea, wrote *The Beauty of Mauna Kea*, there were no telescopes on the mountain, no carloads of tourists looking for snowboarding adventures, no new-age religious practitioners (well, maybe a few) roaming the sacred heights and there was no road to the summit. These developments accelerated until there were 13 telescopes on the summit and plans to build an enormous new facility, the Thirty Meter Telescope (TMT), in this decade.

The TMT was not the first telescope to be opposed by Kānaka Maoli traditional religious practitioners, but the sheer size of the project, coupled with a well-coordinated legal challenge by several organisations, brought that opposition into plain view and sustained it over several years. This culminated in a massive protest involving hundreds of people interfering with attempts to break ground at the site in 2015, with handfuls of protectors holding vigils on the frigid summit for weeks at a time, dozens of arrests and renewed pledges to oppose the project to the end and to prevent the desecration of that mauna.

How does one desecrate a sacred place? Or, to ask this another way: what is sacred about Mauna Kea? When government officials, astronomers and even puzzled onlookers ask that question, it is not always an innocent query. If there is something specifically sacred about a place, where precisely is it located? And based on what practice and history is such sacredness claimed? As Kānaka, we often find ourselves unable to explain kapu (sacred) to Americans, for the same reasons that separate our perspectives and understanding of a mele like *Aloha ʻOe*. That Americans could trivialise and commercially exploit a song that has such meaning and history for us and *never understand* the depth and compelling message it contains have been amply demonstrated over and over again.

Kapu is our word for sacred and things forbidden. But even here the English translation fails to capture the depth of the word. Mauna Kea is not a forbidding place. Our storytellers and composers have long connected themselves to that mauna with deeply intimate gestures of affection. To us, what is sacred is beautiful and what is beautiful is true (thank you, Keats). And sometimes what is true can only be known and partially shared.

There is only one more thing I can share with you and I cannot be sure whether what I have written has moved or shaken you, or convinced you of anything. If you are to carry something away from this essay, it should at least include the understanding that the Kānaka Maoli are still quite alive, we still draw our sustenance and personalities from the ʻāina and from our memories of kupuna (ancestors), and we have grown more conscious of our distinctiveness, learning from the moʻolelo and mele we remember and the ones we continue to create.

Poliahu i ke Hau

Poliahu I ke hau
Kuaehu I ka ipo
With your cold descending down
I am a statue in your arms
On the silent windy slope
I stand beneath your gaze
Auhea ka wahine?
I call out your name

E Mauna Kea
I wander neath the stars
Without knowing who they are
And sleep before I see thee
hovering on the sea

Nānā wale i ka lani
As you search among the stars
Auhea o Waiau?
Nalowale i ka mauna.
A hoʻi aʻe ʻoe
I ka poli o ka wahine
Ulupiʻi me ka ʻōnea (trembling and desolate)
Who weeps for her love?[7]

---

7   Composed by Jonathan Osorio, unrecorded, 2015.

2

Beauty beyond the Eye of the Beholder: The efficacy of Indigenous seasonal calendars in northern Australia

Emma Woodward[1]

Indigenous peoples across Oceania face diverse resource management issues. The Indigenous and traditional knowledge systems that drive local resource management are both unique and complex. These knowledge systems also share important commonalities: the strong observational, practice-based method in which they have come into being and continue to be enacted and tested; the spiritual and metaphysical belief systems that underpin much resource management practice; and the unique phenological basis for resource management that is intimately woven within a detailed understanding of biology, hydrology and meteorology. These systems of knowledge have sustained consecutive generations by adapting continually, if incrementally, to the local context over time. This chapter reveals key similarities and differences between aspects of two Australian Aboriginal resource management systems, derived from the Gooniyandi and Ngan'gi sets of language groups, to demonstrate both the complexities of the systems and the convergence and divergence of resource management knowledge (in form and content) within a tropical northern Australian context. The knowledge was collated through research partnerships between the

1   This project received funding from the (former) Tropical Rivers and Coastal Knowledge (TRaCK) research program. Many thanks to Dion Fleming, who arranged the map.

author and senior Aboriginal knowledge-holders from the two language groups and communicated via seasonal resource management 'calendars'. The potential of these calendars to act as tools that communicate resource management knowledge is discussed within the broader regional context of local and Indigenous-led resource management and the potential and possibilities for beyond-local resource management knowledge-sharing. While, ultimately, resource management solutions will only be ecologically sustainable and socially enduring if they take account of distinct local contexts and cultures, local resource guardianship might be further empowered and enhanced through learning how other local resource managers deal with broadly similar issues and contexts. A necessary foundation for such cross-situational learning are tools that facilitate knowledge transmission, together with the networks that can facilitate knowledge-sharing and interaction across cultures.

Introduction

Indigenous ecological knowledge (IEK), also known as traditional ecological knowledge and Indigenous knowledge, has been referred to as 'a cumulative body of knowledge, practice, and belief, evolving by adaptive processes and handed down through generations by cultural transmission, about the relationship of living beings (including humans) with one another and with their environment' (Berkes et al. 2000: 1252). From an Indigenous perspective, IEK is a way of living in which the core aim is to sustain the healthy functioning of people and Country through relationships of reciprocity (Holmes and Jampijinpa 2013; Woodward and Marrfurra McTaggart 2019) and is therefore best understood 'not as a discrete, stand-alone entity, but rather as tangible systems of knowledge, meanings, values and practices deeply embedded in Indigenous cultures' (Smallacombe et al. 2006: 7). IEK comes into being, and is strengthened and renewed, through the many diverse ways Indigenous peoples regard and act out their relationships with one another, with their lands and environments and with their ancestors (Smallacombe et al. 2006).

Surveys of the literature on IEK emphasise the way it is transmitted and the longevity of its use. There is an emphasis on continuity and cumulative acquisition of knowledge generated by communities heavily reliant on natural resources (Berkes 2012). While IEK has been passed down through generations, it is also a living, dynamic force that is adaptive and innovative (Goodall 2008; Smallacombe et al. 2006; Wohling 2009).

In Australia, Indigenous peoples have been active custodians of the continent's vast land and seascapes for more than 65,000 years (Clarkson et al. 2017), and each of the more than 250 Australian Indigenous language groups has developed their own unique knowledge base for managing the resources within their clan boundaries (Flood 1999). The actions of Aboriginal custodians in managing and looking after Country are diverse (Hill et al. 2013; Russell-Smith et al. 2009; Woodward 2008). Most of the more than 100 formalised Indigenous land and sea ranger groups in operation across Australia have formed from community-driven action with some degree of assistance from Aboriginal land councils, Aboriginal corporations, government agencies, local community organisations and nongovernmental organisations (NGOs) (Altman et al. 2007; Muller 2008; Putnis et al. 2008; Storrs and Cooke 2001; Woodward 2008). Each group draws on its own unique, locally specific system of IEK to achieve day-to-day land and sea management (see Dhimurru 2008; Wunambal Gaambera Aboriginal Corporation 2010).

Many more individuals and family groups also play a significant role in managing their Country on a daily basis by being on Country; sharing stories and songs about Country; observing and engaging Country through conversation; maintaining sacred sites; and enacting knowledge to collect plant and animal resources and preparing these resources for consumption, medicinal purposes, construction and arts and crafts (see Farrelly 2003; Lowe and Pike 2009; NMA 2010). Each of these activities is executed by drawing on a locally specific IEK system based on an intimate and unique understanding of the local environment (Rose 1996, 2000). Much of this environmental knowledge has been built on over generations of continued observations of weather systems and their resultant influence on plant and animal lifecycles. This knowledge has in large part contributed to successful resource harvesting and the continued survival of Aboriginal groups in often harsh environments. The observation and interpretation of seasonal meteorological, hydrological and biological events and cycles, and the interconnections within and between each, have also resulted in a diversity of complex, often highly localised resource management systems.

There has been increasing interest from scientists, governments and NGOs to engage with IEK for its potential insights into natural resource management (NRM) issues including climate change (Agrawal 1995; Berkes et al. 2000; Bohensky and Maru 2011; Ens et al. 2015; Huntington 2000; Krupnik and Jolly 2002; Liedloff et al. 2013; Nakashima et al. 2012; Prober et al. 2011). This is partially because of the geographically and temporally more extensive nature of IEK than research-based knowledge, particularly in regions where Indigenous livelihoods are reliant on natural resources and where there has been long and widespread Indigenous occupation and observation (Fraser et al. 2006; Gadgil et al. 1993; Garde et al. 2009; Ziembicki et al. 2013). The inclusion of Indigenous knowledge in NRM holds significance beyond scientific or broader societal merit. Acknowledgement and adoption of IEK contributes to social justice for, and the sovereignty, autonomy and identity of, Indigenous peoples (Bohensky and Maru 2011).

Given the extensive nature of IEK, there are relatively few cases where it has informed the creation of NRM policy, including that related to water resources (for reference to the adoption of Māori cultural indicators for monitoring river health in Aotearoa New Zealand, see Tipa and Teirney 2006). Prober et al. (2011) argue that inadequate cross-cultural means of organising and communicating IEK have limited its effective inclusion in management decisions, while Bohensky and Maru (2011) suggest that scientists who can span both knowledge systems ('intercultural knowledge-bridgers') can prove effective in achieving successful Indigenous–Western science knowledge integration.

Calendars have been used to organise and represent much-simplified forms of Indigenous and local knowledge systems (Coulter et al. 2012; Davis et al. 2011; McTaggart et al. 2009; Mukherjee 2002; Prober et al. 2011). Calendars can be defined as inscribed condensations of knowledge about cycles (Birth 2012) and are organised by logics that adopt certain ideas over others. For example, the foundation for the Gregorian calendar—the internationally accepted civil calendar—is the solar year, while many other calendrical forms follow the lunar cycle (see, for example, Lefale 2010; Roberts et al. 2006). Environmental cycles work independently of the Gregorian calendar, and those who intimately depend on the environment for their livelihoods look for local environmental signs to guide their activities, rather than set dates (Birth 2012). There are well-documented ethnographic cases of both environmental and astronomical cues being important in marking cycles (Clarke 2009; Lefale 2010; Roberts et al. 2006). While it has been hypothesised that non-Gregorian calendars, which follow environmental and astronomical cues, are of direct interest and use to natural resource managers, government policymakers and the broader public, little direct evidence of their use is available.

This chapter draws on aspects of two knowledge systems, documented in the form of 'seasonal calendars' of aquatic resource use, to reveal the complexities of the systems and the convergence and divergence of Aboriginal resource management knowledge (in form and content) within a tropical northern Australian context. The chapter also aims to highlight the potential of seasonal calendars as tools for cross-regional knowledge-sharing and learning.

Methods

This research responded to the concerns of Aboriginal custodians of the Daly River and Fitzroy River catchments (see Map 2.1) that they were not being effectively included in government-run regional water planning processes that could impact on their future water use and associated values and interests (Jackson 2004). As part of this project, the author worked with four Aboriginal language groups from the Northern Territory and Western Australia between 2008 and 2012 to document Indigenous aquatic resource use, IEK, and seasonal aspects of that knowledge to increase understanding of local Aboriginal interests in freshwater and associated values (Jackson et al. 2011, 2012; Woodward et al. 2012).

The methods by which the author and senior Aboriginal knowledge-holders subsequently partnered to document and compile local seasonal calendars of aquatic resource use are described in detail in Woodward (2010) and Woodward and Marrfurra McTaggart (2015). Participatory research methods were engaged and, due to the relatively long time frame of research engagement (more than three years) and significant resourcing, the research partnerships were able to evolve slowly and focus in accordance with the interests of all participants (Woodward and Marrfurra McTaggart 2015).

The first seasonal calendar to be compiled, the Ngan'gi seasons calendar, was initiated by Ngan'gi-language elder Patricia Marrfurra McTaggart (Woodward 2010; Woodward and Marrfurra McTaggart 2015). Following the compilation of this first calendar, many other Aboriginal language groups have been inspired and motivated to work with the author and other collaborators and facilitators to create their own seasonal calendars (see, for example, www.csiro.au/en/research/indigenous-science/indigenous-knowledge/calendars).

A critical aspect of the methodology was the ability of the author and senior Indigenous knowledge-holders to engage in gradual conversation, which over time created opportunities to reveal detailed descriptions of seasonal happenings—hydrological, ecological, meteorological and metaphysical. The ability to recall this knowledge, and the depth of description, was greatly strengthened by immersion in Country—in place and during the season/s for which the associated events were being observed and recalled (Woodward 2010).

The research project obtained human ethics research approval from Charles Darwin University (Australia) (in the absence of a similar approvals process for the author's host organisation, CSIRO, at the time of the research). The project was governed by a research agreement with the Kimberley (Aboriginal) Land Council for the work undertaken with Gooniyandi language speakers and was directed by Nauiyu Incorporated, a group of Aboriginal representatives from Nauiyu community, for the work undertaken with Ngan'gi language speakers.[2]

---

2   The Indigenous seasonal calendars referred to in this chapter were co-created with the author. They are the Indigenous Cultural and Intellectual Property (ICIP) of the people and communities or Indigenous knowledge-holders who shared them. The Indigenous knowledge-holders assert ownership, authority and control over the ICIP expressed in the language names, stories, knowledge about plants, animals and seasonal connections, as well as the seasonal visual representation, in the calendar. The Indigenous knowledge-holders are sharing their calendars and ICIP embedded in them for educational outreach only—namely, to increase awareness, respect and recognition of their culture, knowledge and practices and for use by the public, students, teachers and schools, universities and cultural institutions in learning. If you wish to reference the seasonal calendars, please acknowledge and properly attribute who and where the ICIP came from. You can find more information at: www.csiro.au/en/research/indigenous-science/indigenous-knowledge/calendars.

Results

Seasonal calendar I: Gooniyandi seasonal knowledge of the Fitzroy Valley region, Western Australia

The regional hub of the Fitzroy Valley is the town of Fitzroy Crossing. In 2009, approximately 2,700 people lived here in about 45 Aboriginal communities scattered throughout the valley (Morphy 2010), including at the settlement of Muludja, where the authors of the Gooniyandi seasonal calendar reside (see Plates 2.2 and 2.3).

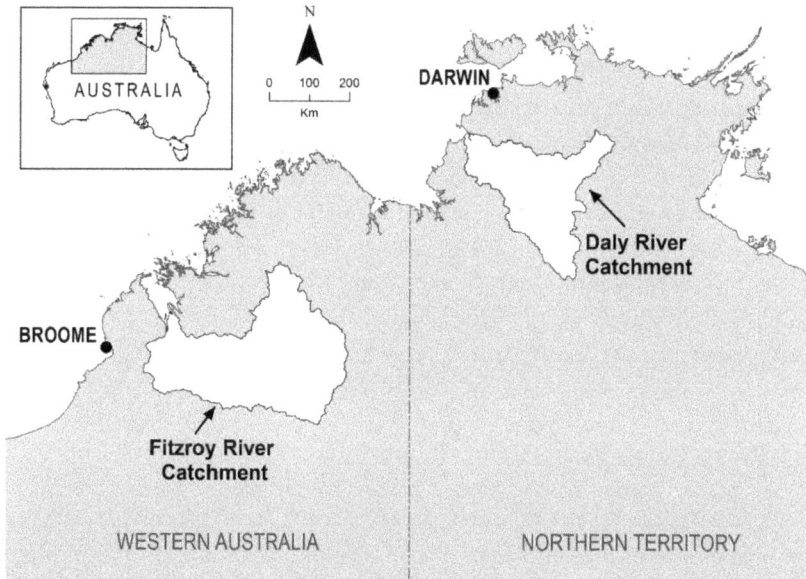

Map 2.1: Location of the Fitzroy River and Daly River catchments within which the Gooniyandi and Ngan'gi seasonal calendars were created.
Source: Dion Fleming, CSIRO.

Aboriginal people make up 80 per cent of the Fitzroy Valley's population. The valley crosses seven ethnolinguistic areas, making it a culturally, linguistically and politically diverse region (Toussaint et al. 2001). These different language groups hold a strong sociocultural connection to land and water in the region (Toussaint et al. 2001) and Indigenous groups continue to express a responsibility to care for all water sources (Toussaint 2008;

Yu 2003). Fish and fishing are extremely important to the Traditional Owners of the Fitzroy River (Thorburn et al. 2004; Toussaint 2014). An unparalleled understanding of the diversity of fish found in the Fitzroy River is highlighted by the recognition of almost all the fish of the river by individual Aboriginal names in the languages of the Bunuba, Gooniyandi, Ngarinyin, Nyikina and Walmajarri peoples (Morgan et al. 2004).

The Fitzroy River is a highly variable hydrological system, with the river ceasing to flow in some years (Kennard et al. 2010). Deep groundwater-fed permanent pools, separated by shallower reaches, occur along the river's length and provide crucial ecological refuges during exceptionally hot, dry conditions. The surrounding landscape is dotted with natural springs, which, as permanent water sources, hold strong cultural significance for local Aboriginal people (Yu 2003).

Key features of the Gooniyandi seasons calendar

The key senior Aboriginal custodians who engaged in the co-creation of the Gooniyandi seasonal calendar, entitled *Mingayooroo—Manyi Waramggiri Yarrangi, Gooniyandi Seasons, Margaret River, Fitzroy Valley, Western Australia*, and who showed, shared, documented and confirmed the inclusion of components of Gooniyandi ecological knowledge were June Davis, Mervyn Street, Helen Malo and Issac Cherel from Muludja Community on the Margaret River (a tributary of the Fitzroy). Many other senior Gooniyandi people were approached by this core group to discuss the creation of the calendar, to secure their approval and blessing for the calendar to progress and to check the knowledge displayed in the calendar against their own ecological understanding.

The Gooniyandi seasons calendar contains three main seasons: Barrangga (the very short season of very hot weather), Yidirla (the wet season time when the river runs) and Moongoowarla (cold weather time). Moongoowarla is further divided into two subseasons: Ngamari, 'female' cold weather time, which is characterised by cold days and cold nights; and Girlinggoowa, the 'male' phase of mild cold weather (see Davis et al. 2011). The calendar can be viewed online at www.csiro.au/en/research/indigenous-science/indigenous-knowledge/calendars/gooniyandi.

The most intensive harvesting occurs during Yidirla (wet season) (see Table 2.1) and Moongoowarla (cold weather time) (see Table 2.2). Barrangga is the season of very hot weather that is said to have arrived once both lagarndi (witchetty grubs) and bingga (sugar leaf) are available (see Table 2.1). Larger fish such as sawfish and barramundi, which are trapped in the shrinking pools within the river channel, stop taking the bait and 'won't bite'. As the weather heats up even more, the smaller fish such as black bream and catfish also stop biting and it is difficult to catch any fish. At this time, people will harvest mussels that move to the banks and shallower reaches, driven by the hot weather. The hot weather stimulates the growth of goorlibi (the bush banana, *Marsdenia viridiflora*) and heralds the availability of yimarli (the sand fig, *Ficus opposita*) and bawooloo (bush carrot) seeds, which will be collected and ground into damper.

A subseason within Barrangga is Yirrirrinyi—the very hot period at the end of the season just before the rains arrive. This period is defined by the heat-haze dancing on the horizon. There is no water and it is hard to dig for soaks (to source underground drinking water); leaves shrivel and birds can die at this time. The average daily maximum temperature is above 40°C (104°F); the air is heavy and it is hot even in the shade. This period is known as Boordbara and people look for lightning in the towering white clouds, which will tell them that rain is on the way. Large boomerang-shaped clouds called wiray warn of a big storm coming.

A series of showers and storms can occur in Fitzroy River country before the river runs for the first time of the wet season; this first rain is called Barrabarra and causes many different types of eucalyptus trees to shed their bark. It gets very hot after this first rain. This rain also causes the flowers of girndi (the black plum, *Vitex glabrata*), to fall to the ground. Fireflies (also called 'girndi') are indicators for the fruit ripening; the flickering of the fireflies at night is said to 'cook' the fruit and make it ripe.

Moonggoowarla, the season of cold weather, is also the season of fat fish and animals: jarloomboo (red dragonflies) appear at the beginning of the season to tell you sawfish are fat. Goorjali (march flies) arrive when all garwi (fish) are fat and protect langarra (freshwater crocodiles) as they lay their eggs. The seedheads and bulbs of lilies are also collected now and roasted in the coals before eating, while the flying fox comes searching for nectar-filled flowers and is also eaten during this season.

However, once the Moonggoowarla wind starts blowing from the east and the weather starts to cool, fish are said to 'shut their mouths' and it can be a hard time to catch fish. But when the wind changes direction and the Garrawoorda blows from the south, this is a sign to start fishing for sawfish.

Table 2.1: Gooniyandi seasons calendar: Barrangga (very hot weather) to Yidirla (wet season time)

Barrangga: Very short season of very hot weather; hot days, hot nights		Yidirla: Wet season time when the river runs	
The season of Barrangga has arrived when both lagarndi (witchetty grubs) and bingga (sugar leaf) are available.	Yirrirrinyi is the very hot time during Barrangga. Heat-haze is dancing; there is no water around; it's hard to dig for soaks, leaves shrivel and birds can die.	The first rain of Yidirla is called Barrabarra. The rain causes the bark of bilindi, walarri, boorngga, thalngadi, yilangi, galardiwa and other eucalypts to peel. It gets very hot after the first rain.	After the eucalypts' bark has peeled, yidiyidi (cicadas) emerge, while jaalinyi (moon grubs) come out after the first flood.
During Barrangga, the pools in the river channel continue to dry and get smaller. When people fish in these pools, trapped galwanyi (sawfish) and barlga (barramundi) will not bite, while gooloomangarri (catfish) and jambinbaroo (black bream) will run for the bait. Fish for galwanyi and barlga in deeper river sections.		It is difficult to catch boornda and other baitfish at the beginning of Yidirla; you can only get tiny baitfish on hooks. Jaalinyi (moon grubs) and big blue-wing grasshoppers are used for bait.	Bawaloo (bush carrot, *Portulaca pilosa*) is collected now and roasted before eating.
			Wilarrabi and diwiwi (turtles) lay eggs in the mud on the sides of the riverbanks when the water is still flowing.
Nganyjarli (bush tomato) ripen now; they are ready when white and soft.	Jambinbaroo (black bream), gooloomangarri (catfish) and longtom stop biting towards the end of Barrangga.	Barndiwiri is the first rainstorm that arrives from the north. It is associated with the Jangala skin group.	Garn gi (white currant) is fruiting and ready to be collected. Jirloowoo (river fig) is also ripe. The fruit falls into the water when the river flows for the second time, feeding turtles and fish. You must be quick to get the fruit before the pigs and birds!
Boordbara is the hot and humid time when the air is heavy and it is hot even in the shade. People look for lightning in the towering white clouds, which will tell them rain is on the way.	The bambira tree (*Atalaya hemiglauca*) flowers at the same time as langarra (freshwater crocodiles) lay their eggs. When the flowers fall to the ground, the eggs hatch and the young join their mothers in the river.	Darloo (bush mango) grows in the hill country and is ripening now.	
		The flowers of girndi (black plum), grow in the first rains, before being washed down to the creeks. The flickering of fireflies (also called girndi) is said to be 'cooking' the fruit and making it ripe.	

Barrangga: Very short season of very hot weather; hot days, hot nights		Yidirla: Wet season time when the river runs
Now is a good time for ngawaya (freshwater mussels) as the hot weather makes them move to the banks of pools and billabongs. They can be boiled and the solution drunk to treat cold sick.		When the river and creeks are running, it is good fishing for gooloomangarri (catfish) and bigger fish — try for baya (stingray), galwanyi (sawfish), jambinbaroo (black bream), barlga (barramundi), wilarrabi and diwiwi (long-necked and short-necked turtles). Turtles lay eggs in the mud on the sides of the riverbanks when the water is still flowing.
Good turtle fishing time.		
When the red seeds of the jirndiwili tree (*Erythrina vespertilio*) fall to the ground, you know a big rain, the wet season, is coming.		
Bawaloo (bush carrot) seeds called blayiwarri are ready to be collected and ground into flour for damper.	Wirayi are the boomerang-shaped clouds that can be seen at the end of Barrangga. Wirayi warn of a big storm coming. Manyboo are the white 'cotton-wool' clouds that come from the spring-country during the middle of the wet season.	Moogoomoogoo is the quiet rain that falls with no wind, thunder or lightning. It is a nice rain to fish in. After the big wet, there is light foggy rain called boolinyji. This is the last rain of the wet season.
Butterflies tell you bambilyi (wild passionfruit, *Capparis lasiantha*) is flowering.		Marroora (Leichhardt pine, *Nauclea orientalis*) is fruiting now.
		Jawandi is the last rainstorm of the wet season and comes from the south.
Yimarli (black sand fig, Ficus opposita) is ripe and ready to eat when it turns purple-black.		

Table 2.2: Gooniyandi seasons calendar: Moongoowarla (cold weather time)

Moongoowarla: cold weather time			
Ngamari: Female cold weather time (cold days, cold nights)		Girlinggoowa: Male cold weather time (mild)	
Gooloowa is the rain that falls after the monsoons have finished and as Ngamari (female cold weather) starts.	Wawanyi (goanna), girwili (water goanna), nyarlangarri (king brown snake), yilimi (black-headed python) and nganthanany (rock python) are all fat and ready to be hunted.	When the crow calls, the weather is moving into Girlinggoowa.	Gooroo (freshwater mangrove, *Barringtonia acutangula*) is flowering now. It is said that galwanyi (sawfish) eat the flowers when they fall into the river in the wet season, making them fat and their guts pink.
		Collect the seedheads and 'chestnuts' of joomboowa and garrjari (lilies) and roast in the coals.	

Moongoowarla: cold weather time			
Ngamari: Female cold weather time (cold days, cold nights)		Girlinggoowa: Male cold weather time (mild)	
Jarloomboo (red dragonflies) appear at the beginning of Moonggoowarla to tell you galwinyi (sawfish) are fat. Goorjali (march flies) arrive when all garwi are fat and protect langarra (freshwater crocodiles) as they lay their eggs. It is a good time for laari (bony bream), gooloomangarri (catfish), wilarrabi (long-necked turtle), barlga (barramundi) and boornda (spangled perch).			Nganyjarli (bush tomato, *Solanum chippendalei*) is flowering.
The knock-em down rain comes now after the big river flow of the wet season. This storm from the east is called Joongoorra.	All kangaroos: thirwoo (hill kangaroo), wandjadi (little river kangaroo), woombanangi (short-eared wallaby), goombirna (left-hand nail-tail wallaby) and bandalngarna (red plain kangaroo) are fat and breeding. It's a good time for hunting, but leave those animals carrying joeys.	When joolwooljidi (*Bauhinia cunninghamii*) flowers, you know it is turning to hotter weather. Drink the nectar from the flowers.	A big mob of flowers around tells you that biriyali (conkerberry, *Carissa lanceolata*) is ripe. The wood is used for smoking babies and anyone who is sick.
Gawi (fish) are said to shut their mouths as the weather cools and the Moonggoowarla wind starts blowing from the east. This can be a hard time to catch fish.		Kangaroos and wallabies are moulting now, getting ready for the hot weather.	Paperbark trees flower all year around and bees make nyarlinya (honey) in the bark. This sugarbag is called darlarli.
Wajarri (the boab tree, *Adansonia gregorii*) shoots new leaves with the first rains of Yidirla (the previous season), before flowering and then fruiting during Moonggoowarla. When the fruit is green, it is roasted in ashes before eating. The nuts and fruit flesh are eaten when dry. Wajarri is a good medicine for stomach upsets.		Gawi (fish) start to carry eggs as they lose their fat.	
Joornda (bush onion, *Cyperus bulbosus*) is an important food that grows straight after the rain and can be dug up until hot weather time. Joornda attracts animals and a Gooniyandi person might use a special stone or Dreamtime place to ask for joornda to grow where they want to hunt for these animals. These places are very significant to Gooniyandi people.		As yirndi (flowers) bloom, the woonggoorroonba (flying fox) comes searching for nectar and stays until barrangga. There are plenty of native bees making hives and janga (honey) now. Both woonggoorroonba and janga are eaten now.	
Start digging for boorngga (yam), jarrandi (bush carrot) and birla (yam).	Goordida (bush orange, *Capparis umbonata*) fruits in the hot weather. The breeze carries the sweet smell of ripe goordida, allowing you to find the fruit. The leaves of goordida are used for smoking babies and young children to keep them strong.		

Moongoowarla: cold weather time		
Ngamari: Female cold weather time (cold days, cold nights)		Girlinggoowa: Male cold weather time (mild)
Galamooda, the favoured bush turkey, is fat now after eating grasshoppers during Yidirla. Gananyanja (emu) and joowooloogoo (whistling duck) are also fat and good eating now.	As the rain finishes, the wind changes direction and Garrawoorda blows from the south. The water is high; it's a good time for fishing for galwanyi (sawfish).	Limirri (spinifex wax) is being made by ants and can be collected throughout the year.

Seasonal calendar II: Ngan'gi seasonal knowledge of the Daly River region, Northern Territory

The term Ngan'gi refers to two closely related Aboriginal languages, Ngan'gikurunggurr and Ngen'giwumirri, which are spoken in the Daly River region. The name Ngan'gikurrungurr is etymologically a compound of ngan'gi, meaning 'language', 'story', 'word', and kurungurr, which is both the name of a particular swamp in the 'myil' swampland and the general term for deep, dark water, as found in the main channel (Marrfurra McTaggart et al. 2014).

The Daly River catchment supports a population of about 10,000 people, with Aboriginal people comprising about one-quarter of the population. The river holds significant economic, recreational, cultural and spiritual values for the 10 Aboriginal language groups who live along it (Jackson et al. 2011).

The perennial Daly River provides important habitat for a rich diversity of fish, reptiles and streamside vegetation (Schult and Townsend 2012). Flooding of wetland habitats occurs during the four to five months of the distinctly seasonal 'wet' period. The largest extent of flooding in the Daly River typically occurs between February and March, with water on the floodplains receding to large wetlands by approximately June and then to perennial waterholes by August (Jardine et al. 2012). The climate is dry monsoonal, characterised by uniformly high daytime temperatures: mean monthly temperatures range from 22.3°C to 37.4°C in October and from 15.5°C to 31.2°C in June (Marrfurra McTaggart et al. 2014).

The Ngan'gi seasons calendar was compiled with Ngan'gi speakers in the community of Nauiyu Nambiyu, which translates to 'coming together in one place' (Farrelly 2003). Residents originate from several different Aboriginal homelands and together speak at least 10 different Aboriginal languages.

Key features of the Ngan'gi seasons calendar

The key senior Aboriginal custodians who partnered with the author to co-create the Ngan'gi seasons calendar were Patricia Marrfurra McTaggart, Molly Yawulminy, Catherine Bamul, Dorothy Daning, Kitty Kamarrama, Benigna Ngulfundi, Maureen Warrumburr and Mercia Wawul. Many other senior Ngan'gi language speakers were approached by this core group to discuss the research, provide contributions and confirmation of documented knowledge and give approval and their blessing for knowledge to be displayed in the calendar.

The Ngan'gi seasons calendar displays 13 seasons in each annual weather cycle, with the length of each season determined by the duration of events that define that season (see McTaggart et al. 2009). As such, the timing of Ngan'gi seasons can vary from year to year as the onset and duration of seasons can be significantly different each year (and dependent on regional and national weather systems). Other time-specific weather events are recognised by Ngan'gi people and may be thought of as 'subseasons'. For example, Memenyirr is a short season informed by the action of yirrng (pig-nosed turtle) as she moves her feet up and down to prevent them burning when she lays her eggs in the scalding sand during the hot and humid seasons of Ngunguwe and Lirrimem (Woodward and Marrfurra McTaggart 2019). The Ngan'gi seasons calendar can viewed online at: www. csiro.au/en/research/indigenous-science/indigenous-knowledge/calendars/ ngangi.

The Ngan'gi seasonal cycle is strongly tied to the lifecycle stages of the local speargrass, wurr (*Sorghum intrans*). The eight seasons related to the speargrass are listed here with their literal translations (see Marrfurra McTaggart et al. 2014) and linked observations:

- Wurr bengim tyerrfal = 'grass seeds sprout' (early wet season, January). The stick insect, amisyawuni, comes out and bush potatoes, misyawuni, are available for harvesting.

- Wurr wirribem dudutyamu = 'grass cheeks swell' (mid wet season, February). The seedheads hang heavily on the grass stems and knock together making a sound, 'taddo'. This tells you the rain is nearing its end.

- Wudupuntyurrutu = 'seeds have burst open' (late wet season, February–March). It is now fruiting season; all fruits are ripe and ready for gathering, while the magpie geese lay eggs on floating mats of wild rice.

- Wurr wirribem filgarri = 'grass stems redden but the seeds are still on the grass' (end of wet season, March). As the big wet subsides, there are lots of anganggurr (prawns) in the river and creeks.

- Wurr bengim miyerr = 'grass seeds fall' (dry season starts, April). The wind starts blowing from the east, which is a sure sign that the dry season is starting; ayiwisi (dragonflies) arrive to greet the new season, telling people it is barramundi fishing time.

- Wurr bengin derripal = 'grass knocked flat' (early dry season, May). Rain is still falling and it is a good time to harvest the eggs of anganni (magpie goose) as there is still water around to support the floating nests. This time of year is known to be good for catfish.

- Wurr tisyari = 'grass dry' (mid dry season, June). The grass is dead and dry and ready for burning. The magpie geese eggs are hatching and angankurinimbi (water goanna) are about.

- Wirirr marrgu = 'new burnt grass ash' (mid dry season, July). Black ash from the first fires is on the ground and people have a 'good feeling' about going hunting as it is not too hot.

As revealed, each of the life stages of the speargrass is an indicator for likely weather events, the lifecycle stages of other plants and animals and for the availability of food resources, which subsequently guide harvesting behaviour (see Tables 2.3 and 2.4; McTaggart et al. 2009; Woodward et al. 2012).

Table 2.3: Ngan'gi seasons calendar: Ngunguwe to Wurr wirribem filgarri

Ngunguwe	Lirrimem	Kudede	Wurr bengin tyerrfal	Wurr wirribem dudutyamu	Wudupuntyurrutu	Wurr wirribem filgarri
Ngunguwe means 'mirage'. It is very hot and humid with no rain. A heat shimmer can be seen during the middle of the day. Burrowing animals retreat to their holes, telling people the season of Lirrimem is coming.	Very humid period of the 'build-up' just before thunder is heard. The river water is warm. Afiti (cicadas) sing, calling out for rain.	The first rains come; start of the monsoon and the wet season. Angaga (tree frog) comes out.	Start of wurr panangalan (speargrass) cycle. The time when speargrass seeds begin to shoot.	The season when wurrmuy (speargrass heads) are swollen and hanging heavily. 'Taddo' is when the wurrmuy knock together and open, telling you rainfall is nearing the end. The river is at maximum height; come into Nauiyu community by boat.	Wurrmuy are puffing open. 'When the river rises, it's time to collect fruit.' Good fruiting season.	The time of the year when speargrass stalks start to die and turn a reddish colour – a sign the dry season is coming. Seeds are still intact.
Munggun munggunnyi (whirlwind) season	Migaga (cluster fig) fruiting and yirrng (pig-nosed turtle) eating it as it drops into the river.	Mundupun (green ant queens) are ready for eating.	Amisyawuni (stick insects) come out. Misyawuni (bush potato) available for gathering. The river is clear.	Awarrapun (saltwater crocodile), anganifinyi (echidna) and anganfepinimbi (rock python) hunting time. Anganifinyi and anganfepinimbi are sometimes found sharing the same burrow.	Fruits ready for gathering: midamurri, mimeli (black currant), miwerrmisya, miwisamuy (white currant) and mundupan (bush cucumber).	As the big wet subsides, there are lots of anganggurr (prawns) in the river and creeks.
Pods of yeninggisyi (red kapok) are brown and cracking open, signalling ewerrmisye (freshwater crocodile) eggs are starting to hatch (too late to collect them to eat).	Ewerrmisye (freshwater crocodiles) hatch as the shoots of new trees emerge. They leave the nest for the first time. The newborns are called mirringgi marrgu, which also means 'new leaves'.	Ngalwangga (short-necked turtles) and yirrng (pig-nosed turtles) hatch with the first rains while atyalmerr (barramundi) sink down into the river as they know the storms are coming.	Afganifinyi (echidna) and anganfepinimbi (rock python) are fattening up.	Mumuy (long yam) digging time, and throughout the wet season.	Anganni (magpie geese) are laying eggs on floating wurrfugar (wild rice) grass mats.	

Ngunguwe	Lirrimem	Kudede	Wurr bengin tyerrfal	Wurr wirribem dudutyamu	Wudupuntyurrutu	Wurr wirribem filgarri
Yerrwurumbi (ghost gum) bark starts peeling; adany (sharks) are fat and ready to catch. When the river level is really low, it's a good time for adany, emelpe (stingray) and sawfish.		Turtles start moving after being in hibernation. They are 'happy to be going back into the water'. They are still fat and still good hunting.				
Very good time for hunting turtle.						
Duny (*Terminalia macrocarpa*) is flowering.	Yerrmanggi (freshwater mangrove) is flowering.					
Duny is fruiting.						
Yirrng (pig-nosed turtle) are laying eggs. Memenyirr is the season name that refers to yirrng constantly lifting her feet as she lays her eggs in the burning-hot sand.						

Table 2.4: Ngan'gi seasons calendar: Wurr bengim miyerr to Walkity denta

Wurr bengim miyerr	Wurr bengin derripal	Wurr tisyari	Wirirr marrgu	Wangi	Walkity denta
Seeds are brown and start to fall. The wind starts blowing from the east. The dry season is starting.	All the seeds have fallen from wurrmuy. 'Knock-em-down' electrical storms knock down the speargrass.	Speargrass is dead and dry and ready for burning.	Dry season and burning grass time. Black ash from the first fires is on the ground. 'Good feeling' about going hunting and looking for turtle as you don't get too hot.	Time of the north-westerly sea breeze – a peaceful wind that brings good fishing and turtle hunting in the evenings.	Yerrwurumbi and yeninggisyi (red kapok) flowering; collect ewerrmisye (freshwater crocodile) eggs, which are being laid now.

Wurr bengim miyerr	Wurr bengin derripal	Wurr tisyari	Wirirr marrgu	Wangi	Walkity denta
Ayiwisi (dragonflies) arrive to greet the new season and tell people the dry season is coming. Ayiwisi also tell people it's a good time for barramundi fishing.	Wadat (flying fox) babies are seen clinging to their mothers.	Angankurinimbi (water goanna) about.	Dagum is the fog and dew that are present in the mornings. The fog is a good sign to go fishing.		
			Collect minimindi (waterlily), miwulngini (red lotus lily), midugu (water chestnut), mifetyen (peanut-like seeds) and mibuymadi (bush banana).		
Anganni (magpie goose) egg collecting.	Anganni (magpie goose) egg collecting.	Anganni (magpie goose) eggs hatching.	Good fishing time: awin (back bream), epelen (archer fish), adilmi (mullet), anganggurr (cherabin prawns), and creek fishing for atyalmer (barramundi).		
Agurri, the big black kangaroos that live in the hills, wake with the arrival of ayiwisi and sing the wind, blowing it from the east.	Awunytyerryin'gini (baby catfish) are seen around wunytyerr (cane grass); the two are thought of together. Good time for catfish.		Young birds are seen. Eperperr (Burdekin ducks) are seen walking in single file with their young.	Duny (Terminalia microcarpa) is flowering. Wayarrfiriny (paperbark) is flowering. Awayirrwurr: the migration of dany (short-necked turtles) and malarrgu (long-necked turtles) on the full moon, from the smaller billabongs as they dry up, to the larger billabongs and river.	
Minimindi (waterlily) opening; the smell of the lily on the wind clears and cleans the air and the spirit.	Anganggurr (cherabin or freshwater prawns) carrying eggs.		Angantyamu (bush turkey), emengginy (goanna) and tyirraty (wallaby) hunting time.	Afungi (mosquitoes) and angannisyi (king brown snake) emerge with the sea breeze.	
			Good turtle hunting.		
Aniyen (sand frogs) burrowing as awerrbawurr (ant lions) build their nests.			Afurra (mussel) and amurriyi (crab) collecting.		
Awuyi (possums) and efekimi (bandicoot) hunting all through the dry season.					

Discussion

The seasonal calendars demonstrate that knowledgeable Ngan'gi and Gooniyandi people draw on finely tuned resource-use strategies informed by an understanding of the interplay between local meteorological and hydrological phenomena and the resultant impacts on a wide array of aquatic species, their life histories and behaviours.

The two geographical areas from which the case study calendars originate exhibit different weather and hydrological systems, resulting in unique flora and fauna. These differences contribute to the unique Indigenous knowledge contained within these two calendars and hint at the diversity and extent of ecological knowledge held by Indigenous groups across the region. However, the comparison of these two calendars critically reveals commonalities across language and cultural groups, raising their potential efficacy as tools for revealing and communicating Indigenous knowledge, and for managing and monitoring the natural systems in which the knowledge is embedded.

Both language groups draw on a suite of environmental observations that are indicators for the occurrence of different life stages of many of these aquatic species. For example, Ngan'gi people look for the flowering of the red kapok tree to tell them that freshwater crocodiles are laying their eggs and it is time to dig them up; once the seed pods of the same tree are seen to be browning and cracking open, the crocodile eggs are known to be cracking open and egg-collecting season has finished. Similarly, Gooniyandi people (more than 700 kilometres away) look for the flowering of the Bambira tree (*Atalaya hemiglauca*), which indicates that freshwater crocodiles are laying their eggs, but as the flowers fall to the ground, the eggs hatch and the young join their mother in the river. This tried and tested observational system reduces a knowledgeable person's harvesting effort, as they won't attempt to hunt, fish or gather particular species before observing environmental signs that indicate that effort is likely to be met with success.

Seasonal calendars as water planning tools

The purpose of creating the seasonal calendars was to reveal in a visually engaging way local Indigenous values related to water and aquatic systems. The seasonal calendars clearly and effectively communicate the variability in the use of aquatic systems throughout the year—an important factor to consider when planning for future water use in a catchment. A key driver of Ngan'gi and Gooniyandi temporal and spatial aquatic resource use is the accessibility of different aquatic habitats. Flooding in the Fitzroy River region is largely contained to the river channel, allowing Gooniyandi people ready access to the river for fishing; Gooniyandi people visit and fish the main river channel throughout the year. For Ngan'gi people, the Daly River breaks its banks most years and people must travel into Nauiyu community by boat as the water floods the many tributaries and inundates the roads and bridges leading into the community. In the wet season of 2015–16, the community was evacuated for a fortnight when the river's peak flow reached 15 metres and the entire community was flooded. There are several months during the wet period, between Wurr wirribem dudutyamu and Wurr wirribem filgarri, when the focus of resource harvesting is away from the swollen river, targeting echidna, rock python and long yam in the rocky hills. As the dry season progresses and the water levels drop, fish and crustaceans are targeted in the main river channel, while turtles and magpie geese are hunted along the muddy margins of floodplain billabongs.

There is consistent interest in developing northern Australia's tropical rivers to support economic development, including agriculture and mining (Australian Government 2015). The seasonal calendars reveal that the hydrological dynamics of the two river systems strongly influence both temporal habitat suitability for species and spatial accessibility for harvesting. These factors drive the targeting of aquatic resources by knowledgeable people during the different phases of the annual hydrological regime. Any impacts on water flows (from regional agricultural development or climate change, for example) will obviously also impact on local Indigenous resource use (Barber and Woodward 2018; Jackson et al. 2011; Liedloff et al. 2013), and at least initially impact on the effectiveness of the underpinning IEK system. This provides a clear argument for the creation of seasonal calendars as tools that clearly demonstrate the local Indigenous presence, use and values of tropical rivers and the intimate knowledge systems that underpin this use and management.

Seasonal calendars as tools for articulating climate change

Although both seasonal calendars are from the wet-dry tropics of northern Australia, the ecology, hydrology and climate of the homelands of Ngan'gi and Gooniyandi people are significantly different—and this is reflected in a direct comparison of the key species harvested (as described in Tables 2.1–2.4). While the resource-use strategies described in each calendar differ, as they are based on interpretations of highly localised observations, there are several similarities and instances where the methods for determining the availability of key species converge. It is this shared understanding that provides a possible common platform for pan-regional discussions about observed environmental change. The following examples highlight commonalities between Gooniyandi and Ngan'gi ecological knowledge systems, where similar indicators are adopted to interpret seasonal change, in which (G) represents Gooniyandi observations and (N) represents Ngan'gi observations:

1. Insects indicating the availability of resources (other species), including:
   – Red dragonflies appear at the beginning of the cold weather to tell you sawfish are fat (G).
   – Ayiwisi (dragonflies) tell people the dry season is coming and they should get ready for barramundi fishing (N).
   – Amisyawuni (stick insects) appear at the same time as misyawuni (bush potato) are ready (N). The small stems of the bush potato look like the body of the stick insect; hence, the two species share the same core Ngan'gi name (Marrfurra McTaggart et al. 2014).
   – The flickering of fireflies is said to be 'cooking' the girndi fruit and making it ripe (G).

2. Animal physiology and behaviour indicating changing weather, including:
   – When the crow calls, the weather is moving into Girlinggoowa (cold weather time) (G).
   – Burrowing animals retreat to their holes, telling people the season of Lirrimem is coming (N).
   – Afiti (cicadas) are heard singing, calling out for rain; the big rains of the wet season will be here soon. Their loud call indicates that humid weather is here and there will be willy-willies or whirlwinds and mirages will be seen (N).
   – Barramundi (fish) sink into the river as they know the storms are coming (N).

3. Plant phenology and physiology indicating the animal species to be hunted, including:

   – As flowers bloom, the flying fox comes searching for nectar—and is eaten now (G).

   – Bambira flowers at the same time as freshwater crocodiles lay their eggs. However, when the flowers fall to the ground, the eggs are hatching and the young are joining their mother in the river (and it is too late for egg harvesting) (G).

   – Yeninggisyi (red kapok) flowers tell people to collect ewerrmisye (freshwater crocodile) eggs (N).

   – When yerrwurumbi (ghost gum) bark starts peeling, adany (sharks) are fat and ready to catch (N).

4. Resource availability indicating seasonal change, including:

   – When lagarndi (witchetty grubs) and bingga (sugar leaf) are both available, the season of Barrangga has arrived (G).

   – When joolwooljidi flowers, you know it is turning to hotter weather. Drink the nectar from the flowers (G).

5. Wind as an indicator of resource availability, including:

   – When the Moonggoowarla wind starts blowing from the east, the weather cools and fish are said to shut their mouths (poor fishing) (G).

   – When the Garrawoorda wind starts to blow from the south (as the rain finishes), it's a good time for fishing for sawfish (G).

   – The north-westerly sea breeze is known as a peaceful wind that brings good fishing and turtle hunting in the evenings (N).

   – Afungi (mosquitoes) and angannisyi (king brown snake) emerge with the sea breeze (N).

6. Plant physiology indicating weather change, including:

   – 'Taddo' is the name of the sound the speargrass seedheads make when they knock together and open, telling you rainfall is nearing the end (N).

   – When the red seeds of jirndiwili (*Erythrina vespertilio*) fall to the ground, you know a big rain, the wet season, is coming (G).

7. River flows (hydrology) as an indicator of resource availability, including:

   – 'When the river rises, it's time to collect fruit' (N).

- When the river level is really low, it's a good time for shark, stingray and sawfish (N).
- When the river and creeks are running, it's good fishing for catfish (G).
- The fruit of the river fig falls into the water (and is ripe) when the river flows for the second time (G).
- Moon grubs come out after the first flood (G).

8. Weather events as indicators of resource availability, including:
   - Short-necked and pig-nosed turtles are known to hatch with the first rains of the season while barramundi (fish) sink into the river as they know the storms are coming (N).
   - The fog and dew, called dagum, are seen during the dry season months as a good sign to go fishing (N).
   - Once the first rain of the season has caused the eucalypts' bark to peel, cicadas emerge (G).

Drawing from these observations, seasonal calendars could provide the basis for monitoring changes to the climate in three ways.

First, climate change has already led to shifts in phenology in many species distributed widely across taxonomic groups (Visser and Both 2005). It has been proposed that many species are becoming 'mistimed' due to climate change. The resultant decoupling of food web phenology will potentially have severe consequences, including loss of biodiversity (Visser et al. 2004). Western-style management of environmental systems has historically been limited by reductionist analysis: when the ecological, hydrological and socioeconomic components of a natural system are studied in isolation, research processes rarely succeed in effectively bringing the components back together to assess potential change in the interconnections within the system (Gadgil et al. 1993).

The seasonal calendars clearly demonstrate at some level the connections and understanding between different life stages of plants and animals (phenology) to indicate for the timing/availability of seemingly unrelated species. It is possible these species share a higher-order connection that is yet to be fully appreciated by Western science. Bringing together diverse Indigenous understandings of phenology from across the region might prove insightful when building a picture of how climate change is impacting, and might impact, these connections and how resilience can be built in response.

Second, and related to the first point, is the observance of insect behaviour as an indicator for food resources. Insects have limited ability to regulate their body temperature and it is thought that tropical insects may already be closer to their physiological limits for tolerating high temperatures and drought (Bale and Hayward 2010). Changes in insect behaviour because of climate variance are likely to be more evident where insect behaviour is used as an indicator for resource harvesting. Insects including stick insects, march flies, fireflies, cicadas and dragonflies are used as seasonal indicators by Gooniyandi and Ngan'gi people. Building on common understandings of insect behaviour across knowledge systems over a broader regional scale could lead to more rigorous early-warning signs of environmental (including climatic) change.

Third, astronomical events provide a reliably consistent time frame against which any deviation in the observation of coupled phenological events can be measured. For example, while not addressed in the Gooniyandi and Ngan'gi seasonal calendars, lunar phases are used to indicate the availability of resources in many Indigenous resource-use calendars. The Māori maramataka is a calendar based on the phases of the Moon. The different phases act as indicators of appropriate times for the onset or cessation of various activities, including harvesting specific species and planting crops (Roberts et al. 2006).

For such knowledge to be easily shared it must be in a form that promotes its communication across cultures and languages.

Community use of seasonal calendars

A seasonal calendar, while often a highly simplified representation of ecological knowledge systems, can powerfully demonstrate to others the extent and complexity of Indigenous resource use, management and knowledge. A key driver for Gooniyandi and Ngan'gi Elders to create a seasonal calendar was the desire to see their knowledge displayed in a form that would engage with other members of their language group and facilitate the intergenerational transfer of local ecological knowledge.

To facilitate this, all-weather A0-size, central-rotating calendars were mounted in communal areas in Muludja and Nauiyu communities (Plates 2.1, 2.2 and 2.3). Large posters were hung in the classrooms of local schools and copies were sent to regional boarding schools and other more distant schools where it was known that Ngan'gi-speaking children attended. Both calendars played a significant role in revealing to other people in the community the knowledge held by the Aboriginal contributors to the calendar (Woodward and Marrfurra McTaggart 2015; Woodward and McTaggart 2019).

The calendars had an immediate impact on local children, with residents of Nauiyu noting the children were 'really interested in that seasonal calendar' and could be heard saying the 'different speargrass cycle names' displayed on the calendar as well as Ngan'gi-language names for fish and animals documented in the poster (Woodward and Marrfurra McTaggart 2015; Woodward and McTaggart 2019).

The calendars also received much support, interest and attention beyond the communities who created them, and far beyond the intended sphere of influence of the research project (Woodward and McTaggart 2019). Several thousand copies of the calendars were distributed nationally and internationally in the five years after their completion and have been used as a tool to generate interest in Indigenous peoples and their knowledge systems, from primary to tertiary education levels. For example, one school association paid for their own print run of six different Indigenous seasonal calendars that had been compiled by the author by 2013 (200 of each), so they could broadly distribute them as learning tools throughout their classrooms.

At the same time, it is important to remember that the seasonal calendars are only partially communicative and are not intended to displace interpersonal communication and collaboration. Hence, the greatest impact is likely to result when calendars are used as a tool by their owners to facilitate communication and knowledge transfer.

Conclusions

The seasonal calendars reveal detailed knowledge of the interconnections between seasonal river flows, animal behaviour, meteorological phenomena and phenological observations that Ngan'gi and Gooniyandi people draw on to enact their unique aquatic resource-use strategies throughout the year. Comparison of the Ngan'gi and Gooniyandi seasonal calendars shows that, while the knowledge systems constructed by the two Indigenous groups are unique, there are strong parallels in their structure and form, as well as the types of indicators and environmental cues that are drawn on to indicate resource availability.

The seasonal calendar framework was found to be a particularly useful tool for capturing and communicating Indigenous knowledge and resource use associated with water. The calendars promoted the intergenerational sharing of Indigenous knowledge (within the language group) and communicated information to non-Indigenous people interested in learning more about Indigenous knowledge systems (Woodward and Marrfurra McTaggart 2015).

Given the interest in the applicability of IEK to climate adaptation and resilience, further investigation into the merit of a seasonal calendar framework to provide the foundation for documenting and sharing observations of environmental change at regional and pan-regional scales is warranted—specifically, as a tool to raise awareness of the impacts of climate change on local Indigenous resource use.

Davidson-Hunt (2006: 609) poses the question: what would a forum look like that could bring together knowledgeable individuals into a social learning process that would allow them to co-produce the meaning of changes in the land?

In the instance of a pan-regional Indigenous network, a user-friendly digital platform might support sharing, learning and adaptive responses between Indigenous peoples—particularly where changes, evidenced by Indigenous groups via new and unusual patterns emerging within their seasonal understanding of the environment, are shared to build a collective voice for action. Such a platform could act as a forum for linking individuals from different organisations so that a new knowledge network, or learning community, emerges (Davidson-Hunt 2006). With seasonal calendars of resource use as a foundation, such a platform might also support wider collective recognition of Indigenous peoples' diverse and complex ecological knowledge systems, and their critical ongoing role in environmental management.

Plate 2.1: Children interact with the Ngan'gi seasons calendar at Nauiyu Nambiyu. An A0-size all-weather rotating version of the calendar was installed on the outside of Merrepen Art Centre.

Photo: Emma Woodward.

Plate 2.2: The Gooniyandi seasons calendar.

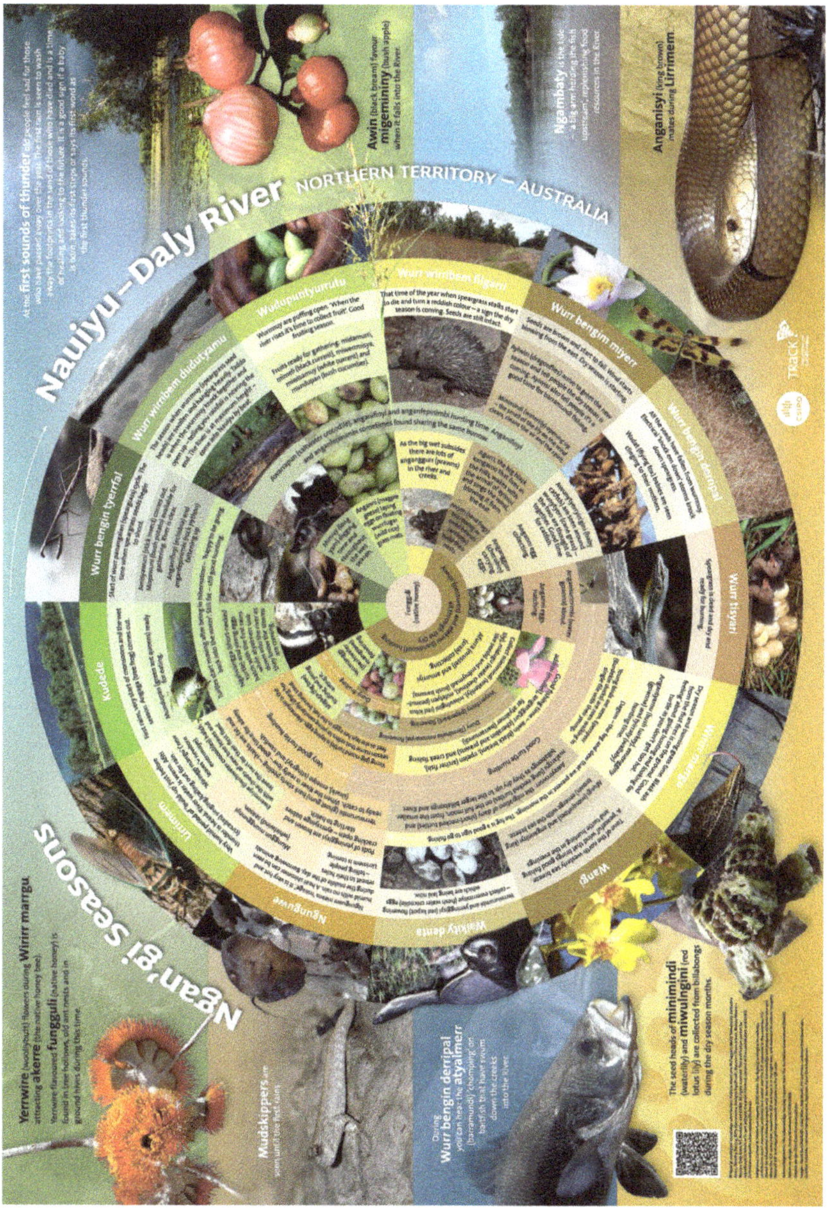

Plate 2.3: The Ngan'gi seasons calendar.

3

Knowledge and Practices of Growing Wild Edible Plants in 'Amis Home Gardens: Content and social distribution of a traditional ecological knowledge system of 'Etolan, south-eastern Taiwan

Su-Mei Lo and Jer-Ming Hu

Introduction

This chapter explores the rich knowledge, use and management of wild edible plants in the home gardens of the 'Amis of 'Etolan, an Indigenous community on the south-eastern coast of Taiwan.[1] We focus on the description of plant species and their functions in the sociocultural contexts in which their collection, cultivation and circulation are practised. In our analysis, the social distribution of this knowledge and the crisis in its transmission are at the centre of our argument. The knowledge of wild

1   We want to express our highest gratitude to all our working partners in 'Etolan village who supported our research from the beginning, especially the age-group Lakancun that the first author of this article joined in 1998. This research has been sponsored by the project 'Traditional Ecological Knowledge and the Resilience of Social Ecological System: Memory, Representation and Articulation of Knowledge in Edible Wild Plants and Spear Fishing of the 'Amis of 'Etolan, East Taiwan', Ministry of Science and Technology, Republic of China (MOST 106-2420-H-002-015-MY3).

edible plants among the 'Amis is an excellent type of traditional ecological knowledge system and demonstrates the rich meaning of sociocultural practices of local knowledge.

In the introduction to their book *Indigenous Environmental Knowledge and its Transformations: Critical anthropological perspectives*, Roy Ellen and Holly Harris (2000) summarise the main characteristics of Indigenous environmental knowledge (IEK). They stressed that IEK is transmitted orally or through imitation and is the consequence of practical engagement in everyday life. It is also place-bound knowledge. All these characteristics make IEK very different from written and universal knowledge systems. Therefore, we would like to stress here the importance of the notion of locally bound knowledge and the representation and understanding of it within the social, cultural and place-bound contexts of wild edible plants. These provide a necessary methodological background that helps us understand the strong resilience embedded in this 'Amis environmental knowledge.

This study incorporates ethnographic method, participant observation, results from plant identification and community analysis. We attempt to work through literature surveys and field studies, under cross-disciplinary evaluation of the ethnobotanical research from both anthropological and botanical perspectives.

Site of study

'Etolan is an 'Amis community north of Taitung City in south-eastern Taiwan. In 2016, the village was home to 2,492 residents, 1,179 of whom were 'Amis (Tonghe Township Office 2016: 398, 447). The 'Amis are the main Indigenous group in Taiwan, with 208,525 people, representing approximately 37 per cent of the Indigenous population.[2] The average 'Amis community usually consists of 500–1,500 individuals, residing mostly on the plains of eastern Taiwan. Their lands are not protected by law, which restrains the free exchange that applies to Indigenous reserved areas in the mountains, where Tayal and Bunun people live. Collective fishing and hunting were central rituals of the 'Amis before Japanese colonisation. As a result of the banning of guns for collective hunting, only collective fishing is still undertaken today. The 'Amis people largely maintain the

---

2   Sourced in 2017 from the Department of Statistics, Ministry of the Interior, Republic of China (available from: www.moi.gov.tw/stat/node.aspx?cate_sn=-1&belong_sn=7460&sn=7503 [in Chinese]).

traditional daily and ritual use of coastal resources, including individual fishing and the collection of edible shells and seaweeds, and they have a rich knowledge of non-domesticated vegetables. Most families maintain farmland with a wetland that contains a micro-universe of different food resources even though most of the residents are no longer professional farmers. The importance of staying close to the practices related to their land and environment is evident and considered central to being a 'real 'Amis'. This value reveals itself clearly in the renewed trend among the younger generation of learning personal vegetable collecting, fishing and hunting skills. This knowhow is also important in reducing reliance on cash income in their everyday lives.

Plate 3.1: 'Etolan on the south-eastern coast of Taiwan.
Photo: Jer-Ming Hu.

'Amis have lived in the community of 'Etolan on Taiwan's east coast for more than 400 years, while most of its Chinese residents arrived after a calamity on the mid-west coast of Taiwan in the 1950s. From the 1960s, the local 'Amis population migrated initially to major harbour cities such as Keelung and Kaoshiung for pelagic fishery work and, in the 1980s, to New Taipei City, Taoyuan and the outskirts of other major urban areas on the west coast for construction and factory work. The lack of local educational resources has also driven younger generations to migrate to Taiwan's major cities. In 2013, the percentage of the 'Amis Indigenous population residing in metropolitan areas had risen to 44.94 per cent—a situation similar to that in 'Etolan, where half the 'Amis live outside the village and many among them constantly travel between their homeland and a metropolitan residence for work. However, the diaspora tends to maintain their strong village identity and assemble around their village membership associations. Almost every 'Amis tribal community has an association in the main cities. These associations use the name of their original community and maintain unity through their participation in urban cultural festivals and competitions. Their connection with their tribal community is also very strong.

The 'Amis were a matrilocal society but have gradually become patrilocal since their migration in the 1970s. While women and their brothers still undertake family and lineage work, collective community work is considered the responsibility of men's age-group organisations. In 'Etolan, this organisation has played a central role in the recent traditional territory movement (Lo 2010, 2015). It is a general 'Amis social group system based on age and gender.[3] Only men may be recruited at the age of preparation for initiation. Women participate in only some of the communal activities after they are married, when they are considered members of their husband's age group. This organisation is tribal and territorial and forms an indispensable social network in addition to clan relatives in communal life, and plays an important role in collective social protests for traditional territory within the 'Amis community. Before Japanese rule, the male age organisation was the unit in charge of collective tribal affairs in every 'Amis village (Chen 1989). In 'Etolan, each age group is bestowed with a unique name according to an important historical event, which is decided by the elders and chief of the tribal community (kakita'an). These groups were greatly limited under Japanese rule as collective work such as clearing the ground for slash-and-burn horticulture, collective hunting and collective fishing were seen as barriers to Japanese control. In 'Etolan, the age organisations have persisted through time, although, in the 1940s, there was a population outflow due

---

3   Among Taiwanese aboriginal peoples, 'Amis and Puyuma are the only two who retain this traditional system. Other plains peoples like Siraya and Makatao have left these traditions far behind. Some Indigenous societies, like that of the Paiwan, have so-called youth organisations, but they are deeply influenced by Japanese and neighbouring 'Amis systems.

to the Sino-Japanese War in China and South-East Asia. From the 1970s, migration flows in search of better economic opportunities in the cities or to study outside the village made it difficult to persist as before.

Wild edible plants of the 'Amis of 'Etolan

We conducted a walk-through observation of the community's living areas in 'Etolan. Having evaluated the different types of collecting behaviour and cultivation, we selected 10 home gardens and their main cultivators to interview. We interviewed about 40 informants, most of whom were older than 50 years. Below this age, knowledge of traditional practices is limited. We revisited some sites in different seasons to investigate variation. We also invited age-group friends to accompany us on a forest survey to collect dengac (rattan heart, *Calamus quiquesetinervius Burret*) and organised marine algae collection with older women at two different sites. When one-on-one talk was difficult for some informants, we invited their age-group friends or clan relatives to join us. Through this kind of plant collecting and food sharing, we also had the chance to better understand the exchange networks of the surveyed home gardens and of wild edible plants.

The 'Amis are famous among Taiwan's Indigenous peoples for their use of many wild plants. Their home gardens are a rich combination of wild edible plants and domesticated vegetables. 'Amis home gardens usually contain the cultivated domesticated vegetables that are also common in other parts of Taiwan, such as mustard (*Brassica juncea (L.) Czern.*), luffa (*Luffa cylindrica (L.) M.Roem.*), pumpkin (*Cucurbita moschata Duchesne*), bitter gourd (*Momordica charantia L.*), chilli peppers (*Capsicum annuum L.*), oriental onions (*Allium chinense G. Don*), ginger (*Zingiber officinale Roscoe*), taro (*Colocasia esculenta (L.) Schott*), sweet potatoes (*Ipomoea batatas (L.) Lam.*) and several types of bean (*Phaseolus spp.*). The 'Amis also show a preference for certain landraces that are rarely found elsewhere, such as bitter gourd (Plate 3.2). This is a small, green landrace that is planted on the border fence of the home garden as it prevents the intrusion of other plants. The southern 'Amis particularly like the bitter gourd and often use its leaves for seasoning and to add bitterness to their dishes. In another example, the 'Amis in 'Etolan prefer their type of oriental onion, which is a landrace they claim as Indigenous.

Plate 3.2: Bitter gourd, with yellow flowers and ribbed fruit.
Photo: Jer-Ming Hu.

Plate 3.3: The view from an 'Amis home garden.
Photo: Jer-Ming Hu.

In addition, all 'Amis home gardens maintain several semi-domesticated edible plants. During our participant observation, we noted certain plants being spared during clearing to prepare the land for planting. The species kept include tatukem (black nightshade, *Solanum nigrum L.*), sama' (wild lettuce, *Lactuca indica L.*), kadipangan (wild amaranth, *Amaranthus viridus L.*) and tapuwacay (corn sowthistle, *Sonchus arvensis L.*)—all of which are common in lowland Taiwan. Sometimes wild plant species from the mountains were selected for transplanting into home gardens, such as lukuc (bird's nest fern, *Asplenium australasicum (J.Sm.) Hook*) and pahko (vegetable fern, *Diplazium esculentum (Retz.) Sw.*). Both these vegetables are planted in the shade of luffa, fruit or breadfruit trees. Alternatively, these ferns are cultivated under black netting (Plate 3.3).

The utilisation of wild edible plants also includes some species recently naturalised in Taiwan. For example, ebolo (hikoki, *Crassocephalum crepidioides (Benth.) S. Moore*) was said to be introduced by the Japanese during World War II as famine food for their army because of its high productivity without needing much agricultural attention. This is also why the 'Amis call it hikoki, meaning 'coming from the airplane', as the Japanese spread the seeds by aircraft. It one of the varieties 'Amis commonly consume daily. A list of the plant species most used as vegetables in 'Amis home gardens and fields is presented in Table 3.1. Among the 20 species, 15 can be considered 'wild', while the remainder are domesticated. Five of the plants, along with a cyanobacterium (explained later), are shown in Plate 3.4. Except for the spices (oriental onion and chilli pepper), the other 18 species have a more or less bitter taste—an important trait we will discuss later.

Table 3.1: Most common vegetable plants in an 'Amis home garden

Family	Scientific name	Common name	'Amis name
Amaranthaceae	*Amaranthus viridus L.*	Wild amaranth	Kadipangan
Amaryllidaceae	*Allium chinense G. Don**	Oriental onion	Kenaw
Apiaceae	*Oenanthe javanica (Blume) DC.*	Java water dropwort	Dateng no paylang
Arecaceae	*Calamus quiquesetinervius Burret*	Calamus rattan	Dengac
Aspleniaceae	*Asplenium australasicum (J.Sm.) Hook*	Bird's nest fern	Lukuc
Asteraceae	*Bidens alba (L.) DC*	Shepherd's needles	Kasipiray
Asteraceae	*Crassocephalum crepidioides (Benth.) S. Moore*	Ebolo	Hikoki

Family	Scientific name	Common name	'Amis name
Asteraceae	Emilia sonchifolia var. javanica (Burm.f.) Mattf.	Sowthistle tasselflower	Kadawangay
Asteraceae	Ixeris chinensis (Thunb.) Nakai	Rabbit milkweed	Datimtimay
Asteraceae	Lactuca indica L.	Wild lettuce	Sama'
Asteraceae	Sonchus arvensis L.	Corn sowthistle	Tapuwacay
Athyriaceae	Diplazium esculentum (Retz.) Sw.	Vegetable fern	Pahko
Cucurbitaceae	Momordica charantia L.	Bitter gourd	Anengelay
Euphorbiaceae	Manihot esculenta Crantz	Cassava	Kaysiafa
Fabaceae	Lablab purpureus (L.) Sweet*	Hyacinth bean	Dadubien
Fabaceae	Psophocarpus tetragonolobus (L.) DC*	Winged bean	Fadas
Pontederiaceae	Monochoria vaginalis (Burm. f.) Presl	Heartshape false pickerelweed	Kasemaay
Solanaceae	Capsicum annuum L.*	Chilli pepper	Linkiu
Solanaceae	Solanum macrocarpon L.*	African eggplant	Kakurut
Solanaceae	Solanum nigrum L.	Black nightshade	Tatukem

Note: This table lists the most common vegetable plants collected in the 'Amis home gardens in our survey. Five species that only occurred in cultivation (not naturalised) are marked with an asterisk.

The central social networks of lineage and age groups offer a network for the exchange of different plants and seeds. 'Amis also tend to collect varieties they like while visiting friends or travelling, all of which increases the diversity of plants in their home gardens. There is even one interesting plant, large-calyx trichodesma (*Trichodesma calycosum Collett & Hemsl.*), which is common in two other Indigenous societies in Taiwan, the Paiwan and Puyuma, which travelled across ethnic borders to be planted in some home gardens in 'Etolan. We found this plant every time we visited an 'Amis family with some Paiwan affinity. In another case, a fern grown at mid-to-low altitudes in Taiwan, called salipa' no maymay[4] (Wallich's brake fern, *Pteris wallichiana J. Agardh*), was sometimes sold to 'Amis by the Hakka group living in the neighbouring mountains, since it was not suitable to grow in 'Etolan village. This fern has a quite strong bitter taste and a sticky texture after cooking. The fern is not known to be consumed by other ethnic groups in Taiwan, including by Minnan or Hakka people.

---

4   This means the form of the Wallich's brake fern is like the duck's paw (salipa'). 'Maymay' means duck.

Plate 3.4: Examples of the wild vegetables used in 'Amis households in 'Etolan.

a) sama' (wild lettuce, *Lactuca indica*); b) hikoki (ebolo, *Crassocephalum crepidioides*); c) anengelay (leaves of bitter gourd, *Momordica esculentum*); d) tatukem (black nightshade, *Solanum nigrum*); e) kadipangan (wild amaranth, *Amaranthus viridus*); f) kimuduay (mother's tears, *Nostoc sp.*).

Photos: Jer-Ming Hu.

Below are brief descriptions of three of the home gardens we surveyed, for which the informants outlined the cultivation history of their plants.

Case 1: Home garden of Ci-Hongay[5]

Plate 3.5: The home garden of Ci-Hongay, viewed from the south-west, as in Plate 3.3.

Photo: Jer-Ming Hu.

This home garden is large (~140 metres x 160 metres) with a varied landscape, including a wetland, a small pond and minor hill slope, and sits beside a stream (Plate 3.5). More than 90 species of plants were recorded, including 30 cultivated trees and 15 domesticated vegetables—for example, oriental onion, chilli pepper, tomato, celery, mustard and taro. Ten of the other 45 species are commonly used as vegetables, and most can be identified by the numbers in bold type in Map 3.1.

The main cultivator, Hongay, is 56 years old and took over this home garden from her uncle and father. During the day, especially in the hot season, the family stays in the open-air shelter of the home garden. Hongay told us she grew several of the wild vegetables to exchange with other families and her close age-group friends, such as kadawangay (lilac tasselflower, *Emilia sonchifolia var. javanica (Burm.f.) Mattf.*), tapuwacay (corn sowthistle, *S. arvensis*) and Java water dropwort (*Oenanthe javanica (Blume) DC*). She is a very talented gardener who enjoys trying new species she obtains from friends as well as maintaining the traditional wild edible plants. At our third

---

5   The 'Amis names of informants in the article are pseudonyms to protect their privacy.

visit to her garden, she showed us her new crop, Bermuda arrowroot (*Maranta arundinacea L.*), which she brought back from the other 'Amis community in the valley. An aquatic cyanobacterium, kimuduay, nicknamed 'mother's tears' (*Nostoc sp.*), which Hongay grows in a pond near a stream, is very popular among the 'Amis. Hongay obtained her kimuduay from another 'Amis village, named Torik, north of 'Etolan, and it has grown well. Family members and friends like to exchange something from their own garden for the kimuduay and other villagers also know Hongay has it in her garden. Occasionally, some of the local restaurants providing Indigenous cuisine place orders for wild vegetables from Hongay's home garden. Some plants, such as water hyacinth (*Eichhornia crassipes (Mart.) Solms*), are grown to feed ducks and chickens, which are also fed with older wild vegetables that have not been collected.

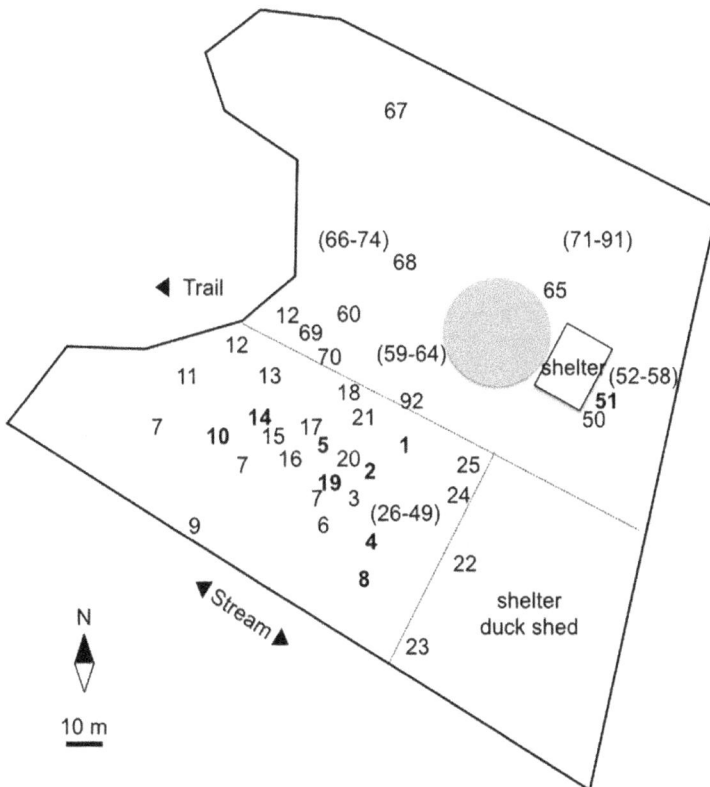

Map 3.1: The layout of Hongay's home garden.

Note: The numbers correspond with the plants found in this survey. 'Core' vegetable species (listed in Table 3.1) are numbered in bold type, while those not used for food are marked with an asterisk: 1. Oriental onion (*Allium chinense*); 2. black nightshade (*Solanum nigrum*); 3. fennel (*Foeniculum vulgare*); 4. sowthistle lilac tasselflower (*Emilia sonchifolia v. javanica*); 5. wild lettuce (*Lactuca indica*); 6. Java water dropwort (*Oenanthe* javanica); 7. taro (Colocasia esculenta); 8. vegetable fern (Diplazium esculentum); 9. water spinach (Ipomoea aquatica); 10. ebolo (Crassocephalum crepidioides); 11. cassava (Manihot esculenta); 12. papaya (Carica papaya); 13. garland chrysanthemum (Glebionis coronaria); 14. sowthistle (Sonchus oleraceus); 15. lettuce (Lactuca sativa); 16. lawulann; 17. rabbit milkweed (Ixeris chinensis); 18. celery (Apium graveolens var. dulce); 19. chilli pepper (Capsicum annuum); 20. Okinawan spinach (Gynura bicolor); 21. mango (Mangifera indica); 22. breadfruit (Artocarpus altilis); 23. paper mulberry (Broussonetia papyrifera); 24. common bean (Phaseolus vulgaris); 25. luffa (Luffa cylindrica); 26. carry me seed (Phyllanthus amarus)*; 27. Jersey cudweed (Laphangium affine); 28. creeping woodsorrel (Oxalis corniculata)*; 29. wild amaranth (Amaranthus viridis); 30. fleabane (Conyza sumatrensis); 31. asthma plant (Euphorbia hirta)*; 32. Henry's crabgrass (Digitaria henryi)*; 33. Indian goosegrass (Eleusine indica)*; 34. smut grass (Sporobolus indicus var. major)*; 35. windmill grass (Chloris barbata)*; 36. Paddy's lucerne (Sida rhombifolia)*; 37. alligator weed (Alternanthera philoxeroides)*; 38. passion flower (Passiflora edulis); 39. umbrella sedge (Cyperus alternifolius)*; 40. camphor tree (Cinnamomum camphora)*; 41. white leadtree (Leucaena leucocephala)*; 42. Chinese mulberry (Morus australis); 43. East Indian crabgrass (Digitaria setigera)*; 44. elephant grass (Pennisetum purpureum)*; 45. bowgrass (Cyrtococcum patens)*; 46. Cinderella weed (Synedrella nodiflora)*; 47. Asiatic dayflower (Commelina communis)*; 48. flossflower (Ageratum houstonianum)*; 49. Asian minor bluegrass (Polypogon fugax)*; 50. longan (Dimocarpus longan); 51. Formosan quinoa (Chenopodium formosanum); 52. Shepherd's needles (Bidens alba); 53. citrus (Citrus sp.); 54. small tomato (Solanum lycopersicum); 55. white-flesh fig (Ficus virgata)*; 56. guava (Psidium guajava); 57. golden rain tree (Koelreuteria elegans ssp. formosana)*; 58. parasol leaf tree (Macaranga tanarius)*; 59. jiaogulan (Gynostemma pentaphyllum); 60. southern giant horsetail (Equisetum ramosissimum); 61. water hyacinth (Eichhornia crassipes); 62. artillery plant (Pilea microphylla)*; 63. duckweed (Lemna aequinoctialis); 64. banana shrub (Magnolia figo); 65. poison bulb (Crinum asiaticum)*; 66. banana (Musa x paradisiaca); 67. betel palm (Areca catechu); 68. green bamboo (Bambusa oldhamii); 69. coconut (Cocos nucifera); 70. bird's nest fern (Asplenium australasicum); 71. fragrant manjack (Cordia dichotoma); 72. Malabar chestnut (Pachira aquatica)*; 73. rat-tail willow (Justicia procumbens)*; 74. avocado (Persea americana); 75. fish poison tree (Barringtonia asiatica)*; 76. umbrella tree (Pandanus odoratissimus); 77. mile-a-minute vine (Ipomoea cairica)*; 78. parasitic maiden fern (Cyclosorus parasiticus); 79. bishop tree (Bischofia javanica); 80. yellow palm (Dypsis lutescens)*; 81. bittervine (Mikania micrantha)*; 82. coat buttons (Tridax procumbens)*; 83. big sage (Lantana camara)*; 84. blue morning glory (Ipomoea indica)*; 85. rose natal grass (Melinis repens)*; 86. skunkvine (Paederia foetida)*; 87. great morinda (Morinda citrifolia); 88. dragon fruit (Hylocereus undatus); 89. southern sandspur (Cenchrus echinatus)*; 90. shell ginger (Alpinia zerumbet); 91. water cabbage (Pistia stratiotes); 92. agave (Agave sp.); 93. kusamaki (Podocarpus macrophyllus)*.

Source: Jer-ming Hu.

Case 2: Home Garden of Ci-Nikar

The second home garden is medium-sized (~14 metres x 12 metres) and is adjacent to two houses. The land was initially intended to be used for a new building, but the landlord could not find enough money to build and eventually it became a home garden. The main cultivator, Nikar, is 68 years old and has another plot of land on a hillside where she cultivates only pumpkins. She has an agricultural background and has always worked in the fields. She lives close to one of her sons but is very independent. She used to collect her vegetables, domesticated or wild, from the garden and sell them door-to-door in the community. She told us this was easier and more efficient than sitting for the whole morning at a street stand. Nikar enjoyed and felt comfortable working in the gardens. We recorded 59 species of plants, half of which were edible species (Map 3.2). Most have been cultivated and likely transplanted from other places—for example, papaya (*Carica papaya L.*), anengelay (bitter gourd, *M. charantia*), pumpkin (*C. moschata*), taro (*C. esculenta*), oriental onion (*A. chinense*), cassava (*Manihot esculenta Crantz*) and hyacinth bean (*Lablab purpureus (L.) Sweet*). Others, like kadawangay (lilac tasselflower, *E. sonchifolia v. javanica*), tapuwacay (corn sowthistle, *S. arvensis*) and tatukem (black nightshade, *S. nigrum*), are likely naturally occurring and maintained in the field. The 'Amis name for cassava is kaysiafa, which is an imitation of the original word—a common occurrence among other Indigenous languages. 'Amis cook cassava like sweet potatoes, by boiling or steaming.

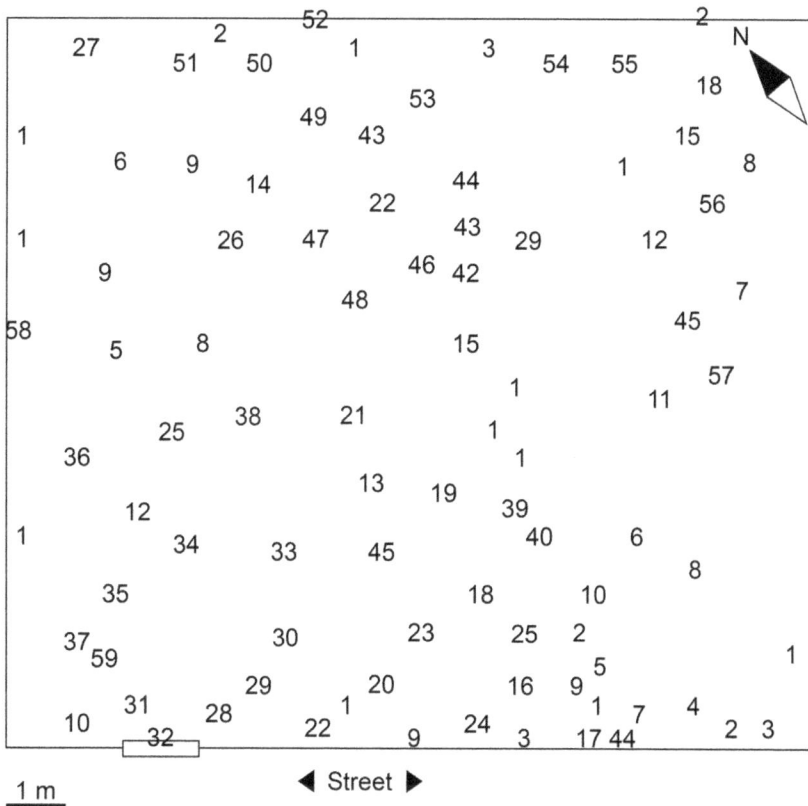

Map 3.2: The layout of Nikar's home garden.

Note: The numbers correspond with the plants found in our survey: 1. Papaya (*Carica papaya*); 2. Hyacinth bean (*Lablab purpureus*); 3. Madeira vine (*Anredera cordifolia*); 4. Geranium aralia (*Polyscias guilfoylei*); 5. Wild lettuce (*Lactuca indica*); 6. Black nightshade (*Solanum nigrum*); 7. Wild amaranth (*Amaranthus viridis*); 8. Sweet potato (*Ipomoea batatas*); 9. Bitter gourd (*Momordica charantia*); 10. Luffa (*Luffa cylindrica*); 11. Sowthistle (*Sonchus oleraceus*); 12. Ebolo (*Crassocephalum crepidioides*); 13. Creeping woodsorrel (*Oxalis hyllanthus*)*; 14. Shepherd's needles (*Bidens alba*); 15. Windmill grass (*Chloris barbata*)*; 16. Indian chrysanthemum (*Chrysanthemum indicum*); 17. Smoketree spurge (*Euphorbia cotinifolia*)*; 18. Chilli pepper (*Capsicum annuum*); 19. Chinese mesona (*Platostoma palustre*); 20. Poinsettia (*Euphorbia pulcherrima*)*; 21. Pumpkin (*Cucurbita moschata*); 22. Common bean (*Phaseolus vulgaris*); 23. Mexican marigold (*Tagetes erecta*)*; 24. Cabbage palm (*Cordyline hyllanth*)*; 25. Taro (*Colocasia esculenta*); 26. Oriental onion (*Allium chinense*); 27. Cassava (*Manihot esculenta*); 28. Saka siri (*Canna indica*); 29. Mo tsao (*Desmodium caudatum*); 30. Blackberry lily (*Belamcanda chinensis*); 31. Corn sowthistle (*Sonchus arvensis*); 32. Ceylon spinach (*Talinum triangulare*); 33. Cockscomb (*Celosia cristata*)*; 34. Madagascar periwinkle (*Catharanthus roseus*)*; 35. Tomato (*Solanum lycopersicum*); 36. Sugar cane (*Saccharum officinarum*); 37. Winter melon (*Benincasa hispida*); 38. Mustard (*Brassica juncea*); 39. Asthma plant (*Euphorbia hirta*)*; 40. Bowgrass (*Cyrtococcum patens*)*; 41. Henry's crabgrass (*Digitaria henryi*)*; 42. Lilac tasselflower (*Emilia sonchifolia v. javanica*); 43. Darkleaf hyllanthus (*Phyllanthus debilis*)*; 44. Bush creeper (*Cayratia japonica*); 45. Celery (*Apium graveolens var. dulce*); 46. Egyptian crowfoot grass (*Dactyloctenium aegyptium*)*; 47. Maize (*Zea mays*); 48. Fennel (*Foeniculum vulgare*); 49. White leadtree (*Leucaena leucocephala*)*; 50. Skunkvine (*Paederia foetida*); 51. Shell ginger (*Alpinia zerumbet*); 52. Longan (*Dimocarpus longan*); 53. Indian acalypha (*Acalypha indica*)*; 54. Fringed spider flower (*Cleome rutidosperma*)*; 55. Fleabane (*Conyza sumatrensis*); 56. *Chamaesyce hypericifolia**; 57. Indian goosegrass (*Eleusine indica*)*; 58. Betel (*Piper betle*); 59. Vegetable fern (*Diplazium esculentum*).

Source: Jer-ming Hu.

Case 3: Home Garden of Ci-Lisin

The final home garden case study are two small plots (3 metres x 1 metre and 5 metres x 5 metres) for vegetables near the family residence (Map 3.3). We recorded 20 species in these two plots, and 15 of them were present in the smaller plot. Although only six wild vegetables were found, most were typically used by the 'Amis—for example, sama' (wild lettuce, *L. indica*), tatukem (black nightshade, *S. nigrum*), anengelay (bitter gourd, *M. charantia*), kadawangay (tasselflower, *E. sonchifolia v. javanica*) and datimtimay (rabbit milkweed, *Ixeris chinensis (Thunb.) Nakai*). Tatukem and sama' are mixed with eggplants, which was the main cultivated plant of the season (May–June), but Lisin, our 50-year-old informant, told us she liked to add some of this unpretentious collection to flavour the cultivated plants like luffa, or just to cook a soup with many different wild edible plants. What she described is a common trait of 'Amis cuisine. Across the road from Lisin's house, she also has a slightly bigger plot, in which she was clearing the ground for planting seasonal beans like hyacinth bean (*L. purpureus*). On the ground, we observed some common varieties that had been cut down to make space for the summer-cultivated vegetables.

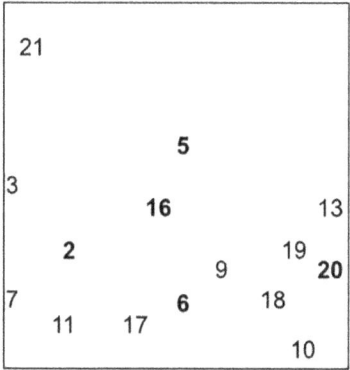

◀ Street ▶

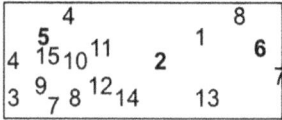

1 m

Map 3.3: The layout of Lisin's home garden.

Note: The numbers correspond with the plants found in our survey. 'Core' vegetable species (listed in Table 3.1) are numbered in bold type, while those not used for food are marked with an asterisk: 1. eggplant (*Solanum melongena*); 2. wild lettuce (*Lactuca indica*); 3. skunkvine (*Paederia foetida*)*; 4. fringed spider flower (*Cleome rutidosperma*)*; 5. black nightshade (*Solanum nigrum*); 6. bitter gourd (*Momordica charantia*); 7. rabbit milkweed (*Ixeris chinensis*); 8. carry me seed (*Phyllanthus amarus*)*; 9. darkleaf phyllanthus (*Phyllanthus debilis*)*; 10. asthma plant (*Euphorbia hirta*)*; 11. creeping woodsorrel (*Oxalis corniculata*)*; 12. windmill grass (*Chloris barbata*)*; 13. Henry's crabgrass (*Digitaria henryi*)*; 14. bowgrass (*Cyrtococcum patens*)*; 15. prostrate sandmat (*Euphorbia prostrata*); 16. hyacinth bean (*Lablab purpureus*); 17. corky stem passionflower (*Passiflora suberosa*); 18. Egyptian crowfoot grass (*Dactylocternium aegyptium*); 19. pink woodsorrel (*Oxalis debilis*); 20. lilac tasselflower (*Emilia sonchifolia v. javanica*); 21. shepherd's needles (*Bidens alba*).

Source: Jer-ming Hu.

Comparison and further remarks

In these three selected ethnographic case studies, we observed an extended home garden with more than 90 species and/or varieties of plants in a season—an example of a normal-sized home garden for harvesting and possible exchange. While the garden may be extremely small, such as Lisin's, outsiders may overlook the importance of its productivity and catering to ethnic tastes. For the 'Amis people, who are so good at using wild edible plants in their home gardens, this is an essential model of micro-land management, which allows them to live well and healthily and maintain social exchange networks. Many informants told us they did not need to go to the market or grocery store for their daily consumption needs because their gardens provided sufficient food.

We also found that bitter-tasting vegetables were a distinct feature of specialised 'Amis home gardens. 'Amis particularly like bitter tastes and enjoy mixing different landraces in one dish to produce very rich, bitter flavours. For example, while many Chinese people like luffa fruit because of its natural sweetness, and sometimes serve it with clams to increase the flavour, the 'Amis add the leaves of anengelay (bitter gourd, *M. charantia*) to their luffa-based soup to enhance the bitterness. In addition, even if there are some landraces transplanted in their home gardens, like the pahko, lukuc and dengac (*Calamus quiquesetinervius*), they prefer wild landraces because of the stronger bitter taste. The preference for bitter-tasting vegetables could be derived from a cultural adaptation in human chemical ecology, as a chemical cue for disease resistance. Such a phenomenon has been discussed for various ethnic groups by Timothy Johns (1990).

We have also compared the species our informants used in the village of 'Etolan with those recorded in the 'Amis area of Hualien, in north-eastern Taiwan, by Shue-Yue Wu. Wu is a native researcher of the 'Amis in Hualien who published a book on 'Amis wild edible plants (Wu 2000). Some species, like small bittercress (*Cardamine flexuosa With.*) and goose starwort (*Stellaria aquatica (L.) Scop.*), are commonly used in northern areas (Wu 2000: 181–82), but are not used by the 'Amis in 'Etolan and adjacent communities. About 20 per cent of the names used for the same plants differ between these two regions—an interesting trait of this locally bound and transmitted Indigenous ecological knowledge. Furthermore, as more and more exchanges occur between people and migration increases, the preferred plants of the 'Amis migrate, too. One interesting newly introduced plant is African eggplant (*Solanum macrocarpon L.*). Our informants in 'Etolan are sure it was only introduced from Hualien in the past five to 10 years. There is a sizeable, recent plantation of it in the next village, attesting to its popularity, and seeds are exchanged so it can be grown in home gardens. The very bitter taste of African eggplant certainly fulfills the southern 'Amis preference. The African eggplant has also been introduced to north-western Taiwan in recent years by 'Amis immigrants, according to research on Sa'owac, in Taoyuan, on the Tahan River in northern Taiwan (Lu 2015).

Motorcycles and cars facilitate field harvesting. Even when 'Amis people live in urban areas in the north or west of Taiwan, it is not difficult for them to discover new collecting grounds in their neighbourhood. In addition, low-temperature express delivery services facilitate the provision of the tastes of home for 'Amis migrants in urban settings. In our interviews, several informants mentioned this was the best and most convenient way to deliver wild edible plants and fermented local products, like siraw (fermented raw meat) or fermented bamboo shoot with green chilli peppers, to their families or friends living elsewhere. New methods of preservation during transportation make these tastes from home accessible elsewhere. The new techniques here play a novel role in reconnecting the 'Amis diaspora with their cultural flavours, maintaining a collective memory of food outside 'Amis lands.

There has been a small market in 'Etolan selling wild edible plants to local consumers and travellers on the main road since the spring of 2015. Some vendors seemed to be more interested in chatting with visitors than conducting commercial activity. The prices were reasonable for everyone. Villagers saw this as a good opportunity to access vegetables without having to collect or cultivate them. We also found piles of tatukem (black nightshade, *S. nigrum*) on the small trucks that came from Taitung City to sell cultivated vegetables to the 'Amis. These Han vegetable sellers knew 'Amis were willing to buy it when they did not have time to collect it themselves. We have visited another site, Fafokod, on the east coast, 15 kilometres north of 'Etolan, where there has been a daily roadside market for wild edible plants for a decade. These markets sometimes stimulate the cultivation of varieties of commercialised wild edible plants in home gardens. The local government recently built a bamboo shelter to encourage villagers to sell the harvest from their home gardens to tourists. It is worth noting that while certain wild species like the bird's nest fern have been commercialised, the less bitter landrace is grown in large quantities for the general market, while the 'Amis persist with their preference for the more bitter varieties.

Another noticeable phenomenon is that the 'Amis migrants take and grow their favoured wild landraces when they move to the cities in the north and west of Taiwan. These plants are clearly important cultural agents. In Lu's (2015) research on Sa'owac, we also see that the agency of Indigenous migrants to re-create traditional home gardens with semi-domesticated wild edible plants remains strong at the margins of urban environments. These are grown not only for consumption in these new locations, but also as a way of feeling like real 'Amis. This practice is a matter of cultural identity and social resilience.

Conclusion

Traditional ecological knowledge (TEK) is a cumulative body of knowledge, practices and belief systems. TEK is also community-specific, place-based and accumulates over time through the sharing across generations of experiences and knowledge about the relationships of living things (including humans) with one another and with their environment (Berkes et al. 1995; Berkes 2012). Accommodating Fikret Berkes's research method for adaptive socio-ecological systems, we have also chosen the term 'traditional' to designate the dynamic relationship between humans and nature. In *Sacred Ecology*, Berkes (2012: 4–9) clearly redefined the term 'tradition' in these practices, comparing numerous authors in anthropology and ethnobotany, such as Eugene S. Hunn (1993) and Michael Dove (2002), to emphasise that *traditional* not only refers to cultural continuity transmitted in the form of attitudes, beliefs, principles and conventions of behaviour and practice; it is also cumulative and open to change. Therefore, tradition and change are not incompatible; rather, TEK is a dynamic system that opens possible discussion about social resilience and social learning. In our case, we can see how ethnic tastes and home gardening practices persist through time in the everyday lives of the 'Amis people of 'Etolan. Some new plants like ebolo and African eggplant have been included in local home gardens thanks to the 'Amis preference for bitter flavours. Nevertheless, by comparing the names of plants used in different areas, we can perceive that each 'Amis community is a repository of their local and traditional ecological knowledge such as that of wild edible plants. This is a biocultural memory embedded in food and a sense of place that nurtures their agency to resist the homogeneity of industrialised food and economic pressures. Agrobiodiversity conservation might be the hidden product of this resistance (Nazarea 2013; Nazarea and Rhoades 2013). The neglected importance of home gardens as hotspots of agrobiodiversity and cultural diversity has been increasingly stressed in conservation. The Global Strategy for Plant Conservation (GSPC 2002) pushes the conservation of 'the genetic diversity of crops and other major socio-economically valuable plant species, while maintaining the associated Indigenous and local knowledge' (Galluzzi et al. 2010: 3635–36; GSPC 2016). The role of home gardens must be stressed more in the development of Indigenous societies. There is obviously much more left to be done in home garden research. The crisis in the transmission of TEK is also perceived strongly by community members themselves. Facing changing lifestyles, the neglect of cultural difference in the national education system and urban migration, the young generation of 'Etolan 'Amis can hardly maintain the same way of living and the rich knowledge of wild edible plants of their parents and grandparents. However, since 2007, in a training camp for young girls held before the traditional annual Kiluma'an ritual, the organisers have integrated traditional skills of collecting wild edible plants from the home garden and shells from the intertidal zone. This collective training through age-group organisations is to some degree replacing the central role of families in the transmission of TEK, however, the collection of plants and shells is regarded publicly as gendered knowledge for 'Amis women.

Mark Hobart (1993: 13) has pointed out that Indigenous knowledge distribution is very often segmented and socially differentiated by gender and age. In the case of knowledge of wild edible plants, 'Amis women and men have certain abilities in distinguishing the varieties of plants, although it is more common for women to be in charge of their family's garden. Men's hunting and fishing skills are highly valued and are considered demonstrations of their ability. In contrast, the ability to collect wild plants has never been considered important in 'Amis society; it is viewed simply as a common, daily activity. This also reflects the commonly undervalued contribution of women's daily labour to food preparation. It is easy for researchers to neglect the importance of such experiences. Some traditional knowledge can only be learned through ritual practices (Ellen and Harris 2000: 5). As rituals can support TEK, their disappearance can affect the original knowledge system. In the 'Amis case, cultivation of the main crop, millet, was one such knowledge system before the 1940s (Lo 2005). It is quite paradoxical that the core knowledge about such an essential crop did not survive. The rich cultural knowledge of millet, its landraces and their cultivation have been all but lost with the disappearance of cultivation systems in most 'Amis societies. In contrast, the everyday knowledge of wild edible plants endures due to ongoing practices and utilisation in daily cuisine. The cases of millet and of wild edible plants demonstrate how such cultural knowledge enhances people's lives.

4

Traditional Pacific Agrosystems and Sustainability into the Future: Vanuatu as a case study

Vincent Lebot and Stuart Bedford

This is a plea to policy-makers not to ignore the traditional economy of Melanesia and other parts of the Pacific when considering options for future development. We must shift our thinking to considering the traditional economy not as a problem to be solved, but rather as an enormous asset to be utilised. (Regenvanu 2009: 33)

Introduction

Across the Pacific region, there are increasing concerns about the sustainability and resilience of island economies, rapidly growing populations, public health and the impacts of climate change (SPC 2011; WHO 2010; World Bank 2014b). Associated with all these factors is future food security, which without doubt represents a major challenge. There is a general trend of increasing reliance on imported food and a general decline in traditional knowledge relating to gardening practices (Feeny 2014; Taylor et al. 2016). Pacific Island governments and their representatives often favour encouraging and supporting commercial crops that are not connected to traditional agrosystems and, in many respects, work against them. This is partly related to the influences of the cropping and economic structures introduced during the colonial period but is also sometimes seen as a solution to the increasing importation of foods such as rice. The planting of rice was instigated and encouraged well before, and has continued since, Vanuatu's independence in 1980, and it has repeatedly failed (Weightman 1989: 252–54; for a discussion of the wider Pacific, see Sharma 2007). In 2016 and 2017, the Vanuatu Department of Agriculture promoted sending thousands of cattle to various islands in a largely unmonitored program. In 2017, it instigated a program to encourage farmers to plant potatoes as a commercially viable crop. Farmers on Tanna were wary as a previous departmental program encouraging them to plant ginger was unsuccessful as there was no readily accessible market.

Many Pacific Island societies are grappling with these issues but the debates both inside and outside the respective countries are often devoid of historical depth or deeper understanding of traditional agrosystems (Regenvanu 2009: 32). Pacific Island populations before European contact were far larger than they are today (Kirch and Rallu 2007) and were almost wholly sustained through different gardening techniques and cropping systems. The island of Aneityum was once described as the 'Easter Island of Melanesian agriculture' (Groube 1975) due to the extensive and spectacular remains of irrigated terracing and channels associated with taro gardens found there. The island was thought to have had a pre-contact population of between 3,500 and 4,000 people, losing 90 per cent of that number by 1900 (Spriggs 2007). In 2009, it had a population of 915 (VNSO 2009). Marine resources were also a major component of some diets and animal husbandry played an important role not so much in daily diets but related to ceremonial activities. Such traditions included not only accommodating the population's required daily consumption needs, but also providing significant surpluses that were integral to ceremonies and trade and exchange networks. These extensive and often intensive gardening systems have been highlighted particularly in the remnant irrigation systems of Solomon Islands, New Caledonia and Vanuatu and the dryland systems of Hawai`i (Bayliss-Smith and Hviding 2012; Bedford et al. 2018; Kirch 2002; Ladefoged et al. 2011; Sand 2012; Spriggs 1981). The irrigation systems of these regions are considered some of the most productive gardening systems on record anywhere (Spriggs 1981; Weightman 1989). We argue here along the lines of the epigraph above— that a focus on traditional Pacific agrosystems is most likely to provide more secure and sustainable food security into the future. While there have been increasing calls recently for such a realignment in Vanuatu (Regenvanu 2009; Wood 2016), which is the focus of this chapter, it remains to be seen whether the historical trend since independence of increasing food imports and expanding commercial crops can be reversed.

The globalisation of the food trade contributes directly to the production of greenhouse gases. Cereals produced with very high levels of inputs and in large quantities by a few major exporting countries are transformed and transported using fossil fuels to consumers located far from production areas (Shiferaw et al. 2013). Vanuatu represents a textbook case, since the per capita consumption of imported cereals (white rice and wheat flour) is constantly increasing while these products cannot be produced locally. With its increased dependence on imported foods, Vanuatu's contribution to the production of greenhouse gases is also growing (van Groeningen et al. 2012; Neue 1993; Pandey and Agrawal 2014). This form of consumption also weakens the country's position in international discussions on climate change. Often considered a vulnerable victim of climate change, Vanuatu could rapidly emerge as an active contributor because of new diets that encourage the massive importation of food products with high carbon footprints. These new diets also produce dramatic effects on the health of Vanuatu's population. As vividly emphasised by Joel Simo, an organiser of the recent Slow Food Festival on the island of Tanna, in contrast to traditional foods, '[f]ast food is quick and easy, but fast food also leads to a fast death' (Wood 2016).

Traditional agrosystems have been changing rapidly during the past few decades. Some village communities are now neglecting local food crops in favour of cash cropping and the establishment of perennial commercial plantations (such as coconuts, cocoa, coffee) or pasture to generate the necessary incomes to purchase imported foods (Siméoni and Lebot 2012). Changes in diets, high demographic pressures and land saturation are increasing the competition between the two types of agrosystems: food crops and cash crops. Questions about agrobiodiversity management and the protection of genetic resources are challenging in current conditions. As communities are focusing on coconuts for copra, cocoa, coffee and kava, they neglect their species-diverse traditional food gardens.

The aim of this chapter is to explain how the redevelopment of local food-cropping systems in Vanuatu will not only improve food security but also increase the country's ability to sequester carbon and thus enhance its credibility in international climate debates. We will attempt to describe the traditional Melanesian cropping system that was developed over 2,800 years before European contact to manage environmental risks and to strengthen food security during an era when generous Western aid was unknown to local populations. We will also discuss how traditional techniques could be used to strengthen smallholders' capacity to adapt to climatic change.

Vanuatu's food-crop systems

Vanuatu comprises 80 islands stretching about 900 kilometres in a north-westerly to south-easterly direction (Map 4.1). The archipelago covers a total area of about 12,280 square kilometres, consisting entirely of islands of volcanic origin, most of which rise more than 700 metres above sea level. Geologically, these islands are between 10 and 20 million years of age and, as the archipelago is at a crossroads between species-rich continental islands (Solomon Islands, Fiji and New Caledonia), its flora were introduced from these source countries on ocean currents, the wind, floating rafts and by bats and birds. Because there were no major herbivores, plants could diversify and evolve through natural adaptation to diverse natural habitats without other constraints. Successive botanical expeditions conducted since the first European visits to these islands have collected and identified approximately 1,200 Indigenous plant species. Among these, many are edible fruit and nut trees, palms and ferns, which represented a major resource facilitating the settlement of the first colonisers and first predators (humans and pigs) approximately 3,000 years ago (Lebot and Sam 2019).

The South-West Pacific is a geographic zone under the influence of regional climatic instability (the so-called El Niño and La Niña phenomena and frequent cyclones) and is subject to high rates of seismic activity (producing acid rain and volcanic ash) (for Vanuatu, see Siméoni 2009). Numerous environmental risks have led local populations to develop resilient and sustainable traditional agrosystems. Several important food crops domesticated further north in New Guinea and Solomon Islands were introduced as vegetative propagules carried in canoes. This was the case for the greater yam (*Dioscorea alata*) and taro (*Colocasia esculenta*), which were traditionally the main crops, along with a leafy vegetable, aibika, also called 'island cabbage' (*Abelmoschus manihot*) and bananas (*Musa spp.*) (Walter and Lebot 2007). All species are asexually propagated and vegeculture characterises these systems. Vegetatively propagated plant species do not develop tap roots and are therefore highly vulnerable to strong winds and drought. The discontinuous extent of food gardens in the forest affords some protection from wind, soil erosion and the spread of crop pests and diseases. However, cyclones frequently sweep through the archipelago, with the resulting destruction of or damage to crops.

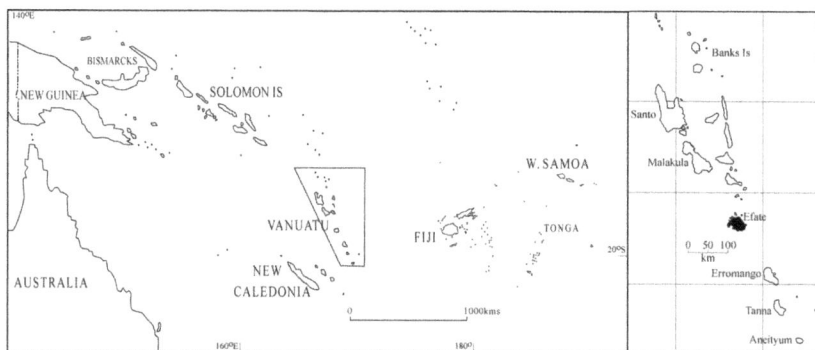

Map 4.1: Map of Vanuatu and the region.
Source: Map by Stuart Bedford.

The slash-and-burn rainfed gardening that was developed in the pre-European era (Barrau 1958) is still practised, however, with less intensity. Such gardens are most often associated with yams on the drier areas and taro in the more humid zones, but many other foods are also intercropped, including bananas and plantains, sweet potato (*Ipomoea batatas*), sugar cane (*Saccharum spp.*), kava (*Piper methysticum*), aibika, leafy vegetables and other minor species. Once a plot is cleared, it will be cultivated for about three years and then abandoned for a longer period due to weed infestation or, rarely, because of a significant decline in soil fertility. Most root crops are very efficient converters of solar energy into carbohydrates and their harvest does not extract important amounts of minerals from the soil. Depending where the cropping system is established, on the leeward or windward side of the island, taro or yams are planted first, generally in September–November, and harvested 10 months or so later. In the hole left by the harvest of their underground organs are planted sweet potato cuttings, as the species does well during the cool season. American species introduced after first contact, such as cassava (*Manihot esculenta*) or cocoyam (*Xanthosoma sagittifolium*) are established in the second and third years and the plants will be kept between one and three years, acting as food banks along with bananas. So, the plot is abandoned progressively and a fully fallow period does not begin at a precise time.

This shifting cultivation system needs to be associated with arboriculture of local fruit and nut species (see Table 4.1), resulting in a resilient agroforestry system aimed at risk management. When production needs to be increased for social purposes (weddings, custom ceremonies), it is done by opening new plots rather than enlarging the existing ones, which would increase their vulnerability to damaging strong winds or lengthy drought. The small size of the plots surrounded by useful tree species is seen as protection against adverse environmental changes. Small, irrigated taro terraces established along perennial streams are also surrounded by protective trees. There are several variations in the organisation of the hydraulic system to suit the topography of the area and the cultivation practices. These irrigated plots may be used continuously for 20 years or so before being abandoned for a similar period and restored (Plates 4.1 and 4.2).

In the 1800s, the introduction of new food-crop species had a positive impact on agro-ecosystems. Cassava, African yam (*D. cayenensis* and *D. rotundata*) and cocoyam have been widely adopted on all islands. Their agronomic performances are such that these species are often replacing traditional ones because of their ease of cultivation. The most striking characteristic of these food production systems is that they are based on vegetatively propagated plant species. True botanical seeds are produced by the cultivated plants but are unknown to farmers, and these staple food crops (roots, tubers, bananas and plantains) are always propagated using vegetative propagules: stems, tubers, corms or cormels, and suckers or runners. This is also true for breadfruit varieties (*Artocarpus altilis*) propagated by root cuttings and for aibika, kava and sugar cane propagated by stem cuttings.

These multi-strata systems host numerous species with different varieties, planted simultaneously and successively, and with various dynamics of production to ensure a continuous supply from the garden over time. The plots are rainfed, with annual precipitation ranging from 1,800 millimetres in the south of the archipelago to more than 3,000 millimetres in the north. Plots are generally kept clean and weeded by hand until the harvesting of the taros and yams seven to nine months after planting. Cultivation operates on very small plots. All useful trees species—and there are many— are preserved to be used as living yam stakes or windbreaks. For most useful trees, volunteer plants can be transplanted from the forest into cultivated plots or their surroundings. Within these, various annual species are established simultaneously: yams, aibika, bananas and giant taro (*Alocasia macrorrhiza*). This system works with minimum input, plants are established one by one and weeding, planting and harvesting are done simultaneously so the working day's outputs are optimised. Agrobiodiversity is often about translating a balance of interactions between asexual propagation and species association.

Plate 4.1: Irrigated taro plots, Maewo Island, Vanuatu.
Photo: Stuart Bedford.

Plate 4.2: Abandoned irrigated taro terraces, Col des Roussettes, Bourail, New Caledonia.
Photo: Stuart Bedford.

Epigenetic factors are playing a role more important than that for sexually propagated crops as there are clonal successions. Vegetative propagation has permitted the accumulation of clonal somatic mutations that characterise a great number of traditional varieties but also capture volunteer plants found growing spontaneously within plots when weeding or returning from fallow cycles (VandenBroucke et al. 2015a). In fact, the agrobiodiversity found within these systems is truly remarkable at the specific and intraspecific levels (Walter and Lebot 2007). At the functional level, this is translated into better stability to cope with climatic, parasite and economic changes occurring in the wet tropics. In these agrosystems, producers use intraspecific diversity to optimise the performance of the system (susceptible varieties interplanted with resistant ones to act as filters against pathogens, early and maturing varieties mixed together, and so on). Furthermore, and because of limited means, producers cannot open large areas and the increase of the cultivated area presents some risks (because crops become more distant from the forest curtain).

The issue is, however, quite complex and the genetics of asexually propagated species necessitates a peculiar approach: varieties presenting very different morphotypes can in fact belong clonally to the same genotype (that is, a gene controlling anthocyanins pigmentation is activated or not) and vice versa; some varieties can be polyclonal and are therefore hosting different genotypes although they present the same morphotype. It is consequently necessary to use molecular markers to characterise this genetic diversity (VandenBroucke et al. 2015b). If sexually propagated species have attracted numerous contributions, studies regarding asexually reproduced plant species are unfortunately quite scarce, to say the least.

In food gardens, the main staple crops are grown on land periodically cleared of its natural cover, to which it returns for several years of fallow after three years of cultivation. These food gardens provide most of the population with a high degree of food security (Map 4.2). Families frequently have several gardens and the dispersion of garden sites reduces the risk of the entire food supply being lost to a cyclone or a severe drought due to El Niño.

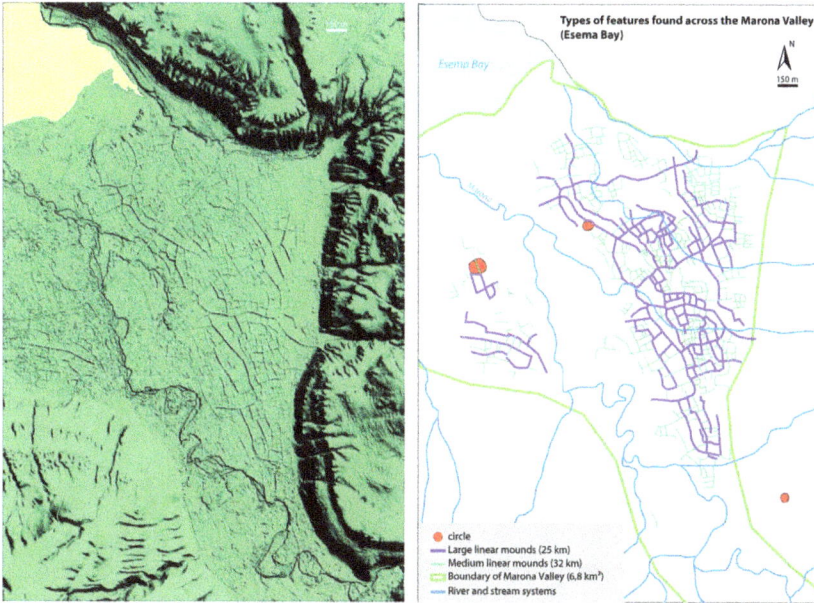

Sources: LiDAR survey - DEM, Ministry of Lands, Vanuatu. Drawn by Patricia Siméoni.

Map 4.2: Remnant agricultural systems, Marona Valley, Efate Island, Vanuatu.

Source: Map by Patricia Siméoni.

How was the food cropping system developed?

Clonally propagated plant species (roots and tubers, bananas, sugar cane, island cabbage) were introduced with the first settlers for their outstandingly high-yielding performance well known by the Lapita people. All were domesticated in northern Melanesia. However, because they do not develop taproots, they need tree curtains for protection. The rationale was therefore to intercrop these fragile clones under multipurpose local trees, many of which were naturally edible and non-toxic. Agroforestry was therefore common sense, especially as logging represented a serious investment in the absence of adequate tools. The development of these systems was therefore the most rational approach to favour fast and sustainable adaptation of recently arrived communities. The propagation rate of the crops after arrival was also critical. Introduced clones producing carbohydrates had to be associated with protective trees because their vegetative propagation ratios

89

(the number of propagules available per plant for replanting) were very low and settlers could not afford to lose them. Most yam species produce only one or two tubers per plant. Taro are better propagated with their 'headsets' (base of petioles) and there is only one per plant. It is consequently easy to assume that carbohydrate supplies (from taros and yams) were irregular before planting materials were sufficiently bulked and that, for a few years after arrival, communities were mostly foraging the abundant and diverse flora for edible fruits, nuts or palm hearts. In so doing, they learnt which trees to protect and replant, especially as many of these species were similar to the ones known further north in Solomon Islands.

Agroforestry systems exploited by Indigenous populations are now threatened by rapid change. Several significant changes have occurred over the past 100 years or so. American root-crop species have been adopted: cassava, tannia and sweet potato. They are now important foods and are virtually free of pests and diseases in Vanuatu. A few high-yielding yam species and cultivars have also been introduced, including the African *D. cayenensis* and *D. rotundata* and several superior cultivars of *D. alata* originating from other islands or countries. Cocoyam is far less labour intensive than yams. A second planting of yams would require holing, mounding and staking whereas cocoyam is simply planted in the depressions that remain after the first harvest of yams. New World species could be regarded as having been added to the yam system in a way that has produced minimum disturbance while increasing garden yields, especially in the second and third years of production. However, we can observe a significant trend in some villages where local food production is not considered a priority and these American species are now planted as early as the first year, replacing yams.

It is difficult to predict accurately what the ongoing and rapid climatic changes will impose on producers. The traditional Vanuatu multispecies food garden, involving small plots surrounded by forest, is fairly drought resistant, can conserve moisture and is protected from desiccating dominant winds and from diseases through intercropping. These traditional systems are sustainable and this can be explained by the discontinuous nature of cultivation that, so far, has benefited from the length of the fallow. The limited population relative to the amount of arable land, the small size of these gardens and the minimum tillage practices that prevent soil erosion, even on slopes, are also possible explanations for their sustainability.

Possible means of improvement

The productivity of these gardens is impressive considering the low inputs. Traditionally, producers visit their plots between three and five times a week and, during a two–three-hour session, they weed, plant and harvest to optimise their visit, as the time spent to reach the plot on foot can be up to three hours depending on location. At present the bulk of production is grown for household self-sufficiency. The produce is also consumed as part as traditional exchange arrangements. It is estimated that food gardens supply 70–85 per cent of villages' calorific needs, depending on location. However, with growing urbanisation, trade in traditional food staples is developing and these gardens therefore have potential for commercial exploitation.

To support smallholders to adapt to ongoing changes while improving, or maintaining, the productivity of these traditional systems, it is necessary to attempt to answer several important questions:

1. At the country scale: How is agrobiodiversity influenced by demographic factors? What are the spatial and temporal consequences of the ongoing and rapid changes?

   – It is hypothesised that accurate mapping of the soils' agronomic potential, combined with population and rainfall distribution, should allow a first assessment of different zones—those of high and low human pressure and maybe of rich and poor agrobiodiversity. Recent studies have shown that populations are already established on good soils. In the absence of roads and transport, farmers now must walk for several hours to reach fertile land as most plots close to their villages have been exploited for decades without sufficient fallow periods to restore fertility.

2. At the local level: How is agrobiodiversity influenced by land use and management? Is the area occupied by perennial cash crops a constraint on the development of local food crops? Are they the focus of farmers' attention and are the local food crops losing their position in daily diets and consequently in agrosystems? What is the incidence of perennial-crop incomes on these diets (that is, why should farmers cultivate root crops if they can instead purchase rice and bread)?

   – Mapping the local land use of village communities should improve the assessment of local constraints. Current observations indicate that most villages are now surrounded by coconut or cocoa plantations or pasture (or pasture under coconuts) and food production cannot be associated with these areas because: 1) many food-crop species are not shade-tolerant, 2) the soil under coconuts is compacted by their root systems and intercropping is difficult, and 3) it is difficult to protect food crops from cattle. Consequently, food production must be established in areas far from villages.

3. At the plot level: What are the direct impacts of farmers' strategies at their plots' level? How are plant species intercropped? What are the cropping cycles?

   – We formulate the hypothesis that by measuring agrobiodiversity with different indexes, taking into consideration more variables than the interspecific richness but also integrating intraspecific genetic diversity and the area constraint (number of species, varieties and/ or individuals per unit of area), these new indexes should improve the quantification and therefore the comparison of different levels of agrobiodiversity in different locations. We present in Table 4.1 a list of species frequently found in food gardens. Most are established as vegetative propagules, but many are replanted from neighbouring forest, and some grow spontaneously and are protected.

4. At the cultivated species level: How is the genetic diversity of asexually propagated plant species (those for which the human factor has the most significant impact) threatened? What is the impact of farmers' strategies on the genetic diversity of asexually propagated plant species and what happens when some varieties are not propagated?

   – We hypothesise that if we accurately measure genetic diversity with reliable co-dominant molecular markers, we can assess the extent of allelic diversity present in the plots, which is sometimes quite different than what is observed at the morphological level. It has been observed that, for a given species, the extent of allelic diversity present within one island is quite narrow and needs to be broadened to strengthen smallholders' capacity to adapt to climatic changes (Lebot 2013).

Conclusions

In the Pacific, the major food crops are roots and tubers (yams, cassava, sweet potato, taro), all of which produce high yields of carbohydrates per individual plant (from 2 to 4 kilograms). These compounds exist in the form of sugars, starch and fibre. People who have a diet high in carbohydrates are less likely to accumulate body fat than those who have a diet low in carbohydrates and high in fat. The energy density of diets rich in carbohydrates is lower because they contain per unit of weight fewer calories than fat. In addition, fibre-rich foods are bulky, thus nourishing, and quickly cause a feeling of satiety. People who have a diet high in carbohydrates are less likely to overeat. These food crops in the Pacific were traditional but are currently neglected. Their development will have three direct impacts: 1) improving diets and health, 2) contributing to food security, and 3) increasing carbon sequestration in the producing countries, reinforcing their arguments about the need for climate change action internationally.

These plants, unlike cereals, do not need to exhaust important resources in the soil (or to absorb those released by fertilisers) to produce high yields per plant. Grown with very low input, they are remarkable converters of solar energy into carbohydrates stored in their underground organs (corms, roots or tubers). This performance is due to their architecture; unlike cereals, such plants do not need to mobilise resources to build the stems necessary to support their heavy aerial storage organs: ears or panicles of grain. They have large leaf surfaces that transfer through photosynthesis sugars to a sink where they are easily stored underground without physiological constraint. The carbon footprint of their cultivation is therefore very low. With increasing levels of carbon dioxide in the atmosphere, these plants are assets for carbon sequestration in Pacific countries when cultivated within traditional agroforestry systems.

The production of food and agricultural products needed by Vanuatu's rapidly growing population represents a major challenge. In some islands of the archipelago, this challenge could be met by cultivating new land that is under forest. However, on most islands, there is limited scope for increasing the area under cultivation. There are numerous reasons for that, including the land tenure system, the absence of roads and/or the topography of the land available. In most cases, increased production will have to come mainly from the intensification of the existing agricultural land. In Vanuatu, the intensification of food gardens also faces several limitations imposed by weeds and the exhaustion of soil fertility. As most farmers do not use fertilisers and/or herbicides, the use of improved cultivation techniques combined with improved rotation, cover crops and intercropping is a necessity. However, while there are indeed challenging obstacles, there is also ample evidence from the past, in the form of remnant agricultural landscapes, that Vanuatu's highly perfected traditional gardening systems once sustained a much larger population even than that of today (Map 4.2).

Table 4.1: List of plants found in agroforestry systems of Vanuatu, their frequency and importance

Scientific name	Bislama name	Type of plant	Species diversity[1]	Frequency in food gardens[2]	Species propagation (planted, protected, spontaneous)[3]	Average no. cultivars per plot[4]	Rank[5]
Adenanthera pavonina	Fumbisu	LIGN	2	1	1	1	
Albelmoschus manihot	Aelan kabish	HERB	5	2	3	3.5	3
Alcalypha grandis		LIGN	2	1	1	1	
Allium cepa	Anion, shalot	HERB	4	1	3	2	4
Alocasia macrorrhiza	Navia	TUB	4	1	3	1	4
Annanas comosus	Paenapol	HERB	5	2	3	1	4
Annona muriata	Corossol	LIGN	3	1	2	1	4
Antiaris toxicaria	Melek tree	LIGN	3	2	1	1	
Arachis hypogea	Peanut	HERB	4	1	3	1	4
Artocarpus atilis	Bred frut	LIGN	6	3	3	4	3
Artocarpus heterophylla		LIGN	2	1	1	1	
Baringtonia procera	Navele	LIGN	5	3	2	1	4
Brassica rapa	Waet bun	HERB	4	1	3	2	4
Burckella obovata	Naduledule	LIGN	3	1	2	1	4
Canarium indicum	Nangai	LIGN	4	2	2	1	4
Canmaruga dorata	Nadigor	LIGN	3	2	1	1	
Capsicum annum	Kapsicam	HERB	5	2	3	1	4
Capsicum frutescens	Pima	HERB	5	3	2	1	4

Scientific name	Bislama name	Type of plant	Species diversity[1]	Frequency in food gardens[2]	Species propagation (planted, protected, spontaneous)[3]	Average no. cultivars per plot[4]	Rank[5]
Carica papaya	Popo	LIGN	4	3	1	3	3
Citrus grandis	Pamplimous	LIGN	4	2	2	2	4
Citrus limon	Lemon	LIGN	3	1	2	2	4
Citrus reticula	Mandarin	LIGN	4	2	2	1	4
Citrus sinensis	Aranis	LIGN	4	2	2	2	4
Cleidion piciflorum		LIGN	2	1	1	1	
Coconus nucifera	Kokonus	LIGN	6	3	3	1	3
Codiaeum variegatum		LIGN	2	1	1	1	
Colocasia esculenta	Wota taro	TUB	4	1	3	2	4
Cordyline fruticosa	Nangaria	LIGN	3	1	2	1	
Cucumis sativus	Kukumber	LIAN	4	1	3	1	
Cucurbita maxima	Pampkin	LIAN	4	2	2	1	3
Cucurbita moschata	Courge	LIAN	4	1	3	2	
Cycas rumphii	Namele	LIGN	2	1	1	1	
Dendrocnide latifolia	Nangalat	LIGN	4	3	1	1	
Dendrocalamus giganteus	Bambu	HERB	3	1	2	1	3
Desmodium umbellatum		LIGN	2	1	1	1	
Dioscorea alata	Soft yam	TUB	6	3	3	6.3	1
Dioscorea bulbifera	Buebue yam	TUB	5	3	2	2.3	3

Scientific name	Bislama name	Type of plant	Species diversity[1]	Frequency in food gardens[2]	Species propagation (planted, protected, spontaneous)[3]	Average no. cultivars per plot[4]	Rank[5]
Dioscorea nummularia	Strong yam	TUB	6	3	3	6.1	1
Dioscorea rotundata	Martinik yam	TUB	4	1	3	1.1	3
Dioscorea transversa	Maru yam	TUB	5	2	3	2	1
Dioscorea trifida	Afrika yam	TUB	4	1	3	1.3	3
Dracotomelon vitiense	Nakatambol	LIGN	5	3	2	1	4
Dysoxylum arborescens		LIGN	2	1	1	1	
Dysoxylum gaudichaudianum	Stingwood	LIGN	2	1	1	1	
Endospermum medullosum	Waet wud	LIGN	2	1	1	1	
Erythrina variegata	Narara	LIGN	3	1	2	1	
Ficus septica	Nabalango	LIGN	4	3	1	1	
Ficus wassa		LIGN	2	1	1	1	
Fluggea flexiosa	Namamao	LIGN	5	3	2	1	
Garuga floribunda	Namalaos	LIGN	2	1	1	1	
Glaodichro sp.		LIGN	2	1	1	1	
Gliricidia sp.	Gliricidia	LIGN	4	1	3	1	
Gyrocarpus americanus	Waet wud	LIGN	2	1	1	1	
Heliconia indica	Liflaplap	HERB	5	3	2	1	
Hibiscus floribundus	Nalalao	LIGN	2	1	1	1	
Hibiscus tiliaceus	Burao	LIGN	5	3	2	1	

Scientific name	Bislama name	Type of plant	Species diversity[1]	Frequency in food gardens[2]	Species propagation (planted, protected, spontaneous)[3]	Average no. cultivars per plot[4]	Rank[5]
Inocarpus fagifer	Namambe	LIGN	5	3	2	1	4
Ipomoea batatas	Kumala	TUB	4	1	3	3	2
Kleinhovia hospita	Namatal	LIGN	4	3	1	1	
Lactuca sativa	Laituce	HERB	4	1	3	1	4
Licuana grandis	Lif umbrella	LIGN	2	1	1	1	
Lycopersion	Tomato	HERB	4	1	3	1	4
Macaranga sp.	Navenue	LIGN	5	3	2	1	
Mangifera indica	Mango	LIGN	5	3	2	2	4
Manihot esculenta	Maniok	TUB	6	3	3	2.9	2
Metroxylon	Natangora	LIGN	5	3	2	1	4
Micromelum minutum		LIGN	2	1	1	1	
Morinda citrifolia	Noni tree	LIGN	4	1	3	1	4
Musa spp.	Banana	HERB	5	3	2	7.5	1
Myristica fatua	Red wud	LIGN	2	1	1	1	
Pandanus tectorius	Pandanus	LIGN	4	1	3	1	4
Persea americana	Avokado	LIGN	3	1	2	1	4
Phaseolus sp.	Bin	LIAN	4	1	3	1	
Piper methysticum	Kava	TUB	5	2	3	2	3
Piper nigrum	Pepa	HERB	4	1	3	1	4

97

Scientific name	Bislama name	Type of plant	Species diversity[1]	Frequency in food gardens[2]	Species propagation (planted, protected, spontaneous)[3]	Average no. cultivars per plot[4]	Rank[5]
Pipturus argenteus		LIGN	2	1	1	1	
Pometia pinnata	Nandao	LIGN	5	3	2	1	4
Pongamia pinnata		LIGN	2	1	1	1	
Psychotria anaityensis		LIGN	2	1	1	1	
Psychotria trichotoma		LIGN	2	1	1	1	
Pterocarpus indicus	Blu wota	LIGN	2	1	1	1	
Saccharum edule	Naviso	HERB	4	1	3	1	3
Saccharum officinarum	Sugaken	HERB	4	1	3	2	3
Saccharum sp.	Waelken	HERB	4	2	2	1	4
Sechium edule	Chouchoute	LIAN	4	1	3	1	4
Semeocarpus	Naholas	LIGN	2	1	1	1	
Solanum variegatum	Pico	LIGN	2	1	1	1	
Spondias cythera	Naos	LIGN	5	2	3	1	4
Sterculia fijiensis	Open frut	LIGN	3	1	2	1	4
Syzygium maccense	Nakavika	LIGN	5	2	3	1	4
Terminalia catappa	Natapoa	LIGN	2	1	1	1	4
Theoroma cacao	Kakao	LIGN	6	3	3	1	4
Trema orientalis		LIGN	2	1	1	1	
Trichosanthes cucumeria	Snake bin	LIAN	4	1	3	1	4

Scientific name	Bislama name	Type of plant	Species diversity[1]	Frequency in food gardens[2]	Species propagation (planted, protected, spontaneous)[3]	Average no. cultivars per plot[4]	Rank[5]
Vanilla planifolia	Vanila	LIAN	4	1	3	1	4
Veitchia spp.	Palm tree	LIGN	2	1	1	1	
Xanthosoma sagittifolium	Fiji taro	TUB	6	3	3	2.6	1
Zea mays	Korn	HERB	4	1	3	1	4
Zingiber officinale	Ginga	HERB	3	1	2	1	4

HERB = herbaceous

LIAN = climbing or creeping vine

LIGN = woody and lignified

TUB = tuberous

[1] Species diversification in Vanuatu (1 = very low, 6 = very high).

[2] Occurrence of the species in plots (1 = low, 3 = high).

[3] Type of establishment in food gardens.

[4] Average number of cultivars found within species in food gardens.

[5] Sociocultural importance of the species for smallholders.

Source: Adapted from Walter and Lebot (2007).

Section Two: Reviving the land and the sea

Introduction: Knowledge applied—Reviving the land and the sea

Paul D'Arcy and Daya Dakasi Da-Wei Kuan

Section Two continues the theme raised in Chapter 4 of effective engagement with the world and processes generated from beyond Indigenous-controlled zones. This section's four chapters outline barriers to more effective use of Indigenous concepts of resource management. The section also shows the promise of how effective mobilisation and integration of Indigenous knowledge and approaches into wider management practices can help restore degraded ecosystems. Another distinct feature of the Pacific is the extent to which Indigenous peoples also exercise influence over marine ecologies, especially coastal fisheries. This section largely focuses on marine ecosystems to more clearly articulate the relative strengths of Indigenous peoples' more intimate conceptions of the sea and its creatures compared with Western, state-focused conceptions. The latter treat the ocean as an economic commons differentiated only by generalised state regulation of 200-nautical-mile exclusive economic zones (EEZs) administered for the national interest. In open oceans beyond EEZs, voluntary compliance regimes for harvesting the sea prevail. Here, the main nation-state concern is freedom of passage for vessels rather than the rights of marine ecosystems and their inhabitants. The economic theory underlying global trade argues against the idea of commons on the grounds that an area owned by no-one will be protected by no-one. The consequences of this so-called tragedy of the commons have been increasingly seen across the Pacific as the Pacific Rim's industrial waste is dumped into the ocean to become someone else's problem. At the same time, highly sought-after and profitable marine resources such as tuna and shark-fin have been pillaged on the high seas under voluntary compliance regimes outlined in regional agreements that lack tools for monitoring and enforcement (Erikson et al. 2014; D'Arcy 2014; Aqorau and Papastavridis 2015; Aqorau 2016; FAO 2016; MRAG Asia Pacific 2016).

Visayan scholar Regina Macalandag begins the section by discussing the hurdles Indigenous minorities face in having their voices heard in public debates about resource use in modern nation-states. Few Indigenous people sit on bodies determining policies and practices for ecosystems they have lived in for millennia and with which they are intimately familiar. Macalandag's focus is the Badjao sea peoples, who once roamed across most of island South-East Asia (modern Indonesia, Malaysia and the Philippines) in their houseboats (Sopher 1965). They were truly a people on and of the sea, who gained an intimate understanding of tides, currents, species, seasonal changes and maritime weather patterns. Today, most live a semipermanent existence on their houseboats or in stilt-houses in intertidal zones because government regulations and fishery officials restrict their sustainable practices. In the past, the Badjao sustainably harvested the ocean, allowing stressed resources to recover by moving to areas with resources of relative plenty. Now, rigid boundaries define marine protected areas (MPAs) to allow fisheries to recover from overfishing by increasingly impoverished local fisherfolk with limited mobility and distant-water fishing fleets, which the Philippine Navy lacks the capacity to monitor and police. Effective monitoring of MPAs is restricted by the disproportionate power in the hands of a few local families with multiple economic enterprises and thus limited incentive to rehabilitate the fishery, while dwindling catches and a lack of local economic alternatives for most others reduce their ability and incentive to monitor the fishery (Fabinyi 2011). As Macalandag astutely notes: 'Enmeshed in a negotiated space of coastal resource management, their practical knowledge is often denigrated in favour of a modernist paradigm of resource management amid the call for inclusion of Indigenous customary practices in conservation efforts.' Badjao interactions with and understandings of the sea are shown to be holistic, based on Indigenous cosmologies of respect in which the fortunes of natural and human worlds are interwoven, but also profoundly informed and empirically based. Macalandag argues that such locally and culturally informed perspectives are vital for effective marine ecosystem recovery and management, which must be inclusive to be effective. The environment and Indigenous peoples are protected with comprehensive national legislation in the Philippines, but it is poorly enforced by under-resourced government bodies that only partly represent both stakeholders and knowledge-holders. One Badjao informant expressed frustration that most representatives are male and meetings are held in English rather than local languages or Tagalog, the national language.

In Chapter 6, Gumbaynggirr community leader Chels Marshall details a similar process in Australia. She notes that Aboriginal peoples are marginalised in the management of marine areas, which remain predominantly the domain of government-appointed bodies of scientific experts. Aboriginal peoples are consulted about cultural aspects of the environments in question and may even occupy minority roles on decision-making bodies. Australia remains far from the ideal of effective, equal co-management by governments and Indigenous peoples as practised in neighbouring Aotearoa New Zealand in recent decades. Marshall investigates how Australia might move towards this ideal and what benefits it might bring. She notes that MPAs can be an effective tool for marine conservation and ecosystem recovery when properly focused. She notes that the total lack of application of Aboriginal cultural practices and principles to marine ecosystems despite their now widespread use on land is particularly noticeable in coastal parks like Booderee National Park in southern New South Wales.

Deeply versed in traditional Gumbaynggirr ecological knowledge, university trained in ecological science and having worked in national parks for most of her adult life, Marshall is ideally qualified to propose how Australia's and other settler governments might move to more inclusive and more effective resource management regimes. She outlines the current government system of mapping and defining resource zones and the protective action categories under which they should fall as well as criteria on which decisions are made. She then demonstrates that similar mapping can be done using Indigenous criteria, which are not necessarily incompatible with Western science–based mapping and conservation principles, as the existence of such dual or combined systems shows. Marshall outlines how Aboriginal mapping and planning can be drawn using geographic information system (GIS) technology—after the implementation of interactive and culturally appropriate data collection allows information that was hidden in minds to protect it from prying colonial eyes to be freely given, as already detailed in Chapter 4. Like all preceding chapters, Marshall's notes how the cosmologies bonding peoples to land and sea enhance inclusive and more effective marine conservation. Locally specific cultural engagement with the environment is not incompatible with national legislation or international marine science. One of the key features of Marshall's emphasis on the need for more inclusive management is her community education for all ages, as epitomised by her permanent exhibition on Aboriginal seasonal calendars in the Australian Museum in Sydney.

Next, Tamatoa Bambridge, Patrick Rochette, Takurua Parent and Pauline Fabre show this desired future in action in their discussion of the Teahupo`o MPA. This outcome is the result of conservation partnerships between marine scientists and local communities at the French Centre of Island Research and Environmental Observatory (CRIOBE) on Mo`orea, French Polynesia. CRIOBE and the University of California Berkeley Gump Station in the neighbouring bay, as noted in the opening tribute to Papa Mape, have worked closely with communities to establish locally managed conservation regimes primarily administered by local communities but utilising marine scientist expertise. Bambridge et al. also pioneered a return to Indigenous resource management practices based on integrated land and sea management. They note these systems are based on the concept of rāhui—'a sacred decision to protect an area and/or a resource, whether on land or lagoon'. They go on to note that the 'rāhui has spiritual as well as economic and social dimensions'. Rāhui temporarily banned the harvesting of certain areas or species during vulnerable times to allow the stock to recover or to increase its numbers in anticipation of increased harvest needs for pending religious ceremonies. This was possible because of the integrated management of the entire resource base of these remote islands and the close observation of ecosystem health by fisherfolk, farmers and especially tahu`a (specialist knowledge experts). The chapter details how in 2008 the residents of the community of Teahupo`o in the district of Taiarapu in southern Tahiti decided to construct a hybrid governance model based on the traditional rāhui system to enhance ecological and social resilience, working in pluralisticly with existing state legal frameworks and in close collaboration with marine scientists. The results were almost immediate and positive in terms of enhanced social resilience, economic empowerment and ecological resilience.

This Teahupo`o model has now spread across French Polynesia. In his 2016 edited collection, *The Rāhui*, Bambridge demonstrated the widespread continuation of rāhui practices and principles across much of the eastern Polynesian Triangle, bounded by the Hawaiian Archipelago, Rapa Nui and Aotearoa New Zealand. The ultimate measure of success for the rāhui may be its ability to ameliorate the consequences of climate change. It arose to manage one of the most resource-poor environments on Earth, where colonists literally had to bring most of their food crops with them and practise sophisticated agriculture making extensive use of irrigation, mulching and complementary farming as well as fish farming and covering risk through propagating and planting a wide variety of food crops. Landscapes and even nearshore seascapes such as those in Hawai`i contain predominantly introduced dietary flora and fauna.

This second section ends with an examination of how Micronesian youth in the community of Kuchawa in Chuuk are responding to climate change by mobilising to enhance environmental capacity. Their first focus has been cleaning up serious issues of waste management and compromised or diminished water supplies. The global culture of mass consumption, nonbiodegradable packaging and waste, combined with mass industrial processing driven by fossil fuel consumption, is heating the planet to harmful levels and threatening water and food security in many localities. Another detrimental effect of these processes is the increasing frequency of storms because of ocean warming. Storm surges and typhoon-induced inundation will increasingly threaten crops and pollute groundwater, as the authors note occurred during Super Typhoon Maysak in 2015. This chapter therefore forms a bridge between this section on reviving and sustaining environments through sustainable development and the next, on responses to climate change. As global warming takes hold, cleaning up pollution and reviving ecosystems through sustainable practices like the rāhui are needed to offset heat-induced plant and fish stress and the rising frequency and intensity of storms. Fish such as tuna and corals are sensitive to even one degree of variation in average water temperature, while crop production tends to diminish with each rise in average annual temperature and reduction in annual average rainfall (Bell et al. 2016; Carpenter et al. 2008; Gattuso et al. 2014). Community-level action is again emphasised, but in conjunction with allies across the globe—academic, nongovernmental and governmental.

However, the authors make it clear that, ultimately, such projects succeed or fail because of meaningful local empowerment in terms desired by local actors. The authors note that 'an inclusive approach is needed that incorporates traditional community practices and knowledge and encourages youth innovation and leadership'. It is a message that all aid donors and local, national and international agencies need to take on board, and Chapter 8's detailed account of how their project was structured and the responses it led to is a valuable guide that deserves a wide readership, and which echoes concerns noted in Chapter 3 on the need to provide young people with future prospects and meaningful roles to ensure the social coherence and viability of Indigenous communities. All three authors—Mymy Kim, Zag Puas and Nicholas Halter—worked on the project they discuss while they were doctoral students in Pacific history at The Australia National University and all had previously taught in Chuuk. Halter now lectures in Pacific history at the University of the South Pacific's Laucala campus in a department in which community–university exchanges are a cornerstone of teaching. Kim has returned to her native Federated States of Micronesia to work on community and national projects, while Puas teaches at Pacific Islands University and heads the Micronesian Institute for Research and Development focusing on food security for climate change resilience, as is discussed further in the next section.

5

The Badjao and the Sea: Indigenous entanglements with coastal resource management— The case of the 'settled' sea nomads in the Philippines

Regina Macalandag

> Here, almost all fishing areas have been 'sanctuarised'.
> — Interview, Badjao fisher, May 2018

In their entanglements with coastal resource management, Indigenous peoples articulate the significance of cosmological and other sociocultural ideas to policies and on-the-ground struggles for coastal resources and the current challenges of the impacts of climate change. Confronted with these confounding and unfamiliar cosmologies, contemporary governments often muddle their own espoused participation/inclusion framework, creating a state of ambivalence or crisis for Indigenous peoples. Sea-based Indigenous peoples are both inside and outside this framework. Enmeshed in a negotiated space of coastal resource management, their practical knowledge is often denigrated in favour of a modernist paradigm of resource management amid the call for inclusion of Indigenous customary practices in conservation efforts.

The Indigenous conception of a 'seaworld without borders'—the known *anthropological cosmology* (Campion 2017) of sea nomads—inclines towards the notion that the sea is free for all and one cannot separate stewardship of nature. This cosmology has always been at loggerheads with states that have endeavoured at length, through slaughter, fortune and political capital, to gain access to open waters while also marking territorial boundaries. Globalisation, captured in the concept of a 'world without boundaries' (Tsing 2011)—artfully designed to transcend borders—has become a convenient justification for the unending accumulation of wealth by governments and corporations. This is translated into property rights regimes embedded within social, political, cultural and economic contexts. The rapid commercialisation of Philippine waters demonstrates the influence of this concept on resource use and governance. Employing a 'modernist' paradigm, the prevailing structure 'assumes that ecosystems are characterized by linear relationships and that only a market approach, emphasizing private ownership of resources will ensure stewardship and responsible resource use' (Palsson 1998).

This chapter argues for the role of Indigenous knowledge in restructuring an inclusive environmental governance landscape and for attention to be given to changing sociocultural inequities around inclusivity-oriented management frameworks. The chapter is divided into four parts. Theme one talks about the entanglements of the marginal Badjao fishing community who have moved to Panglao Island and the tensions materialising from the statist discourse of modernity vis-a-vis Indigenous cosmologies, especially on resource rights and management. Here, I contextualise further these entanglements by taking a historical perspective. As an interpretive exercise in dispelling essentialist constructions and understandings of these entanglements, I also take a reflexive note of my own connection with the Badjao and their place. Theme two describes Badjao cosmology and relations with the sea based on perspectives drawn from interviews and the literature. Theme three points out the disconnect between the sea-oriented Badjao and the practices and rhetoric of the state and other actors in coastal resource management. Theme four considers the potential for accommodating Badjao sense and sensibilities and their contribution to coastal resource management. The chapter concludes by emphasising the importance of genuine recognition and inclusion of sociocultural connections in coastal resource management. The consideration for inclusion is necessary if these management frameworks are to be transformed to support marine resource revival and sustainability.

Entanglements

The analytical case is focused on the Badjao. Dubbed 'sea nomads' (Sopher 1965), the Badjao have lived at sea in their houseboats and roamed the waters of South-East Asia for hundreds of years to fish and trade. Much of the key scholarship on the sea peoples of South-East Asia incorporates valuable detailed ethnographic data about various groupings of sea and boat-dwelling communities, including but not limited to Sopher's *The Sea Nomads* (1965), Bottignolo's *Celebrations with the Sun* (1995), Sather's *The Bajau Laut* (1997), Nimmo's *Magosaha* (2001) and Chou's *Indonesian Sea Nomads* (2003). This set of literature offers a record of the past as well as a glimpse into their current way of life amid continuity and change.

At present, very few of these people remain nomadic (Sather 1997). For various reasons, many of the sea-nomad, turned-boat-dwelling, turned-sedentary Indigenous peoples of the Philippines have moved north to the country's major urban centres. But host coastal communities, and particularly their local governments, often are at a loss as to how to deal with these transient/migrant sea-based indigenes from the south and find them out of place in their current settlements. While accommodating the Badjao as internally displaced people, local governments at the same time adopt an insulated and disengaged position from their Indigenous citizens, to whom their development policies seem inaccessible and, at times, inappropriate.

The rights of Indigenous peoples of the Philippines have been generally protected under the Indigenous Peoples Rights Act of 1997. But the liberal modernist logic and language behind the law, anchored in private property concepts and territorial boundaries, hold problematic assumptions that homogenise both land-based and sea-oriented Indigenous peoples, resulting in their exclusion. What becomes of a people who have been used to mobility in the vastness of the sea and a life of territorial unboundedness now forced to live a sedentary lifestyle and apportioned resources? How are sea-based and mobile sense and sensibility accommodated within and among the land-based sedentary majority? The issue of ancestral waters or the habitual home base and fishing grounds, for example—a significant concern for sea-based Indigenous peoples—has not been duly considered under the law, which remains vague and ambivalent towards this, with repercussions in many areas of policy and practice. This case raises complications about how the concept of ancestral waters should be applied, if at all, when the sea nomads convert to sedentary life away from their home base.

The question arises from opposing rationalities and has typically reflected mainstream majority societies vis-a-vis Indigenous concerns. An analogous demonstration of such a clash of logics between governments and the Bajo, the sea peoples of Indonesia, is best described by Stacey's (2007) *Boats to Burn*. In this work, she argues that Australian Government thinking is based on its own outdated yet still influential view of Indigenous peoples as 'enemies' and 'threats' to natural resources, rather than as the key to their sustainability. This kind of consciousness, primed by the lack of understanding of the historicity and the current realities of Bajo fishers, has ill informed its maritime policies, especially in the treatment of Bajo fishers. The exclusionary management regime has thus produced ineffective policies that have not deterred Bajo fishers from engaging in restricted activities within the Australian Fishing Zone.

This situation has gripping similarities with that obtaining among the Badjao fishers in the Philippines. In search of a better life, a group of Badjao families landed on Panglao Island in Bohol Province in the central Philippines about 30 years ago from the Sulu Archipelago, in the south. They set up stilt-houses along the shores of Totolan, a barangay[1] within Dauis, one of the two municipalities on Panglao Island. The island has provided rich fishing grounds for its inhabitants and its pristine beaches catapulted the province to fame as a prime ecotourism destination in the country.

Panglao Island forms part of the Bohol Marine Triangle, an area spanning more than 112,000 hectares of significant biodiversity including 11 of the 22 species of marine mammals found in the Philippines, three of the world's eight species of sea turtle, rare and endangered species of pelagic fish (whale sharks, manta rays and stingrays), seahorses and giant clams, rare shells and several migratory birds (Samonte-Tan et al. 2007). To preserve the triangle's natural conditions, the government declared certain portions of Panglao Island a protected seascape in 2003, amending two laws: Proclamation No. 2152 of 1981, which declared parts of the country Mangrove Swamp Forest Reserves, and the National Integrated Protected Areas System (NIPAS) Act of 1992.

The shore-based Badjao community of Totolan is adjacent to the wharf area of the province's bustling capital city, Tagbilaran. Tagbilaran City and Dauis share a lively channel abuzz with fishing boats, interisland passenger and cargo vessels, racing dragon boats, fish traps belonging to marginal

---

1   The smallest administrative division in the Philippines.

fisherfolk in the area, fluvial parades on feast days to honour a Catholic saint, the Bantay Dagat ('sea patrol') doing its rounds and other activities. The Totolan Badjao community lives alongside the local inhabitants, the larger Visayan[2] society.

As a Bisaya (Visayan) myself, I grew up on this island and call it home. As the site of my research on the Badjao, the area holds both old and new insights that shape my understanding of the intricate connections between culture and biodiversity as well as the political—or what we currently frame as governance. These insights are built on me seeing the place and its people— the Badjao community included—at various times, through various lenses. This includes as a kid who used to go swimming at the cosy lookout point over the wharf area, as a young adult going moonlight paddling by the channel with fellow kayak enthusiasts and as a university lecturer doing immersion and outreach in the area. Later, my involvement became much more purposive, including as a nongovernmental organisation (NGO) worker advocating for environmental governance while a reclamation site along the channel was being cooked up by the local government and some business interests for recreation and commercial development; as a master's student researching the Badjao community; and, most recently, as a doctoral researcher. Although informed by this background, most of the analyses in this work, however, are generated from fieldwork carried out in 2018 and 2019 using participant observation, semi-structured interviews, life stories, informal conversations and examination of relevant documents and other sources.

The analysis also brings further attention to the Philippines, whose coastal resource management efforts began in the 1980s through community-based projects. As the beginnings of ecological disaster had been noted in the Philippine marine environment, social scientists called for community-based coastal resource management—'a community initiated, run and controlled social organisation as [an] essential instrument in giving meaningful expressions to the views, interests and demands of the rural poor' (Ferrer and Nozawa 1997: 1). Yet, year after year, the country has faced severe challenges in managing its coastal resources, particularly as one of the most typhoon-ravaged countries in the Asia-Pacific, with poverty-

---

2   Visayans (Visayan: Mga Bisaya; local pronunciation: [bisaja]) or Visayan people are a Philippine ethnolinguistic group native to the Visayas, the southernmost islands of Luzon, and many parts of Mindanao, and are the largest ethnic group in the geographical division of the country (National Statistics Office 2003).

stricken coastal communities (dispersed Badjao communities included), degraded mangrove forests, battered coral reefs, rising sea levels, increasing pollution rates and declining fisheries. The Philippine marine environment and coastal resources continue to be degraded and at risk (Ferrer and Nozawa 1997)—something that is intensified by the impacts of climate change. Although integrated coastal resource management is expanding in the country and holds the potential to reverse such trends, the marine Badjao peoples' participation remains marginal and their interests entangled yet sidelined.

Badjao cosmology and relations with the sea

On rare occasions, the Badjao make it into the national news as saviours of locals caught in a maelstrom at sea during the typhoons that perennially hit the Philippines. Children of the waves, so to speak, the Badjao have mastered the sea and possess intimate knowledge of its tides, currents, depths, reef formations, inhabitants and the lunar and monsoon cycles that aid them in navigation (Sather 1997). A national social welfare officer noted in an interview in June 2018 how in one coastal village in the province of Batangas, north-west of the Philippine archipelago, Badjao Indigenous knowledge of swimming amid strong tidal currents has been used to rescue some drowning local villagers.

The Badjao world view manifested in their everyday life is intimately linked to the sea and islands. The interface between sea and land informs their collective representations of orientation and direction expressed in their reference to 'landward' and 'seaward' or 'inland' and 'ashore' as well as in their ordering of identities as 'people ashore' versus 'sea people' (Sather 1997: 92). Theirs is a 'sea-world without borders', where sea peoples moved easily between Sabah, the southern Philippines, eastern Kalimantan and Sulawesi—that is, before the enforcement of national boundaries (Sather 1997: 87).[3]

---

3   Writing about the Bajau Laut of Semporna, Sather (1997) notes that before 1963, the importance of citizenship was not immediately apparent to many villagers who were accustomed to travelling and often paid extended visits across national boundaries. This changed in the years following Malaysia's independence when large numbers of Bajau Laut found themselves classified as aliens and subject to several legal disadvantages.

This maritime heritage and world view—akin to the first law of ecology, that everything is connected to everything else (Commoner 2020)—has allowed the Badjao to peacefully coexist with the sea by adapting to its moods and impulses. The Badjao community in Totolan has not forgotten this kinship with the sea. Once or twice a year, Badjao fishers go out to sea to make offerings (usually of food such as cassava, sweet potato and banana) to ask for a bountiful harvest or to appease sea beings in case of a death at sea (Interview, Badjao woman Ruth, May 2018). They have thrived through centuries from its resources by showing this respect for the sea (Interview, Badjao woman Ruth, May 2018). The sea is a vital element in their survival as a people, so they have long considered themselves as its custodians. Their relation to the sea has the character of stewardship of nature. This acculturated faculty to be guardians of the marine habitat around them increases the chances of marine life to regenerate along their natural course—including adapting to climate change impacts.

The Badjao are known to be seasoned boatmen. In an afternoon of life-story telling, Elijah, one of the young Badjao fishers I met during fieldwork, recounted a scene at the pier near the Badjao village. In a fun boat race—Bisaya versus Badjao—talk quickly decided the Badjao team would win. The Badjao contenders, however, only placed second. This was a funny incident for the Badjao, who laughed for having their reputation precede them.

This anecdote aside, the Badjao are also acknowledged for their boatmaking skills and speargun fishing. Handed down from their ancestors, these skills are a testament to how they have fully mastered their coastal environment. This accumulated wisdom, however, informs them to not throw caution to the wind; they sail only on suitable waters and go out to sea in pairs to minimise risk. They have fashioned the speargun and other fishing implements (for example, wooden fins that act like slippers underwater and homemade wooden goggles for diving)[4] that enable them to take advantage of the marine resources around them with minimum impact (as opposed, for example, to net fishing, which does not discriminate its catch). As habitual freedivers, they have conquered the skills for staying deep underwater for long periods (Wonder Badjao 2017). The extraordinary physicality and

---

4   Badjao fishers employing spearfishing and freediving are featured in *Earth Day Diary*, a documentary that showcases and celebrates the ability of certain communities to coexist with some of the toughest landscapes on Earth (Wonder Badjao 2017).

technical expertise required to engage in this daily toil can only come from 'a people living in pure harmony with the rhythms of the sea' (Wonder Badjao 2017).

'Cordoning' the sea and the management disconnect

From sea nomads to shore-based sedentary peoples, they have grappled with borders and boundaries put in place by mainstream society. Indigenous knowledge and the long and intimate relations of the Badjao to the sea are relegated to the periphery, akin to the 'subjugated knowledges' articulated by Foucault (1980) that are often dismissed and disqualified by the more dominant knowledge of those in power.

The language of borders and boundaries inundates contemporary mainstream living: nation-state, national, subnational, regional, provincial, municipal, village. Not surprisingly, this language of division is reflected in the control and policing of natural resources, notwithstanding the acknowledgement in the *2001 Philippine Coastal Management Guidebook* by the Department of Environment and Natural Resources that 'fisheries and their habitats cannot be managed separately' (Aguilar 2004: 960). For example, a dichotomy exists between fisheries and coastal resource management despite recent laws and integrated efforts such as the Fisheries Resource Management Project, the Coastal Resource Management Program, the Fisheries Sector Program and the Coastal Environment Program (Aguilar 2004).

This compartmentalised regime is further actualised through the creation of protection zones that cordon the sea into marine protected areas (MPAs), which are:

> any specific marine area that has been reserved by law or other effective means and is governed by specific rules or guidelines to manage activities and protect the entire, or part of, the enclosed coastal and marine environment; and marine sanctuaries—in an MPA where all extractive practices, such as fishing, shell collection, seaweed gleaning and collecting of anything else, are prohibited. (Post 2016: 32)

Driven by their unfamiliarity with coastal resource management zones, which are alien to their way of life, and wilful acts of defiance, Badjao fishers now and then commit restricted acts within the boundaries of MPAs despite exposure to some degree of knowledge of the Philippines' environmental rules and regulations. A day in the life of a Badjao fisher in Totolan reveals this difference in cosmology and relations with the sea:

> We go out to sea from five in the afternoon then come back at seven in the morning. We reach as far as Siquijor [a neighbouring province] or midway through Oslob [a coastal municipality in another neighbouring province]. Our fish catch had been plentiful for a long time but has dwindled in recent years. We felt the decline especially compared to when we first arrived here in Bohol. There was so much fish [*sic*] during those times. Today, there are already a lot of fishers. Arrests are rampant. There are already [marine] sanctuaries. We don't have this idea of a sanctuary. We just go fishing and if there are lots of fishes in one area, that is where we always fish. We move from one place at sea to another. For us, we depend on where the tidal currents are. Wherever there is a current, there are fishes. We follow the current. (Interview, Badjao fisher and head of Totolan Badjao community, May 2018)

A study by Pollnac et al. (2001) revealed that while MPAs are widely advocated as a means of managing coastal resources and touted as the most efficient tool for the management of overexploited coastal resources in developing tropical countries, only 20–25 per cent of the more than 400 MPAs in the Philippines (600 MPAs in 2015, according to Post 2016) are successful. While this is concerning, the study also attributed the overall success of the MPAs to: 1) the relatively small population size; 2) a perceived crisis in terms of reduced fish populations before the MPA; 3) successful alternative income projects; 4) a relatively high level of community participation in decision-making (high on the democracy scale); 5) continuing advice from the implementing organisation; and 6) inputs from the municipal government (Pollnac et al. 2001). Many of the MPAs are accordingly 'dysfunctional "paper parks"' that are not effectively managed (Pollnac et al. 2001: 7). Multi-stakeholder engagement is a vital ingredient in these coastal resource management initiatives. However, MPA managers are predominantly men of the major ethnic groups, as revealed in the following observations on the attendance at a high-level workshop held in 2003:

> Thirty resource managers representing 26 MPAs attended and shared their experiences. Twenty-two of them came from Mindanao while eight were from the Visayas. They were mostly male, married and Roman Catholic in religious affiliation. In terms of the age level, 19 participants were in the 31 to 50 years category, 10 were above

50 while only one was below 30 years of age. As regards educational attainment, five were college graduates, nine had some college education, five were high school graduates, six had some secondary education and five were elementary graduates. Most of the resource managers have lived in their respective barangays for more than 20 years and only a few had lived in other places for short periods. About 50 per cent of the participants were barangay captains (local officials) and a majority of participants were members and officers of local fishermen's groups and related people's organizations. (Indab and Suarez-Aspilla 2004: 5)

Although these projects espouse a participatory framework, unequal participation—not social inclusion—has become the norm, and headcounts inform the priorities for these coastal resource management efforts. The marginal (both in number and in social status) Badjao fishers are rarely present at these workshops. In addition to their enduring invisibility, one Badjao fisher complained that even if they are invited, these workshops are conducted in English—a language that is foreign to them. Badjao fishers in Totolan often justify incursions into marine sanctuaries during lean days by referring to their marginal participation in rules that ignore their economic needs. The head of the Totolan Badjao village, a fisher himself, shared his thoughts on the declaration of extensive marine sanctuaries in their area:

> We were not included in the crafting of the local ordinance about marine sanctuaries. I think that was done at a time when tourists flocked through the municipality. That is why at present, everywhere you go out to sea within the municipality, you get fined. We only knew about the ordinance when we got arrested. We were fined PHP2,500 just by entering the marine sanctuary. We had to pay so we won't be put in jail. We had to borrow money for the fine. We won't have any other work if we don't go on fishing. (Interview, Badjao fisher and head of Totolan Badjao community, May 2018)

The village head said it was only after this incident that the Badjao fishers were called to a meeting with the authorities to inform them of the new ordinance. But the infractions remained, and they continue to pay fines whenever they are apprehended. For the Badjao fishers, it is a choice between the lesser penalty of being fined and the greater penalty of losing their livelihood. This limited and insecure livelihood feeds into the cycle of poverty that further undermines coastal resource management efforts.

Another Badjao fisher related how spearfishing has declined with the zoning of fishing grounds into marine sanctuaries. Those who enter a sanctuary risk being shot by the sea patrol; so far, one Badjao fisher has been killed. Other local fishers do the same, however, Badjao fishers complain that the Bantay Dagat authorities arrest them more often than non-Badjao fishers and readily attribute any illegal entry into the sanctuaries to the Badjao. Other Badjao fishers resort to hazardous fishing practices as compressor divers for commercial fishers. Clifton and Majors (2012: 716) conclude that 'while Indigenous peoples and ethnic minorities are frequently perceived as allies of conservation efforts, their inclusion in these initiatives remains a problematic process'.

Accommodating Badjao sense and sensibilities

Despite resorting to sedentary living onshore, the Badjao's intimate relationship with the sea has not diminished. The sea remains a natural extension of their life—a refuge, not simply a resource. Sedentary living has set the Badjao in proximity with land-oriented communities and, inevitably, in conflict with these neighbours' rules.

Studies from South-East Asia (Clifton and Majors 2012; Stacey 2007; Acciaioli et al. 2017) note how Badjao fishers figure among those associated with illegal and destructive fishing practices such as blast fishing, cyanide fishing, coral mining and the harvesting of protected species. They are depicted as perpetrators of coastal resource mismanagement through overextraction and use of destructive fishing methods. But in the Philippines, as in the rest of South-East Asia, the Badjao are only a small minority of the population and are responsible for a marginal amount of fishing (Nagatsu 2007, in Clifton and Majors 2012; Nagatsu 2013). In the Philippines, their small numbers betray their overall footprint on coastal resources compared with the majority of non-Badjao marginal fishers in the country. This means a 'tragedy of the commons' scenario in coastal resource management—blaming degradation on marginal fishers—is misleading and simply reductionist.

The sociocultural, political and economic dimensions of these reports deserve more scrutiny. Moreover, the inclusivity of coastal management efforts must be examined—the importance of which is highlighted by examples of resource conflicts between the Badjao and other groups. The reach of modernist development theory coupled with neoliberal globalisation draws a cultural faultline against Badjao cosmology. This division is apparent in the way Badjao are often found at the bottom of the commercial fishing pyramid as illegal compressor fishers and, for example, in their resultant displacement when commercial cultivation of agar-agar or seaweed (a major export commodity in the Philippines) was introduced in the Sulu Archipelago (Nimmo 2001). Changing perspectives is an almost impossible task given the dominant notion of development has 'achieved the status of certainty in the social imaginary so much that it is difficult to conceive of reality in other terms' (Escobar 1995: 5). As a totalising project, this allows no apparent path for the Badjao other than entering this type of development, even in conservation and coastal resource management, under the onslaught of global pressures and influences.

Translating this further scrutiny into a more informed perspective would also require looking at the positive practices of Badjao fishers rather than simply focusing on adverse resource use. Badjao fishing deserves attention. Modern methods—for example, the use of fine mesh nets, dynamite, poison and compressors—have reduced marine resources faster that the Badjao's customary fishing practices. According to Nimmo (2001), the Badjao (Sama Dilaut) are the best fishers in Tawi-Tawi (the southernmost part of the Philippines) in terms of the versatility of their fishing methods and the variety of their catch.

When asked how the urban Badjao's relationship with the sea and mobility figure in the mainstream schema of development and governance, a Philippine government official pointed to the need to build on Badjao knowledge and ways of doing things, especially as the government embarks on an inclusive resource management program for local development:

> [W]e have not really come to a point that we are able to understand their patterns of movement and how they themselves understand that pattern of movement that is so inherent in them. My sense is that mobility is dynamic, not just physical mobility. For example, perhaps livelihood initiatives are not working because their very sensibility is [that] things are not permanent. We can introduce several but let them figure out how they will move from one type of livelihood to another. Their life pattern is based on a sensibility of generations and generations of 'moving people'. Their way of thinking must also be moving. If they are the type who shift from one place to another or are used to adapting from one sea to another, perhaps even how

they work with their crafts is also moving. You really have to engage, when dealing with all these challenges with the Badjao. You really have to work with where they are. The work of capacity-building and development will take much more time. There is a need to work with other agencies. (Interview, Department of Education staffer, June 2018)

This sentiment indicates that some officials already agree on the need for inclusion. However, improving the conditions of Badjao fishing communities still requires engagement on the ground. What is apparent is the forfeiture of their sense and sensibilities in favour of the limiting of contemporary mainstream management frameworks. The Badjao should be not passive objects, but active subjects and genuine participants in coastal resource management.

Inclusive marine revival

The case of Indigenous entanglements with coastal resource management is a lesson in empathy: entering the world of the Badjao and recognising Indigenous knowledge of the sea and their potential contribution to thinking about and doing coastal resource management. Understanding this cultural connection—being Indigenous to the sea—could hold the key to addressing changing Badjao relations with the sea and the exclusionist tendencies of mainstream stakeholders and advocates of coastal resource management. It is a reminder of purpose and a nudge to the government to reframe its understanding of diversity and difference, its connections and changing realities.

The contemporary Badjao fishing communities gain from acquiring the knowledge, information and values necessary to navigate mainstream configurations of coastal resource management. Acknowledging the inclusion of Indigenous peoples' interests in legal obligations to mainstream policy and practice is critical. This means truly understanding Badjao peoples' despair over their exclusion from mainstream occupations. This recognition requires renegotiation of coastal resource management frameworks, principles and practices to account for the changing realities of mobile-turned-sedentary sea nomads who have moved to areas other than their 'ancestral waters' or original home base. While co-management principles have been successfully enacted in various communities, there is still much to be done to ensure productive co-management.

Marine sanctuaries have gained popularity and support as a management tool for marine revival and sustainability; however, lessons can still be drawn from Badjao fishers' participation. Indigenous knowledge not only retains important links with the past, but also serves as a vital source of information about changes at sea, climate change impacts at the community level and Indigenous resilience-building strategies. Coastal resource management could shed its technocratic, prescriptive nature by incorporating more contextual factors such as the knowledge, innovations and practices of Indigenous communities who have, for so long, lived in direct contact with the sea and nature.

6

The Importance of Aboriginal Marine Park Management Concepts for Australia

Chels A. Marshall

Australia has one of the largest marine jurisdictions in the world, containing a vast array of diverse and unique biological and physical features (Director of National Parks 2013). There are also many Aboriginal individuals and groups who continue to identify themselves as Traditional Owners of maritime estates in Australia and who are keen to have their rights to ownership and management of marine estates recognised (Rist et al. 2014). This traditional or customary right among maritime Aboriginal peoples includes the development of platforms and processes that enable us to be more directly involved in marine estate establishment, management and decision-making processes.[1] At present, Aboriginal peoples' involvement in the establishment and management of marine reserves in Australia falls well short of what we Aboriginal custodians of traditional marine estates desire and, as will be discussed in this chapter, well short of what is in the best interests of marine ecosystems as they relate to cultural and national interests.

Like many other Indigenous marine peoples throughout the world, Australian Indigenous communities have a profound reliance on, attachment to and responsibility for their customary marine tenure. In many coastal areas of Australia, Aboriginal people have a deep affiliation with the ocean, where

---

1   In this chapter, 'Aboriginal', 'traditional' and 'Indigenous' are used interchangeably, depending on context.

marine dominion is embedded in cultural practices and social constructs and contributes to the composition of our identity. It is interpreted in many areas as part of the traditional estate, with cultural responsibilities, identity, ownership and access to resources parts of that cultural attachment (Smyth 2001). The ocean provides spiritual, cultural, social and livelihood benefits to both Aboriginal and non-Aboriginal communities. The sea is seen somewhat as a common domain that is managed by governments in cooperation with relevant stakeholders on behalf of the commons (Smyth 2001). However, there continues to be a large blue space between the understanding of Aboriginal peoples' ideology and world view of marine management in Australia, and the scientific principles applied to protect and manage such maritime areas.

Why is it that Aboriginal people do not have greater involvement and authority in the marine estate, particularly protected areas? Why are ecological cultural management ideology and obligation not facilitated and incorporated into marine park establishment? This chapter seeks to understand why these have not occurred and then explores some of the potential prospects and benefits of reversing this marginalisation of Aboriginal peoples in marine conservation policy and practice. In understanding how marine protected areas evolved, I will first go back to examining the original development of marine reserves in Australia—the functions, establishment and construction processes—to provide a background framework for better understanding how Aboriginal values and interests are applied. I will also endeavour to pinpoint where the obstructions lie from an Indigenous perspective and propose a process for how to move forward.

The protected area co-management arrangements in Australia are still evolving. However, there is still disparity in the ratio of co-management and ownership between terrestrial areas and the marine domain (Bauman and Smyth 2007). In many parts of the world, policymakers, legislators, marine managers and Indigenous peoples have attempted to reconcile marine protected area (MPA) governance and management with that of Indigenous peoples (Rist et al. 2014). Within Australia, there are informal and formal local and regional agreements and memorandums of understanding that apply to specific areas or use agreements under native title legislation. This chapter therefore does not claim to be comprehensive on Aboriginal rights legislation but looks at Aboriginal marine interests and contexts to contribute to protected area management, marine conservation and resource management. It also focuses on examples that reflect current trends in frameworks for several marine jurisdictions. It aims to highlight formal arrangements as they appear in agreements and legislation related to MPAs as well as the construct of marine reserves and the opportunity for Aboriginal principles to parallel Western ideologies in science and resource management.

After 78 years of marine parks in Australia, there are no existing models of marine planning that allow for culturally identified marine ecosystem protection or formal joint management of MPAs. A key issue facing marine conservation today is how to develop and implement governance approaches that are both effective in achieving conservation objectives and equitable in fairly sharing the associated benefits with the Aboriginal owners of Australia.

Development and establishment of MPAs in Australia

Australia's first marine park was established in 1937 at Green Island, in Queensland, with the second declared over Heron and Wistari reefs in 1974. This process began in 1906 when Green Island was declared a recreational reserve under the authority of Cairns Council. The next step was the declaration of a fauna sanctuary in 1934; then, in 1936, management control was transferred from Cairns Town Council to the Queensland State Government. In 1937, Green Island was declared a national park. In 1974, Green Island Reef was declared a marine national park by the Queensland Government, with 1981 seeing the Green Island Reef zoned a Marine National Park 'B' with Buffer Zone (extending out 500 metres from the edge of the reef) under the *Great Barrier Reef Marine Park Act*. Interestingly, throughout this time, the 15-hectare island has continued to support a fishing industry, recreation, mining of reef corals to make lime for use on cane fields, jetty construction, ferries, hotels, resorts, an underwater observatory, theatre, retaining walls, a crocodile farm, luxurious resorts, boats, seaplanes, catamarans, a desalination plant—all in all, a lot of commercial activities and infrastructure not exactly compatible with its offshore waters' legal designation.

Green Island is also the traditional estate of the Aboriginal Gunagandi and Mandingalbay tribes, who utilised this cultural seascape for sustenance and significant ceremonies. Essentially, it was managed under Aboriginal law and custom before 1906. In a process repeated across Australia, pre-existing Aboriginal management practices are often acknowledged but rarely incorporated into management principles.

Functions, establishment and construction processes

Australia has a federal system of government in which legislative power is divided between the Commonwealth (federal) government and six state and two territory governments. The limited topics on which the Commonwealth Parliament has power to enact legislation are set out in the Australian Constitution. Most marine tenure in the states is legally within waters covered by the exclusive economic zone (EEZ). Near shore, each state formulates legislative structures to authorise state MPA systems. Commonwealth waters start at the outer edge of state waters— generally, 3 nautical miles (5.5 kilometres) from the shore (territorial sea baseline)—and extend to the outer boundary of Australia's EEZ, which is 200 nautical miles (370 kilometres) from the territorial sea baseline. The Commonwealth Parliament has the power to enact legislation in relation to Australia's marine territories. The *Environment Protection and Biodiversity Conservation Act 1999* (*EPBC Act*) is the Commonwealth legislation relating to marine territories.

Within the many planning frameworks of Commonwealth, state and territory governments, the marine reserve management planning documents identify Aboriginal heritage as a component of significance and value. The criteria applied aim to address the objectives of the *EPBC Act*, which recommends that administering authorities:

- recognise the role of Indigenous peoples in the conservation and ecologically sustainable use of Australia's biodiversity
- promote the use of Indigenous peoples' knowledge of biodiversity with the involvement of, and in cooperation with, the owners of the knowledge.

The Marine Reserves Network forms part of Australia's National Representative System of Marine Protected Areas (NRSMPA), the establishment of which has been under way since 1998, when the federal, state and Northern Territory governments agreed to its creation. The states and the Northern Territory continue to create MPAs in their coastal waters, while the Australian Government establishes MPAs in Commonwealth waters around Australia.

The NRSMPA also aims to meet Australia's international commitments as a signatory to the Convention on Biological Diversity to establish a representative system of MPAs within Australia's EEZ. It is accepted that the creation and management of marine reserves are an important strategy for the conservation and ecologically sustainable use of the marine environment:

> Marine reserves, when well designed and managed effectively, make an important contribution to maintaining the overall health and resilience of our oceans. The primary goal of the NRSMPA is to establish and manage a comprehensive, adequate and representative system of marine protected areas to contribute to the long-term ecological viability of marine and estuarine systems, to maintain ecological processes and systems, and to protect Australia's biological diversity at all levels. (Director of National Parks 2013: 7)

Where do the obstructions lie?

A critical component missing from the marine estate and from the management of Australia's marine zone is appropriate and meaningful recognition of Aboriginal peoples and our historical and ongoing role in the management of and connectivity with these marine zones. Deficiencies in representation and participation by Aboriginal people in decision-making, along with the inadequate protection and management of Indigenous cultural approaches in marine estates, result in misrepresentation, diminished opportunities to own and control inputs into policy and legislative processes and inconsistencies in legislation and policy across the country. The results of this structural setup are lost opportunities and constraints between regions—often with disadvantageous consequences for Indigenous peoples.

Underpinning the Aboriginal desire for improved and holistic sea country management is the development of models of governance that provide scope for the management of intragroup and intergroup relationships. The strongest and most basic desire is recognition of the Indigenous view of holistic land and sea management that includes people and culture—in other words, sea country is more than just 'sea' (NAILSMA 2012). The inherent absence of cultural laws and protocols when dealing with Aboriginal maritime estates and the lack of government expertise on processes and recognition of cultural laws and protocols extend to planning and management of marine resources. These deficiencies then act as deterrents to Indigenous communities to be proactive in MPA decision-making structures and deny equitable sharing of the benefits.

The current lack of application of Aboriginal cultural laws and protocols omits the Indigenous holistic concepts of ecosystem management in a cultural landscape/seascape context. Western tenure structures created by various government agencies impose a regulatory structure that acknowledges Aboriginal use rights in one domain and not in the other. A good example is the terrestrial Commonwealth Booderee National Park, which adjoins the NSW Jervis Bay Marine Park. While co-management occurs on land, it is not extended to the marine estate, thus ignoring traditional territories and obligations. This arrangement inherently fails to fully protect Aboriginal cultural integrity of the landscape/seascape, as highlighted by Farrier and Adams in their 2011 publication, *Indigenous–Government Co-Management of Protected Areas: Booderee National Park and the national framework in Australia*. This constitutional division of powers and legislation not only impacts the integrity of cultural practices and sustenance, but also increases the economic, social, cultural and spiritual impacts along with the long-term ecological viability of the area. This framework also ignores the fact that historical and continuing Aboriginal practices in many areas along the coastal fringe have contributed to the evolution of the ecosystem processes and habitat complexes.

The most important and immediate need to rectify this flaw is the development of a framework for Indigenous governance setting out the appropriate institutional and legislative platforms for Aboriginal processes, and detailing Aboriginal interests and rights, values, significance and associations. Such a framework should also detail contextual integration into MPA strategic planning processes. This would provide a rational and equitable tool for the establishment and acknowledgement of Indigenous rights and values in sea country adjoining already Aboriginal-owned lands.

How are marine parks developed? Developing the framework

The National Marine Planning Framework is developed collaboratively between the legislative government body (state, territory or federal government), its agencies, the affected local government/s, industries reliant on profits or losses from the proposed protected area and scientists. The community representative component is there primarily to input perspectives or views that are not necessarily projected or affiliated with the proposed protected area.

The Australian marine planning model notes that:

- Bioregional marine planning is a relatively new concept worldwide.
- Planning concepts and traditions in marine planning models are based on managing activities within the capability of the ecosystem.
- The key assumptions behind the current models are that the available data reflect:
  - the ecological parameters fundamental to the functions of the ecosystem and the biological diversity
  - the spatial distribution of the ecological parameters of the ecosystem.

The key assumptions behind the model are that the data available reasonably reflect:

1. The ecological parameters fundamental to the function of the ecosystem and its biological diversity.
2. The spatial distribution of the ecological parameters of the ecosystem.

The aims of the model are to:

- zone the planning area based on ecological criteria
- identify and define the spatial boundaries of the zones.

The current methodology and standard steps in the development of a marine reserve and plan are:

1. Collect, create and collate spatial data for the planning area.
2. Sort spatial data into appropriate resource-use categories of social, economic, and cultural and heritage. These data are collected from various and numerous sources, including other government agencies, businesses and communities (one that is marginalised is represented in the process to always emphasise diversity). The environmental data are used for the development of the marine planning model with social, economic, and cultural and heritage values to support it.
3. Geographical information system (GIS) layers of environmental data are created to form ecological variables.
4. Planning areas and spatial summary of data are conducted.
5. Planning unit spatial layers are linked to the ecological variables and grouped into ecologically rated zones.
6. Impact analysis using the spatial data is undertaken to determine use areas.

Consequently, there are no existing models of marine planning in Australia that allow for culturally identified marine protection, protection of cultural species or joint management of marine ecosystems. There is room for the above formula or process to also apply to cultural values where there are Aboriginal cultural interests in the environment, resources, species and areas/sites within the proposed or existing MPA. The same layers of spatial conservation and protection are applied to sites of ecological, natural, customary, resource and geomorphological significance. At present, the scope of cultural interest or value is somewhat an add-on as part of the community consultation process and not so much a starting point inserted as a value or asset variable that is mapped as part of the spatial distribution parameters within the ecosystem.

The standard operating processes of these government-controlled departments involve:

- desktop review
- consultation with stakeholders
- redefining policy positions
- coastal and marine planning and development frameworks
- strategic assessments
- application of science (habitat and ecosystem mapping).

When initial zoning occurs, ecologically rated (ER) zones seek to:

- establish boundaries defined along ecological criteria rather than administrative or jurisdictional boundaries
- recognise the complex interactions between ecological levels including across varying scales such as habitats and regions
- focus management on the maintenance of ecosystem integrity.

The zoning system consists of four ER zones, distinguished by the highest diversity of marine, coastal and estuarine habitats and species that occur within a marine planning area. The ER zones are graded as follows:

- ER1 Zone: containing the highest diversity of marine, coastal and estuarine habitats and species.
- ER2 Zone: containing a high diversity of marine, coastal and estuarine habitats and species.

- ER3 Zone: containing a moderate diversity of marine, coastal and estuarine habitats and species.
- ER4 Zone: consisting of areas for which the available scientific data are inadequate to identify their importance to the maintenance of biodiversity, ecological health and productivity of the ecosystem.

Aboriginal rights, interests and obligations in the marine environment

Making real progress in advancing Indigenous rights and management in the marine environment requires interpretation and evaluation of what these rights are and how they should be applied and integrated into the framework and planning and then transferred to management and policy within Australia's MPAs. It also requires a more Indigenous perspective of progress and sustainable development, and real advancement of Indigenous entitlements to the control of marine jurisdiction. There are documented examples from the past 78 years on which to draw of the work and application of traditional mechanisms, along with the commitment and successes of Aboriginal and Torres Strait Islander peoples' application of their world view and current approaches to the management of sea country. These examples include research and monitoring of the sustainable use of biological resources, which demonstrate that the empowering and application of Indigenous concepts and practices have contributed to the success of marine protection and biological functioning of marine habitats in Australia (NAILSMA 2012).

The following discussion looks at 'progress and advancement' from an Indigenous perspective and draws on a sea country meeting held in 2012, where land and sea managers from around Australia met at Mary River in the Northern Territory to discuss issues affecting Aboriginal sea country management in Australia. The workshop provided an opportunity for Aboriginal and Torres Strait Islander peoples from around Australia to discuss current issues, aspirations and cultural obligations as sea country owners and managers. It also aimed to explore options for increased Indigenous engagement in sea country management and to develop and articulate the views of delegates on an appropriate national Indigenous sea country management framework.

The consistent theme of the meeting was Aboriginal peoples' desire to increase our participation in the management of the marine estate, from increased opportunities to own and control inputs into policy and legislative processes, along with establishing processes, to increasing resources, capacity and powers for individual groups directly involved in management on Country (NAILSMA 2012).

The legislative constructs that surround MPA management are essentially derived from colonial frameworks. Globally, policymakers, marine managers, legislators and Indigenous peoples increasingly seek to attempt to reconcile MPA governance and management with Indigenous peoples (Rist et al. 2014). Due to the varied tenure regimes and interests within Australian marine governance systems, the ability to insert Aboriginal world views and cultural paradigms is somewhat confronting and exposing.

The momentous turning point for Indigenous peoples in Australia was the Mabo native title case in the High Court of Australia, which overtured the legal doctrine of *terra nullius* or 'nobody's land', which was the main assumption underlying Australian legal rulings on land and sea title. This significant moment provided legal recognition in Australian law that Aboriginal and Torres Strait Islander peoples continue to hold rights to their lands and waters that extend from traditional laws and customs. The *Native Title Act 1993* provides for the recognition of native title on land and in the sea.

Despite this legislation, there is a consensus view among Aboriginal peoples that Indigenous sea country aspirations and requirements are still not being met (NAILSMA 2012). This is especially troubling given the original native title claim to which the Mabo ruling pertained was by the Meriam people over sea country in the Torres Strait. The second significant determination was the native title declaration over Blue Mud Bay in the Northern Territory in July 2008. In this case, Australia's High Court ruled Traditional Owners have exclusive access rights to waters on Aboriginal land in intertidal zones. Aboriginal land is privately owned; it is not Crown or public land. Permission must be obtained in accordance with the *Aboriginal Land Rights (Northern Territory) Act 1976* before entering these lands (NLC 2022).

Indigenous peoples taking control of the intertidal zone was unprecedented in Australia. The decision was described as the most significant ruling for Aboriginal landowners in the 27 years since the High Court's Mabo decision in 1992. Since 2008, an interim management arrangement has been in place giving commercial operators and recreational fishers permits, and licence-holders free access, to those areas. This has been governed by NT Fisheries, which has been authorising access to the intertidal zones. Traditional Owners want to retrospectively control that access and the associated governance arrangements.

Many of these sea country areas are in remote sections of Australia's jurisdiction and join terrestrial areas where Indigenous communities have ownership. A recent exception is the native title determination for Yaegl on the north coast of New South Wales in August 2017, which saw the first determination for native title rights and interests over areas of sea in that state. After 20 years of negotiations, the Yaegl people gained 'non-exclusive' rights, which means they do not own the land or sea, but they have 'non-exclusive' rights to use it. Non-exclusive native title rights include the right to access, hunt, fish and carry out ceremonies in the area. This 'right' exists in line with the rights of other stakeholders to access and enjoyment, with the government having the right to effectively protect and manage the area. Existing lawful users of the area—such as protected area reserve managers, holders of fishing licences and members of the public—continue to enjoy the same rights in the area (DPI 2017).

Another evolving mechanism for joint management is the establishment of Indigenous protected areas (IPAs). Examples of governance bridging tenure and authorities are occurring in the Dhimurru IPA in the Northern Territory and Girringun Region IPAs in Queensland. This Indigenous-driven, collaborative, non-legislative approach to dedicating, governing and managing coastal areas and MPAs can serve as a model in other nation-states for Indigenous peoples wishing to use a protected area governance framework to support the contemporary management of their traditional marine and coastal estates (Rist et al. 2014).

Despite these examples, the consensus view that still resonates throughout Aboriginal Australia is that Indigenous sea country aspirations and requirements are not being met and there is a need for a national voice and a national organisation to bring together these objectives (NAILSMA 2012). Any negotiation process to this end requires sufficient monetary and human resources to enable the equitable participation of the Indigenous owners of Australia in the development of policies, the setting of allocations and the management of regulatory schemes that may evolve into social and cultural, ecological and economic needs. It also requires capacity within the Aboriginal community to participate and sustain the prolonged time frames associated with legislative and legal processes.

At the national Indigenous sea country forum held in 2012, the delegates wrote a statement to the Australian state and territory governments. The statement outlined that, as Traditional Owners, they had inherent and pre-existing rights to make decisions about cultural landscapes and the management of biological resources in Australia. It emphasised that theirs is a holistic cultural approach to management, including land, sea country, freshwater, spiritual aspects, cultural aspects and intellectual property, with which Aboriginal and Torres Strait Islander peoples are intrinsically entwined. This statement also outlined to government the need to review current legislation, policies and practices and shift towards new initiatives to identify obstacles and remove impediments, with the view of fully involving Aboriginal and Torres Strait Islander peoples in the control and management of the marine environment and associated biological resources and systems (NAILSMA 2012).

Australia is a signatory to the Convention on Biological Diversity through the *EPBC Act*. Under the convention, participating governments agreed to acknowledge and give full account to the following:

- In accordance with the Convention on Biological Diversity (CBD), Indigenous peoples must have a central role in the development, implementation and evaluation of policy and legislation or administrative measures that may affect their estate. Of key importance is Article 8, 'In-Situ Conservation', and particularly Article 8(j), which states:

  Subject to National legislation, respect, preserve and maintain knowledge, innovations and practices of Indigenous and local communities embodying traditional lifestyles relevant for the conservation and sustainable use of biological diversity and promote their wider application with the approval and involvement of the holders of such knowledge, innovations and practices and encourage the equitable sharing of the benefits arising from the utilization of such knowledge, innovations and practices.

- Article 10, 'Sustainable Use of Components of Biological Diversity', particularly Article 10(c), which states: 'Protect and encourage customary use of biological resources in accordance with traditional cultural practices that are compatible with conservation or sustainable use requirements.'

- In accordance with Article 19 of the United Nations Declaration on the Rights of Indigenous Peoples, we must have a central role in the development, implementation and evaluation of policy and legislative or administrative measures that may affect us concerning our estate.

- In accordance with Articles 26 and 32 of the UN Declaration on the Rights of Indigenous Peoples, we affirm that:
  - Indigenous peoples have the right to the lands, territories and resources that they have traditionally owned, occupied or otherwise used in acquiring.
  - Indigenous peoples have the right to own, use, develop and control the lands, territories and resources that they possess by reason of traditional ownership or other traditional occupation or use, as well as those that we have otherwise acquired.
  - States shall give legal recognition and protection to these lands, territories and resources. Such recognition shall be conducted with due respect to the customs and traditional land tenure systems of the Indigenous peoples concerned.
  - Indigenous peoples have the right to determine and develop priorities and strategies for the development and use of our lands or territories and any other resources.
  - States shall consult through our representative institutions to obtain our free and informed consent before the approval of any project affecting our lands or territories and other resources, particularly in connection with the development, utilisation or exploitation of mineral, water or other resources.
  - States shall provide effective mechanisms for just and fair redress for such activities, and appropriate measures shall be taken to mitigate adverse environmental, economic, social, cultural and spiritual impacts. We are also aware of the following instruments that support the aspirations of Aboriginal and Torres Strait Islander peoples:
    - *EPBC Act*
    - Ramsar Convention
    - Nagoya Protocol
    - Addis Ababa Principles and Guidelines
    - Akwé: Kon Guidelines.

Science-based decision-making and Indigenous practice

Many government department reports and publications state their desire to better recognise and support culturally significant marine and coastal areas, especially those already being managed by Indigenous communities (IUCN 2013). An inherent issue arises, therefore, where there is no inclusion of Aboriginal values in ecological value assessments and Western scientific methodologies are to the forefront of the planning applied.

Western scientific and Indigenous approaches have been applied in partnership in some cases with promising results. A prototype of this process is the Teahupo`o MPA discussed in the next chapter. Here, a hybrid system based on the old Polynesian custom of rāhui was initiated to enhance both social and ecological resilience along with ecological connectivity for the first time in French Polynesia. The simple shift in hegemony through recognition of the legitimacy of traditional experts and their role in the contemporary management of resources and territories helped reverse postcolonial inequities and dramatically improved the ecological health of the MPA administered in this way. Facilitating local community conceptual recognition and election to governance bodies gave traditional knowledge and the traditional experts that represent it a place in the formulation of the MPA's establishment framework. This also provided the ability to legitimise the development of cultural maps, which then allowed exploration of International Union for Conservation of Nature (IUCN) categories by the inhabitants of Teahupo`o to legitimise the rāhui and apply it to resource management and decision-making capacity (Bambridge 2013b).

Another issue in Australia is that the smaller number of MPAs compared with terrestrial equivalents means there is less experience and understanding of applying cultural categories to MPAs. Application of the categories to MPAs has often been inaccurate and inconsistent (IUCN 2013). Traditional Owner groups consider developing and implementing sea country plans an Indigenous-led mechanism to engage in the planning and management of Victorian and Queensland MPAs, including consideration of collaborative frameworks such as Traditional Use of Marine Resource Agreements and IPAs (Smyth 2009; Gidarjil Development Corporation 2021; GBRMPA 2020). Global experience indicates that the conservation and sustainability objectives of MPA managers can be achieved without unduly eroding Indigenous customary rights to access, use and management of marine areas and resources (Smyth 2009).

Aboriginal cultural marine mapping

Indigenous cultures throughout the world have used different forms of mapping, whether drawn on skin, wood or paper (De Hutorowicz 1911). Gladwin (1970) noted that Micronesians created stick charts that showed complex representations of ocean tides and currents. Other expressive forms of culture, such as the Hawaiian Hula, use body movements to embody experiences and events (Wood 1992). In the Hawaiian case, the traditional steps of the Hula express the creation and codes of culture.

In Australia, Aboriginal peoples have developed songlines to sing their land into existence, which also draw mental maps of historical events, significant places and claims to territory (Chatwin 1987). Another type of mapping applicable to Aboriginal culture is oral, which explains people's world view of how the land and seascapes were organised and utilised. The sense of kinship to the natural environment is often based on strong spiritual connection with ancestors and the land/water where ancestors were buried, as well as on subsistence needs. This intimate connection with nature is very hard to digitise, as Calamia (1999) found when reflecting on Pacific Islanders' oral maps, as these may reflect less physically apparent social behaviour and cultural aspects of marine resource use and conservation. Oral cultures also utilise spatial references or landmarks, such as waterways, headlands and mountains, which are more amenable to cartographic representation. Cultural mapping must therefore go beyond strict cartography to include cultural resources other than land: 'anthropological, sociological, archaeological, genealogical, linguistic, topographical, musicological and ecological and botanical' (Poole 2003).

More recently, spatial information has been used for understanding interrelationships between traditional human societies and ecological processes (Calamia 1999). The application of GIS technology in marine cultural resource documentation provides an opportunity to assemble information about species, habitats, seasonal patterns and cultural values in a spatial manner. The application of cultural mapping alongside ecological mapping allows:

1. development of a predictive model of spatial Indigenous cultural use and associated resource products in shallow-water marine environments
2. identification of key environmental variables as indicators of cultural resource use and management, producing habitat maps with indigenously defined habitat classes and connected cultural associations, providing cultural perspectives on resource management
3. highlighting of the intimate and intricate knowledge of ecosystems, species and the physical fundamentals of place
4. identification of species and locations (tangible and intangible) of cultural significance.

The mapping of Indigenous attachments to place and significance is a relatively new approach to securing tenure, managing natural resources and strengthening culture, with origins in Canada and Alaska during the 1960s. Each mapping objective has a variety of methodologies that range from highly participatory approaches with village sketch maps to highly technical methods using spatial and technological equipment, GIS and remote sensing (Chapin et al. 2005). Such tools can complement the Indigenous systems traditionally used to store and transfer knowledge and information.

These data systems of cultural knowledge also require a framework for application, management and access. The values that are attached to traditional and contemporary knowledge include relationships with ocean attributes including habitat, ecosystems and species, cultural elements such as totems, connections in spirituality and belief systems and how these elements are integral to the sustenance of local resources, use, access and responsibilities for territories/homelands.

It must be acknowledged that understanding and documenting customary resources, systems and processes operating in the marine environment and traditional coastal landscapes are not easy tasks. The multilayered cultural systems of the many language groups involved, and the interconnectedness between cultural biodiversity, social and cultural values, and social systems, require a multidimensional assessment. The information obtained provides a basic introduction to Indigenous governance systems in marine environments. Both qualitative and quantitative data must be compiled, including on ecological knowledge, areas of significance and connection and known resources, with examples of connection in traditional estates and associated knowledge systems of country and creation. The spatial mapping of resource information in two and three dimensions can provide a resource tool that incorporates attributes of cultural connection into current management systems in the coastal and marine environment. It also provides insight into analysis or theories of restriction as harvest principles as they relate to species biology and ecology, ecological sustainability management and cultural concepts of biodiversity.

The framework and data analysis would primarily aim to link the concept of interconnectedness between cultural biodiversity, social and cultural values, and the relationship of the changing variables of the coastal and marine environments within each group's 'country'. The connection between ecological knowledge, cultural use, resource information and ecological habitat communities is mapped in terms of spatial multidimensional data. These data are used for spatial representations and applied through a commonly used spatial resource information tool, incorporating cultural knowledge and values into a management system with data manipulation to show Aboriginal cultural associations including existing marine and coastal environment data and site-specific information.

The framework and process proposed above are similar to and compatible with those of current scientific ecological assessments. In 2008, Lauer and Shankar undertook an assessment of the practical application of Indigenous ecological knowledge along with remote-sensing analysis to construct marine habitat maps. Outcomes from this study showed that remote-sensing techniques produced culturally defined marine habitats that could be useful in socio-ecological processes and management decision-making and planning (Lauer and Shankar 2008). Marine resources were managed and knowledge was accumulated and conveyed on species biology, ecology, habitat and ecomorphology, influencing such things as seasonal indicators, harvest times based on abundance and potentially high nutrition and protein yield, and interrelated ecosystem dynamics, to ensure abundant resources.

While it is possible to make maps that show various forms of marine cultural associations and values, including cultural connections, marine system habitats and cultural resource associations, there are limits to cultural mapping. Given the available software and resources, the comprehensive attributes and variables involved in Aboriginal maps are not capable of representation. The inherent issue lies in the limits of mapping cultural connections of spiritual origin—not an attribute that can be easily delineated, represented or displayed. The application of cultural spatial data systems does, however, highlight the complexity of associations (in time and space) and, most importantly, the layers of resource management and protection mechanisms.

The context and relevance of information can primarily lead to a focus on elements and variables where relationships can be detailed in a systematised manner. The secondary component requires developing a system to translate oral data into a spatial format by extracting explicit details of resource and habitat and associated linkages or secondary variables into feature point locations or polygon areas. Such mapping is a means of consolidating research undertaken into traditional and cultural uses of coastal and marine resources and illustrating it in a two and three-dimensional visual record, such as the author produced for the permanent display of Gumbaynggirr resource management principles in the Australian Museum (Australian Museum 2014).

Although TEK is recognised as important, effective and widespread application remain elusive (Tengö et al. 2011). Indigenous ways of knowing are holistic, acknowledging the 'interconnectedness of physical, mental, emotional and spiritual aspects of individuals with all living things and with earth, the star world, and the universe' (Lavallee 2009). Conventionally framed resource management approaches can contend with factual observations, past and current land uses and some traditional land management systems, but do not effectively grapple with issues of cosmology (Houde 2007). Current geospatial techniques and technologies have limited potential to represent Indigenous cultural knowledge and may have detrimental effects because they de-emphasise, ignore or devalue concepts that are of central importance to Indigenous cultures, including the ubiquity of relatedness, the value of non-empirical experience, access and the value of ambiguity over binary thought (Hi`iaka Working Group 2011). Calamia (1999) states that Indigenous peoples have an enormous contribution to make; however, he continues that traditional knowledge is complementary to Western science and not a replacement for it (Knudtson and Suzuki 1992).

Conclusion: The efficacy of Indigenous environmental management principles

There is increasing awareness—indicated in the international Convention on Biological Diversity—of the critical need for IEK to help achieve environmental sustainability. Many scholars emphasise the practical and ethical importance of retaining and applying IEK. The IUCN's program on traditional knowledge for conservation (IUCN 1986) summarises five practical and tangible benefits of TEK:

- it may provide new biological and ecological insights
- in resource management, rules and rote procedures are often just as good as Western scientific prescriptions
- in resource management, rules and rote procedures are often just as good as Western scientific prescriptions applied in protected area and conservation education
- in environmental assessment, where those dependent on local resources for livelihoods are in a better position to assess the true costs and benefits of development.

Indigenous marine cultural values emphasise resource sustainability and layered partitioning and security. Issues of climatic alteration, species displacement, pollution, increased population and coastal development are current and accumulative. Indigenous perspectives and values on marine ecosystems provide another light on how these systems can be managed. This change revolves primarily around the psychology of people and their resource values and connections.

While effective co-management of Australian marine areas remains embryonic, processes elsewhere in our region suggest this limited progress is due more to assumptions and attitudes than to basic incompatibilities between Western and Aboriginal marine management practices and principles. Community-based conservation such as IPAs and locally managed marine areas are increasing throughout the Pacific Islands as conservation and management specialists argue for the incorporation of conservation frameworks that recognise sea-based culture areas to enhance protection of the marine environment (Cordell 1991, 2007; Govan et al. 2009; Bambridge 2013a; Bambridge et al. 2019). This trend is based on the efficacy of both the social and the ecological benefits observed.

This chapter has argued that the use of cultural mapping to identify Indigenous values and practices is a vital and achievable means of increasing knowledge and awareness of Aboriginal concepts and knowledge among Australian marine policymaking bodies. For Aboriginal concepts to effectively partner with Western science—as occurs more and more on land—greater decision-making powers must be conveyed to Aboriginal guardians of sea country for effective co-management of Australia's marine spaces. Such a process would complement education in revealing a different psychology, perception and perspective of the marine environment that highlight holistic values and interrelated connections, as well as the complexities of the personal principles at play. Effective empowerment of Aboriginal sea country managers will not only enhance conservation, but also address the inequity inherent in the current governance of Australian marine areas.

7

Integrated Indigenous Management of Land and Marine Protected Areas in Teahupo`o (Tahiti, French Polynesia): A way to enhance ecological and cultural resilience

Tamatoa Bambridge, Marguerite Taiarui, Patrick Rochette, Takurua Parent and Pauline Fabre

Introduction

This case study retraces the implementation and development of an integrated management area (land and sea) in Taiarapu, French Polynesia, based on an old Polynesian custom called rāhui. Traditionally, rāhui is a sacred decision to protect an area and/or a resource, whether on land or lagoon. The rāhui has spiritual as well as economic and social dimensions. In 2008, the community of Teahupo`o (a small district in the south of Tahiti Iti), decided to create a management plan for their territory to increase its social and ecological resilience. Land and lagoon toponyms were recorded, along with the associated tahu`a (ancient specialists), and scientists have been mobilised to devise the patterns and frontiers of the integrated coastal areas to be protected. Moreover, the governance of this territory integrates decades of missionary and colonial influences. To strengthen the legal basis of the new rāhui system, the community decided to create a hybrid model of governance, in which local norms based on rāhui, with the participation of traditional experts and the local population, interact with the state's legal framework borrowed from the IUCN's MPA typologies. This has created a legal pluralist model of governance that has already increased social resilience and fostered the creation of an integrated MPA over land, lagoon and coral reefs. In addition, thanks to this plural governance pattern, the economic and cultural activities now planned in and outside the MPA are carefully chosen to enhance ecological resilience.

Analytical framework

Across the Pacific, legal pluralism—which is understood as 'the presence in the social field of more than one normative order' (Griffiths 1986: 8)—is a structural element of the governance of marine and terrestrial resources (Ward and Kingdom 1995; Boege et al. 2008; Govan 2008; Govan et al. 2009; Bambridge 2009, 2013a, 2013b). Limited studies have addressed issues of ecological and social resilience, taking into account this structural context (Barrière 1996; Fisher et al. 2009; Bambridge 2013a). Social and ecological resilience are generally defined as the ability of social and ecological systems to withstand disturbances without changing their structure, function, feedback or identity (Walker et al. 2006; Adam et al. 2011), and be flexible in responding to changing environmental and social contexts (Redman and Kinzig 2003; Bohensky and Maru 2011). However, it seems clear that no system, ecological or social, can return to its previous state after disturbance.

Analysing ecological and social resilience in the context of legal and cultural pluralism requires consideration of the economic, cultural, social, political and plural normative contexts, incorporating land and marine aspects. As such, traditional knowledge and practices should be incorporated into the study of social and ecological resilience (Bohensky and Maru 2011). This would reduce the gap between data collected by social scientists and ecologists' ecosystem models (Folke 2006).

In Teahupo`o, social and ecological resilience can be analysed as social constructions built daily according to specific institutional and human terms, historically situated. As elsewhere in Polynesia, here, discourses and practices refer to the island territory including the inland side (pae uta, literally 'mountain side') and seaward side (pae tai, literally 'sea side').

The analysis of practices in the light of subsequent developments illuminates the perception and understanding of a management model integrating land, sea and coral reefs. Social resilience manifests primarily by 'working on memory' about rāhui (the traditional Polynesian spatial management of resources).

It is important to discuss here how this pluralism is articulated locally and in what ways a cultural and legal hybridisation process allows, at two different scales, the history of governance and collaboration between institutional and Indigenous science, including traditional knowledge, to increase the social and ecological resilience of the territory.

The poor integration of normative and cultural aspects in previous studies of resilience has encouraged the formation of a multidisciplinary team to conduct this program at Teahupo`o. The team included researchers in the humanities (Polynesian civilisation, oral history, linguistics, anthropology, fisheries law, geography), ecology, remote sensing and mathematical tools applied to the space (Bambridge 2008–11).

Two main approaches have been used. A qualitative method based on fieldwork and surveys helped to identify and define the territory, actors, knowledge and management issues (Bambridge 2009; Bambridge 2008–11). A quantitative survey using statistical processing and geographic information from the general census of the population was used to quantify information and compare it with qualitative analyses of field surveys (Campaner 2010). The results of the two types of surveys were compared to refine the choice of variables and the sociocultural development of indicators for the management of protected areas.

The mapping tool (GIS) integrated the information shown in Figure 7.1.

The choice of Taiarapu, encompassing the associated towns Teahupo`o (East Taiarapu) and Tautira (West Taiarapu), was determined by the cultural issues that arise there, some of which date back to pre-European times: conflicting use of resources and space over a relatively homogeneous area (conflict over lagoon resources, issues related to the use of a border between the two territories), and the increasing urbanisation of this part of the island (construction of a port and an industrial area, residential and agricultural developments, and so on).

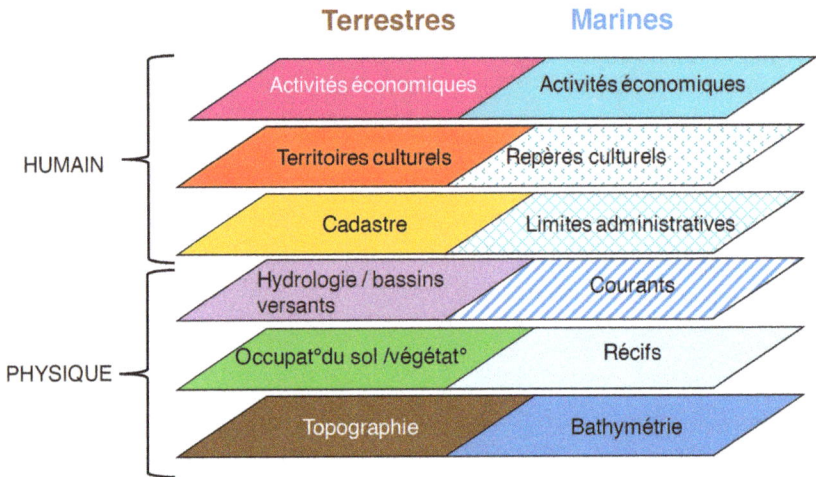

Figure 7.1: GIS mapping tool information.

Humain = Human
Physique = Physical
Activités économiques = Economic activities
Territoires culturels = Cultural territories
Reperes culturels = Cultural landmarks
Cadastre = Landownership registration
Limites administratives = Administrative boundaries
Hydrologie/bassins versants = Hydrology/watersheds
Courants = Currents
Occupat du sol/végétat = Land use/vegetation
Récifs = Reefs
Topographie = Topography
Bathymétrie = Bathymetry

Source: Jean-Brice Herrenschmidt (ddatpacific@gmail.com).

After a brief presentation of the study area, the first part of the chapter is devoted to the history of this island society and its present links with rāhui (the traditional system of land management and resources). This will allow us to show how rāhui is now used to build social resilience.

The second part will be devoted to the mechanisms currently being implemented in terms of governance (participatory management and the involvement of traditional experts or tahu`a) and the construction of a hybrid framework for state and local management to increase social and ecological resilience.

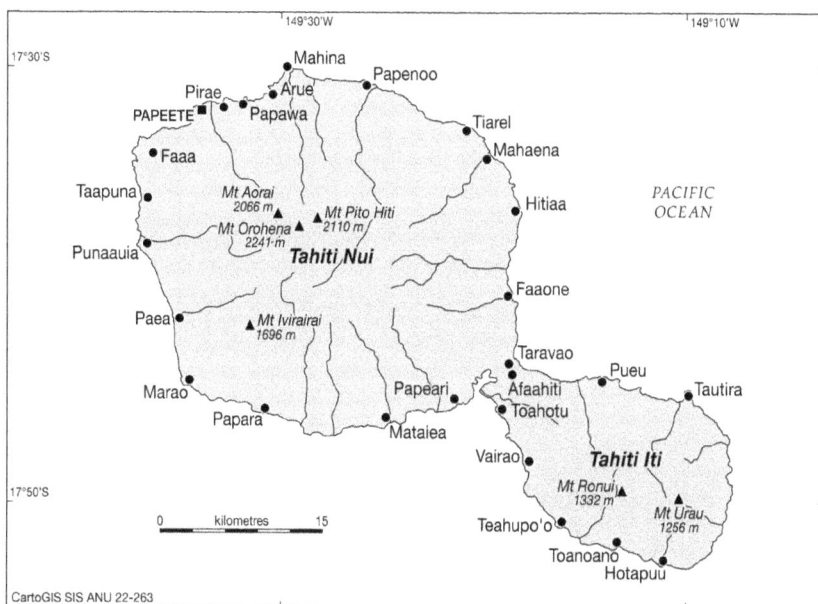

Map 7.1: Map of Tahiti (Teahupo`o is at bottom right).
Source: CartoGIS SIS ANU 22-263.

The study area

Teahupo`o, a municipality associated with west Taiarapu, is at the southern end of the island of Tahiti. With 1,289 inhabitants (ISPF 2007–17), the district is divided into three sociologically distinct geographic parts: the 'village', the 'fenua `Aihere' and the 'pari'.

Table 7.1: Population dynamics of Teahupo`o study area, 2007–17

	2002	2007	2012	2017
Taiarapu West	**6,081**	**7,007**	**7,706**	**8,078**
Change over five years (%)	0	+15.20	+9.90	+4.80
Change over 10 years (%)			+26.70	0
Teahupo`o	**1,194**	**1,321**	**1,289**	**1,419**
As a percentage of municipality population	19.60	18.80	16.70	17.60
Change over five years (%)	0	+10.60	−2.50	+10.00
Change over 10 years (%)			+7.90	0

Source: ISPF (2007–17).

Most of the population of this municipality is concentrated in the village. Over the past decade, the population increase in Teahupo'o has been 7.9 per cent, compared with 26.7 per cent for the whole of the west Taiarapu municipality.

The village enjoys the conveniences of the modern world in terms of capital goods, infrastructure and means of communication. The fenua 'Aihere, between the coast and inland peaks, has its western limit in the coastal part of Mahora peak while its eastern limit is the pass of Tutataroa. There is a buffer between the village and the pari (mountain cliff or steep slope). Few people live there. This part of the Tahitian coast boasts large wet valleys, attracting new economic interests and secondary residences. More and more people are building homes here.

The pari was probably quite densely inhabited until the nineteenth century (Rodriguez 1995), but was abandoned due to the regrouping of the population into villages by missionaries. This place is for many people an area of great cultural value—a reservoir of biodiversity for traditional care, hiking trips and fishing—and also has numerous archaeological sites, testifying of the heroic history of the peninsula.

Many changes have affected the life of the village, mainly in terms of the influx of non-residents, the opening of a marina, increased housing in fenua 'Aihere and annual surfing competitions that are internationally publicised. Since the 1980s, the village space has grown steadily in the direction of fenua 'Aihere.

The main activities in Teahupo'o are agriculture and fishing, and there are 324 family businesses. These figures often hide the reality that many activities are seasonal and not practised for much of the year. The number of tourist operators also varies depending on the time of year. It is mostly on the Teahupo'o site, during the international surfing competition that takes place each year, where, for a few weeks, a substantial amount of the population will be oriented towards providing tourist services: renting out houses, driving boats, acting as tourist guides, and so on.

History, rāhui and pluralism

To understand the patterns of land use in Taiarapu, one must consider the territorial and political boundaries of the eighteenth century. The district of Tairapu holds a special place in Tahitian mythology. The island of Tahiti was believed to be a fish that detached from Havai`i (Raiatea). According to Henry (1968: 454–60), Mahine, the ari`i (chief) of Huahine and Tamera, a famous tahu`a (priest-specialist), recalled how Tahiti became separated from Havai`i, travelled like a fish and settled again as fenua (land) when it arrived at this destination. It is likely this historicity is recent (no earlier than the seventeenth century) and emerged at Opoa (Raiatea) at a moment when the atua (god) Oro became more important in Polynesian history. The place where we worked, Matarufau, was considered to be the head of the fish, whereas Hotuārea, in the district now called Fa'a`ā, is the tail of the fish. Thus, in many ways, this history is considered the point when Tahiti became more independent and autonomous in relation to Havai`i's gods and social organisation.

In Taiarapu, there were six political and territorial federations whose boundaries were included in each confederation, depending on shifting alliances. The territory of the present town of Teahupo`o, which was not yet its name, was part of the Confederation of Teva-i-tai ('Seaward Teva'), who were allies of the Teva-i-uta ('Inland Teva'). Together, these Teva, under the authority of the chief of Papara, who was also chief of Teva-i-uta, was the most powerful coalition on the island of Tahiti. In the second half of the eighteenth century, the territory of Taiarapu (where the first Catholic mission was established by the Spaniards) played a crucial role in Tahitian history. The ari'i Vehiātua was the chief of Seaward Teva (Teva-i-tai). Vehiātua was closely linked to another young ari`i, Tu, who ruled the north of Tahiti and had previously made a coalition with Vehiātua's father to remove the maro `ura (a belt of red feathers and the honorary badge of the supreme power of Tahiti) from Inland Teva. The victory that freed Seaward Teva from the tutelage of Inland Teva took place in 1769 after the passage of James Cook. This battle saw the defeat of the ari`i Amo and his wife, Purea (written as Oberea by Cook), whose ancestral district was Papara on the southern coast of Tahiti Nui. Thus, the tumultuous history of Teahupo`o was intertwined with the transformation of the centres of power in Tahiti until the advent of Pōmare, who formed the first Christian Tahitian dynasty, which ultimately centralised political power within a unitary state.

In line with the Tahitian tapu (spiritual restriction), the rāhui was probably the most important attribute of ari`i in their management of populations, territory and resources (Bambridge 2013a). Strictly speaking, rāhui is a sacred ban imposed by the chief on a specific area for a certain period. The logical order of rāhui was economic, political and religious. Its aim was to impose temporary restrictions to renew the area's resources in preparation for a large and prestigious circulation of goods, to demonstrate the reality of power and human networks (Oliver 1974; Devatine 1989; Rigo 2004).

During the evangelisation of Tahitians after the defeat in 1812 of the chiefs attached to the old social and religious order (Taaroa 1971; Ellis 1972), missionaries drew up legal codes designed to get rid of the old religion and weaken the ari`i system. One measure was the suppression of the rāhui in the first half of the nineteenth century. Many of the prerogatives of the ari`i were transferred to a new institution, the To`ohitu ha'avā (literally, 'seven judges'), who were non-ari`i (Newbury 1967). This declining trend in the power of the ari`i and ancient Tahitian structures served French interests following the establishment of a protectorate in Tahiti and its dependencies from 1842. Although the rāhui was restored, the distinction between the French and native administrations disappeared, which resulted in the ari`i losing significant land rights and their control of the rāhui, while the selection of district chiefs was now conducted by election.

Land registration

Registration of property title in Teahupo`o was made under the influence of a decree on 24 August 1887, following the annexation of Tahiti and its dependencies in 1880. Claims organised between 1890 and 1891 resulted in 331 titles or tōmite in Teahupo`o. The first land register was established in 1935 and updated in 2008, excluding the mountainous areas. The application of the 1887 decree to the registration of property excluded claims relating to the lagoon—a result of the fact that the Western legal standard was at odds with traditional Polynesian ones, under which marine and land territories were appropriated by extended families. Since the late nineteenth century, under French administrative rules, the official design of the territory of Teahupo`o has neglected cultural aspects, which locals still consider disruptive.

Rāhui: Symbol of social and ecological resilience

For today's actors in Teahupo'o, rāhui is the preferred instrument to restore the economic, social and political resilience deconstructed by two centuries of missionary and colonial influences. It is therefore important to show how this resilience is built locally by considering multiple, sometimes contradictory, influences.

It is interesting to note the extent to which people in Teahupo'o now view the rāhui as a mechanism for social resilience in terms of land and marine resource management. This is perceptible not only in discourse, but also by observing unspoken attitudes that demonstrate commitment to an old institution. Thus, when the central government and the municipality of Teahupo'o decided to set up a general plan for the maritime area in 2004, locals greeted it with indifference. The ultimate sign of its failure was that it was consistently and negatively compared with the rāhui.

As in much of eastern Polynesia, in Teahupo'o, the rāhui is very present in the minds of the inhabitants when management of marine and terrestrial resources is discussed (see Bambridge 2013a). During group meetings or individual surveys conducted by our team to discuss the management of the commune's territory, a local expert, Papa Mote, clearly captured a policy framework for managing land and resources. He spoke bluntly in Tahitian:

> If I am the ari'i here, it's me who decides the harvest period. It is the ari'i who share the resources and the harvest goes to the ari'i … even if it was you who planted it. This is the word of ari'i. Here at Teahupo'o, it certainly existed. If your territory is rāhui, do not touch it. You can have access to another place. All resources in the sea and on the land were rāhui.

The rāhui restriction is here clearly linked with a political dimension of resource management. It includes terrestrial and marine areas, and implies authority, a body of rules and behaviours adapted to respect an institution. The rāhui refers more to a logic of sovereignty than to a property logic (Colin 2008; Jacob and Le Meur 2010).

Many actors in Teahupo'o expressed the need—like other attempts in neighbouring districts—to restore a 'priority mastering of land' (Le Roy 2011, 2013) as well as community control of the lagoon. If the lagoon's resources must be managed, it is a community space for the benefit of its stakeholders. Our investigations have indeed helped to highlight the different categories of traditional expertise that correspond with two types of control over territory (Bambridge 2013a). 'Specialised mastering' is specific expertise associated with a field of activity (fishing, culture, agriculture, pharmacology) in a territory. 'Priority mastering' is the ordering of society (person or tahu`a-specific extended family, and so on) to allow access to certain areas or resources. This involves privileged access to specific uses of an area and should not be confused with absolute rights or fixed ownership as in the civil law tradition.

The cultural and legal hybridisation process for strengthening social and ecological resilience

Local ways of characterising territory by encompassing the continuity of land and sea contrast with the duality of state standards regarding the land (private property) and the lagoon (public domain). Thus, the toponymies developed by experts (tahu`a) in culture, fisheries, traditional medicine and agriculture form a space of ecological and cultural coherence, including the land and the lagoon.

The representation and use of the public maritime domain are examples of local norms in Teahupo`o. According to the State of French Polynesia, lagoons are in the public domain. Successive autonomy laws have enhanced the transfer of competence to Polynesian authorities for the protection and management of lagoon areas (Cazalet 2008). This 'official law' (Chiba 1998), however, does not correspond with Tahitian norms from the pre-European period, nor does it correspond with contemporary local norms based on *habitus* in the sense of Bourdieu (1986b: 40). Paralleling the practical experiences of law (code) and regulation (Bambridge and Vernaudon 2013), Tahitians often feel state rule is alien and established largely for foreign interests. In this regard, several interviews we conducted were interesting for the beliefs expressed that the legislation on the maritime public domain was clearly anti-Tahitian. The same pattern applies to Teahupo`o regarding ownership of rivers and springs, which the state considers to be in the public domain yet are subject to appropriation and use by local actors based on longstanding use and affiliation (for example, the freshwater source carrying the name and history of a group).

Map 7.2: Map of local names in Teahupo`o.

Source: Patrick Rochette in Bambridge (2008–11: Report 2).

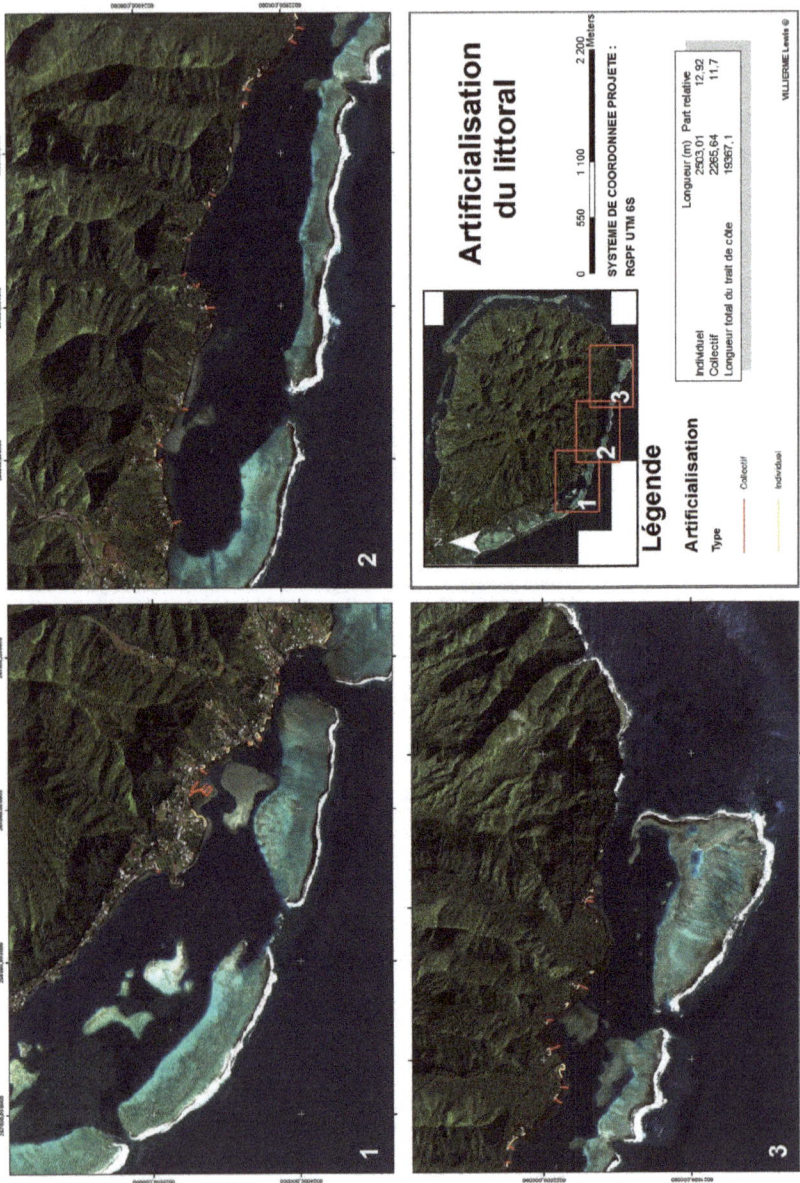

Plate 7.1: Artificial modification of the Teahupo'o coastline.

Source: L. Villierme in Bambridge (2008–11: Report 1).

This poses a fundamental problem for the public authority, which does not seem to have sufficient legitimacy to impose the rules of the public domain. However, the low acceptance of rules of public property, the significance of collective and private ownership of the coast today, combined with population growth in the municipality of Teahupo`o, have led to significant human modification of the coastline. In total, considering both collective (public embankments, docks) and individual, generally unauthorised coastal modifications, more than 4.7 kilometres of hitherto common-access-only Teahupo`o coastline is now artificial.

These figures are important considering Teahupo`o has a reputation as a wild place, preserved from the 'evils' of civilisation. The artificial coastline now represents about one-quarter of the territory of the district of Teahupo`o—a ratio that has significantly increased in a decade (Raynal 2004). This is likely to reduce the ecological resilience of the district because it destroys beaches and areas that protect juvenile marine species that are necessary to repopulate the lagoon.

Considering the previous human and ecological dynamics, the populations of Teahupo`o decided to respond to these disruptions by creating a protection framework to promote cultural and ecological resilience based on the rāhui.

Rāhui, hybridisation and co-management

'Stakeholder participation' is a controversial notion because it encompasses very different realities, ranging from simple consultation of stakeholders through to the implementation of co-management processes in which actors retain a high degree of autonomy and freedom of choice (Gregory et al. 2008; Deroche 2008; Le Meur et al. 2012). It is in the context of this second interpretation that our research team worked with populations of Teahupo`o to consider different management scenarios for protected land and sea known as contemporary rāhui pratices (Fabre et al. 2021). The people's desire was to design a framework that combined the security of state law to provide the necessary legal certainty for the sustainable development of the territory and enabled management of this area according to the rāhui standards, as it is recalled by local people. Our team invited various leaders of the administration of French Polynesia to show the people of

Teahupo'o the possibilities, advantages and disadvantages of each option. Three main tools were discussed: the urban code, the fisheries code and the environmental code.

Through our meetings, the first two proposals were subsequently excluded by actors because they did not allow land and sea management by the people; the process was legally controlled by the government, with locals simply asked to give their opinion on the implementation of management plans. However, the third option, the environmental code, is more flexible and provides six rating categories borrowed from the IUCN that allow a local management committee relative autonomy in its organisation and decision-making, as long as local actions do not contravene the general framework.

After discussing the advantages and disadvantages of different classification categories (I to VI), those present at the meetings in Teahupo'o wanted to implement category VI, which provides priority (Table 7.2) to the sustainable use of resources and ecosystems, ecological functions and the preservation of species and genetic diversity.

Table 7.2: IUCN implementation categories proposed to Teahupo'o residents

Management objectives	Ia	Ib	II	III	IV	V	VI
Scientific research	1	3	2	2	2	2	3
Protection of endangered, rare species, etc.	2	1	2	3	3	-	2
Preservation of species and genetic diversity	1	2	1	1	1	2	1
Maintenance of ecological functions	2	1	1	-	1	2	1
Protection of specific natural/cultural elements	-	-	2	1	3	1	3
Tourism and leisure	-	2	1	1	3	1	3
Education	-	-	2	2	2	2	3
Sustainable use of resources	-	3	3	-	2	2	1
Preservation of traditional cultural features	-	-	-	-	-	1	2

1 = primary objective
2 = secondary objective
3 = potentially achievable goal
- = not realisable

The main advantage of category VI noted at the meetings lay in the fact it could integrate at the same level actors such as fishers and farmers, whereas other categories did not prioritise these actors. It should be noted that French Polynesia had never previously implemented a category VI classification. The choice involved protecting the nearshore as a nursery for fish in partial continuity with the terrestrial protected area in place since 1952, and the participation of traditional experts throughout the process, as a demonstrated commitment to the hybrid solution for environmental protection desired by the people of Teahupo'o. This appears to be a syncretic solution in that it integrates traditional management methods (rāhui) into an existing legal framework that was not originally designed for this purpose.

When considering the management rules proposed by the representatives of the people and traditional experts, the characteristics of this hybridisation clearly show the logic of rāhui. Concerning the rules to be applied to a classified site, the assembly recalled the consensus reached between residents and stakeholders in the period 2009–11, and vowed that all types of fishing should be banned, year-round, as well as all swimming, except in a strip approximately 50 metres wide along the coast. These types of prohibitions recalled the sacred traditional rāhui at Teahupo'o, in which no exception is tolerated. At the same time, the total bans are justified by the difficulties of monitoring the area. In a similar context in the Marquesas, Ottino-Garanger et al. (2016: 45–46) recall:

> The practice of Kahui/rāhui provides an accurate definition of the scope of their [chiefs' and priests'] power of coercion and initiative. Not heeding the prohibitions set by the chiefs and priests is tantamount to offending and arousing, through them, the wrath of the network's ancestors. There is always an extreme disproportion between the nature of the transgression—such as eating a forbidden fruit, for instance—and the harshness of the penalty, which is often lethal. In this instance, it is less about punishing an individual fault than demonstrating the ancestral power of the network.

Another new aspect is that the prohibitions apply to marine and coastal areas, while the rules on land use—governing access to the territories of traditional pharmacopeia in the Faaroa Valley and fishing for īna'a (gobies) at the Vaipoiri River mouth—were not changed.

Local principles of continuity were recognised, such as the interlinking of land and sea, to respect the local community's belief that cultural resilience cannot be separated from ecological resilience. Thus, the protection of spaces does not mean banning access to this space, except during ritual cycles; it necessarily implies the maintenance of traditional routes. For example, the Faaroa Valley in the proposed classification is the place where you will find much of the area's endemic biodiversity, and where experts of traditional medicine (tahu'a rā'au) obtain the necessary ingredients to make their medicines (rā'au). Prohibiting entry would mean losing an important living aspect of social and cultural heritage that improves health in the community. Preserving access to the mouth of the Vaipoiri River allows traditional populations to continue practising seasonal fishing for īna`a, which is an important part of the cultural heritage of these populations.

Similarly, regulating access to sanctuaries like the Vaipoiri and Faaroa valleys would not make sense to people if the same system was not also applied to marine spaces. For locals, their names recall their marine inventories and the historical and contemporary importance of these places. In the logic of rāhui, places are protected not for the benefit of humanity, but to allow fry to find a place of refuge to become adults and later feed the population. Environmental protection of the area and maintaining the cultural resources of the community are interrelated and inseparable.

Map 7.3: Map of land and sea use zones in Teahupo`o and Tautira districts.
Source: Campaner (2010).

Interaction with traditional scientific knowledge as a mechanism for social and ecological resilience

Another aspect of building social and ecological resilience in Teahupo'o is collaboration between researchers, traditional experts and local populations (see also Davis and Wagner 2003). Developing a scientific approach to the service of people is not simple as it requires collaboration between disciplines such as history, geography and ecology, to answer questions from actors and help them in their decision-making, without replacing them, about what to protect, the terms of protection, the co-management of land, as well as providing them with the tools to assess the social and environmental development of protected areas.

As such, one of the major contributions of science to the collaboration with the people of Teahupo'o has been to recognise the legitimacy of traditional experts in the management of resources and territories. In a postcolonial context in which these same experts (tahu'a) have historically been ignored or marginalised by missionaries, colonial authorities and local administrations, the simple task of social representation conveyed by our scientific team and the promotion of traditional knowledge represented a profound change. This approach has also been crucial for defining the scope of occupancy, the places that should be protected and the relevant actors who should be included on a management committee. Thus, the legitimacy of these tahu'a was made possible through strict adherence to intellectual copyright, and it led to the development of cultural maps of sacred places suitable for accessing traditional medicines and annual fisheries. These social and ecological maps are not disclosed without the consent of the relevant tahu'a. This work with tahu'a has facilitated their consensual recognition by the people of Teahupo'o who elected them as members of the future management committee.

From a legal anthropological perspective, this work offers a pragmatic and opportunistic view of the relationship between 'official law' and 'unofficial law'. The IUCN categories were not designed to suit local needs in terms of cultural patterns of resource management, but they were used by the inhabitants of Teahupo'o as a means of legitimising the rāhui. The local community was concerned not about the possibility of the rāhui being recognised in official law, but about applying it in a very practical way to suit local needs and, in so doing, preserving their decision-making capacity.

Conclusion

The Teahupo'o case is symbolic. Not only was it the first time a hybrid form of resource management had been implemented in French Polynesia, but also its success has much wider implications. To be fully effective and efficient, other rāhui must be developed to enhance ecological connectivity at a larger scale. The rāhui approaches used in Tahiti Iti provide strong evidence that considerable benefits arise from increasing the scale of contiguous areas managed in this way. Expanding the scale of rāhui management into neighbouring districts enhanced spillover effects in terms of both social resilience and ecological continuity between inter-linked ecosystems. Similarly, hybrid management forms have thrived due to normative and cognitive interactions among stakeholders within this enlarged ecological-management area.

Most protected area models are based on the protection of habitats and resources, and not the integration of culture and connectivity in relation to ecological resilience. This case study has shown how a local population has built a model of hybrid management, combining social and ecological resilience to consider the broader context of cultural and normative pluralism. More fundamentally, social resilience and ecological resilience are inseparable from the space under protection, especially when these spaces are occupied by human communities with a strong cultural identity. The cultural and legal pluralism that dominate many situations in Oceania and the world in general must also be considered when building protected areas. The evidence suggests that this approach is a necessary condition for social acceptance, the effectiveness of actions and, ultimately, the sustainability of management methods.

8

Indigenous Youth Responses to Water and Waste Management in Kuchuwa, Federated States of Micronesia

Myjolynne Kim, Gonzaga Puas and Nicholas Halter[1]

The global debate about climate change and its impacts has brought renewed attention to the unique challenges the Pacific Islands face, but in so doing, the experience of local communities and actors has often been overlooked in favour of developing national and regional strategies. In response, an international research collaboration led by the Micronesian & Australian Friends Association (MAFA) initiated a project in 2016 that focused on the impacts of climate change at a grassroots level in a relatively understudied region of the Pacific. Specifically, it focused on climate change adaptation in the Micronesian village of Kuchuwa, with the aim of recording Indigenous youth responses to water and waste management. Lessons learned from this project show that an inclusive approach is needed that incorporates traditional community practices and knowledge and encourages youth innovation and leadership.

1   This research was made possible by a PACE-Net Plus grant from the European Commission in 2016. We also acknowledge other members of MAFA who supported this project, including Manuel Rauchholz (University of Heidelberg), Rebecca Hoffman (University of Munich), and Paul D'Arcy, Roannie Ng Shiu, Ingrid Ahlgren and George Carter (The Australian National University). Last, but certainly not least, we are grateful to the people of Kuchuwa for their generosity and trust. Kinisou chapur.

The impacts of climate change in Kuchuwa

The devastating impact of Super Typhoon Maysak in the Federated States of Micronesia (FSM) in 2015 provided a stark reminder of the vulnerability of these islands to climate change. The FSM comprises four major island groups totalling 607 islands, 65 of which are populated. Although the four main centres—Chuuk, Kosrae, Pohnpei and Yap—are volcanic, most of the outer islands are low-lying atolls. Maysak not only demonstrated the dangers posed by sea-level rise to the coastal fringes of islands but also destroyed crops, damaged infrastructure and exacerbated waste-control measures, contaminating water supplies and aiding the spread of disease. Even the foreign aid sent to the FSM in the form of shelters and food supplies, though necessary, has unintentionally contributed to the islands' urgent landfill problem.

Waste management is one of the most neglected problems among the raft of issues that rising sea levels threaten to unleash on Pacific Island coastal communities. Poor waste management threatens population health, deters tourism and affects the economic development of Pacific Islands. This was the case in South Tarawa, Kiribati, which had a waste crisis in the late 1990s due to the absence of engineered landfill sites, prompting a series of regionally funded waste-collection initiatives in the early 2000s (SPREP n.d.). Though some recycling initiatives were successful in reducing aluminium cans and polyethylene terephthalate (PET) bottle waste, the Asian Development Bank (ADB 2014) reported that nappies and electronic waste remained a growing problem, with 26 per cent of waste still being disposed of onsite, 35 per cent illegally dumped in the sea or lagoon and only 1 per cent recycled. Toxins from rubbish can leach into the freshwater supply, which is already very limited. Funafuti in Tuvalu is a demonstrative case, suffering such contamination from sources including pig faecal matter, human faecal matter from leaking septic tanks and open defecation, rotting biological matter and heavy metals from solid waste. Combined with saltwater intrusion caused by king tides and drought, Tuvalu has periodically experienced states of crisis and is considered one of the more vulnerable Pacific Islands as a result (Office of the Auditor-General 2011).

Micronesians are closely connected to the waters that surround their islands. During his address to the United Nations General Assembly in 2012, then FSM president Emanuel Mori noted: '[O]ur livelihood, our economy, our culture and our way of living are tied to a blue economy' (Mori 2012).

Seventy per cent of the FSM's population and economic infrastructure are in coastal areas and 17 per cent of the population lives on outer islands or atolls, all of which are particularly vulnerable to typhoon damage, sea-level rises and variation in rainfall patterns (FSM Permanent Mission 2008: 6). The FSM has a rich tradition of maritime navigation. It is one of the few places in the Pacific that continues to practise traditional navigation—famously demonstrated by Mau Piailug of Satawal, who led a cultural revival of seafaring in Polynesia in the 1990s. Today, Micronesians rely on the ocean for subsistence and nearshore commercial fishing, especially in the islands distant from the main population centres. Foreign-based fishing is the country's top export and fees from foreign vessels fishing in FSM waters represent a major source of income (FSM Permanent Mission 2008: 4). Seafaring also has deep cultural implications for Micronesians. Oceanic practices such as fishing and sailing are embedded in cultural lore and processes of identity construction.

Climate change has several impacts on the FSM, most clearly demonstrated by natural hazards such as storms, droughts, floods and sea-level rise. The threat of sea-level rise is so severe that President Mori joined a petition to the UN General Assembly in 2008 that stressed the threat of climate change to 'our security and our territorial integrity' (Mori 2008). In fact, it now seems more than likely that, by 2100, the sea level will be 1.2 metres higher than today; and the fastest rates of sea-level rise from 1993 to 2010 were measured in the tropical Western Pacific—in Micronesia (Nunn 2013: 143). Population growth in the FSM has placed increasing pressure on limited food resources, including fish stocks and agriculture, as well as affecting the price and affordability of food. Similarly, freshwater supplies are often at risk due to climatic changes, saltwater intrusion, ageing infrastructure and growing demand. The Australian Government's Pacific Adaptation Strategy Assistance Program (PASAP 2011) recently focused on this issue in the FSM, drawing attention to the benefits of introducing drought and salt-tolerant food species and sustainable farming methods. Other human activities related to resource efficiency and raw materials, such as land clearing, logging, dredging, mining and the uncontrolled disposal of waste, impact the everyday lives of those living in the FSM.

Despite an awareness of these challenges, attempts to encourage more sustainable practices have been slow and inconsistent. For example, a national audit in 2010 revealed that seven years after the formation of the FSM Infrastructure Development Plan, there had been 'minimal progress towards implementation of a solid waste management infrastructure project'

(FSMOPA 2010). Solid waste management remains a major challenge in the FSM because of the small size of most islands and the importance of an uncompromised subsistence agriculture base for most citizens' daily food requirements, demonstrating the need for a new community-based approach. FSM is also the nation most affected by typhoons, with the majority of the world's typhoons passing through its territory. This means inadequate waste management increases the risk of storm damage compromising surrounding ecosystems and agricultural systems.

In Chuuk State, where 50 per cent of FSM's population is spread across various volcanic islands and sandy coral atolls, many of these climate change impacts require urgent attention. Its economy is reliant on fishing and tourism, with many international divers coming to visit the unique shipwrecks in the lagoon. These remnants of World War II may be popular attractions, but they pollute the reefs and waters with their toxic oils and rusting hulls. They are also sources of dynamite, and dynamite fishing remains a common activity despite its highly destructive ecological impact. Inadequate waste management has led to wide-scale pollution in Chuuk. The reliance on foreign imported products is a symptom of modernity that has led to the proliferation of disposable goods. This waste has been discarded in various and inconsistent ways—sometimes buried in landfill, repurposed as building materials or for coastal land reclamation or used as fuel. Human waste is another concern, with limited sewerage infrastructure in place, despite the successful development of modern composting sanitation systems in other parts of the world. Chuuk has significant potential to be a site for implementing a human/animal dry-waste processing system that has flow-on benefits for agriculture (that is, producing fertiliser). In addition, renewable energy technology has been slow to reach Chuuk, which continues to rely on diesel generators and kerosene. Most Chuukese use very little energy because of the high cost of electricity, but this has led to the logging of native vegetation, such as mangroves, for fuel. The situation in Chuuk suggests more work needs to be done to understand how modern technology and knowledge can connect with traditional environmental practices.

The unique challenge Chuuk faces from climate change is its isolation. It is serviced by a limited number of shipping and air networks, thus creating extraordinary costs for the transportation of people and materials and making the cost of implementing climate adaptation projects prohibitively expensive. Though this is commonly recognised by foreign aid stakeholders, the cost of repairing and maintaining equipment is often overlooked.

Machinery is abandoned on islands because replacement parts are too costly or because locals have not been trained to repair specialist equipment. As a result, projects tend to have a limited shelf life.

In comparison with other Pacific nations, the FSM receives less funding for climate change projects and is often overlooked in favour of its close neighbours Palau, the Republic of the Marshall Islands and Kiribati. The Asian Development Bank (ADB 2011) Pacific Climate Change Program funded only Cook Islands, Solomon Islands and Palau, and the Australian Government–funded Pacific Adaptive Capacity Analysis Framework (USP 2012) selected Micronesian field sites in Palau and Kiribati only. According to the Global Environment Facility (GEF 2022), 43 national projects have been completed or approved for the FSM compared with 46 for Palau, 49 for the Marshall Islands and 55 for Kiribati. To date, Micronesia has accessed $27.6 million of the Green Climate Fund (GCF 2022), while Kiribati has received $28.6 million and the Marshall Islands has received $55.5 million. Other programs, such as the Kyoto Protocol Adaptation Fund (UNFCCC 2021) and the Pilot Program for Climate Resilience (CIF 2016), have no Micronesian projects at all. The need for more funding has slowly been recognised, with the Secretariat of the Pacific Regional Environment Programme (SPREP) Adaptation Fund Board approving US$9 million for 'enhancing the climate change resilience of vulnerable island communities in Federated States of Micronesia' (SPREP 2017a), although only six outer islands were selected, two of which were the Chuukese islands of Satawan and Lukunor.

This reflects the broader shift in academic debates about climate change since the 1990s, in which 'adaptive capacity' has increasingly considered 'vulnerability-led' approaches, rather than the traditional 'impacts-led' strategy (Erikson and Kelly 2007; Wisner 2004). This shift has seen a greater input from the social sciences in assessing climate change and a consideration of non-climate factors that shape abilities to adapt to climate change. Recent community-led projects in the FSM demonstrate the success of this approach, such as the climate change initiative led by the Micronesia Conservation Trust and the Nature Conservancy as part of a regional intergovernmental program known as the 'Micronesia Challenge', which was established in 2007.

President Mori in 2008 argued that climate change must be approached 'from a holistic perspective rather than limiting it to the dimensions of sustainable development, to humanitarian or technical issues, or to economic or environmental issues' (FSM Permanent Mission 2008: 8). Yet, local and Indigenous knowledge are yet to be included in policies on disaster risk reduction or climate change adaptation and the wealth of documented knowledge and practices has not led to increased efforts to make use of this knowledge to enable communities to increase their resilience. What has been missing from this holistic perspective is a greater social science approach—one that considers human capital, social capital, belief systems, world views and values, and an awareness of how Micronesians have dealt with climate events in the past. This approach is valuable because it acknowledges the human capacity to respond to climate change rather than assuming a passive reaction.

The Kuchuwa Youth Water and Waste Management Project

The Kuchuwa Youth Water and Waste Management Project (hereinafter the Kuchuwa Project) began in late 2015 when a dialogue was established between the MAFA research team and the village of Kuchuwa, on Tonoas (Dublon) Island in Chuuk (Truk) Lagoon. The MAFA team consisted of researchers from Germany and Australia, drawn mostly from the social sciences and with considerable expertise and knowledge of Chuukese language, culture, history and politics. Four of these members travelled to Chuuk in January 2016 to conduct the main component of the project under the leadership of two Chuukese PhD scholars, Myjolynne Kim and Gonzaga Puas. Given the absence of climate change data for Chuuk State, it was determined to initially focus attention on the Chuuk Lagoon to link up with government officials and NGOs based in the capital, the main island of Weno (Moen).

Initial assessments made on Weno suggest the local impact of existing approaches to climate change is limited. Foreign stakeholders have tended to focus on youth engagement thus far—indicated by a range of illustrated educational pamphlets produced by the International Organization for Migration and a series of workshops and a public billboard funded by the Pacific Resources for Education and Learning. The effectiveness of such programs is questionable. Though these educational materials promoted water conservation and quality, residents were generally unaware of how to test for water quality or how to respond to drought (with most acknowledging they were reliant on bottled water as a backup source).

Likewise, though educational programs have encouraged the need for local waste management strategies, public rubbish collection services are limited and most Chuukese dispose of waste individually and indiscriminately. The challenge of waste disposal is made difficult by the availability of cheap imported nonbiodegradable products, and efforts to establish a recycling program have been intermittent. Consultations with members of the state government, Chuuk State Water and the Department of Meteorology confirmed there was limited coordination on climate change programs, producing inconsistent results, duplication and confusion.

Despite these challenges, the structure of Chuukese society is a key asset that can strengthen efforts to adapt to climate change, although it has been largely overlooked until now. Chuuk is ethnically diverse, with clan and lineage connections spreading beyond its current political boundaries. As Manuel Rauchholz (2011: 53) argues, these cultural and linguistic ties are crucial to the 'sharing, corporate holding, and use rights to the most important natural resources available such as land (islands) and reefs', and are a system that Micronesians fall back on in the event of natural disasters. Acknowledgement of these important cultural connections and the idea of reciprocity and exchange that underpins them is essential. Rather than being an obstacle, Micronesian ethnic diversity promises the key to developing a more sustainable and localised approach to climate change.

For this reason, the MAFA research team focused its efforts on a community assessment in Kuchuwa, which consisted of a youth-led needs assessment and gap analysis, followed by a workshop designed to mobilise youth and community leaders to build their capacity to understand and respond to climate change. Kuchuwa was chosen as a case study for its relative distance from the capital and because of cultural ties between the village and one of MAFA's Chuukese leaders. This was crucial in building collaborative relationships with the Kuchuwa community elders and the local youth council. Trained in anthropology and history, the MAFA team incorporated an ethnographic approach to research that was consistent with cultural expectations and responsibilities. This involved living in the Kuchuwa community for a week, visiting individual households, visually inspecting the island to identify environmental hazards and needs, meeting elders and building relationships of trust and mutual respect. Community participation in planning the more formal workshop component was integral; the details and parameters of the program were agreed on by the community elders before it began, and they informed the village of the project, invited the key leaders and youth participants and mobilised the village to prepare the necessary logistics.

The first day of the workshop consisted of a formal welcome and introduction ceremony, which gave village elders the space to comment on the issues before the group discussions began. These formalities were significant because they observed important cultural protocols and, in so doing, the project was condoned and legitimised by the community. During the second and third day of research, youth participants were split into groups to identify water and waste risks and develop management strategies that incorporated the Indigenous knowledge and practices shared by their elders the day before. Groups were asked to quantify the types and amount of waste their households produced, how much water they used and how it was sourced and to complete a mapping activity to identify key water sources and waste disposal areas in the village. Participants were encouraged to formulate new strategies for managing water and waste to present to the broader community as part of a competition the next day. This participatory research was useful for allowing the MAFA team to draw on their extensive knowledge of Chuukese language and culture to present specific issues in ways that were meaningful to the youth.

On the final day, the MAFA team discussed climate change adaptation strategies used in other parts of the Pacific, with an emphasis on community consultation and planning. Groups then gave creative performances in front of the whole community, explaining the impact of climate change as they understood it, identifying a particular risk related to water or waste in Kuchuwa and potential adaptation strategies to manage it. Prizes were offered as incentives, with items such as fishing and sports equipment, a brush-cutter and a chainsaw carefully chosen to be shared and to benefit the whole community. Each group made a public commitment to implement one strategy in their community in the next three months.

Lessons learnt

Though small in scale and scope, the Kuchuwa Project confirmed the need to rethink current approaches to climate change adaptation in Micronesia. Our conclusions were based on informal interviews and ethnographic fieldwork and were supported with statistical data gathered from a questionnaire provided to the youth participants. This questionnaire was based on other climate adaptation surveys funded by AusAID under its Community-Based Climate Change Action Grants program, and was written in English and Chuukese. Forty-one questionnaires were completed and an estimated 81 people attended; the discrepancy can be explained by people attending only one day and non-youth groups who participated. Further information can be found in the official report (MAFA 2016). Future efforts to develop local climate change management and adaptation strategies that incorporate Indigenous knowledge and practices should focus on three issues: improving educational outreach, supporting youth leadership and encouraging meaningful community engagement.

Education

Improving educational outreach is an important first step to expand the percentage of the local community who are aware of and involved in climate change adaptation. During the project, the MAFA team observed a lack of climate change education and awareness in Chuuk, which was compounded by the competing and overlapping activities of foreign NGOs and donor groups. Though some NGOs have been active in Chuuk in the climate change space for some time, it is not clear whether information is reaching communities at a grassroots level, as demonstrated in Kuchuwa. Before the workshop began, participants were asked what they thought climate change was. Their responses demonstrated that although the majority understood the concept broadly, the latest scientific information about the localised impacts of sea-level rise or temperature change had not been communicated clearly by governments or scientific agencies in vernacular languages. For example, an understanding of El Niño and La Niña, which can have important impacts on water supplies in Micronesia, was limited. The Kuchuwa Project preceded the FSM Government's proclamation of a state of emergency due to high levels of drought, and our research suggested that few Chuukese were aware of the dangerous drought conditions that could be caused by El Niño and had no water conservation plans in place. Although 58 per cent of Kuchuwan respondents said they had learnt about climate change from another program, government agency or community group, a similar percentage (56 per cent) noted they had never talked about the issue with others at home, school or elsewhere. These responses suggest that, although information about climate change is gradually being made available, it is not yet penetrating at the deeper level required to change habits.

This trend can be seen in the formal education system in Chuuk. There have been some positive efforts to include climate change in the school curriculum, and the Department of Education in Chuuk State has been attempting to implement reforms to comply with national standards since the early 2000s (Chuuk Department of Education n.d.; Jaynes 2010; Chuuk Advisory Group on Education Reform 2013). This has been a controversial and divisive process, however, among Chuukese communities. Kuchuwa's only public school was closed because of these reforms. Educational facilities are poorly funded and Chuuk is frequently judged to have the lowest standards of education in the FSM (according to Western measures). Climate change materials produced in the local language may not be read due to low levels of literacy, which are compounded by lack of resources and access to information or the internet. The education system inhibits the development of the skilled workforce that is needed to implement and maintain new water and waste management technologies, and the 'brain drain' continues to affect Micronesian migration patterns.

The lack of a formal education does not mean Chuukese people are oblivious to changes in their local environment. On the contrary, Chuukese communities possess sophisticated and deep knowledge of the maritime and agricultural resources on which their livelihoods are based. Though children may not understand the scientific details of climate change, they learn from a young age how to manage their local environment effectively—knowledge that is often passed down by the elders through oral traditions. For example, the Kuchuwa youth participants were knowledgeable about the different types of taro, when to plant and harvest them, and the location of the most arable soil on the island. Fishing is a major employment sector for the people of Kuchuwa and many participants commented on the noticeable changes to fish stocks that were likely caused by the changing climate.

Acknowledging this local knowledge is an important first step in climate adaptation given the region is relatively unknown and understudied by the global scientific community. With the government struggling to rebuild in the wake of Typhoon Maysak, local communities are particularly vulnerable to other climatic changes like drought and there is a lack of access to technical and scientific solutions. Thus, there is a need to encourage the sharing of knowledge between Micronesian communities and researchers and foreign counterparts. These collaborations will not only raise the profile of Micronesian communities in the international academic community, but also connect Chuukese communities to a broader network of sponsors and organisations and facilitate a translation process that unites academic research with local community knowledge and practical applications.

The Kuchuwa Project reinforced the importance of this translation process. In this case, translation applies not only in the linguistic sense, but also in translating across cultures. This was done by allowing adequate opportunities for community forums in which information could be debated. In the Kuchuwa case, MAFA leaders facilitated these forums, answering questions and 'bridging the gap' between Western knowledge and local practices. In some cases, this cross-cultural translation was significant in clarifying misunderstandings—for example, when discussing the use of batteries for fishing torches, it became apparent that some participants were unaware of the dangers posed by the leaching of battery acid or the effect of toxins when using battery acid to make tattoos. This reinforced the need to agree on waste disposal sites that would limit potential toxins affecting food sources. In another case, a discussion of the properties of plastics revealed that some families were burning or cooking with plastics, unaware of the potential health risks. Thus, the message of minimising the use of nonbiodegradable plastics was justified as both a health and a waste management issue.

The Kuchuwa Project also demonstrated that local communities are willing to adopt new technologies if they are shown to be cost-effective and sustainable. In Kuchuwa's case, the introduction of 'rocket stoves' was popular because they could be cheaply made using local materials and they reduced reliance on disposable propane gas canisters. Similar enthusiasm was shown for the bio-sand water filtration systems that were demonstrated at the workshop, particularly because these could be easily produced and maintained. These simple and practical solutions were developed in other developing countries but had not been 'translated' into a Micronesian context. Other technologies could be introduced provided adequate training and explanation are given to communities to demonstrate their cost-effectiveness and sustainability.

Youth

Another key to formulating climate change adaptation strategies is targeting youth and supporting the development of young leaders in the community. Not only do youth represent a large proportion of the Chuukese population, they also form an important part of Chuukese society as future custodians of the land. The Chuukese word for 'youth' is fanufan, which translates literally as 'light of the world'. Like other parts of the Pacific, in Chuuk, there is a so-called youth bulge and, combined with high levels of unemployment, the wellbeing of young Chuukese is a great concern. In Kuchuwa, the elders considered youth important for community renewal, particularly in dealing with contemporary issues such as education and climate change.

Youth participation was identified as a crucial factor for the success of the Kuchuwa Project. The enthusiasm and energy that young people contributed changed the group dynamic, creating a positive and excited atmosphere that encouraged innovation and creative solutions among their peers and families. Youth were eager to discuss the merits of cultural traditions and practices but were also open to challenging or reforming conventional ideas. By framing the approach as one in which youth were the central focus, it was also possible to discuss complex and sensitive cultural issues with the consent of their peers and elders. This was significant given the politics of land and resource ownership can often hamper creative problem-solving efforts. Feedback from the community suggested youth were effectively engaged with the content because they were able to discuss issues openly with their peers and there was broad consensus that proactive community action to manage water and waste was necessary for future prosperity. After the workshop, youth participants organised themselves to become a chartered youth organisation and arranged clean-ups in Kuchuwa. Given the ethnic diversity in Micronesia and the potential conflicts that can arise when discussing issues related to climate change, encouraging and empowering youth to consider climate change adaptation are the most effective strategies moving forward.

Another benefit of focusing efforts on youth participation is that potential leaders can be identified and empowered. In the Kuchuwa Project, a key factor in this empowerment process was the involvement of the two Chuukese researchers, Myjolynne Kim and Gonzaga Puas. Not only were they crucial in planning the project from conception to implementation, but also during the workshop they were important Chuukese role-models for the youth, demonstrating the benefits of higher education and the potential for youth leadership, as well as embodying MAFA's project philosophy of incorporating Indigenous knowledge within Western frameworks. Their participation contributed to a strong sense of community pride, especially as Myjolynne had family ties to the community. This workshop provided Kuchuwa youth not only an opportunity for peer mentoring by Myjolynne and Gonzaga, but also a forum for them to become leaders among their peers, and we identified several individuals who showed real promise.

This process of nurturing potential leaders is vital to future endeavours in the region and offers the opportunity to increase political participation, encourage gender equality and involve youth in community forums and decision-making.

Community engagement

The development of climate change adaptation strategies needs to be a communal endeavour that encourages meaningful community engagement. This is important for encouraging Indigenous ownership of programs and outcomes. Many climate change programs and policies in the Pacific recognise this, however, it is not always applied in practice. A community-centred approach driven by local actors and initiatives is arguably more effective and sustainable than a top-down approach from external organisations. In Chuuk's case, climate adaptation plans at the state and national level are limited by inadequate funding and a cumbersome bureaucracy, and we argue that donor groups working directly with local villages and communities are more effective in supporting adaptation.

Future initiatives that occur at the grassroots level, emphasising community leadership and participation, are essential to build a sense of community pride and ownership. One advantage of a communal endeavour is that it encourages diverse groups to negotiate and agree on the challenges they face and promotes local ownership of the solutions required. Communal ownership is ultimately important for encouraging solutions that embody cultural values and traditions, rather than applying artificial Western ideas and practices. These traditional networks are also important for mediating potential conflict within communities. In Chuuk's case, lack of access to technical and scientific solutions is only part of the challenge; our research argues that community practices often undermined foreign donors' attempts to impose environmental reforms, which was a result of those donors failing to address the interrelated human, social and cultural factors that are closely tied to climatic and ecological hazards.

The Kuchuwa Project placed significant emphasis on formally recognising community leaders (both traditional and political) at the beginning and end of the workshop. By observing the proper cultural protocols, potential conflict was minimised and youth participants were reassured that the project was sanctioned by their elders, rather than imposed. The sense of communal ownership was crucial to the management of water and waste specifically because they are challenges that can only be solved by community action. Most Kuchuwa residents draw their water from communal wells or natural sources in the higher mountain valleys. Some villages have laid long, narrow PVC pipes from the springs to each house. Although some elders could recall times when mismanagement polluted the water sources, in most villages there was no apparent water management being applied. Villages and households did not have water conservation plans, pipes were not tapped to conserve water and there was no village-coordinated effort to control access or limit pollution upstream. In terms of waste, there was no community plan or disposal site for villages, no garbage bins or collection service, no recycling facilities and no discernible pattern of waste distribution. Most rubbish was discarded according to the preferences of individuals or households, and some did not understand the potential dangers of their waste disposal practices, such as from the leaching of chemical toxins into soil and water and air pollution. Thus, the advantage of a community-based approach is that it allows programs to be developed to suit a specific local context. Focusing on Indigenous knowledge and practices will drive further innovation in climate change management at a local level.

Encouraging community engagement is difficult and often context-specific, but lessons from the Kuchuwa Project point to successful strategies. First, allowing the community to plan the workshop themselves increased local participation. Community members were able to negotiate with schools and families to encourage attendance and, although the workshop was publicised as a 'youth' event, anyone on the island was welcome to attend. The workshop was held in a communal house and the open setting allowed people to watch from outside and participate when they felt comfortable. This was especially important for the village elders, who were able to supervise and participate in the workshop from the edges of the wut (communal house), offering unique insights to the youth, reinforcing our messages and legitimising our presence. Even the prizes offered as incentives for participation were carefully selected to be shared by the community.

Effective community engagement was also ensured by the key involvement of local actors. In this instance, Myjolynne Kim's family connections in Kuchuwa were important for legitimising the project and for monitoring the progress of Kuchuwan youth afterwards. Although other climate change adaptation programs may incorporate evaluation processes, their effectiveness will be limited unless they have key local actors invested in the monitoring process.

Conclusion

The impact of climate change on Micronesia may have gained global attention and acknowledgement in recent decades, but the ways in which it affects the daily lives of Chuukese are largely unknown and understudied. This project attempted to address this gap as part of a broader goal to ensure Micronesians are at the centre of discussion and debate, rather than the periphery (Puas and Halter 2015; Puas 2021). Climate change is one of many contemporary issues that could benefit from more Micronesian-led research, and social scientists can play an important intermediary role between Western science and traditional communities. Given Micronesia is host to such a diverse range of cultures, in which every island is home to different communities and facing different climate challenges, a communal approach is vital. Meaningful community engagement can only be achieved by an inclusive approach that acknowledges and respects traditional knowledge and practices to ensure the long-term sustainability of climate change adaptation strategies. In Chuuk's case, focusing on education and youth offers the best possibility of encouraging future innovation and leadership.

Section Three:
Local Responses to
Climate Change

Introduction: Knowledge contested—Local responses to climate change

Daya Dakasi Da-Wei Kuan and Paul D'Arcy

Low-lying atoll nations in the Pacific are already experiencing the existential threat that climate change poses to humanity. Section Three details how atolls have been inundated multiple times in the past decade—something that has not happened in living memory across three generations. Inundation floods and rots crops and compromises groundwater for considerable periods until rainfall can replenish and refresh the slim water table lying atop a saltwater base beneath atolls. All chapters in this section focus on how Pacific Indigenous peoples are actively seeking to protect and climate-proof their island homes through traditional means, while at the same time lobbying through diplomatic channels and the media to persuade the rest of the world that a lot more can be done to protect them.

The section opens with a chapter from geographer and development specialist Jenny Bryant-Tokalau. She focuses on the disjuncture between responses made by external parties to the threat of climate change inundation, with or without Pacific government support, and those made by local communities most at risk from inundation. She concludes her opening paragraph by noting that 'when it comes to dealing with the spectre of climate change, the voices of those most likely to be affected are often ignored'. She goes on to observe that Pacific Islanders have always responded creatively to variable environmental conditions, which was what made them such successful colonisers. As has been already noted in this volume's Introduction, the theme of active adaptation rather than passive victimhood runs deep in Pacific studies, as is perhaps best articulated in Pacific historian Dave Chappell's seminal 1995 article on this theme, 'Active Agents versus Passive

Victims'. Bryant-Tokalau uses two case studies of planning for future inundation to demonstrate the complexity involved and how such planning often neglects the lessons of the past. The first example is of modern, high-tech floating cities proposed by various global enterprises, and the second is Kiribati's multiple-scenario planning, which includes purchasing some of these proposed floating islands from a Japanese corporation and partial or permanent relocation of the population to other nations. She then discusses the varied success of artificial island-building and reinforcement, noting the most successful mimic nature, as demonstrated in Chapter 10 by Zag Puas. The massive stone city of Nan Madol, built into a lagoon on Pohnpei, and multiple villages on artificial islands in the Lau and Langalanga lagoons of Malaita in Solomon Islands demonstrate the immense capacity of traditional Pacific societies to mould their landscapes and seascapes. Bryant-Tokalau discusses how the Government of Kiribati purchased land in Fiji for a future refuge despite significant division of opinion within Kiribati over this purchase and little investigation of possible domestic alternatives for the increasingly flood-prone main population centre of Tarawa. The purchase of largely poor-quality mountainous land incapable of supporting the potential refugee population of tens of thousands of I-Kiribati raises serious concerns about due diligence. The chapter concludes by noting that most future planning has been done without significant investigation of past Indigenous practices of successfully colonising and improving atolls.

Zag Puas's chapter examines similar debates in the Federated States of Micronesia. He looks to the past in seeking solutions to climate change threats and notes several cost-effective and simple proven solutions that can be applied and maintained at the local community level. He advocates combining a selective adaptation of previous generations' knowledge with the Kuchawa village strategy outlined in Chapter 8, involving young people learning from elders and taking over the implementation and administration of projects. Puas, a native of the low-lying Mortlock Islands in Chuuk State, begins by noting increasing concerns about natural disasters related to climate change. He also notes that FSM sits in Typhoon Alley, through which the majority of the world's typhoons pass, so natural disasters have always loomed large in community and government consciousness. National legislation recognised the threat posed by natural disasters, but also marked a realisation that local communities will have to play a major role in preparing for and coping with such events. The strategy for which Puas argues focuses on two elements: protecting islands from encroaching seas through salt-resistant plant barriers and traditional seawalls; and increasing self-reliance by developing more locally grown drought and salt-resistant crops. In both elements, elders' advice on old, proven methods such as buffer trees, suitable food crops and seawalls radically different from modern designs were used and proved highly successful. FSM has also sought likeminded allies regionally and internationally to pursue its self-sufficient, sustainable and low-energy agenda.

Finding empathetic external allies also requires ensuring external players have Pacific needs and Pacific concepts conveyed directly to them by Pacific peoples. In Chapter 11, Māori academic Lynette Carter explores myths and realities in the portrayal of Pacific peoples in the era of climate change and in debates about their possible futures as climate refugees. In particular, she challenges the Western idea that statehood, nationhood and citizenship rights are tied to residence in territorially discrete areas with hard borders, that land is the basis of residence and that intervening seas between shores are mere passages between places of residence. As Carter notes, for Pacific peoples, identity, place and territory are intimately linked to land, people and sea in a fluid, seamlessly interwoven relationship. Travel between geographically extensive social networks was common in many Pacific Islands and mobility continued into the colonial era and after independence as many islanders moved to larger economies on the Pacific Rim in search of work to fund home communities through remittances. Locality changed, but identity remained, linked back always to the cultural landscapes and seascapes of ancestors. This fluidity of identity and affiliation with a special location or interconnected locations does not mean Pacific peoples are ready to abandon their ancestral homes. The Majuro Declaration signed by Pacific Island nation leaders on 5 September 2013 committed them to taking a global lead in reducing greenhouse gas pollution to facilitate being able to remain in their island homes. Carter ends by noting that greater recognition of Pacific cultural concepts and historical patterns of belonging must be taken by the global community in viewing options for Pacific peoples.

In Chapter 12, Samoan academic George Carter reflects on problems faced and strategies used in Pacific Island climate diplomacy. Carter was a member of his nation's delegation to the 2015 twenty-first Conference of the Parties (COP) of the United Nations Framework Convention on Climate Change (UNFCCC) in Paris. Carter argues that this event was a coming of age for Pacific political agency on the world stage, when the 12 Pacific states involved agreed to speak and negotiate with one voice as a regional coalition. Carter begins by outlining the complex nature of managing negotiations between the 197 signatories to the UNFCCC. In such large and diverse organisations, parties tend to negotiate by forming coalitions of common interest. Carter then returns his focus to the Pacific and traces the evolution of Pacific political agency at the regional level from 1971 through to the runup to this watershed moment for Pacific diplomacy in Paris. He notes that Pacific regional organisations began to intensify their climate change lobbying in earnest only after the Pacific Island Forum's Niue Declaration on Climate Change in 2008. The failure of COP15 in Copenhagen brought a new urgency to Pacific climate diplomacy, culminating in the 2013 Majuro Declaration in which Pacific nations sought to take the lead on the world stage in pushing for effective climate change mitigation to break the COP impasses. COP21 in Paris in 2015 loomed as a major test of global resolve, enhanced by the fact that the year also witnessed major world meetings on the Sustainable Development Goals and development financing. Carter spends considerable time outlining how the diverse Pacific region, including Australia and Aotearoa New Zealand, was able to forge agreed positions in the runup to Paris 2015. They did so by allocating sufficient time and resources to frank and open discussion of points of contention. Even then, the final agreement reflected compromises required to forge consensus, especially for gaining the support of Australia's Abbott government with its strong links to the fossil fuel industry. Once agreement was reached, however, Pacific leaders and delegations were able to be much more assertive on the world stage (Fry 2015b; Fry and Tarte 2016).

9

Indigenous Responses to Environmental Challenges: Artificial islands and the challenges of relocation

Jenny Bryant-Tokalau

Artificially constructed islands have been discussed in recent years in the Pacific as a potential response to dealing with the impacts of climate change and sea-level rise. Acknowledging these international offers, Pacific Island leaders, supported by the Dutch in 2009 and, more recently, the Japanese, have shown interest in the development of, for example, circular islands with enough space for island populations to engage in farming (and hopefully fishing), business, government and normal daily life, as well as platforms tethered to the seafloor. Such plans have been gaining support at regional meetings including the Pacific Islands Forum and some concepts have already been developed with a view to creating real island settlements by 2025. Although these modern artificial islands appear to have the support of some governments, the notion is entirely externally driven. It is apparent that while there is much rhetoric about consultation and community empowerment in many aspects of Pacific resource management, when it comes to dealing with the spectre of climate change, the voices of those most likely to be affected are often ignored.

The futuristic plans for high-tech artificial islands—which may appear fanciful and even unlikely given the complications of sovereignty, land tenure and exclusive economic zones—are not new. When the concept of artificial islands as a possible response to inundation and rising sea levels is raised at regional meetings, the wider and historical context is rarely discussed. Yet, artificially constructed islands have long been a part of settlement history in the oceanic Pacific. Islanders have always actively responded to environmental, social and political changes during periods of human settlement and migration and have long recognised the need to build and expand land. They have done this in many ways, as evidenced by examples such as in the Lau and Langalanga lagoons of Malaita in Solomon Islands (Bryant-Tokalau 2011; Guo 2001; Parsonson 1966).

This chapter uses two case studies to illustrate that planning in the face of rising sea levels is not always straightforward. The first case examines modern offers of artificial islands as one way of facing an uncertain future but demonstrates that people's own knowledge and practices in constructing such islands appear to have been forgotten. In the second case, where Kiribati is looking at many scenarios, including artificial islands, the 'flight' or relocation option is examined. Again, the case looks at implications for community agency and for the proposed host nation. This case demonstrates that, given earlier histories of relocation and adaptation to new cultures and environments, some recent plans for relocation—that might on the surface look like the only sensible future for Kiribati—could in fact be highly detrimental and unworkable, not only to I-Kiribati, but also to the host country.

Background

In 2009–10, there was much media attention given to the Pacific Gyre or Great Pacific Garbage Patch, the floating 'islands of plastic' that are becoming daily larger in two areas of the North Pacific. Dutch conservationists proclaimed possibilities for building islands from recycled materials that would make use of dangerous waste and some saw a future for 'nomadic' islanders continuing their historical mobility:

> [T]hese 'Inhabited Artificial Islands in International Waters' do not need to be static; they could be mobile. Nomads have long roamed the land. Some cultures are based on that. Artificial island states or sub-national jurisdictions could roam the seas. Many islander peoples are already known for their history of sea-based mobility. (Kelman 2010)

At the time, I argued that this concept was misguided on many levels. While it is clearly important to clean up the Pacific Gyre, the notion of peoples of the Pacific fleeing the impacts of climate change on a nomadic quest that would raise complex issues of sovereignty is not a workable approach to today's fast-escalating issues related to environmental change (Bryant-Tokalau 2011). Most important in the debates about Pacific Island sovereignty, knowledge and responses to the impacts of climate change is the need to recognise peoples' histories and past adaptation to such events. 'Plastic fantastic' ideas, as well as the new technological offerings of aid donors, fail to consider historical efforts of Pacific Islanders to respond to the need for and expansion of land. Certainly, some land and island construction was in response to inundation and other environmental factors, but artificial island development was also about power, relationships and influence. Climate-related decline in food resources inevitably led to conflict, meaning people left their homelands in search of other, better-resourced islands. This undoubtedly led to competition for land and, at times, the construction of 'artificial' land.

Modern artificial islands

In 2013, Shimizu Corporation, a Tokyo-based construction company, announced it was devising plans for a city that would float on vast 'lily pads' on the surface of the Pacific (Sunhak Peace Prize 2018). The design is interesting, looking like something that might be devised for another planet in the distant future:

> Each island will be nearly two miles [3.2 kilometres] across, with a central tower rising half a mile to form a 'city in the sky'. The tower will have residential units for 30,000 people and space for offices, services and shops. (Sunhak Peace Prize 2018)

The central shaft will be used to grow vegetables and fruit, with Shimizu aiming to make the city self-sufficient for food. The flat base of the island, which will be tethered to the ocean floor, will have a residential zone for another 10,000 inhabitants, along with forests, beaches, arable land and port facilities.

Single units will be connected to form floating 'cities' of up to 100,000 people. According to Masayuki Takeuchi, the head of the scheme:

> The idea behind the Green Float project was first as a solution to the problem of a rapidly growing human population or as a city that would be immune to earthquakes and tsunami … But we quickly realized that it could save islands from rising sea levels. We are still at the planning stage, of course, but we believe this is a feasible project. (Sunhak Peace Prize 2018)

Despite these plans appearing to be fanciful imaginings, the former president of Kiribati, Anote Tong, held discussions with Shimizu about buying these floating islands to relocate people. Tong is convinced his nation requires a radical solution. He has said that global commitments to reduce the impact of climate change will not help his country:

> The momentum of what's already in the atmosphere will ensure that sea levels rise above our islands. We will be totally devastated … [These are] concerns we jointly share about the increasing severity of the challenges facing our people today from climate change and the slow pace of global action to address them. (Tong 2014)

It could be argued these 'islands' are more an 'installation' than an island in the sense that they are not attached to the seabed, but probably anchored through moorings. The fact these islands could not be considered permanent raises several points in law as, if they are not historically assimilated, they do not qualify as territory (Kardol 1999). These plans seem far too futuristic, with many possibilities for physical and technological failure, not to mention excessive cost. Apart from the obvious comment that such plans are more about aid, relationships and access to resources by donors, they also (if they are genuine plans) do not appear to include any recognition of the fact that most atoll and coastal Pacific peoples are seafarers rather than gardeners.

Despite scepticism, some government officials—facing the prospect of inundation, increased storm surges, relocations and at the very least brackish water supplies—are clearly looking for alternatives. The kind of alternatives they choose, as with much Pacific aid and overseas investment, may depend on who is making the offer, the costs and what will be received in return. In these circumstances, few take time to involve communities in the decision-making process. There is no agency for the people who will be settled on these islands. There also seem to be gaps in the knowledge of what has been tried before and people's capabilities. This chapter will explore the history of artificial islands in the Pacific and what involvement people had in such constructions. Where they had no choice (such as being under the control of powerful chiefs or gods), these earlier societies demonstrate that Pacific peoples have long had the knowledge to adapt to environmental change. Current thinking—not only in academia but also in the reports of the Intergovernmental Panel on Climate Change over the past decade—recognises that it is crucial to acknowledge the 'adaptive capacity' of those impacted by climate change. Relationships, the participation of traditional leaders and churches, and links throughout governments, communities and organisations are essential for strong adaptive capacity in the face of climate change and, indeed, all potential and real environmental challenges. The two cases presented here challenge that recognition of and respect for agency, as well as people's ability to adapt.

To be successful, artificial constructions should mimic the local environment. Some have been successful, such as Nunn's (2009a: 219–23) example of the FSM, where, on the vulnerable atoll of Kapinngamarangi, people manipulated naturally accumulating sandscapes to make them liveable, in the form of Touhou Islet. Obviously not all artificial constructions are successful. Poorly designed modern seawalls and increased coastal erosion are well known around the Pacific. Other forms of artificial construction have required enormous cooperation, possibly even the use of slaves or very powerful leaders with numerous willing commoners to carry out the work required. The case of Nan Madol in the FSM is just one example.

History of artificial islands

Historical and contemporary evidence demonstrate that island states, communities and individuals have, through necessity, created additional land and found ways of dealing with that space. There are contested concepts of ownership but, as will be demonstrated, there is also, over time, much give and take and adjustment by communities.

Nan Madol, Pohnpei

The oft-quoted example of land construction in the Pacific is the case of Nan Madol on coastal Pohnpei. Nan Madol is the ancient centre of the Sau Deleur dynasty of around 25,000 people in Madolenihmw in Pohnpei, FSM. It comprises 93 artificial islets across 81 hectares of sheltered reef near Temwen Island (Ayres 1983: 135; Kirch 2002: 195). The main development of Nan Madol appears to have occurred between 800 and 1500 CE when the huge basalt residential temples were constructed (Ayres 1983: 139). The islets themselves are built of stone, 'with coral and rubble fill, the entire complex bounded … by massive seawalls or breakwaters, some of them incorporating islets' (Kirch 2002: 195; Bryant-Tokalau 2011). The sheer size of the individual basalt slabs used to construct the walls of the tombs and residences is overpowering. The canals threading between and around the structures are large and not at all dwarfed by the basalt constructions, some of which consist of columnar slabs of basalt weighing up to half a tonne each. Kirch (2002: 196) reports that Nanauwas tomb, for example, has a base of 79 by 63 metres, rising 7.6 metres above canal level. As Pohnpei was settled around 1 CE, construction of Nan Madol may have begun at that time, although the megaliths are dated to about 1200–1600 CE (Kirch 2002: 197). The settlement has important sacred significance and there are many stories about the supernatural powers associated with it. There is some debate about how construction occurred and there are similarities with Samoan adze forms (Kirch 2002: 200) and the use of kava, leading archaeologists to speculate on western Polynesian links (pp. 200–1). As frequently recorded, basalt stones and their association with political status, power and sacredness are well known in other parts of Micronesia, such as Kiribati and Marshall Islands, where special stones have great significance. This basalt had to be transported to those island groups from high island sites such as Pohnpei and Kosrae (Goodenough 1986: 561). Research on Nan Madol is ongoing and far from fully explaining its origins, but its purpose may have much to do with power, influence and religion over an area much larger than simply Pohnpei—in effect, a regional power or centre of influence, as understood through the legendary stories of Kachaw or the sky-world (Goodenough 1986: 551; Bryant-Tokalau 2011: 78–79, 2018: 39–40). Such stories are examples of deep traditional knowledge of human adaptation both to the environment and to competition for land. How far such knowledge translates to today's need for adaptation in the face of climate change must be further understood. It is difficult to accept Nunn's (2009a: 221–22) prognosis that the only form of adaptation for modern, more sedentary Pacific Islanders is relocation, but without more understanding and without drawing on the traditional knowledge and practice that do exist, relocation may be the outcome.

Existing artificial islands

Langalanga Lagoon, Malaita, Solomon Islands

On the western side of Malaita in Solomon Islands are the many, several-centuries-old (possibly as old as 1,000 years; Bryant-Tokalau 2018: 103) small artificial islands (or islets) of the Langalanga and Tai lagoons. In this area, where large, steep landmasses often drop straight into the sea, the need for additional land was acute. Over the past 60 years, academics have debated the true origins of these islets. Parsonson (1966) attributed them to the scourge of malaria, necessitating a move by people from the bush of the main island to the clearer air of the lagoons. He also noted that the artificial islets were most often constructed in shallow waters, with deeper water at one end enabling easy fishing from the houses (Parsonson 1966: 5). But the origins and certainly the continuing existence of the islands are likely to be more complex, including the need for protection from enemies, the demand for expansion of living space for coastal people, the bartering of fish for root crops between the 'solwara (sea) and bus (bush) people as well as protection from mosquito-borne diseases.

In her doctoral thesis, Pei-yi Guo (2001) aims to understand how Langalanga people of Solomon Islands conceptualise and appropriate their landscape. In effect, the islets are a cultural symbol that mark how people remember their history. It is difficult to determine, then, whether the islands have continued to exist because of 'the colonial and post-colonial (tourist) gaze [which have] highlighted artificial islands as a locus of interest'. Other research, such as that by Hviding (1998: 259), demonstrates more complex reasons for the continuing existence of these islets, particularly institutionalised exchange between the lagoon and bush peoples, trading fish for root crops. Such exchange has not diminished over time and, indeed, the communities are thriving and continuing as before (Hundleby, Pers. comm., 2014; Bryant-Tokalau 2018: 39–44).

Of particular importance in a discussion of how Pacific peoples have responded to climate change over time is the relationship between peoples of the vast Pacific Ocean. Parsonson (1966: 18), for example, notes the ancient origins of most peoples living on the artificial islands of Melanesia, pointing to their relationship with Polynesian and Micronesian peoples who frequently occupy the 'outliers' in Melanesia such as Ontong Java, Trobriand Islands, Tikopia and Futuna. Parsonson (1966: 18–20) notes a 'strong Micro-Polynesian strain' and cultural affinities such as fishing methods (kite-fishing, for example, as well as outrigger canoes), shell money, the building of houses on piles—but more particularly, the design and decoration of the houses—canoe burial, similar statuary and names originating from Tonga (Lau, Langalanga) as well as the ancient arts of stone-building found throughout Polynesia and Micronesia (Pohnpei, Tonga, Marquesas Islands and Hawai`i). To better understand Solomon Islander use of the landscape and the construction and continuing maintenance of artificial islands, a cultural landscape approach could be used (Walter and Hamilton 2014: 1–10). In discussing community-based conservation, Walter and Hamilton (2014: 2) argue that 'Indigenous communities tend to embrace a more complex and diverse set of environmental values than is often appreciated'. Supporting Guo's view of landscape as memory, Walter and Hamilton discuss the encoding of cultural memories and history, which is then used in socialisation and social reproduction. The authors note that in Solomon Islands (and other coastal communities), shrines and other sacred sites are today not simply viewed as static reminders of the past but are used and remembered in very modern transactions such as over logging or land. Cultural and physical notions of landscape are thus intertwined (Walter and Hamilton 2014: 2).

Considering this approach in the discussion of artificial islands as a response to climate change and other environmental challenges provides more understanding of why and how people move and respond to their landscapes. They are embedded with memories and the past continues to live in the current landscape. Even if people move and construct new homes, memories of ancestral links, ancient voyaging and conflict remain in both stories and actions.

With Pacific populations facing inundation and/or loss of territory, how might the understanding of cultural landscapes and Indigenous knowledge be utilised and what might be possible alternatives? In the following section, I present one case of a modern alternative and demonstrate how it fails to consider people's cultural memory and or recognise the Indigenous knowledge of people who have travelled widely to settle on their islands.

Modern alternatives: Kiribati

Relocation: Kiribati and Fiji future imperfect

The Republic of Kiribati straddles the Equator north of Fiji and Tuvalu. There are 33 atolls and reef islands, and one raised coral island, Banaba. The total land area of 800 square kilometres is spread over 3.5 million square kilometres of the Pacific Ocean. In 2010, more than half of the permanent population of 108,800 (SPC 2013) lived on Tarawa Atoll in the capital, South Tarawa. Banaba's history is especially relevant in terms of forced migration as it was largely ruined by mining for phosphate for use on New Zealand and Australian farms. The Japanese occupied it during World War II and either murdered or enslaved much of the population on Chuuk (then Truk) in Micronesia. After the war, the British colonial administrators refused to return the survivors to Banaba, instead relocating them to Rabi Island, Fiji, which was purchased for them. Today, there are about 5,000 Banabans living on Rabi, with about 300 on Banaba itself.

Kiribati has been inhabited largely by Micronesian peoples since between 3000 BCE[1] and 1300 CE. There has been much interaction over the centuries between Kiribati and countries to the south, especially Tonga, Sāmoa and Fiji, often in the form of invading parties. Although Kiribati is regarded as Micronesian, links with other nations have meant there are strong ties with Polynesian and Melanesian cultures. Indeed, from the late 1930s, I-Kiribati have been relocated both within the nation (to the Phoenix group) and without, to Solomon Islands, largely as a response to environmental change (Tabe 2014).

Kiribati—along with Tuvalu, its partner in colonial times as the British-governed Gilbert and Ellice Islands—is often held up as one of the global poster children of climate change. As an atoll nation, Kiribati already has a limited supply of freshwater, which is caught in tanks from rainfall or sits under the atolls in freshwater lenses. Rising sea levels and increasing inundation are causing saltwater infiltration of groundwater, which is also being contaminated with sewage and leaching from gravesites. The disposal of rubbish is always an issue in atoll countries. Apart from household rubbish, solid waste such as old cars, oil, batteries and plastics, and hospital waste are a difficult issue.[2]

In addition, coastal erosion has meant some villages have been abandoned and the atolls of Tebua and Abanuea disappeared in the late 1990s (Nunn 2009b: 171). Coral reefs are being degraded, both through ocean acidification and overfishing, meaning the peoples of Kiribati, like those on atolls everywhere, are not only losing their livelihoods but also being threatened by greater coastal erosion as the reefs are no longer protecting the islands to the extent they once did. On land, the few crops that grow, such as breadfruit and coconut, are badly affected by saltwater inundation and will die within three months of standing for two or three days in saltwater (Caritas 2014: 23).

Not everyone believes the islands will be uninhabitable in a short period, citing the building up of reefs by 10 to 15 millimetres a year (outpacing sea-level rise) due to natural processes (Webb and Kench 2010). There is also some debate over the media's use of images of large waves crashing into houses, some of which were taken during king tides and show the results of

---

1   See: en.wikipedia.org/wiki/Kiribati.
2   In 1992, when I was working in Kiribati, I encountered hospital syringes (needles) on a sandbar in the lagoon some kilometres from Tarawa.

badly constructed seawalls or causeways that alter the behaviour of waves (Webb and Kench 2010). Foreign scientists are not the only ones to offer alternative scenarios to the image of Kiribati 'drowning'. Naomi Biribo, a geography graduate from the University of the South Pacific and a senior scientist in Tarawa, authored a report that essentially said the widespread erosion and flooding affecting South Tarawa, in particular, was due largely to local human activity, such as overcrowding, coral reef mining and the construction of seawalls and causeways.

Whatever the nature of the impacts of climate change, in the face of potential devastation, Kiribati has been considering various options. These options range from migration within Kiribati itself—such as to Aranuka or North Tarawa, which is much wider and has good protection against the ocean swell according to Kench—or to Australia, Aotearoa New Zealand or other Pacific nations, to doing nothing, adapting and staying put or very expensive engineering solutions such as the construction of suitable seawalls or building up the islands. More recently, the government has been party to discussions with Japanese companies seeking to build high-tech artificial islands. All are fully aware that any reduction in emissions by the people of Kiribati will not alter the outcome since island nations contribute so few emissions and because the die is already cast for global climate change. Kiribati has always been vocal about climate change at international summits and many 'solutions' have been offered to ease their plight, some of which have caused dissent in the community.

In a 2012 masters of communication dissertation by Taberannang Korauaba, it was argued that President Tong's growing focus on climate change, which was centred on his close relationship with the foreign news media, increasingly portrayed the people of Kiribati as victims. Korauaba's key argument was that the victim approach further marginalised people's ability to learn about climate change. But he also noted that there was no connection between what Tong was saying overseas and his government's 2008–11 development plan. Korauaba (2012: Abstract) makes a case that Kiribati is not united on the issue of climate change: 'Traditional, cultural and religious beliefs about land, environment and sea, and division among educated elites and political parties are some of the key barriers to communicating and receiving climate change stories.' There are other implications of the government's top-down approach and lack of communication, including the distribution of climate change funding.

Korauaba's dissertation is refreshing in the global publicity about Kiribati's 'plight'. A recent example of the 'poster-child' scenarios and the international feting of President Tong arose around the purchase of land in Fiji.

The Fiji land purchase

In May 2014, a plan to buy land in Fiji was announced during the first regional joint meeting of the Pacific Platform for Disaster Risk Management and the Pacific Climate Change Roundtable. Kiribati purchased about 2,500 hectares (24 square kilometres) of land in Natoavatu estate near Savusavu on the island of Vanua Levu, Fiji, to ensure 'food security as its own arable land is swamped by the rising sea' (Bryant-Tokalau 2018: 50–52). President Tong said he bought the land so his people would have high ground to go to when the rising sea makes his low-lying nation unliveable. 'We would hope not to put everyone on [this] one piece of land, but if it became absolutely necessary, yes, we could do it,' he told Reuters (2014). For years, Tong claimed at climate change conferences and in interviews that sea-level rise was already claiming a heavy toll on his people, eroding beaches, destroying buildings and crops, forcing the evacuation of a village and wiping out an entire island. His views are echoed by Conservation International, on whose board Tong sits. The residents of 'Kiribati, where the effects of rising sea levels already are being felt, [are] on the front lines of climate change', says its website (Pala 2014b).

I-Kiribati scientists, civil servants and atoll-dwellers are divided over the purchase of the land in Fiji. First, to pay for the land, F$8.7 million was taken from Kiribati's $600 million sovereign wealth fund, the interest from which goes into the national budget. According to former president Teburoro Tito, an examination of the sales deeds of comparable land parcels revealed Kiribati paid four times more per acre than other buyers in the previous few years. Tito believes the price paid was solely for publicity purposes, to highlight Tong's far-sightedness and how serious he was about climate change. Some have described the land purchase as the 'politics of hope' by the Fiji and Kiribati governments, allowing people to develop 'imaginings of migration' (Hermann and Kempf 2017). While such comments may appear as political posturing, there are more serious issues surrounding the purchase of this land.

Although government officials celebrated the purchase, citing the capacity of the land to hold 60–70,000 people, there are many problems. In Fiji, John Teaiwa, the former environment secretary who is a Rabi Islander, said the land made no sense as a food source. It lies in the interior of Vanua

Levu, a mountainous island, far from the atoll environment of I-Kiribati. It consists largely of an abandoned coconut plantation and dense forest on steep hills.

Bryant-Tokalau discusses in some detail the further complications of the Fiji land purchase (2018: 51–53). Apart from difficulties applying agriculture to the site, there is another, supremely ironic[3] and equally serious story associated with this land: it is not uninhabited. Some 270 Solomon Islander descendants of 'black-birded' labourers live on the former estate, invited there in 1947 by the Anglican Church. They were told they could stay indefinitely (if they were practising Anglicans) and have practised subsistence agriculture on 283 hectares, using the rest to graze cattle. The sale means they now have only 125 hectares on which to live. The balance of the land, now sold to Kiribati, would be difficult to farm in any case— something with which the Solomon Islanders agree, claiming the balance of the land could support very few people. They also now must lease the land they have for 99 years, being told by the church that 'that is all they will get'.

The Anglican Church has been accused of failing in its duty to the Solomon Islanders and of taking advantage of an unsophisticated buyer. The church claims people could transform the landscape but appears to have no concern about the future of the Solomon Islanders. Meanwhile, President Tong announced the formation of a committee to study what should be done with the land, saying the purchase marked 'a new milestone' in the government's 'development plans, which include exploring options of commercial, industrial and agricultural undertakings such as fish canning, beef/poultry farming, fruit and vegetable farming' (Pala 2014a).

It is unfortunate the people already living on the land have been so marginalised, but it is also of concern that the people of Kiribati have had such little say in their relocation—if, indeed, it happens. In Kiribati, there is much opposition to the purchase, with people variously accusing the government of spending money on 'foolish things' or being tricked by the Church of England, which they say is gouging 'one of the poorest and most isolated countries in the world'. Others are even harsher, claiming the land purchase was a publicity stunt for Tong to glorify himself. President Tito, a former secretary-general of the Pacific Island Forum, said the fact that Tong described the purchase variously as being for relocation, food security

---

3   This is ironic in the sense that I-Kiribati have close connections with Solomon Islanders, with some relocated there in the 1950s and 1960s (Tabe 2014).

and an investment highlighted that Tong, who was reputed to govern with little parliamentary oversight, had no clear plan. Tito pointed out that after three years of negotiating the purchase of the land (and making no effort to ascertain its value), the first thing Tong announced after the purchase was completed was the appointment of a committee to decide what to do with it.

What could make more sense for I-Kiribati is internal relocation, to North Tarawa, as noted earlier, or even to Christmas Island in the Line Island group. Public comments on the proposal included the view that what Kiribati needed was more coconuts (a staple part of the diet that also provide income from copra), but since people have moved from Tarawa to Christmas Island over the past few years, demand has outstripped supply. Because it takes four years for a sapling to produce coconuts, instead of buying land in Fiji, the government should hire people to plant trees; people emigrating from overcrowded, flood-prone Tarawa would then have not only plenty of space and drinking water, but also a way to earn a living.

It seems that despite international awareness of Kiribati's possible future there is inadequate knowledge of what might be the most sensible options for this nation. When he was president, Tong regularly warned in speeches that climate change would destroy his homeland but he was working hard to obtain compensation from the countries that caused it. People are sceptical and, as one journalist put it, while Tong's warnings of impending doom for atoll-dwellers have brought him a measure of fame abroad and even saw him twice nominated for a Nobel Peace Prize, in Kiribati, there is confusion among some and derision among others. This is a pity as Kiribati, along with other atoll and low-lying nations, and indeed all coastal areas, faces an uncertain future. Tong himself, although often on the global stage making certain the plight of small island nations was recognised, also spoke of wide consultation and the involvement of communities—a fine balancing act for any leader, but debacles such as the Fiji land purchase were not helpful in determining a positive future for all.

As Tong told the UN General Assembly in 2014: 'Let us bring in our youth, let us bring in our women, civil society, the private sector, our traditional institutions. Let us be inclusive' (Tong 2014; see also Bryant-Tokalau 2018: 51–53).

The future: Whose Indigenous knowledge?

The two cases presented here remind us that there are many approaches to facing the impending scenario of rising sea levels, more devastating storms, inundation, the impacts on agriculture and fisheries, a future with limited or no potable water, not to mention the potential loss of not only land but also entire countries. But although we know these scenarios are real (even if some of the visual portrayals are exaggerated), the real questions remain: Should we stay or should we go? And, if we stay, where and how should we live? If we go, will the future location be suitable, and what will be the impact on the moving population and the hosts?

What has been presented are technological solutions of futuristic artificial islands that not only will be extremely costly, but also appear to take no account of how people live currently and their knowledge of the sea and the surrounding environment. Importantly, they pay no heed to people's own technological solutions, their own adaptive strategies such as the kinds of artificial islands and land reclamation that have existed for centuries. Such solutions also ignore current technical knowledge about the state of reefs, how rapidly they grow and the fact that sometimes (as in Kiribati) there are places where people can go without abandoning ancestral lands and the surrounding sea. But 'the only adaptation option of relocation' (Nunn 2009a) is now being presented as a key solution for Kiribati. The purchase of land in Fiji has many negative aspects and, far from 'saving' Kiribati, it may have undesirable implications not only for I-Kiribati, but also for their hosts.

Current responses to sea-level rise have failed to give adequate attention to history and traditional knowledge. People have always moved and adapted to changing environmental circumstances, but this has generally been done with the involvement of the peoples themselves, building on their history. Of course, many of the great migrations and the construction of massive structures such as Nan Madol were most likely orchestrated by a powerful leader or a warring chief. Nevertheless, people in these circumstances also carried with them their own fishing and gardening knowledge. In current times, communities have begun to demand a greater say in their circumstances, yet schemes for futuristic cities and relocation to other countries appear to ignore such demands. It is suggested here that whatever Pacific nations decide about how to adapt to climate change, local knowledge must be considered.

10

The Future of the Federated States of Micronesia in the Era of Climate Change

Gonzaga Puas

The Federated States of Micronesia (FSM) is on the front lines of climate change, especially regarding rising sea levels. Many of its low-lying islands have been subject to increasingly frequent storm surges that have decimated food crops, polluted freshwater wells, eroded shorelines and dislocated many human habitats. Storm surges have also eroded sacred places, destroyed fish weirs and created new roadways between island villages. Other consequences of climate change include coral bleaching, more intense storms, shortages of drinking water, destruction of seawalls and degraded soil fertility. Despite all the destructive forces of nature, Micronesian islanders continue to sustain their environment as they have been doing throughout history. This chapter discusses the experiences of Micronesians and how they are adapting to the consequences of climate change on their own terms. It also focuses on how the FSM plans to mitigate the effects of climate change as much as possible with the resources it has at its disposal to reduce reliance on external partners that might seek to use the country's climate change vulnerability to advance their own interests in the region.

Environmental, economic and climatic realities in contemporary Micronesia

The Pacific cultural region of Micronesia, centred on the FSM, is becoming more prominent in global strategic and environmental discourses as the stage for three externally induced issues: inundation of low-lying islands due to the rise in sea levels; pressure on its tuna fishery because of increasing ocean temperatures and illegal fishing by distant countries; and rising tensions between the world's two economic superpowers, the United States and the People's Republic of China. Micronesians are proactively countering potential threats to their economic and environmental futures and political independence. Rather than being merely victims of questionable policies of other nations, Micronesians are often initiators of innovative solutions to issues that will soon confront much of humanity. The implications of this reconceptualising of Micronesia in world affairs is affecting the orientation of the FSM's relationship with China, the United States, Taiwan and other players.

The FSM forms the north-western part of the region of Oceania. It lies immediately above the Equator, north of Papua New Guinea, south of Guam, east of Palau and to the west of the Marshall Islands. It comprises 607 islands dispersed across a vast oceanic space (Susumu and Kostka 2010: 1). Only 65 of the islands are inhabited, with population size varying from less than 200 in the low-lying islands to more than 35,000 on the mountainous islands. The islands range from small atolls barely exceeding 4 metres above sea level to many high volcanic islands. The total land area of FSM is approximately 700 square kilometres (Henry et al. 2008: 7).

The FSM's exclusive economic zone encompasses 2,978,000 square kilometres. Data published by the Office of Statistics, Budget and Economics Management, Overseas Development, and Compact Management (SBOC) show the country's population is just over 107,000 people, 49,840 of whom were living in the United States as of October 2012. Of those living in the United States, 16,790 were also born there and are referred to as the 'Compact Generation' (SBOC 2010; Kim 2011: 271; Hezel 2013: 33–34; D'Arcy 2014b: 299).

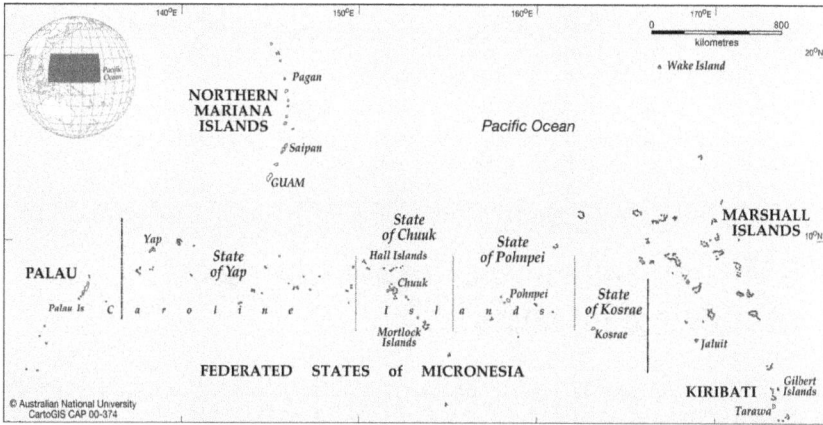

Map 10.1: Map of the Federated States of Micronesia in regional context.
Source: CartoGIS, College of Asia and the Pacific, The Australian National University.

The FSM's climate is tropical and humid with heavy year-round rainfall, especially in the east. The average daily temperature is 27°C, with two seasons: the dry months, generally from May to September, and the windy months, from October to April (Goodenough 1951: 22–23). The Chuukese peoples who form the largest cultural group within FSM call the dry months lerak ('bountiful breadfruit season') and the windy season lefang ('the lean season') (Gladwin 1970: 24–25; Alkire 1965: 44–45; D'Arcy 2006: 14–16, 152–53).

Recent climate change studies have confirmed local observations of deteriorating conditions, indicating that rising sea levels are slowly eroding shorelines and increasing the incursion of saltwater into freshwater wells and agricultural lands (Henry et al. 2008: 38–39; Fletcher and Richmond 2010: 4–5; Susumu et al. 2009: 4–9; Klein 2014). Storm surges occurred intermittently from the 1970s[1] to the 1990s, but were never as devastating as the inundation events in 2007 and 2008, which affected between 50 and 75 per cent of the land for food production and freshwater wells (Susumu and Kostka 2010: 22; Fletcher and Richmond 2010: 9). The first FSM National Communication to the UNFCCC in 1999 noted the increase in:

---

1   I witnessed the surge in 1971 (which was not caused by a typhoon). It destroyed almost half the taro farms in my village of Rewow on the atoll of Lukunor in the Mortlock Islands of Chuuk State. Other surges followed, but on a smaller scale, affecting only the shoreline. Unfortunately, there are no documents recording these events.

the frequency, duration and intensity of *El Niño* droughts, and the need to enhance capacity to address *El Niño* and *La Niña* events. Accelerated sea level rise was identified as a concern over the longer-term ... [Other] concerns were noted as being [the] coral reef ecosystems, coastal zones, waste management ... agriculture and water supply. (Mulalap 2013: 382–83, 386)

FSM responses to climate change: Preserving islands

The FSM's territorial integrity and sovereignty are defined by its constitution, in compliance with international law. Article 1, Section 1 of the FSM Constitution states:

> The waters connecting the islands of the [Micronesian] archipelago are internal waters regardless of dimensions, and jurisdiction extends to a marine space of 200 miles [322 km] measured outward from appropriate baselines, the seabed, subsoil, water column, insular or continental shelves, airspace over land and water, and any other territory or waters belonging to Micronesia by historic right, custom, or legal title. (FSM Government 1979: Art. 1, s. 1)

The nation's islands and surrounding waters, however, are being slowly affected by climate change. The legal implications for territorial sovereignty of submerged islands have still not been seriously considered. For now, the FSM is committed to doing all it can to bulwark its island shorelines against this threat.

Climate change is caused by the industrialised countries, yet has its greatest impact on the low-lying islands of developing nations. It is altering the integrity of fragile environments, especially in low-lying atolls. Traditional methods have been combined with foreign engineering as defence mechanisms to protect low-lying islands from sea-level rise (FSM Government 2009: 2). For example, traditional practices such as the placement of heavy rocks to facilitate the natural flow of currents and wave patterns to minimise shore erosion remain effective adaptation strategies. Another protective measure to prevent beach erosion is the planting of native trees such as rakish (sea-oaks), fash (pandanus) and shia (mangrove) within a metre or so of the shoreline, with heavy debris used to seal the gaps between the plants. These forms of local adaptation and mitigation are used especially to strengthen shorelines where they are susceptible to ocean currents and waves (Henry 5 July 2013).

In the late 1960s, seawalls were seen as the best approach to fight shoreline erosion in the atolls of the Mortlock Islands, and were built based on a model erected by the Japanese. Unfortunately, they were not successful in preventing shoreline erosion. Many local elders had opposed their construction because they required the clearing of native trees and bushes along the shore that naturally prevented coastal erosion. This information was relayed to me by Ring Puas and Alfonis Buluay, who were present at a debate about seawall erection in 1972–73 during a sotang (village meeting) in Relong village (see also Marshall 2004: 68). Many seawalls fell apart within a few months of construction due to changing nearshore currents, as predicted by the elders. A new engineering approach was recommended and seawalls were once again erected. After the completion of the new supposedly well-engineered seawalls, locals started to complain about the changes in the seascape along the shoreline. For example, the habitats of certain fish were disturbed, causing their migration to different parts of the islands. This caused tension between clans as certain fish belong to particular clans by tradition, and the seawalls forced fish into different shoreline zones owned by other clans. This remains a sensitive cultural issue caused by climate change and a lack of consultation with all groups affected.

It was not until the late 1970s when Super Typhoon Pamela hit the Mortlock Islands that the folly of seawalls was extensively exposed to the public (Marshall 2004: 68). The typhoon destroyed the seawalls and saltwater soon found its way into the taro patches, with devastating impacts on agricultural land.

Today, seawalls are still required because of the clearing of vegetation along the coast, but they must be designed differently in keeping with the topographical features of the coastline. The debate over seawall construction is still dividing island communities. In my interview with Marion Henry, a traditional leader from the island of Oneop and the national secretary of the FSM Department of Resources and Development, she said 'seawalls contradicted traditional wisdom because they interrupt the natural flow of ocean currents around the islands, which deposit sand on different shores and thereby increase beach erosion rather than preventing it' (Henry 18 July 2013; Haglelgam 2011).[2] She argued that native shrubs and trees should have been left alone.

More people are becoming receptive to the traditional wisdom propounded by Henry; however, others dispute it and believe seawalls are necessary, but their design must be compatible with the topographical configuration of the islands. In Kosrae, for example, a new seawall design has been implemented with some success in preventing beach erosion. Solid concrete blocks were placed along a beach in a pattern that hugged the natural configuration of the shore. In my discussion with some locals, they said the seawall had prevented beach erosion and withstood big tides and strong storms. It is up to each island to adopt designs that suit local circumstances, but with the support of the national government.

Seawall technology is a modern form of defence that could assist islanders in their fight against the impacts of climate change. However, collaborative approaches between locals and outside experts are required to implement the appropriate technology for local requirements and local ecological, social and economic configurations.

Legislation was adopted in February 2013 to provide a national Integrated Disaster and Climate Change Policy, which relevant government departments were obliged to implement, such as the Department of Resources and Development, the Department of Climate Change and Environment and Emergency Management and the Department of Transportation. It required the president of the FSM to submit a report to congress every year 'on the progress of the implementation of the Climate Change Policy and recommend additional legislation where applicable and necessary' (Congress of the FSM 2013). This illustrates the seriousness of the FSM Government's resolve to tackle climate change by creating a legal framework for the nation to actively implement its adaptation strategies.

Furthermore, the FSM is seeking assistance and support regionally and internationally to ensure its adaptation goals are implemented and strengthened. Geologists Charles Fletcher and Bruce Richmond (2010: 11–12) suggested that adaptation within the FSM could be facilitated by a two-step approach: forming international partnerships to aid adaptation efforts and continuing the development of internal policies focused on

---

2   Henry is also a samol from the Island of Oneop. Congress of the FSM (1983).

building resilient and sustainable communities. International partnerships will need to adhere to local needs based on discussions with both sides, but within a domestic policy framework. Although new concepts exist for creating floating artificial islands and barrier reefs, many are too costly for Micronesians; perhaps they will become a reality when resources from the nation's EEZ are exploited to finance a concept suitable to FSM's circumstances.

FSM responses to climate change: Food security and self-reliance

Food security is one of the main challenges for the FSM Government. Its Food Security Vulnerability Assessment provided a snapshot of what the FSM could look like in the future. The report characterised the FSM economy as aid-dependent, relying primarily on money provided by the United States under the Compact Agreement, as well as from other donor countries like Japan, China and Australia. The report found the compact provides about 65 per cent of revenue for the national government and 75 per cent of revenue for the states. The FSM economy thereby remains in negative growth (Susumu and Kostka 2010: 3). A shift in local thinking is required to ensure self-sufficiency remains a national objective especially in the coming years as climate change impacts become more profound.

Additionally, the construction of public buildings and private dwellings needs to be appropriate for the changes in the local environment, such as variations in temperature and topography caused by climate change. The best possible design for these buildings is one that implements local knowledge and materials, in addition to weather-resistant imported materials and engineering models. For example, shoon fash (pandanus leaves), shoon nu (coconut leaves), soponmei (breadfruit trunks), sopon nu (coconut trunks), shia (mangrove), mosor (seashore plants) and shokis (a very strong tree that grows in saltwater along the shoreline) are best suited to the island environment. Shokis branches are used in traditional house construction, especially for pillars, and can be used for fish-traps as they last for many years. They can withstand tropical weather longer than materials imported from China and Japan, for example. Moreover, local products are cheaper compared with the inflated prices charged for imported materials. Such local knowledge should be incorporated into post-secondary trade qualifications to encourage sustainable building practices.

The government also set up the FSM Food Security Steering Committee, whose role is to enhance coordination and cooperation in food security for the nation and to oversee the effective implementation of future initiatives (Australian Government 2013). In my interview with Gibson Susumu, he noted that during a trip in 2012 to the low-lying atolls in Chuuk, he found many people were close to starvation due to the failure of food crops affected by saltwater. He estimated that on close to 70 per cent of all the islands he visited in Chuuk alone, food production was the main challenge for islanders. Many of the low-lying islands in Yap and Pohnpei were experiencing the same problem (Susumu and Kostka 2010: iii–v).

The FSM Government has been developing its adaptation policies for food security and environmental management. It has suggested the following strategies to sustain food production: switching to different cultivars, improving and conserving soils, increasing water supply by building reservoirs and enhancing rain catchment, improving watershed management, desalination, water management and improving the health of coastal zones and marine ecosystems (Susumu and Kostka 2010: iii–v). New 'concept projects' are also in the development stage and have been put to the national government for consideration.[3]

Actions Micronesians desire from international partners and donors

The FSM's marine resources, especially tuna, are its biggest economic asset. The fishing industry is thus at the heart of its blueprint for future self-sufficiency. It is estimated that the FSM could sustain a yield of more than 100,000 tonnes of marine products annually; however, it lacks the capability to fully exploit this resource. Its fishing industry benefits other countries, such as Japan, South Korea and Taiwan, which pay a licence fee to the FSM Government that is less than 10 per cent of the sale value of the fish caught. The FSM must explore its economic potential in terms of its own resources to deliver important services to its people (Nimea 2006: 1–10).

Capacity-building involves developing a coordinated system of training programs so the FSM can respond to all climate change issues as they arise. The priority is to implement local knowledge as a first line of defence

---

3   New farming concepts—for example, the saltwater-resistant taro project in Kosrae—were also mentioned by Gibson during my interview with him in Palikir, Pohnpei, 13 July 2013.

(FSM Government 2009: 1–3). The various levels of government have been working together to develop new adaptation strategies in anticipation of new climate change challenges. Many foreign governments and institutions are present in the FSM, but they should be mindful of not tying their climate change aid projects to their political objectives, or they risk diplomatic fallout.

Conclusion: Adaptation, development and self-reliance

The FSM's national climate change objective is to harness traditional practices as its first line of defence against the encroaching sea. Climate change issues are the responsibility of the three strata of government in the federation. However, each level works within its own jurisdiction as defined by the nation's constitution. The president, the departments of Foreign Affairs, Resources and Development, and the new national Department of Environment and Climate Change and Emergency Management are working together with their state counterparts such as the environmental protection agencies and historical preservation offices.

Climate change adaptation ranks as one of the nation's top priorities and new laws have been enacted to support this. National government officials have been conducting field studies in all low-lying islands, where support for climate change adaptation and economic and social programs is strong (Susumu 2013). The FSM Government's economic development plans emphasise sustainability and discourage reliance on foreign assistance, except in the use of new technologies to fight climate change impacts. The United States, Taiwan, China and other like-minded countries should be mindful of the clearly articulated needs and objectives of the FSM Government and adjust their aid and development interactions accordingly. The FSM, with the support of genuine external partners, reaffirms its right to exist as a nation under international law, particularly in view of the debate about sovereignty as a result of possible reconfiguration of island territories if islands are overwhelmed by the sea and become uninhabitable (FSM Government 2009: 1–2).

11

'We Are Not Drowning': Pacific identity and cultural sustainability in the era of climate change

Lynette Carter

The chief focus of this chapter is to investigate the impact of climate change on cultural identity and sustainability across Pacific nations. One concept to be challenged is the notion that people must reside within their home territories to be fully of that place—and, consequently, to retain the recognised status of statehood, nationhood and rights. The second challenge is to the notion that Pacific nations are confined territorially to landmasses—thus, excluding territories formed through seamless extensions of land and sea. These notions are not apparent in the Indigenous Pacific way of understanding and knowing about identity, place and territory, which recognises that land, people and the sea are intrinsically interlinked. Both challenges to the contemporary discourse on Pacific climate change are necessary to counter the unfortunate belief that Pacific-dwellers will become climate change refugees from sunken islands with a subsequent loss of statehood and identity.

I have included Aotearoa New Zealand because it is part of the Pacific and forms one apex of the Polynesian Triangle. Māori occupy territory within Aotearoa New Zealand and have acknowledged ancestral connections to their Pacific neighbours, with whom they share similar cultural practices and knowledge frameworks. Therefore, it is important to include them in this discussion, as Māori tribal entities will also face challenges from climate change. It is recognised that Aotearoa New Zealand has different social, political and economic structures to those of other Pacific Island states. However, Māori economic, social and political systems are values-based and rely on specific Indigenous knowledge frameworks to manage resources. In other words, Māori and all New Zealanders are Pacific people, too, and should be able to learn valuable lessons from Indigenous Pacific adaptation measures for climate change challenges.

What I am concerning myself with here is how Pacific Island nations view themselves in the context of being 'a state' and its associated trappings based firmly on non-Indigenous political organisation. The Montevideo Convention on the Rights and Duties of States was put in place in 1933 and entered into force on 26 December 1934. Under the convention, the definition of a state specifies four key criteria that can give rise to the recognition of a specific nation-state: a defined territory, a permanent population, an effective government and the capacity to enter into relations with other states. 'State' is a Western term that has become a necessary fact within the Pacific; it has no direct correlation with Indigenous political systems that are premised on Indigenous knowledge frameworks centred on reciprocal relationships and obligations. Each Pacific Island's recognised power and authority over vast tracks of land and ocean were around long before the Montevideo Convention. Hence, Pacific Islands have their own criteria firmly based on traditional concepts and practices. However, it is the question of how to maintain the Pacific Islands as recognisable entities in a contemporary global context that will be considered here.

To date, there has been much discourse about climate change in the Pacific, a great part of which has also been about 'Small Island Nations', which presupposes the old adage of many dependent small island groupings in a vast sea—a point disputed eloquently by Epeli Hau'ofa (1993). To counter this perspective, I refer to the 'small island nations' as Pacific Island nations, which better describes the nationhood and identity of Pacific-dwellers. When we also consider Pacific perspectives of a seamless territory incorporating land and sea, the territory governed by each Pacific Island enlarges dramatically. Similarly, lumping all populations together as 'Pacific peoples' denies the number of distinct cultural, political and economic entities identifiable through whakapapa (origins and genealogies), history and practices that differentiate each nation. Each has its own recognisable territory, government and population. All these criteria were determined through traditional practices and, since colonisation, incorporate a mixture of Indigenous and non-Indigenous systems and processes.

Before investigating how the Pacific Islands incorporate concepts of nationhood into an Indigenous knowledge framework, there will be a general discussion about the concept of a people–land–sea continuum as informed by Pacific oral traditions about origins and relationships. The oral traditions teach about the collaborative relationships and obligations between people and the land, people and the sea, and the land and the sea; they teach us about those seamless extensions and how they came into being.

People–land–sea as seamless extensions of one another

Across the Pacific, there are oral traditions and histories of how the land came into being—as Patrick Nunn (2003) succinctly puts it: 'either fished up or thrown down' (see also Tregear 1891; Beckwith 1970; Dixon 1916; MacGregor 1937; Westervelt 2009). Many tell of the ancestor Māui fishing for the land and raising it up to the water's surface. The North Island of Aotearoa New Zealand, for example, is known as Te Ika-a-Māui ('the fish of Māui'). Here is one version of the story:

> Katahi ia ka hapai ake i tana hiki ake mo tana ika kia maiangi ake;
>
> He aha tau, e Tonganui
>
> e ngau whakatuturi ake i raro?
>
> Ka puta te hau o ranga-whenua
>
> Ka rukuruku, ka heihei
>
> Ka rukuruku, ka eaea
>
> Oi mokopu Tangaroa meha
>
> Ehara, tarewa ana i runga te ika a Māui; he ika whenua, ko Papatuanuku, anana, takoto ana to ratou waka.
>
> [Then he raised up his raising-from-the-water spell for his fish that it might be raised and grown faint:
>
> What are you doing, Tonganui
>
> Holding on stubbornly with your teeth?
>
> The power of 'Rangawhenua is abroad
>
> Down dives the fish, spray is tossed up,

Down dives the fish, it emerges.

Oi! Mokopu, Tangaroa is utterly weak.

Behold. The fish of Māui is raised up, a land-fish, the earth … their canoe lay on dry land.][1]

The land as a fish and the fisher, Māui, also operated in other parts of the Pacific, such as in these chants from Aitutaki and Rakahanga in Cook Islands:

> Within the circle of the sea,
> It holds a fish of note
> It holds a fish
> O'er which the rainbow arches,
> Spanning the immensity of the Ocean
> It is—my land.
> (Aitutaki chant, in Buck 1975: 52)

> The sea settles,
> The sea recedes,
> It appears, the land appears
> And Māui stands upon it.
> (Rakahanga chant, in Buck 1975: 122)

In Hawai`i, Mangareva in French Polynesia and Tokelau, there are stories about Māui hauling up the land. In Sāmoa, the name for the land-raiser is Ti`iti`i, which recalls one of the names given to Māui in other parts of the Pacific and refers to his origins: Māui a Tiketike o Taranga ('Māui of the topknot of Taranga'). In Vanuatu, the land-raiser is named Wuhngin. The idea of land being hauled up from the ocean floor further establishes the Pacific-wide knowledge that land and sea are one; there is no separation between the land above water and that below. In most stories of Māui fishing up the land, there are people living on the fish as it emerges from the water, hence, people and land came together into the world of light (Te Ao Marama).

Other lands are the result of oceanic forces throwing land down. This is the origin of the South Island of New Zealand. In a Ngāi Tahu story, the southern lands are Te Waka-a-Aoraki ('the canoe of Aoraki'). Aoraki and his brothers were returning to their homeland after visiting Tangaroa's new

---

1   'Maui tiketike-a-taranga: Te Rangikaheke to Grey', GNZMMSS 43, 896-973, Auckland Public Library collection. This version is also reprinted in Thornton (1992).

wife, Papatūānuku.[2] A mistake in the karakia (incantation) led to the canoe being thrown into the sea, where it rested on an underwater ridge. Over time, it solidified, with Aoraki becoming the tallest mountain (Aoraki/Mt Cook) in the long chain of mountains that make up the backbone of the South Island. Aoraki's grandson Tuterakiwhanoa and his companions made the land ready for human occupation. The story progresses to include a version of Māui's arrival and his fishing expedition that produces Te Ika-a-Māui.

What all these stories tell us and indeed reinforce is that land and sea are one and the same. Also, people were already on the land as it emerged and, once they reached the world of light above Tangaroa's domain, they began developing and expanding their home territories. Tangaroa is a prominent figure across the Pacific, linking together the origins of land, sea and people.

Regardless of origin story (throwing down or fishing up), the land and sea are a seamless extension of one another and the origins of people remain intrinsically entwined with the origins of the territory (land and sea). Land, sea and people originated as one entity; the land is often referred to as a parent, such as in the following extract from a letter to New Zealand Governor Sir George Grey in 1853:

> He pani au. Kua mate aku matua; tuku tungane—a Te Hiko.
> Ko taku matua i ora ko taku whenua,
> Hei atawai ia matou aku tamariki.
> [I am an orphan. My parents have died, as has my brother, Te Hiko.
> My living parent is my land,
> Which cares for myself and my children.][3]

Oral traditions provide the reference point to intrinsic associations: the values, beliefs and knowledge of the people who claim origins from them. They also provide a reference point for the extrinsic associations: the lifeways and cultural practices governing the management of resources. Naming and claiming took place equally across both land and sea. All reefs, currents, tides and fishing grounds (to name a few) were considered part of the territory of each island group. These were sometimes contested and fought over, but always were known and utilised as significant territorial resources. Thus:

2　Tangaroa is the god of the seas and all living things within it; Papatūānuku is the Māori name for the Earth.

3　Extract, Letter from Metapere to George Grey, 1853, GNMA 453: *Te Wai-puna-a-hau, Metapere, Akuhata 2 1853*, in Vol. 3, Grey New Zealand Autograph Series, University of Auckland 'Special Collections'.

> [T]he notion of land and sea as one vast landscape, named and identified, will allow the notion of continued sovereignty over resources (land and sea-based) … [that] remain under the protection and sovereignty of the [Pacific] Nations that govern these territories. (Carter 2014: 67)

Over generations, knowledge expands to emphasise growth, exploration and migration—temporary or permanent—to other lands, both within and outside the Pacific region. There are varied reasons given for the movement, including networking, intermarriage for future beneficial alliances, war, population increases straining resources and environmental disasters or challenges.

Travelling is also part of being a contemporary Pacific-dweller and occurs via mapped highways across water, land and air that criss-cross Pacific spaces filled with named places. From the legendary voyages that first peopled the Pacific to outward migration to the Westernised Pacific Rim and to transnational circulation on modern aircraft, there are significant stories of travelling and dwelling outwards in circles from the homelands. These travels mirror those of ancient times and often occur for the same reasons: wealth, trade, adventure and kinship. At the base of all this travel and dwelling away from home are the cultural landscapes that keep people connected. They are the pivot from which travelling occurs and the central reference point for identity, to which we all return either spiritually or physically. They are not abandoned lands and are always referenced as the place of origin and identity:

> The idea of home is not the location in which they dwell; it is the place they are from and hence identity and claim is to that place. Migration or travelling is a temporary absence that does not sever ties that bind them to homelands and the subsequent responsibilities and obligations that go with belonging … [T]ravelling and dwelling away then is a circular process with the homeland as the pivot point for both nationhood and identity. (Carter 2014: 66)

Oral traditions are a key component of Indigenous knowledge frameworks as they transmit cultural patterns, values and lessons intergenerationally across time and space. The past holds knowledge that informs the present as each new challenge presents itself. Indigenous peoples 'have long multi-generational histories of interaction with the environment that include coping with variability, uncertainty and change' (Williams et al. 2013: 8). These multigenerational histories underpin and inform the way

Pacific Island nations understand and operate within their territories. This provides a strong foundation for the mitigation of and adaptation to contemporary challenges such as climate change that allows cultural integrity to be maintained. Indigenous knowledge, then, informs contemporary practices for Pacific peoples in the context of cultural sustainability and confirmed identity.

Indigenous knowledge no longer exists exclusively within a singular global context and has instead become part of the knowledge pathways that parallel those of other nations and cultures. Over time, these pathways must merge to incorporate non-Indigenous knowledge and practices to achieve the best possible outcome for challenges that arise. The merger of these parallel knowledge frameworks will provide a co-production of knowledge for meeting contemporary and future challenges, such as climate change. This co-production will become more important as resources are contested both within and from outside the Pacific region. Davidson-Hunt et al. (2013) note that 'coproducing knowledge in response to environmental change requires new institutional arrangements that provide community control, meaningful collaboration and partnership, and significant benefit sharing'. This can be best demonstrated through the collaborative efforts of countries such as Aotearoa New Zealand, Australia and the United States to provide development aid and programs to Pacific Island nations. The co-production of knowledge will ensure that adaptation and development occur not in isolation, but through complex interactions between different knowledge systems. Most importantly, this will be underpinned and informed by Pacific Indigenous knowledge frameworks and practices, many of which are couched in experiential and local knowledge that are informed by ancestral practices and reworked when changing circumstances come into play. Davidson-Hunt et al. (2013) refer to changing circumstances as a process of adaptation that has been forced on Indigenous societies through colonisation and the globalisation of natural resource markets. In resisting external acculturation of practices and policies, Indigenous peoples have adapted to change by 'incorporating knowledge, practices and technologies consistent with [First Nations] customs and values' (Davidson-Hunt et al. 2013). This has been achieved through developing relationships and networks that, in line with Pacific perspectives, may be useful immediately or later—for example, the Māori concept of whakawhanaungatanga ('managing relationships'), which provides guidelines for forming and sustaining relationships over a non-defined period. This generally requires adherence to a complex system of reciprocity that forms the basis of the ongoing relationship. The concept is also useful for understanding the relationships and network structures formed between Indigenous and non-Indigenous communities, organisations and businesses. The knowledge acquired from external relationships will allow new technologies, values and institutions to be incorporated into Indigenous knowledge frameworks to become part of the Indigenous community's response to environmental change (Davidson-Hunt et al. 2013). It is in this context of co-produced knowledge that adaptation to climate change–induced challenges in the Pacific will be addressed.

Let us return to the focus of this chapter: the challenges to notions of migration and statehood.

In a Pacific Island context, none of the key requirements for statehood can be analysed in isolation from the others. The land–sea–people continuum becomes evident when discussing statehood and identity—for example, if we look at the fourth criteria of the Montevideo Convention (the capacity to enter relations with other states), the relationships that have been built up over generations and that extend across the Pacific territories form the key framework for all other criteria to be met. Hence, the maintenance and establishment of relationships are the starting point for engagement with Pacific Island nations. As mentioned, Pacific relationships include those between land and sea, people and land, and people and sea—all are inclusive and interdependent. The statehood requirement for a defined territory is premised in a Pacific Island context on the history of origins, settlement and resettlement, negotiation, conquest, trade and intermarriage—all of which form the web of interrelating factors determining control over resources, including human resources.

Under the Montevideo Convention definition of the modern state, the key is recognition by other states of the continued control, governance and regulation of their territories and people. Crawford has pointed out that, when determining a state, the size of its territory has no minimum requirement and does not need precisely defined boundaries. The requirement is simply that 'the right to be a State is dependent at least in the first instance upon the exercise of full governmental powers with respect to some area of territory' (Crawford 2006: 46). Crawford goes on to say: '[T]he State must consist of a certain coherent territory effectively governed' (2006: 52). Another important point for territory is that it need not be contiguous: 'little bits of state can be held within another State's territory' (McAdam 2010: 109), such as Vatican City within Rome.

From an Indigenous perspective, Pacific territories have been determined from the first fishing up or throwing down of land, through travelling and networking and continued recognition of groups' power and status. These are regulated through relationships of obligation and reciprocity, including over resources and people, which are informed by past associations, practices and values. These, in turn, provide frameworks for contemporary and future sustainability and growth. Recognition of authority is the basis for parallel Indigenous political, governance, economic and social systems. These may have to incorporate non-Indigenous knowledge frameworks to provide co-production of knowledge for future environmental, economic, social and cultural sustainability, but the Indigenous frameworks must continue to underpin solutions to avoid loss of cultural integrity.

A contemporary Pacific example is the island of Rabi in Fiji, which was acquired by Kiribati to rehouse people displaced through phosphate mining. As noted by Jenny Bryant-Tokalau in Chapter 9, Kiribati has also recently purchased land within Fiji, though this has been fraught with controversy including criticism from I-Kiribati. Controversy aside, Kiribati now owns territory within Fiji as well as its own remaining ocean territories, allowing it to retain the criteria for statehood.

The second criterion for a state is the notion of a permanent population in the defined territory. Crawford (2006: 52) points out that the size of the population is not specifically defined but should be sufficient to render effective government possible, to enable a viable economy and control over its territory. This supposes that the permanent population must reside within the defined territory, but again, as Crawford (2006: 52) points out, this is not an explicit criterion. The idea of belonging to a particular place is firmly embedded in the very identity of Pacific peoples, but that belonging can be in a spiritual or a physical sense, or both. A Māori whakataukī (saying) succinctly sums up the notion that land is an identity pivot point for people coming and going continuously, generation after generation: 'Whatungarongaro he tangata, toitū he whenua hoki [People disappear, the land remains]' (Mead and Grove 2001: 425).

Regardless of where people disappear to, the land will be their central reference for identity and nationhood. The whakataukī upholds the idea that travelling and dwelling elsewhere do not erase one's identifying with a specific homeland. Land remains in physical form regardless of how many people dwell on it. The 'homeland' includes the ocean and the recognised authority of each oceanic group over their specific seaways; Hau`ofa's claim that the land and the sea are one demonstrates that they share the subsequent intrinsic and extrinsic values as prescribed by the associated groups. These sometimes manifest themselves as cultural symbols that provide a recognised and respected link with specific landscapes. Thus, cultural landscapes can also travel to new locations through the symbols that allow a recognised connection to a place and the people who both shaped and were shaped by it. The symbols then become reminders of the cultural landscape and identity of the people who have travelled away (Carter, L. 2010). There is a reciprocal obligation embedded in the relationship between people and place regardless of where those people are, and this will become more important as claims of authority over oceans and land become tenuous in the context of climate change–induced relocation. Subsequently, the acceptance and practice of Pacific travelling challenges the notion that peoples must live permanently within designated territories to be considered fully of that place.

David Gegeo's work on (re)visioning 'place' in the Pacific contextualises the ideas of space and place from the perspective of an Indigenous Pacific-dweller that also has parallels with Māori ways of knowing and acting. Gegeo's (2001: 492) work on Solomon Islands investigates indigeneity as 'a matter of physical space ... or cultural place ... and asks, "how do [Kwara'ae people] negotiate indigeneity in a time of cultural rupture and increasing transnational and interisland migration?"'. His work acts as a convenient framework for investigating notions of 'home' and 'away' in contemporary Pacific society. Gegeo defines place as, among other things, 'one's historical and cultural base'—the physical and geographic location of connection. He maintains that place also indicates 'having connection to land or unconditional right to access land through genealogy and marriage', and provides people attached to that place with an 'unquestioned right to speak on certain matters' regarding the place and the people genealogically connected to it. He also considers place as the seedbed for language, traditions and customs; by connecting with the place, there will be an automatic assumption that the person or people claiming connections to it will have a full understanding of such matters (Gegeo 2001: 493–94). Another important characteristic is that people associated with a place will have 'associated obligations and responsibilities that cannot go unfulfilled'. As Margaret Jolly so aptly noted: 'Those who have followed routes beyond the [ocean] still celebrate their roots back home. Peoples live in both spatialities and contextually deploy metaphors of both groundedness *and* mobility, settlement *and* detachment to articulate their being in the world' (2001: 425).

There are several historical and contemporary examples of populations across the Pacific moving from their state territory during times of environmental disaster. These movements away from the homelands involve calling on established relationships with ancient origins and are part of deliberate networking processes and systems. Paul D'Arcy (2006) describes the sawei system in the Caroline Islands that orders the maintenance of relationships there. One example described by D'Arcy is the movement of the island populations of Satawal and Lamotrek to Saipan in Guam after a severe earthquake in 1849. The refugees were able to settle on Saipan because of historical associations and the establishment of kin in the area. Although the refugees had planned to stay permanently, by 1851, only 267 people remained there, with the rest returning to their islands and 'the links forged with the Marianas [having] added to existing relationships, rather than replacing them' (D'Arcy 2006: 145–50). The value of D'Arcy's work in the Caroline Islands is the detailed description of the reciprocity that has built a network of relationships and obligation—a pattern repeated across the Pacific. Such movement occurred not only across oceanic territories, but also across landmasses. These, too, established intergenerational kin-based connections that enabled movement and periods of resettlement. D'Arcy (2006: 152) explains:

> The configuration of coral islands promoted inter-island ties … [M]any clans had members on a number of atolls they could call on … [T]hese links served as a safety net in case of drought, war, or storms. Each coral island's potential carrying capacity generally exceeded its actual population during optimum conditions, enabling refugees to be accommodated.

D'Arcy also states that 'a highly seasonal pattern of inter-island visits took place', confirming interisland travel as a necessary way of life for Pacific-dwellers. The citizens of Pacific Island nations have travelled and dwelt away from their homelands for millennia; this is part of what it means to be a Pacific Ocean–dweller. In terms of the second criterion for statehood, Pacific Island nations have their own notion of what is a population base, which raises the question of against whose terms and knowledge frameworks will the population criterion be tested? Evident within the historical record of travelling and dwelling away are the means used to maintain the relationships between the homeland, those dwelling there and those who have travelled away. It follows that any means of determining the population criterion other than through a Pacific lens would deny Pacific Island nations their right to determine who is and who is not considered among the permanent population, and what that number must be to maintain effective territorial government and resource management.

Pacific Island nations signed the Majuro Declaration on 5 September 2013 at Majuro in the Marshall Islands. The declaration was developed to highlight the commitment of the leaders of the Pacific Islands Forum to the reduction and phasing out of greenhouse gas pollution, with 'the leaders wanting to spark a new wave of climate change leadership' (PIF 2013). This demonstrated the Pacific nations' willingness and desire to become leaders on climate change adaptation within their region and the wider Pacific. The forum's secretary-general stated:

> So this is a declaration of responsibility. They [Pacific Islands Forum members] have pledged to commit themselves as climate change leaders and to demonstrate this leadership by attaching in this declaration what each is doing as part of their commitment to ameliorate emissions. (RNZ 2013)

This alone indicates that Pacific nations will take a leading role to ensure their own ways of understanding and knowing are at the forefront of climate change mitigation and adaptation in the Pacific.

Conclusion

The climate change dilemma Pacific Island nations face is largely not of their own making; however, the adaptation solutions they choose can be based on their own knowledge frameworks and processes that have been in place for generations. That said, adaptation to environmental change cannot occur in isolation and there will need to be cognisance of external knowledge to develop effective solutions and adaptation measures.

Territory is not just land. Under Indigenous Pacific lore, the land and the sea are one and the same, and form the expanded territorial areas of each state. The status of land territories after sea-level rise 'should not affect the legal status of the entity' (McAdam 2010: 7). The crux of territorial control is, according to McAdam, more about a state meeting the criterion for independence. This ensures the state has control over its affairs and activities within its defined territory and is not regulated by any other state

(McAdam 2010: 20). In the case of the Pacific Island states, then, it is the recognition by other states of the continued control, governance and regulation of their territories that is key.

Just as land and sea extend one from the other, so, too, does the relationship between people and territory, regardless of where most of the population resides. There is a historical pattern of travelling and dwelling that not only has its reference point firmly in the homeland, but also has strengthened and extended culture, identity and claims to nationhood. The examples from the Marianas of the historical planned 'systematic redwelling' (Carter 2014: 67) of human populations have contemporary equivalents that draw on past associations and relationships to ensure cultural and economic survival. The Pacific climate change discourse, then, needs to move away from the idea of climate change refugees forced into permanent migration. Instead, reference to historical and contemporary cyclical patterns of travelling and dwelling away will ensure an Indigenous perspective prevails when considering the notion of a state's permanent population.

Accompanying this is the knowledge of how the Pacific Islands identify and respond to Indigenous ways of understanding territory. This informs the governance and management processes that rely on past, present and future relationships. The discourse must emphasise Indigenous ways of knowing that will help create strategic frameworks for culturally relevant solutions to contemporary and future challenges. So, metaphorically speaking: the ocean is still throwing down and Māui will continue to fish.

The last word should perhaps go to former governor-general of Tuvalu, Sir Tomasi Puapua:

> Taking us as environmental refugees, is not what Tuvalu is after in the long run. We want the islands of Tuvalu and our nation to remain permanently and not be submerged as a result of greed and uncontrolled consumption for industrialised countries. We want out children to grow up the way we grew up in our own islands and in our own culture. (Puapua 2002)

12

Negotiating Political Climate Change Agency in the Pacific Region

Salā George Carter

A common opening statement from many Pacific Island negotiators at the twenty-first Conference of the Parties (COP21) of the United Nations Framework Convention on Climate Change (UNFCCC) was: 'I speak on behalf of the Pacific Small Islands Developing Group, and support the statements made by the AOSIS [Alliance of Small Island States] and LDC [Least-Developed Countries] and the positions of the G-77 China group …' These words reverberating through the negotiation rooms of the Paris Le Bourget Exhibition Centre in December 2015 may sound procedural to many, however, they signified the coming of age of Pacific political agency in international climate change negotiations. For the first time in the 20-plus years of such negotiations, the 14 Pacific Island state signatories[1] to the UNFCCC chose to speak and negotiate collectively as a regional coalition. Before 2015, the positions and voices of Pacific Island states were confined within the consensus of traditional regime coalitions of the AOSIS, LDC and the G-77, which includes China. This begs the question, what factors or processes brought about this collective action on the international climate stage?

---

1   Cook Islands, Fiji, FSM, Kiribati, Marshall Islands, Nauru, Niue, Palau, Papua New Guinea, Sāmoa, Solomon Islands, Tonga, Tuvalu and Vanuatu.

This chapter explores the coming of age of Pacific Island states in climate change negotiations, by tracing their work leading up to the Paris Agreement in 2015. It unpacks the work of Pacific Island states before Paris by asking: what are the processes and forms of political climate change agency in the Pacific region? Although participation as sovereign states is their political right, a deeper analysis of their behaviour before and during international meetings provides illuminating nuances of political agency. Within the study of international relations, political agency is assumed to be 'the practices of a collective, relatively stable actor that is more often than not institutional in form, guided by strategic and instrumental considerations, and transnational in practice and consideration' (Marchetti 2013: 4). This study utilises process-tracing techniques to follow the key moments, meetings, documents and political declarations in an ethnographic study of climate negotiators in 2015[2] to explain the factors and processes of climate change political action/agency by Pacific Island states. The existing literature tends to evaluate the political agency of Pacific states within the international level of the UNFCCC negotiations. It explains their agency through borrowed power, by them establishing coalitions with groups of similar countries like AOSIS or as part the Global South G-77–China coalition, as well as working with third-party media and NGOs (Betzold 2010; Carter 2016; Chasek 2005). This chapter moves beyond the confines of the UNFCCC and explains this political climate change agency at the regional level through the story of preparations for the Pacific negotiations in 2015.

Pacific Island leaders and negotiators were very aware of the global consciousness about achieving a new climate change agreement by the end of 2015. Regional responses from the Pacific in the form of high-level political meetings, declarations and political reform leading up to 2015 were in line with major events within the UNFCCC. The first section of this chapter will trace the efforts of the main Pacific regional organisation, the Pacific Islands Forum (PIF), and the Secretariat of the Pacific Regional Environment Programme (SPREP), especially its major climate declarations, which emphasised their serious investment in the UNFCCC process. This international–regional relationship is further articulated in the latter part of this chapter, which focuses on 2015, by analysing the multiple political declarations and strategic high-level meetings on the road to the Paris

---

2   The author conducted fieldwork in 2015 following the work of Pacific leaders and negotiators in multiple international and regional climate change meetings leading up to (and including) the 2015 COP21 in Paris. The 10 meetings were in Apia, Suva, Port Moresby, Bonn, New York and Paris.

Agreement. The flurry of political activity throughout the year reflected the urgency during the buildup that culminated in the formation of the Pacific Small Island Developing States (SIDS) group at the Paris meeting. These regional declarations are sites of power that help mobilise consensus and action. The more frequently these sites were utilised, the higher were the levels of coherence and group action that resulted.

Regional climate forums

The establishment of the UNFCCC to 'stabilize greenhouse gas concentrations in the atmosphere at a level that would prevent dangerous anthropogenic interference with the climate system' (UN 1992) initiated prolonged and complex climate negotiations. The 1997 Kyoto Protocol put forth a plan committing industrialised countries (Annex 1) to emissions reductions under the principle of common but differentiated responsibilities. In 2001, the Marrakesh Accords were agreed to, which detailed the rules for implementation of the Kyoto Protocol for 2005–12. The failure of the infamous 2009 Copenhagen Climate Change Summit for a post-2012 order (which was salvaged at the next meeting, in Cancún, Mexico, in 2010) meant the Kyoto Protocol would govern the climate regime for the period 2012–20. The 2015 Paris climate conference was to determine the rules of implementation for 2020–30. The difficulty of this never-ending process is compounded by the fact that the issue is of such a magnitude that it can only be tackled by a collective international response, eschewing national interests. Furthermore, for many countries, the impacts of climate change are not noticeable nor widespread enough to create collective political will for action among state leaders. The third issue is that any international solution requires policies that alter the behaviour of billions of people. Although evidence of climate change damage has mounted in the decade since Keohane and Victor's (2011: 7) perceptive analysis of the barriers to collective action just outlined, global actions of the magnitude sought by Pacific leaders remain elusive, although President of the United States Joe Biden's recent Leaders Summit on Climate offers reason for hope in terms of commitments at least.

The 197 signatory parties to the UNFCCC converge on an annual basis at the COP, where they form intrastate political groupings or coalitions. These coalitions are based on traditional alliances, regional affiliations or issue-based groupings that fall under the main division between the

Annex 1 Global North developed countries and the Global South under the G-77 and China group. The 14 Pacific Island states were part of six negotiation coalitions: G-77 and China, the Climate Vulnerable Forum, the LDC, the Coalition of Rainforest Nations, the Cartagena Dialogue for Progressive Action and the AOSIS (Carter 2016). These coalitions have not only enabled states to manage complexity in the UNFCCC regime, but also served as vehicles to carry positions in negotiating outcomes (Chasek 2005).

This tendency for states to negotiate national climate policies through coalitions at the UNFCCC level, balancing domestic and international politics in negotiating an agreement, is best explained by the two-level game-theory analysis by Putnam (1988). However, this assumption excludes a seldom-explored level of analysis in the literature on climate negotiations: the regional level. A consensus on common negotiating positions among Pacific Island states was sought through multilateral regional forums in the Pacific before these positions and strategies were taken to the international level.

In the Pacific, various political forums invested time and energy in preparing for the UNFCCC negotiations. The next section will focus on the PIF and the Pacific's main environmental organisation, the SPREP, and their work in the climate change negotiations space from the 1980s until the end of 2014. These forums have not only been at the forefront of creating and supporting a regional response to international climate change negotiations, but also shaped climate politics and governance within the Pacific.

Pacific Islands Forum

The PIF evolved out of the South Pacific Forum as many Pacific states achieved independence in the 1970s. From its original membership of five states in 1971, the PIF has expanded to 18 member states[3] and territories in the Pacific. International negotiations on climate change within the United Nations in the late 1980s were discussed at PIF leaders' meetings. The 1988 PIF leaders' communiqué highlighted their concerns about the economic and social impacts of a changing environment, and Australia affirmed its leadership in establishing a climate monitoring network for

---

3   The most recent inclusions as full members were in 2016 with the French territories of New Caledonia and French Polynesia. The PIF members are: Australia, Cook Islands, French Polynesia, Fiji, Kiribati, Marshall Islands, FSM, Fiji, Nauru, New Caledonia, Aotearoa New Zealand, Niue, Palau, Papua New Guinea, Sāmoa, Solomon Islands, Tonga, Tuvalu and Vanuatu.

the region (PIF 1988). However, the 1989 communiqué saw an elevation of the emphasis on climate change—in particular, on sea-level rise, to draw the world's attention to how this 'affected the South Pacific, and to represent regional views at appropriate international gatherings, possibly including by way of a resolution in the United Nations General Assembly' (PIF 1989). These conversations in the late 1980s and early 1990s mirrored international discussions about the creation of not only the Rio Earth Summit, but also the UNFCCC, in 1992. For the next two decades, this regional priority became a permanent fixture of the many PIF Secretariat (PIFS) communiqués.

Secretariat of the Pacific Regional Environment Programme

From the 1970s, regional environmental issues were handled by a divisional section of the Secretariat of the Pacific Community, which oversaw work on various regional conventions on the conservation of nature, protection of natural resources and the environment, anti-dumping and pollution. The secretariat evolved into a separate regional intergovernmental agency with headquarters in Apia, Sāmoa, in 1993, and was renamed the Secretariat of the Pacific Regional Environment Programme in 2004. A key governance arrangement for the SPREP and a vital link to the PIFS is the annual SPREP meeting of environment ministers to discuss and establish the environmental priorities for the region. This regional environmental consensus is then consolidated and endorsed at the PIF leaders' meetings. SPREP's mandate expanded from its early 1990s obligations as the principal intergovernmental environmental and sustainable development organisation to include climate change. The secretariat's four key divisions are: Biodiversity and Ecosystem Management, Waste Management and Pollution Control, Environmental Monitoring and Governance, and Climate Change. Intrinsic to SPREP's regional support on climate is its leadership role in providing technical advice and negotiation skills training for member states. The organisation continues to support the 14 Pacific states with their national communications for adaptation work programs and climate change mitigation efforts as party members of the UNFCCC (SPREP 2020).

Interplay and intensification of PIF and SPREP climate change efforts

While SPREP's work program of support for member countries with climate change adaptation, mitigation and policy implementation started to take shape in its first 10 years, it was not until 2005 that work on regional action and political responses intensified. The PIF member states, under the auspices of the SPREP, endorsed the Pacific Islands Framework for Action on Climate Change (PIFACC) 2005–15 as the implementation guide for plans and activities to address climate change in the region (SPREP 2020). The PIFACC created the biennial Pacific Climate Change Roundtable (PCCR) to bring together public, private and civil sectors to discuss and share information on existing climate change–related projects at all levels. The PCCR is a powerful conference and exposition involving climate change leaders, policymakers, practitioners, scientists, communities and individuals working within the climate change space in the Pacific.

The PIF's Niue Declaration on Climate Change in August 2008 was the first regional climate change declaration (PIF 2008). It was a call for global action in support of the multilateral UNFCCC system by strengthening members' contributions to adaptation projects and commitments to reducing greenhouse gas emissions. PIF states were to 'develop Pacific-tailored approaches to combating climate change, consistent with their ability to actively defend and protect their own regional environment, with the appropriate support of the international community' (PIF 2008). The Niue Declaration came about during heightened global political attention to the issue amid preparations for the COP15 in Copenhagen in 2009. The declaration, and the subsequent 2009 PIF leaders' call for action against climate change (PIF 2009), laid out key positions of convergence for the Pacific states to pursue at the talks, such as financing and capacity for adaptation and mitigation projects. Furthermore, it highlighted the necessity to develop capacity and support for negotiators attending the UNFCCC, whereby the SPREP and relevant Council of Regional Organisations in the Pacific (CROP) agencies were mandated to take the lead. This led to the establishment of regional preparatory meetings and negotiator training through the High-Level Support Mechanism (HLSM) for the Pacific as one of SPREP's key functions in its climate change work.

The Pacific's response: The Majuro Declaration

The diplomatic failure at the UNFCCC COP15 in Copenhagen in 2009 saw the establishment of the Ad Hoc Working Group on the Durban Platform for Enhanced Action (ADP) in Durban, South Africa, in 2011, with the task of producing the text for a post-2020 global climate agreement before the COP21 in 2015 (UNFCCC 2011). The ADP's mammoth task had a dual purpose: to execute a strategic, transparent process to reach a global consensus (the Paris Agreement text) among all 196 countries, while implicitly restoring the faith of the global community in the multilateral process through political and climate leadership. The general feeling in the 2011 and 2012 UNFCCC meetings was for the ADP to formulate a text that was not a top-down compliance system like the Kyoto Protocol, but rather, an inclusive, bottom-up approach in which countries submitted their emission targets and financial contributions. This exercise of seeking national contributions towards a global goal would require the same or greater political will than had hitherto been exercised.

The Pacific's regional response to this was the *Majuro Declaration for Climate Leadership* in September 2013 (PIF 2013). The declaration emphasised not only the political will and leadership of the region, but also the willingness and practicality of Pacific governments to experiment at the regional level. Under the stewardship of the Republic of the Marshall Islands as the chair of the PIF in 2013, the Majuro Declaration was an attempt by PIF countries to carry out the ADP's mandate. In demonstrating climate leadership, the then 16 PIF member countries submitted nationally determined contributions and commitment targets (both adaptation and mitigation measures) that would contribute to the global goal (PIF 2013). The declaration was heralded as the 'Pacific's gift' to the world (Manassah 2013) and was presented at the UN Secretary-General's Climate Summit in September 2013 to 'catalyze ambitious climate action and mobilize political will for a universal, ambitious and legally-binding climate change agreement by 2015' (PIF 2013). This declaration and its contributions would prove to be a helpful experiment for the region in materialising and understanding the process of achieving a global consensus on post-2020 actions on climate change to be decided in Paris in 2015.

Pacific climate change leadership in 2015

Events in 2015 exemplify the interplay of international and regional sites of Pacific Island political agency in climate change negotiations. This was a year of high drama and divergence in global climate change politics. Three interrelated UN multilateral agreements were concluded: the Sustainable Development Goals, the Third International Conference on Financing for Development and a text for a post-2020 climate change agreement for the UNFCCC. The ADP process was to conclude by December 2015 at the Paris meeting, but there would be five global preparatory meetings before then. The first was a Geneva session in February (ADP2-8) to compile a text from all positions, which was then streamlined in the negotiation sessions in June (ADP2-9), August (ADP2-10) and October (ADP2-11), with the fifth session in the first week of December (ADP-12) before completion. During ADP preparatory sessions, the work and positions of Pacific countries were carried out through the six traditional UNFCCC system coalitions outlined earlier.

As global climate negotiations intensified throughout 2015, the divergence on climate policy among the PIF members was brought to the surface between island states, on one side, and the continental states of Australia and Aotearoa New Zealand on the other. This divergence has always been apparent within UNFCCC politics, with Australia and Aotearoa New Zealand's priorities aligning with Annex 1 coalitions, while the island states found their voice in the AOSIS and G-77 political groupings. In line with the SIDS Accelerated Modalities of Action Pathway 2014 (SĀMOA Pathway 2015), Pacific Island states entered 2015 prioritising the status of special consideration of SIDS enshrined in a legally binding agreement, a long-term global temperature goal lower than 1.5 degrees, a standalone article and international mechanism to address loss and damage from climate change, and scaling up climate finance pledges before 2020 to support adaptation and mitigation projects (AOSIS 2015).

Oceania 21 Lifou Declaration

The ADP2-8 negotiations in February 2015 concluded with a 90-page working draft 'Geneva text'. Streamlining of the text would become the focus of two regional meetings to discuss and prepare for the next ADP session in June, the first of which was the Third Oceania 21 Summit on sustainable development, held in April in Nouméa, French Caledonia, and funded by the French Government. The summit included all 22 Pacific Island states and territories, including the metropoles of Australia, Aotearoa New Zealand and France. With the French holding the presidency of COP21 later in the year, it was no surprise that climate change negotiations were one of the main priorities of this summit. The key outcome was the Lifou ministerial declaration on climate change, which asserted that there was 'insufficient funding for mitigation and adaptation policy implementation, insufficient capacity building and transfer of technological advances, weakness of existing measures in terms of loss and damages as well as the lack of inclusion of civil society in climate negotiations' (Oceania 21 2015). The declaration was a reaffirmation of the key AOSIS positions, except for that on the long-term temperature goal, which by then included 'limiting global warming to less than 2ºC or even 1.5ºC' (Oceania 21 2015), and no explicit support for the creation of a new loss and damage mechanism. The participation of Annex 1 states (Aotearoa New Zealand, Australia and France) in Oceania 21 highlighted early the key areas of policy divergence on which Pacific Island states would have to focus to bring about a consensus on the 1.5-degree temperature goal and on loss and damage. The summit also provided the regional space, outside the formal UNFCCC process, for leaders and officials to discuss upcoming negotiations.

SPREP High-Level Support Mechanism

The same issues were also the focus of the SPREP HLSM (the first of two HLSM that year) held on the final day of the Pacific Climate Change Roundtable in May 2015. As part of the SPREP policy advice mandate, the HLSM continued the practice of the previous three years of utilising the services of the German NGO Climate Analytics to train and update officials from the 14 island states on the impending ADP process (Climate Analytics 2013–15). The HLSM was a closed one-day session for officials and technical experts to discuss the text and provided an update on the state of play and political dynamics of countries and coalitions in the regime and, more importantly, to strategise how the Pacific countries could engage in the negotiations through coalitions before the next meeting in Bonn. The training utilised seasoned leading Pacific negotiators from the formal UNFCCC process and stressed the importance of a united Pacific voice under AOSIS.

The second and most important HLSM was held in Apia, Sāmoa, in November and brought together state negotiators and ministers as well as representatives from all CROP and Pacific Islands Development Forum (PIDF) regional bodies for political negotiation updates and media training. The intensive three-day meeting was held in a secluded resort to strategise and align coordinating positions before Paris. As always, it was scheduled one month before COP and after the PIF leaders' meeting from which it would receive its regional mandate and priorities.

The formal UNFCCC negotiations at the Bonn ADP2-9 in June achieved very little in streamlining the Geneva text, as discussions focused more on procedures than negotiation. Meanwhile, momentum was building in the Pacific with subregional groupings meeting within a day of each of other in mid-July: the three states in the northern Pacific, Marshall Islands, Palau and FSM; the Micronesian Presidents' Summit (MPS); and the seven-member Polynesian Leaders Group (PLG) of Tahiti, Cook Islands, Sāmoa, American Sāmoa, Tuvalu, Tokelau and Tonga. The climate meeting for the Melanesian Spearhead Group was hosted in 2014. As expected, climate change negotiations and the road to Paris were prominent in both MPS and PLG meetings.

MPS Boknake Haus Communiqué

The MPS was established in 2001 to enable the presidents of Palau, Marshall Islands and FSM to meet each year to discuss 'working together to improve communication and planning on areas of common interest to their nations and to the region' (Gallen 2016). Since the first summit, climate change—or, more precisely, the UNFCCC negotiations and seeking a greater role and voice for Micronesia—has always been part of the MPS agenda. The forum hosted in Marshall Islands in 2015 produced the Boknake Haus Communiqué, which, among many subregional initiatives, set out a plan of action for the three states and their role on the 'road to Paris' (MPS 2015). The three presidents agreed on the positions they wished AOSIS to pursue, especially the 1.5-degree target. Furthermore, it was agreed there would be joint coordination and communication in Paris, with Marshall Islands offering to present a Micronesia pavilion at the COP21 expo to showcase the vulnerability of the islands to climate change and, more importantly, its leadership on climate action at home and its commitments in the international climate negotiation process (MPS 2015).

PLG Taputapuātea Declaration

One day after the release of the Boknake Haus Communiqué, the PLG's *Taputapuātea Declaration on Climate Change* was made public (PLG 2015). Taputapuātea returned to AOSIS's original red-line positions on the 1.5-degree temperature goal and emphasis on mechanisms to address loss of territorial integrity. Diverging from other Pacific calls for action was the Taputapuātea Declaration's Polynesia Against Climate Threats (PACT)—a call to revitalise an issue that had not so far been emphasised in formal negotiations: climate justice (population displacement, natural and cultural heritage) and the importance of oceans (PLG 2015). The PLG differed from other regional groupings in that its members came together more on grounds of cultural understanding than on economic trade matters or integration. This cultural affinity underpins the strong stance on the linkage of climate change to people and culture—and to climate justice, which seems less prominent in other declarations. By the end of the Bonn ADP2-10 negotiations in late August, great strides had been made in reducing the text by half, down to 45 pages. However, procedural questions about insertions to the text continued to slow the process and frustrate negotiators.

PIDF Suva Declaration

At the same time as the Bonn ADP2-10 was happening, the third annual PIDF Summit was taking place in Suva, Fiji. The newest institution in regional politics, the PIDF describes itself as 'distinctively Pacific', in that it is an islands-only organisation that does not include non-Pacific development partners as full members. Despite promoting membership exclusivity, it also practised inclusiveness by incorporating the civil and private sectors in most discussions as equal stakeholders with government leaders.

Under the theme 'Building Climate-Resilient Blue Economies', the 500-plus attendees, including seven Pacific heads of state,[4] the UN special envoy on climate change, the Commonwealth secretary-general, the deputy prime minister of Thailand and observers from non-Pacific governments, were divided into three breakout sessions—government, civil and private—with the task of formulating 'key messages' or priorities for the Pacific to take to the Paris COP21. These suggestions were circulated in a document for

---

4   Fiji, Solomon Islands, Kiribati, Tuvalu, Marshall Islands, Vanuatu and FSM.

further discussion before being compiled as the *Suva Declaration on Climate Change* (PIDF 2015). The declaration returned to the key positions of limiting global temperature increase to less than 1.5ºC, a standalone clause on loss and damage and 100 per cent financing for adaptation measures for Pacific SIDS. In addition, the open, participatory nature of the summit saw prominence given to support and climate action from civil and private sector players and action on gender-based inequality and discrimination.

While the Suva Declaration reaffirmed these key positions, it also went much further in calling for any agreement from the Paris COP to include developing low-carbon sea transport, a moratorium on extractive fossil fuel industries and mechanisms for the payment of ocean and ecosystem services. These three issues were not reflected in the final Paris agreement; not only were they introduced late in the negotiating rounds, but also they were deemed to be outside the parameters of the convention.

Smaller Island States leaders' declaration on climate change action

One week after the release of the Suva Declaration, the mood changed from optimism to uncertainty as leaders converged in Port Moresby for the PIF leaders' meeting. Before all 16 leaders met, the seven-member[5] Smaller Island States (SIS) subgroup met, on 7 September. This subgroup had been part of the PIF institutional framework in the 1980s but was given teeth from 2006 with a formal structure to better advocate for the peculiar needs of this group (PIF n.d.). The SIS leaders usually met separately, but in Port Moresby, their meeting was incorporated into the official program and used the same venue. It was clear from the beginning of the SIS meeting that a political declaration on climate change was required, prompted by a feeling, as one SIS official noted, that Australia and New Zealand 'will water down our positions from the Suva declaration' (PIF 2015).

All previous regional meetings in 2015 (Oceania 21, MSP, PLG, PIDF) and the upcoming PIF leaders meeting had circulated working drafts of a declaration for contributions in advance. However, the Port Moresby SIS declaration was proposed and written in the lunch hour on the day of the meeting (PIF 2015). While reaffirming the position of AOSIS and other regional declarations, the SIS declaration noted that negotiations needed

---

5   Cook Islands, Palau, Nauru, Kiribati, Marshall Islands, Niue and Tuvalu.

to be about more than just economic matters; at the very least, they were also about 'survival and security' (Mou 2015). As the SIS chair, President of Palau Tommy Remengesau Jr, told the media: 'We need to be frank and honest with reality. And the reality is that it is upon us and whether it is 1.5 or 2 percent, we are already seeing the impact of climate change in Small Island Countries' (PIF 2015). The sense of urgency and fear about a watered-down PIF text had already played out in the media and academic circles as a showdown on regional climate diplomacy (Fry 2015a; Cochrane 2015). Despite the numerous declarations from the Pacific, 'it would be the PIF declaration that is read and circulated within the UN' (Sopoaga 2015).

PIF Port Moresby call for climate action

Although Australia and Aotearoa New Zealand participated in Oceania 21, the PIF leaders' meeting in Port Moresby was the occasion in the leadup to Paris for Pacific Island countries to test reaching a consensus with their regional Annex 1 partners. While the plenary session and photo opportunities with leaders were grandiose, jovial affairs, there was some uneasiness among climate change policymakers, as the ADP2-10 had just finished in Bonn over the weekend and the talks were deadlocked. The PIF plenary meeting allowed for frank discussions between state leaders and regional organisations about how they should conduct their work in Paris. The premier of Niue Sir Toke Talagi compared climate change to a 'slow cancer' and proposed that, instead of 'making declaration after declaration, the region needs to be pragmatic' (Talagi 2015). This prompted statements from Prime Minister of Tuvalu minister Enele Sopoaga on the role of a regional diplomatic strategy in coordinating and sharing resources and knowing 'how to speak as one voice in Paris' (Sopoaga 2015). The heads of both the SPREP and the Secretariat of the Pacific Community (SPC) reassured leaders about the one-team approach of the CROP, whose personnel would travel with and support the country delegations.[6] While the plenary meeting reached an understanding on shared support, it was also 'not just one voice but many voices with one message' (Tukuitonga 2015).

This message would come in the form of a PIF declaration. Two months earlier, the Forum Officials Committee had drafted a proposed PIF declaration that was circulated to the Pacific capitals. Two days before the

---

6   The CROP brings together several intergovernmental organisations: SPC, SPREP, PIF, Forum Fisheries Agency, Pacific Islands Development Program, South Pacific Travel Organisation, University of the South Pacific, Pacific Aviation Safety Organisation and the Pacific Power Association.

PIF leaders' retreat, a special drafting group met multiple times to finalise the text. Australia, Aotearoa New Zealand and Papua New Guinea were able to fly their negotiators from the ADP2-10 Bonn sessions to participate in the meetings of the drafting group. One participant in the drafting sessions noted that the expertise and strategic manoeuvres of these technical experts gave their countries the upper hand in 'playing with [the] text … [D]espite the passion and willingness seen on some of [the] Pacific faces—they couldn't push hard enough'.[7] The draft negotiations were completed on 9 September and delivered to the leaders' retreat for final approval.

The outcome was the Port Moresby PIF Leaders' *Declaration on Climate Change Action 2015*. On the surface, it seemed most of the key requests were listed, including the 1.5-degree temperature cap and the loss and damage requirement. But on closer inspection, while the 1.5°C figure was listed, the declaration followed the language of the UNFCCC COP20 decision on 'holding the increase in global average temperature below 2°C or 1.5°C above pre-industrial levels' (UNFCCC 2014). On the issue of loss and damage, the text was ambiguous on two grounds: while it was listed as a stand-alone issue, this did not mean it had a stand-alone clause in the agreement; and the text did not support a new mechanism for loss and damage, but rather only continuing the work of the Warsaw International Mechanism for Loss and Damage. As expected, given the hardline stance of the Australian Government of Tony Abbott, any mention of a moratorium on coalmines and fossil fuels or mechanisms on sustainable sea transport did not make it into the final text. Rather, the text was obscured by jargon and layers of textual diplomatic manoeuvring. The declaration attempted to hide the divergence in positions by inserting into the text the terms '1.5 and Loss and Damage', which was called 'creative ambiguity' by some commentators (Fry 2015b).

Conclusion: Political climate agency in the Pacific region

The account here of regional political action on climate change negotiations resonates with the thesis outlined in the emerging 'new Pacific diplomacy', which more assertively represents Pacific Island interests in global forums. This new approach emphasises collective action by Pacific states using an

---

7   Pacific Island negotiator, interview by George Carter, 2015.

'assertive attitude, the emphasis on Pacific Island control of the diplomatic agenda, the creation of new institutions, its appeal to regional identity, and its concern with negotiating global agendas that are impacting Pacific societies' (Fry and Tarte 2016: 3). This chapter reveals a new form of diplomatic behaviour since 2009 in which Pacific states have been proactive in regional political climate action. This climate leadership has not been limited to the international UNFCCC level, but, more importantly, has been formulated in and sourced from multiple sites of regional and subregional power. Furthermore, this chapter's analysis of agency sheds light on the underappreciated and under-researched role of regional informal negotiation processes in the global climate change regime.

While the regional and subregional meetings and their respective declarations act as forums to share and strategise positions, they are also sites for socialisation and open, informal processes of negotiations. Leaders, negotiators and observers were in constant contact throughout 2015, refining and testing positions with one another. The year's meetings provided them with a platform to create relationships and networks that would prove helpful in negotiations once they arrived in Paris.

While the main regional sites were limited to the PIF and the SPREP before 2015, during that year, a wide variety of old and new institutions sought to become involved in building political will. All political forums in the Pacific were mobilised, from the subregional (MPS, PLG, Melanesian Spearhead Group,[8] SIS) to new institutions (PIDF) and traditional ones (PIF, SPREP). While there was little or no coordination between the meetings throughout the year, a pattern of importance emerged. Most of the meetings in the early half of the year were subregional, at which there was little or no divergence of opinion, while the meetings at the end of the year were political and tense in nature, before culminating in the premier PIF meeting that brought together the 16 Pacific leaders. The participation of Annex 1 nations Australia and Aotearoa New Zealand, with their differing climate policies, provided an opportunity for the other 14 Pacific states to test key positions on the issue of loss and damage and the long-term temperature goal. The outcome not only indicated what positions would survive, but also tested leaders' and negotiators' assumptions about global negotiations still to come.

---

8   The Melanesian Spearhead Group's position on climate change is linked to its *Declaration on Environment and Climate Change*.

This chapter also illuminates the extraordinary leadership abilities and proactive diplomatic experiments Pacific states were willing to take to show the world their commitment to the UNFCCC regime. The various declarations were not just consensual statements for the region, but also calls for greater political commitments and will from the global community. The Majuro Declaration was a political experiment in which the Pacific was the first region to try to emulate a multilateral agreement with individual country targets. This bottom-up approach, instead of the usual top-down compliance system, would go on to be replicated in the final Paris Agreement.

The coming of age of a Pacific coalition in the UNFCCC may be explained by the maturity of its work within the international climate change frameworks, which was a product of regional preparations at multiple sites of power. The regional negotiation processes acted as a clearing house for positions to take to the international UNFCCC. The high frequency of meetings socialised both state leaders and negotiators and offered lessons on how to achieve consensus on key positions and how to formulate effective collective action.

Section Four:
Pacific Lessons
for Humanity

Introduction: Knowledge adapted and shared—Pacific lessons for humanity

Paul D'Arcy and Daya Dakasi Da-Wei Kuan

This final section examines how local Indigenous strengths can be used to enhance engagement with the world without compromising social cohesion and environmental systems. This section also suggests that the various accommodations between local values and global engagement discussed have beneficial application beyond the worlds reviewed. This section begins with a review of how Māori farming enterprises are responding to government incentives and directives on greenhouse gas mitigation by a team consisting of Steve Wakelin, Phil Journeaux and Graham West, and led by Māori economist Tanira Kingi. The chapter also discusses how Māori have successfully balanced their collective social organisation and cultural development objectives with modern business principles in the export-focused rural sector of Aotearoa New Zealand. This combination of traditional values and modern business practices has much wider applicability in the Indigenous Pacific. The high number of owners per economic unit can potentially render decision-making cumbersome, however, and has required the formation of governance structures such as trusts and incorporations. The authors note that Māori collective landownership structures rose out of traditional practices. Today, their governance structures primarily take the form of trusteeships, committees of management or directorships of entities arising from government compensation payments for past state injustices in breach of the 1840 Treaty of Waitangi between the Crown and Māori.

It is only in the present generation that the New Zealand Government has acknowledged the 150-year history of forced alienation and occupation of Māori land by European settlers and the immense suffering and social dislocation caused (Kawharu 1977; Walker 2004; Ruru et al. 2011; Ruru 2018; Māori Land Court 2022). The government has recently made available incentives to reduce greenhouse gas emissions. Māori entities face competing pressures to intensify output for income generation through profitable, yet environmentally problematic, pastoral activities such as dairy farming and diversifying into other forms of production with lower environmental impacts. Collective landownership has proven compatible with good business practices. This successful combination of social values and sound business practice has enabled the social and cultural values desired by collective stakeholders to be inserted into objectives such as restoring and establishing wetlands or the expansion of Indigenous forestry. These activities may generate lower cash revenues but return higher cultural values by supporting diverse ecosystems. The reduced revenue is not of a magnitude to threaten business viability and, in fact, often enhances long-term prospects for sustainable ecosystems and economic returns.

The next chapter in this section, by Bougainville community development researcher Anita Togolo, examines how Indigenous social organisation influences the growing of crops for subsistence and income-generating export. Indigenous land tenure was less disrupted by colonial rule in Papua New Guinea than in Aotearoa New Zealand and Indigenous peoples remain the overwhelming majority of the population and still have tenure over 97 per cent of the land. Despite Papua New Guinea's considerable mineral, forest, agricultural and marine wealth, most of the population remains rural and practices subsistence agriculture, partly supplemented with cash cropping. Togolo examines a longstanding debate among economists and anthropologists about whether customary collective land tenure inhibits economic development or whether privatisation of land offers the best means of ensuring adaptable and resilient modernising economies (Crocombe 1971; Finney 1973; Crocombe and Meleisea 1994; Ward and Kingdom 1995; Fingleton 2005; Fingleton and ToLopa 2008; Weiner and Glaskin 2007). She does so by looking in detail at the traditional matrilineal descent systems and economic output of the Nagovisi and Nasioi peoples of the Autonomous Region of Bougainville. Togolo concludes that the matrilineal systems of the two peoples are flexible and resilient and are a solid foundation on which to develop modern cash cropping. This assessment is based on the experiences with cash cropping of cocoa in Bougainville's fertile soils from the 1960s. She concludes that matrilineal organisation in these cases 'can provide a stable platform for commercial industries and for new opportunities in business development, while helping Bougainville keep its valuable social systems intact'.

Chapter 15 addresses local concerns about retaining young people in Indigenous villages—in this case, among the Tayal community of Cinsbu in Taiwan's rugged, mountainous interior. Authors Ai-Ching Yen and Yin-An Chen argue that skilful and inclusive community action based on traditional principles of collective economic action, organisation and widespread consultation has set the community on the path to sustainable development. This development is driven by community priorities rather than external forces through modifying existing cultural assets to meet changing conditions. Yen and Chen show how moving to organic farming and modifying generations of agroforestry practice to meet current market needs have placed cultivation on a more sustainable footing, supplemented by teaching Tayal ways to visitors and selling traditional weaving and woodwork. This cultural ecotourism centred on homestays has created extra employment across the community as well as increasing the connection between young Tayal and the elders who are the guardians of this learning. These traditional strengths were enhanced by forming a business group to assist in seeking government grants and advise on business planning.

The examples in the previous three chapters of the successful blending of local priorities and adapted external features raise the question of the extent to which the alternative Indigenous practices outlined in this collection have wider applicability beyond their immediate contexts. The next three chapters in this section address different aspects of this potential for transfer and adaptation, both within and beyond the lands and seas of their ancestral diaspora. In Chapter 16, Samoan academic Roannie Ng Shiu and her New Zealand colleague Paul D'Arcy discuss how Indigenous peoples in southern Chile are reaching out to Indigenous peoples in the Pacific to investigate the efficacy of their development models for their own needs. The Chilean Government and the Mapuche peoples, who make up around 10 per cent of Chile's population, have expressed a keen interest in drawing on the success of Māori models of economic empowerment and cultural development. Māori form 15 per cent of Aotearoa New Zealand's population and the Māori economy is worth approximately $50 billion, which represents about 6 per cent of the country's total asset base. Aotearoa New Zealand has a similar export-orientated economy to Chile and the two landscapes share similar habitats as lands that were once joined before humans roamed the Earth. Māori interactions with Indigenous peoples in

Chile have begun to intensify in the past decade, culminating in an official visit to Chile by Minister for Māori Development Nanaia Mahuta in 2019 (Mahuta 2019). Māori-run cultural and ecotourism ventures and business models, resource management strategies and education initiatives have been of particular interest to Mapuche and other Chilean Indigenous peoples (Te Puni Kōkiri 2013; de la Maza 2018). They have also interacted with Pacific success stories such as that of Sāmoa, where tradition and modernity have been reconciled better than most places around the globe in terms of appropriate economic, educational and health measures (Hassall 2018). These links are based on more than shared experiences of colonialism; there is now mounting evidence that the Mapuche have Polynesian ancestry (Ramírez-Aliaga 2010).

In Chapter 17, Ecuadorian sustainable development advocate and member of a community-based environmental NGO in the Galápagos Islands José Guerrero Vela provides a cautionary tale about the potential difficulties of applying environmentally beneficial concepts in contexts different to those in which they arose. Sumak Kawsay, the development model incorporated in the 2008 Ecuadorian Constitution, is based on the Kichwa Indigenous cosmology and can be broadly translated as 'good living'. As Guerrero notes, the Sumak Kawsay concept integrates social and environmental wellbeing as interdependent processes and provides constitutional legal rights to Pachamama (Mother Earth). The disjuncture between consistently principle-based national and international legislation on the one hand and its implementation at the local level in a myriad of political power relations and environmental conflicts on the other has already been noted, especially in Chapter 5. Guerrero Vela provides a detailed example of how non-Indigenous Galápagos fishers' financial losses due to sea lion predation of commercially valued species jeopardised their coexistence with the animals and made implementing the Sumak Kawsay–based national socio-environmental framework problematic. Fisherfolk felt marginalised economically by government legislation and shut out of decision-making bodies on human–nature relations, which were deemed to be the realm of scientists. Guerrero Vela makes the important point that improved human–nature relations will be undermined by a lack of attention to social justice issues. Ironically, further offshore, far greater threats to the fishers' livelihoods went unchecked in the form of massive commercial fishing fleets and the atmospheric and ocean pollution emanating from the fossil fuel–driven global industrialisation that is the source of the current existential threat to planetary life.

Until the time comes when the world's most powerful nations and biggest polluters agree to take effective action to control the pollution and pillaging of the oceans, the Indigenous management regimes outlined in Section Two are allowing some ecosystems and species to survive and even revive within MPAs. The ban on shark-finning in most Pacific Island nation EEZs, for example, has already allowed shark numbers to revive within these refuges, while their open-ocean kin continue to be decimated by industrial shark-finning. Large-scale shark-finning has now reached across the entire width of the Pacific to the shores of the Americas to feed East Asian market demand. The contrast between practice and consequences for sharks is nowhere more apparent than in the Galápagos MPA discussed in Chapter 17. Each dusk, distant-water fishing vessels gather on the boundaries of the MPA to slip across at night and harvest its relatively plentiful fish in numbers far too great for Ecuador's limited number of patrol vessels to halt (Bergen 2016; Alava and Paladines 2017).

Against this background in the ultimate disputed commons—the unpoliced spaces of the Pacific Ocean out of sight of land—marine biologist and artist Melody Tai ends this section by investigating the potential for developing a new global environmental management framework spurred in part by the Ecuadorian legislation Guerrero Vela describes. Tai examines recent debates in academia about whether rising awareness of the existential threat to planetary life from modern global economic practices is altering the way we conceptualise the relationship between society and nature, bringing it more in line with Indigenous peoples' views of and respect for nature. She then looks at how this concept has been enshrined in national legislation and government practices across the South Pacific, in Ecuador and Aotearoa New Zealand, where natural elements such as rivers and the ocean have been given legal personality, which entails legal rights and protections. In May 2015, Secretary-General of the Pacific Islands Forum Secretariat Dame Meg Taylor, became the world's first politically endorsed ocean advocate as the Pacific Ocean commissioner. Legislation alone will not bring about a change of attitude or practice. Legal recognition combined with more frequent mentions in political and educational discourse, as well as highlighting working examples of enhanced social and ecological resilience and recovery, such as those outlined here, offer the best hope for widespread and fundamental change. Attitudes already noticeable among the young show that consensus is moving more in line with Indigenous peoples' views of, and respect for, nature.

13

Collective Land Tenure Systems and Greenhouse Gas Mitigation among Māori Farmers in Aotearoa New Zealand

Tanira Kingi, Steve Wakelin, Phil Journeaux
and Graham West

Introduction

In this chapter, we focus on the link between collective land tenure systems and investment in strategies to reduce environmental impacts, particularly greenhouse gas (GHG) emissions. Collective landownership structures among Māori in Aotearoa New Zealand have evolved from traditional ownership systems since the late 1800s to produce governance structures that include a combination of trusts and quasi-corporate structures under separate land tenure legislation. Recent government policy has focused on the development of underutilised Māori land—in particular, conversion to high-intensity pastoral farming such as dairying. This chapter documents the first stage of a three-year study with a case study of 29 Māori entities (te kāhui aro whenua, or kāhui) in different regions of Aotearoa New Zealand and the underlying principles, values and knowledge systems that influence Māori landowners of these structures. We examine their status in terms of GHG emissions and discuss the consequences of intensification versus diversification into alternative production systems with lower environmental impacts. This chapter does not present the results of the modelled GHG mitigation options for production systems and land use change scenarios. These are outlined in the conference proceedings of the 2016 International Rangelands Conference (Kingi et al. 2016) and the more detailed description of scenarios is presented in a 2020 report for the New Zealand Agricultural Greenhouse Gas Research Centre (Journeaux and Kingi 2020).

The first stage of the study focuses on understanding the legislative background that has shaped the Māori land tenure system and the cultural context that influences governance and decision-making among Māori landowners. The key question we ask is: what is the profile of GHG emissions among Māori farmers? Subsequent reports will document the results of mitigation strategies and the levels of preparedness and willingness to invest in change to reduce GHG emissions. This first-stage report will develop a set of baseline emissions profiles for the case study group and lay the groundwork to explore the influence of cultural imperatives and collective ownership on the design of sustainable production systems.

Māori pastoral agriculture

Māori farmers are a minority in Aotearoa New Zealand's pastoral production sector, with an estimated national contribution of about 8–10 per cent of national milksolids production and 10–15 per cent of national sheep and beef stock units. These statistics, however, are difficult to verify given the lack of 'ethnicity' or 'ownership' identifiers in national industry datasets. Despite the lack of accurate data, the Māori contribution to these industries is increasing, as government-owned farms are returned to Māori control under Treaty of Waitangi settlements (Wheen and Hayward 2012), underutilised land is converted to higher productive uses under government-led initiatives focused on Māori economic development (Te Puni Kokiri 2015) and regional development initiatives are implemented as outlined in the government's Business Growth Agenda (NZ Government 2022).

Increased activity in the pastoral sector will create a greater requirement to increase resource efficiency and farm productivity while lowering GHG emissions. Aotearoa New Zealand ratified the UNFCCC in 1993 and the Kyoto Protocol in 2002 and has committed to submitting an annual inventory of, and reducing, GHG emissions. Aotearoa New Zealand's main domestic policy measure for reducing GHG emissions is the Emissions Trading Scheme (ETS). Forestry entered the ETS in 2008 and the post-farmgate sector of the agricultural industry has been reporting on emissions since 2012, although without facing an emissions liability. The date for the inclusion of the on-farm biological component of the industry is unknown.

The future imposition of GHG emissions charges (or a carbon tax) on Māori farming businesses will have a major impact on the viability of these operations. In some regions, farms are already facing restrictions on or charges for nutrient discharges. The *National Policy Statement for Freshwater Management* came into effect in September 2020 and introduced sweeping changes for regional councils to consult and engage with iwi under the Te Mana o te Wai provisions (Ministry for the Environment 2020). In July 2022, the Climate Change Commission (2022) submitted its statutory Agricultural Progress Assessment advice to the minister for climate change on the He Waka Eke Noa proposal for farm-level emissions pricing. There is a high correlation between nutrient discharge and GHG emissions. This chapter explores how well positioned Māori are to respond to GHG accounting and we investigate the role that cultural values and collective governance structures play in designing farm systems and diverse landscapes that reduce GHG emissions.

The second section provides an overview of the Māori land estate, governance structures and cultural values that are common across the diverse Māori landowning groups. Section three describes te kāhui aro whenua, a case study group of 29 Māori farmers/farming entities in different regions of Aotearoa New Zealand. Section four outlines the GHG mitigation strategies of this group, and we conclude by discussing the influence cultural values and governance structures have on their ability to invest in changes to their production systems that will lead to more resilient, sustainable farms with better environmental outcomes.

Utilisation of Māori land and the business growth agenda

The underutilisation of Māori land has been a focus of industry, government and Māori for several decades or more. In 2013, the Ministry for Primary Industries produced a report on growing the Māori land base (MPI 2013), the recommendations of which were based on a 2011 Ministry of Agriculture and Forestry report on Māori agribusiness (Ministry of Agriculture and Forestry 2011). The 2013 report was responsible for the estimate of

NZ$7.9 billion in additional gross output based on the assumption that 970,000 hectares of Māori land was either underutilised or unproductive and that this land could be transferred into high-value dairy, sheep and beef production.

This figure—subsequently rounded up to NZ$8 billion by the media and policy advisors—is underpinned by an increase in gross output from the 80 per cent of Māori land (or almost 1 million hectares) classified as unproductive or underutilised. The most current assessment of the Māori asset base, from 2020, was estimated at NZ$42 billion (Schulze 2020). This estimate includes assets held by Māori under the Te Ture Whenua Māori, post-settlement treaty entities and assets owned by individuals including businesses and residential properties. The entities in this report are predominantly those entities under *Te Ture Whenua Māori Act 1993* (*TTWMA*).

Māori governance structures and cultural constructs

A description of Māori farming in Aotearoa New Zealand needs to start with a description of the land tenure system. The outline here will be brief given the availability of several references that provide a comprehensive description of Māori land legislation or Te Ture Whenua Māori (New Zealand Parliament 1993; Boast 1999).

Most Māori have a genealogical connection to their ancestral land, while also owning or leasing general land. A key point is that most Māori do not live on or derive a living from their ancestral lands. Because of title fractionation or increases through succession that are registered against titles (Kingi 2009b), the legislative system has resulted in high numbers of owners per title who have small individual interests and very low levels of influence over decision-making. The current estimate is 2.71 million registered interests with an average of 99 owners per title (Te Puni Kōkiri 2014). High numbers of owners not only increase the costs of administration of these land blocks because of the need to establish governance entities (such as trusts), but also mean decision-making is cumbersome and expensive (Kingi 2014). *Te Ture Whenua Māori Act 1993* remains in place and its most recent amendment was in October 2021.[1] The structures used under the current legislation will be described in more detail in the next section (Kingi 2008).

---

1   Available from: www.legislation.govt.nz/act/public/1993/0004/latest/DLM289882.html.

The Māori land estate

The most recent assessment of Māori land estimates a total of 1.77 million hectares owned collectively by Māori hapū (clans or extended family units). Given the space limitations, a comprehensive description is not possible but can be obtained via the Ministry of Māori Development (Te Puni Kōkiri 2014).

Governance structures: Trusts and incorporations

Most Māori farmers (or Māori farming entities) fall into one of two structures: the ahu whenua trust, which is designed to manage blocks of Māori land with multiple owners and is the most common structure used by Māori landowners; and the Māori incorporation, a body corporate with perpetual succession and powers that, in form and basic structure, are similar to a joint stock company. These are registered under the current legislation, the *TTWMA*.

In contrast with New Zealand's pastoral sector, where most farmers are owner-operators, Māori farming is made up primarily of absentee-owner structures that are governed by boards, trustees or committees of management. Decision-making by committee is also a contrast with the average owner-operator structure, where the individual farmer makes most decisions. Māori organisations, in general, will have a governance board and advisors, including farm consultants, accountants and other specialists. Governance skills are therefore critical to the success of organisations that are cumbersome and expensive to maintain, and decision-making is slow given the need to balance multiple objectives. Māori land representatives are charged with the responsibility of protecting the interests of landowners who can number in the thousands. Whenua (land) has a specific role in the cultural identity and social fabric of Māori and therefore decisions about its use must reflect the cultural values and aspirations of the land's owners.

Cultural values and Māori agribusiness

The management of land and water within a Māori framework is a blend of cultural norms and modern practices. Māori knowledge, values and concepts such as tikanga (practice, convention), mātauranga (knowledge, understanding), āhuatanga (characteristics, attributes) and kaitiakitanga (guardianship, stewardship) are often described within holistic frameworks

(Smith 2000). These frameworks acknowledge that increasing productivity in the Māori land-based sector, while also balancing economic growth with the ethic of kaitiakitanga, is a complex issue. Due to the wide range of iwi (tribe), hapū (subtribe) and whānau (family) perspectives, it is critical that the complexity and diversity (nga tini āhuatanga) within Māori communities are retained.

Growth of the Māori agribusiness sector requires the integration of science and Māori knowledge systems while also adhering to iwi/hapū expectations of environmental sustainability. Capturing science and Māori knowledge systems (mātauranga/nga āhuatanga Māori) is essential for Māori to enhance their assets while maintaining the natural capital base and preserving natural ecosystems.

There are many mātauranga Māori frameworks using the core principles of Māori knowledge systems and values. These principles include wairua ('spirituality'), whakapapa ('genealogical connections'), mana ('authority and control') and mauri ('life essence'). These principles are described in Marsden (1975), Best (1982a, 1982b) and Buck (1987).

While each of these concepts and values is intrinsically important in understanding the cultural influences on the decisions that underpin land management and land use change decisions by Māori landowners, there is one principle that captures the essence of the Māori relationship with the natural environment: whakapapa. Whakapapa literally means 'to layer' (Williams 1975) or to recite the interconnected layers between humans, the natural environment and spiritual realms. Genealogical recitation is not restricted to 'family trees' but extends to cosmogony and the personification of natural phenomena. Whakapapa genealogies are central to Māori thought processes and are a pervasive tool for transmitting knowledge. Genealogies are taxonomic structures that attribute order and meaning to existing patterns in nature (Attran 1993) and they also define the relationship between humans and the natural environment.

The influence of these constructs on the behaviour of Māori agribusiness organisations is significant (Kingi et al. 2013)—in particular, the enveloping effect they have on decision-making in relation to investment, diversification, collaboration, environmental management and the development of their lands (Te Puni Kōkiri 2011). There are several recent examples of the influence of values on practice (Kingi et al. 2013; Kingi 2013; Pizzirani et al. 2014; Coffin and Kawe 2011; Morgan 2004). These influences, coupled with the requirement for Māori land to be retained, often result in decisions that place priority on environmental outcomes and intergenerational responsibility.

Te kāhui aro whenua:[2] Māori network

Establishment of the kāhui: Typology

To enable development of emission mitigation scenarios with Māori pastoral farmers, it is necessary to understand the range of emissions profiles of their farming systems.

We have taken a case study approach to developing an understanding of GHG emissions and mitigation potential on Māori pastoral farms. To ensure we have considered the full range of relevant properties, a typology of Māori farms was developed for this purpose. The use of typologies for developing and delivering rural policy is well established (Andersen et al. 2007).

The methods used to define typologies are diverse, including a typology of farms based on physical factors such as soil, climate and topography, farming system (Stats NZ 2008), or categorising landowners and land use decision-makers by structure. The intended application of the typology should guide the approach taken. In the context of GHG mitigation options for Māori pastoral farmers, there are two aspects to consider. The first is determining which mitigation options are technically possible at a biophysical level. This includes the physical location of the farm, the production system and the ownership structure. The second is the implementation stage, which must also consider sociocultural factors in adoption, including the values, priorities and motivations of the owners who influence decision-making. The main purpose of the Māori farm typology is to describe the structure and diversity of the Māori farm resource and to ensure this diversity is captured by a representative sample of farms for further analysis.

---

2   Translated as 'the group focused on the land'.

Typology criteria

Given the specific focus on GHG emissions and mitigation, there is a need to understand the key drivers of emissions and the likely mitigation options. However, it was decided that this information should not be part of the typology criteria but collected later in the research program.

The selection of Māori farms from within these three categories relied on access to data about Māori farms across the country. Because much of the information needed to identify and contact farming entities is held privately and is confidential, the typology matrix required access to information that is not in the public arena. This meant the identification of farms would not follow any rules of statistical sampling and therefore could not be considered a representative sample. Instead, they were identified using the existing networks of Māori land entity collectives and knowledge of the sector from advisors and consultants working in the Māori pastoral agriculture sector.

The matrix used to guide the selection of 30 representative Māori farms was based essentially on three components: 1) the geographic spread of the farms (based on the Māori Land Court regions), 2) the type of farming enterprise (based on the two main pastoral agricultural systems: beef and lamb, and dairy), and 3) ownership structure.

Geographic spread

Māori land under the *TTWMA* is managed under seven Māori Land Court (MLC) districts, as outlined in several papers (Kingi 2008, 2013; Kingi et al. 2013). Subsequent reports will document the results of mitigation strategies and the levels of preparedness and willingness to invest in change to reduce GHG emissions (Journeaux and Kingi 2020).

Given the uneven spread of Māori land across the seven districts, the number of entities selected was consistent with this distribution—that is, higher numbers of entities were selected in Taitokerau, Tairawhiti and Waiariki districts.

Farming enterprise

The entities were selected according to their main land use or business enterprise—that is, dairy or sheep and beef. This may be an oversimplified description of these organisations given that some have interests in exotic forestry, Indigenous forests and other land uses including horticulture. Many of these alternative land uses will contribute to the sequestering of carbon, thereby lowering the total carbon footprint. Given the key research objective is the effectiveness of mitigation strategies that reduce both total carbon emissions for the property and the efficiency of the farming operation to reduce the volume of carbon per unit of output, the decision was made to identify standard pastoral agriculture properties that produce the highest levels of carbon—that is, dairy and sheep and beef.

Ownership structures

Defining Māori farmers is often done using one of two approaches (or a combination of both): 1) the ethnicity of the owner of the farm and/ or 2) the tenure status of the land. However, defining a Māori farmer as a 'person of Māori ethnicity who owns a farm and produces farm produce' is problematic. Many industries do not record the ethnicity of farmers. A more consistent and less problematic method—although there are issues—is to define Māori farmers as entities that own Māori land under the *TTWMA* or land that is owned by an iwi authority or post-settlement governance entities (PSGEs).

The PSGE has emerged in recent years through the ongoing Waitangi Treaty settlement process. This type of entity may be entirely new or built on previous entities—notably, Māori trust boards or mandated iwi organisations (MIOs), with the latter the primary recipients of fishery quota assets allocated via the treaty fisheries settlement (Ward 1999). In addition, numerous iwi and hapū entities have established businesses as providers of social services—particularly in health, education and welfare. The net result is a diverse range of Māori organisations in addition to the landowning trusts and incorporations under the *TTWMA*.

These new iwi–hapū entities have a wider mandate from their tribal constituents and many are leading investment in new technologies and land use change that the more conservative trusts and incorporations would not contemplate. Several recent treaty settlements have involved the transfer of government-owned farms to iwi. These purchases or transfers are likely to continue and, as such, the number of large farms that are owned by Māori will increase over time.

Categorising Māori farms according to scale, diversity and ownership

The categorisation of Māori farming adopted applied a combination of the ethnicity of the owners and the legal status of the land. For the purposes of developing the kāhui, these criteria provide a useful guideline that acknowledges the diversity of tenure and governance structures:

A. entities that own or manage pastoral land that is defined as Māori land under the *TTWMA* (for example, Māori incorporations and trusts)

B. organisations that administer land defined as general land where these organisations are owned by Māori (for example, PSGEs)

C. individual Māori who own or manage pastoral land.

Within these three ownership categories, Māori farming activity can vary significantly. The main categories of farming activity, scale and organisational complexity can be represented as:

- Category 1: Multiple farms, multiple enterprises, multiple structures (*TTWMA* plus limited liability companies).
- Category 2: Multiple farms, multiple enterprises, single governance structure.
- Category 3: Single farm, multiple enterprises, single governance structure.
- Category 4: Single farm, single enterprise.
- Category 5: Owner-operator.

An earlier section outlined the large areas of land that either are governed by small entities or do not have a governance structure. For many of these properties, there are issues that currently take precedence over GHG mitigation, and it was therefore pragmatic to select farms that employed a consultant, advisor or other individual to assist with the compilation of data. Criteria for selection and invitation into the program therefore include:

1. Farms must fall into one of the categories (1–4) outlined above.
2. Farms must fall into one of the groups (A, B or C) outlined above.
3. Pastoral agriculture—for example, dairy or sheep and beef—should be the dominant enterprise in the farm business.

4. The scale or size of the farm is not critical, but the farm should be at least the minimum size for an economic unit to support full-time management staff (a range of sizes was targeted).

5. Geographical spread across tribal regions is preferable.

More dairy than sheep and beef farms were selected relative to their proportion in the total Māori farms because of the recent trend in dairy conversions and their higher level of GHG emissions. Varying proportions of effective farm area and existing forestry area were also desirable given their effect on on-farm mitigation potential. It was hoped the selection criteria would be sufficient to result in a broad range of farm emissions (GHG intensity and total property GHG emissions) as well as identifying a range of feasible mitigation options.

It should be noted that 'cultural values' were not used to differentiate farms or as a basis for selection, and farms were not surveyed for values, aspirations or objectives. This will be carried out in a later stage of the research. A description of a range of generic values as outlined in this section was given to provide the cultural context in which these organisations function; the cultural influences on investment decisions and management practices will vary across the group of 29 organisations/farms and this will be reported in subsequent publications.

Profile of te kāhui aro whenua: Māori network

Based on the typology criteria outlined above, 29 organisations were selected. To protect their identity, only summary descriptions are included below. The small number of 'other organisation types' was not specified as this could also lead to the organisations being identified; they included whānau trusts, limited liability companies and partnerships. The region names are the MLC districts.[3] A simple profile of the 29 farms shows there are 11 dairy farms and 18 sheep and beef properties. The dairy farms were distributed fairly evenly around the country while the four farms in Tairawhiti (east coast of the North Island) were all sheep and beef. The structures were dominated by ahu whenua trusts (18) compared with seven incorporations and four other structures.

---

3   The Ministry of Justice website gives an overview of the districts and towns/cities where the court is located. Available from: www.maorilandcourt.govt.nz/.

Table 13.1: Profile of 29 farms

Organisation type	Farm type	Region	Pasture	Exotic forest	Indigenous forest	Other land uses#	Total size
			(ha)				
Incorporation	S&B	Takitimu	2,200	329	4,682	0	7,211
Incorporation	S&B	Tairawhiti	3,709	0	1,860	1	5,570
Other	S&B	Tairawhiti	2,200	1,900	0	150	4,250
Incorporation	S&B	Taitokerau	2,430	30	0	294	2,754
Ahu whenua trust	S&B	Wairarapa	2,019	27	50	400	2,496
Incorporation	S&B	Taitokerau	2,100	0	0	0	2,100
Incorporation	S&B	Taitokerau	900	0	870	0	1,770
Incorporation	S&B	Aotea	1,128	57	365	25	1,575
Ahu whenua trust	S&B	Taitokerau	1,530	0	0	0	1,530
Ahu whenua trust	S&B	Tairawhiti	1,137	0	117	0	1,254
Ahu whenua trust	S&B	Waiariki	901	0	329	3	1,232
Incorporation	S&B	Tairawhiti	1,158	0	0	0	1,158
Ahu whenua trust	S&B	Taitokerau	773	0	0	306	1,079
Ahu whenua trust	S&B	Taitokerau	728	38	140	136	1,042
Ahu whenua trust	S&B	Waiariki	348	549	55	0	952
Ahu whenua trust	S&B	Waiariki	800	0	0	55	855
Ahu whenua trust	S&B	Taitokerau	521	0	0	0	521
Ahu whenua trust	S&B	Waiariki	415	0	0	100	515
Ahu whenua trust	Dairy	Waiariki	417	10	0	0	427
Ahu whenua trust	Dairy	Waikato	287	0	0	3	290
Ahu whenua trust	Dairy	Taitokerau	250	0	0	0	250
Ahu whenua trust	Dairy	Wairarapa	175	5	9	20	209

Organisation type	Farm type	Region	Pasture	Exotic forest	Indigenous forest	Other land uses[#]	Total size
			(ha)				
Other	Dairy	Aotea	170	0	16	0	186
Ahu whenua trust	Dairy	Taitokerau	180	0	0	0	180
Ahu whenua trust	Dairy	Taitokerau	161	0	10	0	171
Ahu whenua trust	Dairy	Waiariki	152	0	0	0	152
Incorporation	Dairy	Waikato	120	0	7	6	133
Other	Dairy	Aotea	63	0	0	11	74
Other	Dairy	Aotea	67	0	0	5	72

[#] Other land uses include roads, tracks, scrub, wetlands, land under buildings.
S&B = sheep and beef

GHG emissions profile of te kāhui aro whenua

Baseline descriptors of the 29 farms were modelled in Overseer to produce the current GHG emissions of each farm (as of June 2015), then comparisons were made with national datasets including the Ministry for Primary Industries (MPI) GHG stocktake from 2011 to 2012 (MFE 2014). Summaries of the GHG emissions are given in Figures 13.1–13.3. The results of the Overseer modelling of GHG and nitrogen (N) and phosphorous (P) emissions for the 11 dairy farms and 18 dry-stock farms (sheep and beef, S&B) are for the whole property (and include forestry sequestration) and show considerable variability. They must be compared in the context of the land uses of the whole property and will be influenced by the area of bush or plantations in the farm total.

Figure 13.1 gives the distribution and range of GHG emissions and compares dairy with S&B. As reported from other research, dairy emissions are higher than those from S&B and are related to the number of large cows, the use of synthetic nitrogen fertilisers and soil type. The range varies considerably, from 1 tonne to 16.4 tonnes. The very high S&B emitter is a cattle-finishing system with a high stocking rate and crop production system. The analysis of the 29 properties provides a sample of farms to form a benchmark of emissions and gives context to the more in-depth analysis carried out on the four focus farms.

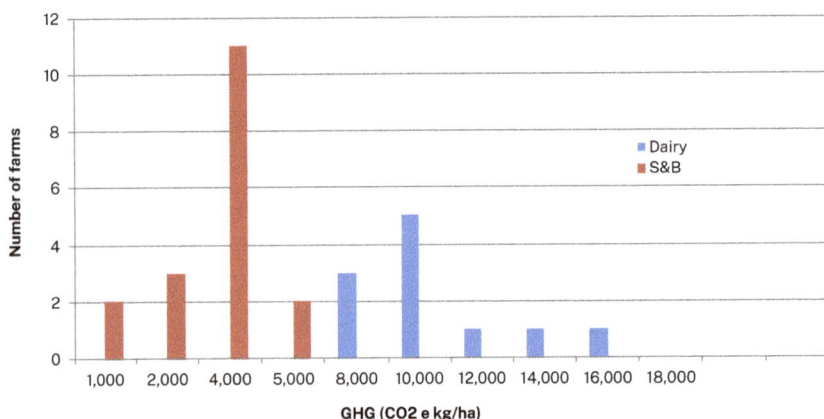

Figure 13.1: GHG emissions by farm type.

Source: Author's work.

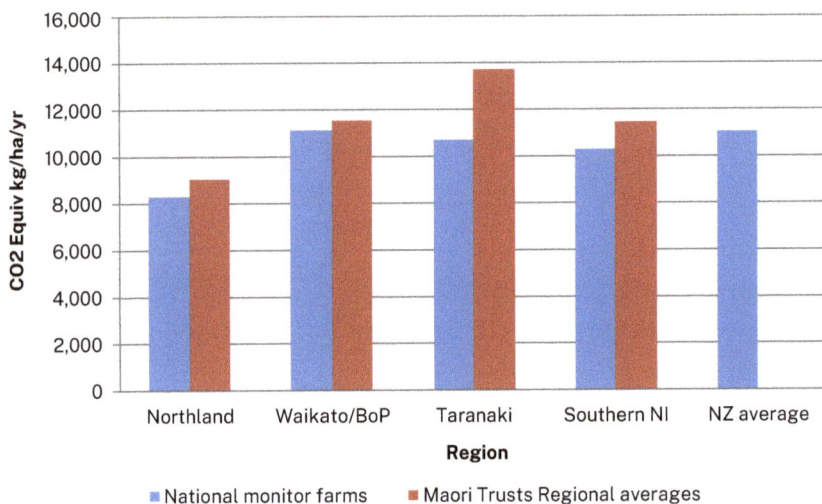

Figure 13.2: Comparison of regional averages for dairy farm GHG emissions.

Source: Author's work.

To give context to these emissions, a national benchmark was sought. The best available is from the national Monitor Farm program assembled in 2011–12, run through Overseer and averaged for each region (MPI 2012). Figure 13.2 gives results that compare Māori dairy farms in this project with the regional estimates from the Monitor farms.

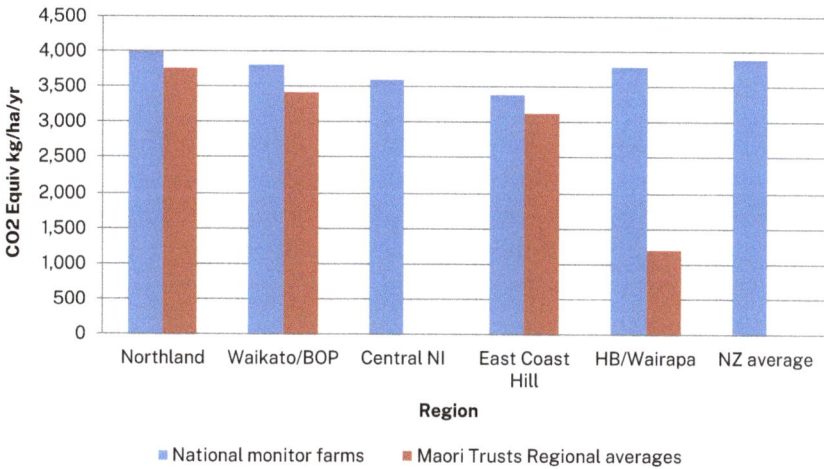

Figure 13.3: Comparison of GHG emissions from Māori S&B farms and national Monitor farms.

Source: Author's work.

The results from the comparisons between the national Monitor farms and the Māori dairy and S&B average need to be interpreted with some caution as comparisons between Māori farms and non-Māori farms can lead to misleading conclusions. The comparisons were based on averages of the Māori farms versus the Monitor farms for regions in the North Island.

Many of the Māori dairy farms were larger than the regional Monitor farms, were running higher stocking rates and the systems were producing and importing higher volumes of supplementary feed. The Māori S&B farms had, on average, lower emissions, largely because they tend to be larger properties and less intensively stocked. The Hawke's Bay – Wairarapa comparison had only one Māori farm profiled so it was difficult to draw any conclusions.

Discussion

Emissions from the agricultural sector make up 46 per cent of Aotearoa New Zealand's total carbon dioxide–equivalent emissions. The largest sources of emissions in 2012 were from enteric fermentation (methane emissions) and agricultural soils (nitrous oxide emissions). The increase in emissions from 1990 to 2012 and from 2011 to 2012 were attributed to the increase in the dairy cattle population. Methane emissions from enteric fermentation make up 86 per cent of Aotearoa New Zealand's total methane emissions and nitrous oxide emissions from agricultural soils make up 97 per cent of the total nitrous oxide emissions (MFE 2014). The challenges facing New Zealand farmers are significant.

Māori pastoral farms are a relatively small proportion of New Zealand's farming properties but their contribution to the Māori land estate is significant. It is therefore critical for the owners of these properties to understand the impacts of their land use decisions on their roles as kaitiaki (guardians). This chapter documents the first year of a three-year program and provides several insights into Māori farming and GHG emissions. The first is the wide range of farming systems represented within the dairy and S&B sectors based on the profile of the 29 farms and the wide range of GHG emission results. Comparisons with regional Monitor farms show the dairy farms in the kāhui were, on average, higher emitters. Further analysis was carried out to model the GHG production system mitigation options and land use change scenarios to understand the impacts on the emissions profiles of the farms and changes in profitability—presented as EFS (economic farm surplus) or EBITDAR (earnings before interest, tax, depreciation, amortisation and rental). These scenarios are presented and discussed in Kingi et al. (2016) and Journeaux and Kingi (2020).

The contribution this study makes to our current knowledge base on the adoption and implementation of mitigation options by farmers is important. GHG science is relatively new and mitigation technologies specific to the reduction of methane and nitrous oxide are still in their early stages. Most of the mitigation options are based on farm system changes that have emerged from the larger body of nutrient-mitigation science. These options include reducing stocking rates, reducing nitrogen fertiliser inputs and reducing forage cropping. Modelling these system changes in Overseer produces lower GHG emissions as well as lower nutrient emissions.

However, the more significant statement of this study is the insight into the interplay between tribally or collectively owned land and the level of preparedness of Indigenous farmers to adopt technologies and invest in system changes to achieve improved farm viability and sustainability. This research provides a snapshot of Māori farms that are engaged in productive systems that contribute to GHG emissions in the pastoral sector. While the emissions profiles share several similarities with the general pastoral sector, there are differences that will be reported in future publications.

A key factor that has emerged in the interactions with the kāhui members is the influence of the ownership structure and land legislation on their decision-making. Most of the farming entities have elected governance representatives in the form of trustees, committees of management or directors of treaty settlement entities. Investment decisions are often made with reference to historical factors, acknowledgement of past owners and the welfare of future generations. Decisions to adopt new technologies or to invest in infrastructure that has both environmental and economic benefits usually need to consider both the limitation of not selling the land (that is, restricted access to debt finance) and the advantages of not selling the land (that is, having a much longer payback period and intergenerational benefits). Many landowners emphasise that their priority is the legacy they will leave for future generations of landowners. Economic success is important but not at the expense of the natural environment.

Recent government initiatives to encourage Māori land into more productive and intensive uses as outlined in the 2013 MPI report rarely consider cultural factors in relation to converting underutilised land to pastoral agriculture. The assumption is made that this land will 'go into either dairy production or sheep and beef farming' (MPI 2013: 6)—enterprises that were assumed to be the highest economic value uses available. This model did not consider other forms of agriculture, such as horticulture or other farming, or forestry. Māori views of the environment and their genealogical relationship with the environment are factors that are often acknowledged in discussions among governors and managers of land blocks; however, incorporating cultural concepts into decision-making frameworks is difficult. The absence of metrics or indicators makes comparisons, rankings and weightings problematic. Development of an emissions matrix (which is under construction by the research team) will enable the comparison of multiple farm system (or enterprise) changes and investments in farm infrastructure to compare the impacts on emissions, economic viability and consistency with cultural values. For example, if enhancing the natural ecosystem biodiversity of the land is important, modelling multiple land uses (including non-productive areas under protection) will provide a more holistic assessment of the property. More importantly, it will balance components that reflect cultural concepts (for example, kaitiakitanga, as reflected in biodiversity and the establishment of wetlands or the expansion of Indigenous forestry) that may have lower cash revenues but higher cultural values by supporting diverse ecosystems.

14

Matriliny under Siege? Exploring the matrilineal descent system in a modernising Bougainville

Anita Togolo

Introduction

This chapter explores the long-running argument among some economists and anthropologists that Indigenous customary land tenure systems inhibit economic development in developing countries. It examines the traditional matrilineal descent systems of the Nagovisi and the Nasioi, two language groups in the Autonomous Region of Bougainville, Papua New Guinea (PNG). Bougainville is one of three islands in the New Guinea Islands region that predominantly follow the matrilineal descent system.[1] In this chapter, the matrilineal descent system of customary land tenure is discussed in the context of land privatisation. Matrilineal descent systems are also considered in a broader context, as an adaptable and resilient foundation for Bougainville's modernising economy. The detailed explanation of the matrilineal descent system is an example of the complexity of customary land tenure practices and how deeply embedded these practices are in Bougainvillean society.

---

1   Matrilineal societies are mainly located in the New Guinea Islands region, including East New Britain, West New Britain, New Ireland and Bougainville. There are also some in Milne Bay Province on Papua New Guinea's mainland.

Some anthropologists have claimed that matrilineal descent-group ownership is fragile, prone to disintegration and incompatible with economic development. Some neoliberal economists claim that economic development can occur only if customary land tenure is replaced with individual property rights. In this chapter, economic development is focused on the production of cocoa cash crops by smallholder farmers.

There has been rapid socioeconomic change in Papua New Guinea since independence in 1975 and, although the mineral resource boom continues, there are indications that economic growth over the medium term will be driven by the non-extractive sector, with the exception of liquefied natural gas production (BPNG 2019: 33). Land continues to be central to people's livelihoods and identity in Papua New Guinea. It is estimated that 85 per cent of Papua New Guineans live in rural areas and are dependent on agriculture for their income and overall sustenance (Armitage 2001: 1). Land is used in various ways, including for subsistence food production, cash-crop production for domestic and export markets, agroforestry, fuelwood and hardwood timber (Bourke and Harwood 2009: 7–8).

Agriculture currently accounts for nearly 20 per cent of Papua New Guinea's gross domestic product (World Bank 2019). The agricultural industry is dominated by smallholder farmers and land is managed through customary land tenure systems (FAO 2019: 12). Approximately 97 per cent of PNG land is customarily owned and 3 per cent is alienated or owned by the state. Currently 14 of Papua New Guinea's 22 provinces produce cocoa. Approximately 20 per cent of the country's labour force (World Bank 2014a: 3) and one-eighth of its current population of 8.6 million people (World Bank 2019) rely on cocoa for their livelihood. In 2018, Papua New Guinea produced 38,000 tonnes of cocoa and cocoa exports earned annual revenue of K300 million (Xinhua 2019).

This chapter first defines customary land tenure and alienated land in Papua New Guinea, then introduces the relationship between customary land tenure and economic development. Following this, structural differences between patrilineal and matrilineal descent group ownership are explained. Additionally, the claims made by some anthropologists that matriliny is incompatible with modern economic development (Douglas 1969; Gough 1961; Murdock 1949), and that it is a fragile institution at risk of being replaced with patrilineal inheritance and succession (Richards 1950; Schneider 1961), are examined.

The next section argues that the matrilineal descent system practised by two language groups in Bougainville, the Nagovisi and the Nasioi, is resilient, primarily due to postmarital residence patterns. These two language groups practise the postmarital residence pattern of matri-uxorilocality—a pattern characterised by a husband's move to his wife's land. Other factors that affect the resilience of the matrilineal descent system will be explained briefly.

Finally, this chapter reflects on modernisation theory and its implications for developing countries. It then looks at Bougainville's cocoa production since the 1960s and considers matrilineal customary land tenure as a platform for future economic development opportunities in Bougainville.

Land tenure systems: Customary versus alienated

Land is integral to the identity and livelihood of Papua New Guineans and vital to the country's economic development. It is important to begin by defining the following key concepts: customary land, customary land tenure, alienated land and cash cropping.

Customary land is 'land owned or possessed by Indigenous nationals, the rights to which are regulated by traditional or customary property right systems' (Jones and McGavin 2001: 28). Customary land tenure systems operate differently from one community to another, so it is important to define what this concept means. For this chapter, the working definition of customary land tenure is 'a balance between group and individual rights and obligations, with land ownership being held at group level and land use being exercised at the individual or household level' (Fingleton 2005: 4).

This system of property rights is well established, appropriate for traditional needs and well understood by its users (Armitage 2001: 3). Customary land rights are obtained through the membership of, or affiliation to, a landowning group. For some groups, membership is traced through the mother (matrilineal descent group system) and for others, membership is traced through the father (patrilineal descent group system). For yet other landowning groups, membership is traced through the mother and father, which is known as cognatic. Types of land rights differ between landowning groups—an example of this is the Nasioi language group discussed later in this chapter. The type of land rights an individual has is determined by their status in the landowning group, clan or lineage. The individual must meet certain obligations to use the land and decisions regarding land must be made as a group (Lakau 1997: 530). The key point is that it is a system that ensures everyone in the landowning group has access to land.

In contrast, alienated land tenure is a largely unfamiliar concept for most people in Papua New Guinea. It is defined as 'land that has been severed from the traditional sector either by compulsory or voluntary processes' (Jones and McGavin 2001: 28). Within the alienated land tenure system, ownership of land is individualised and regulated by the state, with individual title formalised through the courts and legislation (Armitage 2001: 3). This system requires land titling through the process of demarcation and registration. The nature of alienated land means it can be bought, sold or transferred.

The specific form of economic development this chapter discusses is commercial cash cropping. Commercial cash cropping, also known as commercial silviculture, refers to the large-scale planting of perennial tree crops, such as cocoa and coffee. These crops require considerable investments of land, time and labour. The long-term nature of commercial cash crops contrasts with subsistence crops, which are seasonal and impermanent. Subsistence crops are grown for household consumption or for sale at local markets.

Customary land tenure and economic development

This chapter will use the following definition of 'neoliberal' attitudes regarding customary land tenure: '[A] theory of political economic practices that proposes that human well-being can best be advanced by liberating individual entrepreneurial freedoms and skills within an institutional framework characterized by strong private property rights, free markets and free trade' (Harvey 2005: 2).

The key element in this definition is that human wellbeing, inclusive of economic development, is characterised by strong *private property rights*. Private property rights mean individual property rights, as opposed to group ownership through customary land tenure systems. Implementing individual property rights generally requires land to be divided through the process of land titling. Neoliberal economists suggest a system characterised by individual property rights is more likely to ensure economic development and wellbeing, improved welfare and increased incomes (Curtin and Lea 2006). It is argued that the long-term benefit of individual property rights is improved living standards, and assigning economic value to landholdings and property allows individuals to 'participate meaningfully in the business of trade and commerce' (Curtin and Lea 2006: 166). Neoliberal thought supports the concept that the more ambitious and hardworking a person is—whether that be in developing their land or as a wageworker—the more likely it is their income will increase over time. Subsequently, it is said to be more likely that individuals will be able to save money because they are not giving it away to extended family (Curtin and Lea 2006).

Proponents of the individualisation of land claim that poverty and low agricultural productivity are due to the customary land tenure system (Gosarevski et al. 2004: 137). Advocates claim there is a relationship between rapid population growth and the pressure this puts on land availability. It is also claimed that, under customary land tenure, the production of export crops such as coffee, cocoa and copra-oil has fallen behind the annual population growth rate (Curtin 2003; Curtin and Lea 2006: 165). Some neoclassical advocates of individual property rights discuss the relative abundance of land in Papua New Guinea but claim the reason there is a serious shortage of land for development is that almost none of it is available for purchase for agriculture, commercial or residential purposes (Curtin 2003: 6). However, proponents of individualised property rights do not adequately address the fact that much of the land in the country is not suited to commercial cash-crop development as it is mountainous, infertile or waterlogged (Allen 2008: 3).

There have been concerted efforts by the Government of Papua New Guinea and international organisations to individualise property rights in the country. In 1995, the International Monetary Fund (IMF) proposed a land mobilisation program and, as part of its structural adjustment program, advocated for economic recovery. This involved pressuring the government to enact legislation concerning customary land registration (Brown and Ploeg 1997: 515). During that period, the Australian Agency for International Development (AusAID), the World Bank, the IMF and the PNG Government pushed for land reform with several aims in mind (Anderson 2010; Brown and Ploeg 1997): to organise either the leasing of customary land or shifting whole areas of land under customary title into a registered system under which land can be mortgaged or sold (Anderson 2010: 12).

Developments in land reform in Papua New Guinea have not resulted in the government's desired goal to mobilise large areas of customary land for development while empowering customary landowners (Filer 2019).

The National Land Summit held in 2005 resulted in the formation of the National Land Development Taskforce, which made 54 recommendations in 2006. After the summit, significant amendments were made to the *Land Groups Incorporation Act 1974* and the *Land Registration Act 1981* (Filer 2019). The national parliament passed these amendments in 2009, but the lands department delayed their implementation for another three years. Despite the implementation of these two pieces of legislation in 2012, they have not achieved their outcomes. The stated aim of the latest land summit, held in May 2019, was to 'develop a policy, legal and administrative framework facilitating efficient utilisation of customary land for the benefit, first and foremost, of the customary landowners' (Filer 2019). Participants of the summit identified 17 issues and adopted a resolution on each. Filer (2019) says the 17 resolutions 'called for a review of just about every aspect of the current legal and policy framework that applies to the creation of formal titles over customary land and the transformation of such titles into marketable assets'. Two of the 17 resolutions called for the two pieces of legislation to be reviewed, amended again or even repealed (Filer 2019). Despite concerted efforts, it seems the issue of the mobilisation of customary land is no closer to being resolved.

Landowners have two major concerns about land titles: first, that they will not receive adequate compensation from the government (or a resource company); and, second, that the rights of future generations to that land will not be guaranteed (Brown and Ploeg 1997: 515). Despite this, it is important to acknowledge that customary landowners in Papua New Guinea also see weaknesses in the customary land tenure system. Customary landowners can see how at times this system inhibits development at the local level (Martin 2004, 2007), how custom can result in unequal land distribution and how the increasing trend towards father–son land transfers has caused land disputes. However, those in support of this type of land tenure system argue that descent group ownership has provided social stability and security and has helped maintain important cultural practices; people have a social safety net and are able to take risks in 'pursuing education, finding paid employment, investing and other activities' (Lightfoot 2005: 24). Another concern is that major reforms to the customary land tenure system could result in social deterioration through people's permanent alienation from their land.

Land titling—part of the process of customary land registration—can be difficult and time-consuming, and disputes can take years to resolve in court. The division of land into parcels with fixed boundaries is not the way customary land tenure—a system operating for thousands of years—was designed to work. The system of private property rights does not allow for the complexity and range of descent group ownership systems within customary land tenure.

Matrilineal and patrilineal descent systems

The matrilineal descent system can take different forms, but some anthropologists have tended to take a simplistic view of it. It is important to explain the structural differences between patrilineal and matrilineal descent group ownership, as they reflect the complexity of customary land tenure systems.

Matrilineal and patrilineal descent systems are defined as decision-making units, with the fundamental structural difference being the gender through which the lines of authority and group placement run (Schneider 1961). In patrilineal descent groups, both group membership and authority are determined by males. In matrilineal descent groups, although the line of authority runs through males, group membership is determined through the female line (Schneider 1961: 7). To operate effectively, matrilineal descent groups must be able to retain control over both male and female members. Children must develop primary orientation and ties of loyalty to the matrilineal descent group. Male members will eventually succeed to roles of authority, so it is in the interests of the matrilineal group to retain their loyalty (Schneider 1961: 8). Another key difference between patrilineal and matrilineal descent groups is the gender of the individual who marries into the descent group, otherwise known as the in-marrying affine. For matrilineal descent groups, the in-marrying affine is the husband. In most matrilineal societies, an individual must marry someone outside their clan and this arrangement is described as an exogamous one.

Among most matrilineal societies in Papua New Guinea, bilateral cross-cousin marriage is preferred as it reaffirms relationships within the lineage and keeps land within the matrilineage. Bilateral cross-cousin marriage is 'a form of direct exchange marriage in which two lineages or families establish permanent alliances and exchanges through marriages to each other's women' (Schwimmer 1995). Marriage between bilateral cross-cousins occurs in unilineal descent systems where there are paired lineages, and this type of marriage ensures commercial cash crops inherited through the female line return to the original matrilineal clan in the third generation (see Figure 14.1). The cooperation displayed between clans during events such as weddings and mortuary feasts also helps to cement the relationships between paired lineages. In addition, practices such as trade and exchange of shell valuables assist in maintaining these relationships (Togolo 2020).

In the matrilineal descent system, the children of one's father's brothers and one's mother's sisters are known as one's parallel cousins.[2] Marriage cannot take place between parallel cousins because they consider one another 'brother' and 'sister'. An individual can marry the children of their mother's brothers or their father's sisters. This is because they are members of different clans and are known as one's cross-cousins (see Figures 14.1–14.3).

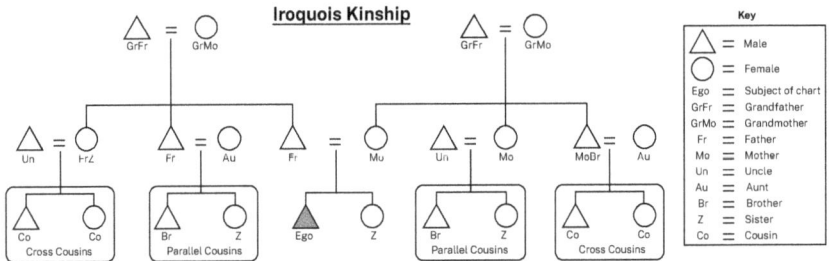

Figure 14.1: Parallel cousins and cross-cousins.
Source: Togolo (2008: 35).

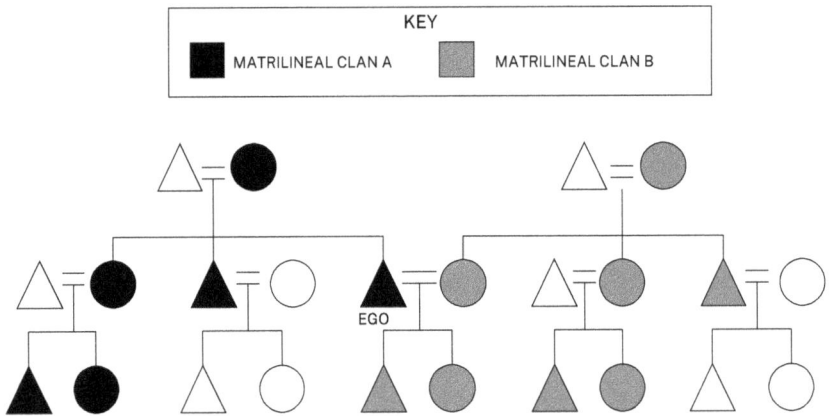

Figure 14.2: Matrilineal inheritance.
Source: Togolo (2008: 35).

---

2   The Iroquois kinship system, found only in matrilineal societies, is one of several kinship terminology systems that have different terms for maternal and paternal relatives based on gender and generation.

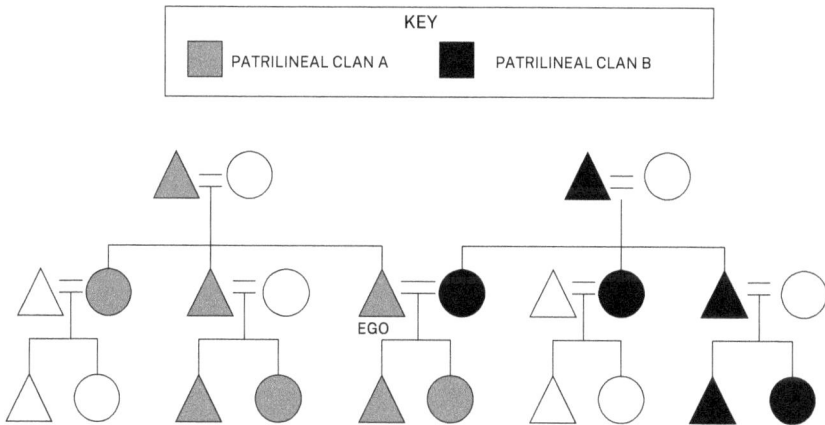

Figure 14.3: Patrilineal inheritance.
Source: Togolo (2008: 35).

Anthropologists' arguments

Some anthropologists argue that matriliny is incompatible with economic development (Douglas 1969; Gough 1961; Murdock 1949). Matriliny is seen as a fragile institution that will slowly be replaced with patrilineal inheritance and succession (Murdock 1949; Richards 1950; Schneider 1961). This argument is based on the view that the universal unit of society is the male-centred nuclear family and that this is the most viable unit of kinship in the modern world. On this basis, scholars claim that the matrilineal descent system is disintegrating. They propose an inherent conflict in the matrilineal system because the father has kinship obligations beyond the nuclear family (Douglas 1969: 122). Scholars in this area also allude to the supposed disintegration of the matrilineal system due to the intensification of commercial cash cropping (Douglas 1969).

Postmarital residence patterns are important in this discussion because they affect how land is transferred from one generation to the next, which has implications for the transfer of land used for commercial cash cropping. Matrilineal societies in most of Bougainville practise matri-uxorilocal residence, whereby on marriage, the husband leaves the land of his clan and moves to and works on land belonging to his wife's matrilineage. In these cases of matri-uxorilocal residence, the man usually does not have to move very far as his clan land may be in the same village or area as his wife's. Where matri-uxorilocal residence patterns were practised, sons (and daughters) were automatically guaranteed rights to their matrilineage land. Another type of postmarital residence pattern in matrilineal societies is matri-virilocal residence, where the wife leaves her clan land and moves to land belonging to her husband's matrilineage. This practice did not always ensure that a son who contributed labour with his father would inherit those crops. While the son resided on his father's matrilineal land, he was working land that was not his own. However, traditionally, there were ways a son could be provided with land, either by permission from senior members of his father's matrilineage (Epstein 1969) or if his mother secured land from her matrilineage through a ceremonial feast (Leslie 2008). In the past, when land was used predominantly for subsistence cropping, the type of postmarital residence pattern matrilineal societies followed was not a significant cause of concern.

Where commercial cash crops are involved, the postmarital residence pattern of matrilineal descent groups can become a significant issue in terms of individual rights versus group rights and residence rights versus descent rights. Land used to grow commercial cash crops requires a lot of labour over a long period and can potentially lock up the land for decades. Men who plant commercial cash crops often retain exclusive rights even after the land has become fallow. In matrilineal societies where matri-uxorilocal residence is preferred, children of the couple live on their matrilineal land and therefore can inherit the land on which the trees are planted, the trees themselves and any land their father has cleared (Nash 1974: 64, 101). In matri-virilocal matrilineal societies, scholars have noted how the intensification of cash cropping tends to increase land disputes for several reasons (Epstein 1969; Ogan 1972)—in particular, the increasing trend of father–son land transfers (Keil 2005: 332). This trend directly contradicts matrilineal land tenure principles in which succession rights are transferred from a mother to her sons and daughters. The trend of father–son transfers has the potential to weaken matrilineal ties (Epstein 1968: 7; Fortes 1950: 261), with cash crops becoming more strongly associated with individual families.

There are some anthropologists who claim matrilineal group ownership is in decline because of several sources of tension. First, they point to the issue of the father's primary interest in his sisters' children, rather than his own children, and potential conflicts that can arise (von Benda-Beckmann and von Benda-Beckmann 2006: 199). Anthropologists such as David Schneider (1961: 16–17) noted the potential conflict between the bonds of marriage and the bonds of descent. Schneider claims a man must choose his priority according to his own matrilineage, rather than his marital relationship, and the wife must prioritise her own matrilineage, and these conditions must be met for matrilineal descent groups to survive. Some anthropologists also note that another potential source of tension is that a man's wife and children are not necessarily under his authority, but under the authority of the male members of the wife's matrilineage—usually the wife's brothers. Anthropologist Audrey Richards (1950) called this source of tension the 'matrilineal puzzle'.

Despite the assumptions made by some anthropologists, economic development does not necessarily lead to the disintegration of matriliny. There are anthropologists who challenge these commonly held views (Douglas 1969; Nash 1974). Among the Nagovisi language group in central Bougainville, Nash (1974) found the intensification of commercial cash cropping resulted in matri-uxorilocal residence (where the husband moves to work on his wife's clan land) taking place more often. In addition, matrilineal inheritance rules regarding land and its use were more strictly adhered to (Nash 1974). Taking these matrilineal descent group ownership issues into account, matrilineal social organisation and land tenure remain strong in Bougainville, as will be addressed in the next section.

Bougainville case study: The Nasioi and the Nagovisi

This section examines the matrilineal system among two language groups in Bougainville, the Nagovisi and the Nasioi, and demonstrates the complex and consistently adaptable nature of the system. These two matrilineal societies also provide an example of the complementary nature of matri-uxorilocal residence and commercial cash cropping.

Bougainville is 1,000 kilometres east of Port Moresby, Papua New Guinea's capital. Bougainville has a land area of 10,620 square kilometres and a population of approximately 300,000 people. It comprises two large islands—Buka in the north and Bougainville, less than 1 kilometre to the south across the Buka Strait—and 168 smaller groups of islands and atolls scattered across 450,000 square kilometres. Bougainville generally has a low population density (Connell 2005: 196), with the exception of Buka and other smaller islands. Bougainville is divided into three main political regions of north, central and south, and 12 local-level government (LLG) areas. The land on Bougainville is of volcanic origin, extremely fertile and well suited to a variety of food crops (see Map 14.1). There are 25 languages spoken in Bougainville, 16 of which are Austronesian and the remaining are Papuan (Tryon 2005: 31; see Map 14.2).

Hanpan
Lemanmanu · Jitopan
Lemankoa · Tohatsi
Lontis
CAPE
DUNGANON · CAPE KOTOPAN
Hanahan
Hagus
QUEEN
CAROLA · Hahalis
HARBOUR
PORORAN I. · Koruso · Gogone
Bel · Gagan · Suhin
YAME I. · Sing
PETATS I. · Lonahan
Turu · Malasang
Kahule · Hangan · Hutjena High School
BUKA PASSAGE
Buka Town · Boria · Hantoa
(Chinatown)
MADEHAS I.
SOHANO I. · Talena
TAIOF I. · MATCHIN
BAY · Siara
TANUVGA I. · Chabai · Chinpats · Tinputz
Porapora · Rugen
SAPOSA I. · Aravia
Hahon

BUKA ISLAND

SOUTH PACIFIC OCEAN

Tinputz Harbour
CAPE L'AVERDY
TEOP I.
Kekesu

Petspets
Kunua · Inus
Sipai · Tekai
Tore · Asitavi · Wakunai

BOUGAINVILLE ISLAND

Amun · Balbi · Ihu
Togarau · Tenekau
Kuraio · Tarara
CAPE MABIRI

Lake Billy Mitchell · Vito
CAPE PUIPUI
Turupei · Bagana · Rorovana · KIETA PENINSULA
ARAWA · TAUTAINA I.
Laruma · Atamo · BAY · POK POK I.
Beirema · Kuka · Kieta
POROATA I. · Torokina · Pakia · Mongontoro
Mom · Karato · Bakawan · Siromba · Kobeinang
Paru · Sirowai · Morona · Panguna · Roreinang
Peru · Kupei · Daratui · Rumba · Aropa
Valley · Kawerong R · Dapera · Guava · Naasioi
EMPRESS · Jaba River · Deomori · Irang · Morangasina · Peiwona · KOROMIRA POINT
AUGUSTA · Pinadu · Orami · Aid Post
BAY · Sikorewa · Pondoma · Sirowai
Moratona · Panam · Takuan · Siorovi
Beretemba · Sovele · LALUAI
MOTUPENA · Pomalate · Lake · POINT
POINT · Bakoran · Loloru · Loloru

Boku · Tokainoi · Oria
Mogoroi · TORAU
DEURO · BAY
Tabago · Lahaia
Mamagata · Tonu · Lake
Altara · Plano · Morou · Muguai
Buin
Malabita
Hill · Toniolei
Laguai · Kangu · Harbour
Patu Patual
MOII A POINT

SOLOMON SEA

○ airport   ▲ volcano/mountain
• village   ⌣ reef

0   kilometres   20

© Cartography ANU 04-008 base

Map 14.1: Bougainville and Buka islands.
Source: Regan and Griffin (2005: xxvi).

Bougainville society is predominantly matrilineal, including all the north, east and west of the region. The following areas are patrilineal: Buin in south Bougainville, Nissan Island, and the Polynesian islands of Taku (Mortlock), Nukumanu (Tasman) and Nuguria (Fead). For many Bougainvilleans, matriliny has been a significant source of identity, as it is a characteristic that sets them apart from other language groups in Papua New Guinea (Ogan 2005: 50).

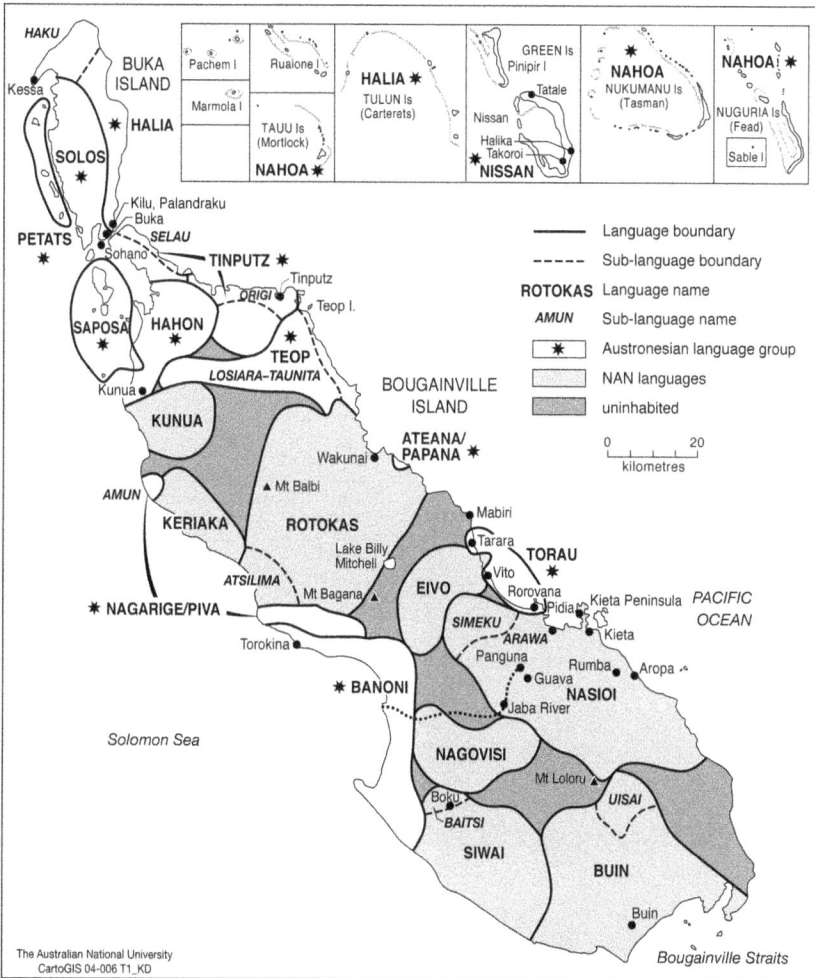

Map 14.2: Bougainville linguistic divisions.

Source: Regan and Griffin (2005: 33).

The Nasioi and Nagovisi language groups are in the most southerly LLG area and both are characterised by high population density, low agricultural potential and problems with law and order, but differ in the way the matrilineal descent system operates and has been adapted to the practice of commercial cash cropping. During the 1960s and 1970s, American anthropologists Jill Nash and Donald Mitchell lived with and studied the Nasioi group, and Eugene Ogan lived with the Nagovisi group. The next section draws on their work during this period and some reflections made by Nash and Ogan on their return to Bougainville post crisis in the early 2000s.

Nasioi

The Nasioi people live in small, discrete villages of no more than a few households, each of which usually comprises a husband, a wife and children (Ogan 2005). Land is abundant and fertile in this area and suitable for growing subsistence crops. Traditionally, the flexible nature of the matrilineal descent system allowed people to move freely to make new gardens, avoid disputes or to abandon a village due to sorcery (Ogan 1972: 13). Every Nasioi belongs to a named matrilineal descent group or clan (muu) and members of each clan are dispersed throughout the Nasioi region (Ogan 1971: 82). Marriage is exogamous, matri-uxorilocal (the husband moving to the wife's matrilineal land) and usually arranged by matrilineage elders to ensure long-lasting relationships between clans. Bilateral cross-cousin marriage between paired lineages and village or parish endogamy—marrying within one's own 'group'—is preferred. This type of marriage keeps land and valuables, such as shell money, within the clan (Ogan 1971).

Nasioi land tenure is based on a complex hierarchy of use rights: 'primary', 'subsidiary' and 'derivative'—a system that differs to the Nagovisi's. A man who clears a tract of virgin rainforest normally gains primary rights to it (Ogan 1971: 84), which includes the right to make gardens and to erect houses, the right to plant tree crops with a longer life than ordinary gardens and the right to allocate sections of garden land to others (Ogan 1971: 84).

Among the Nasioi, there is a clear sexual division of labour, with the men clearing the land and planting permanent tree crops and the women responsible for subsistence gardening. Garden land was allotted to women, with the primary rightsholder's wife or wives taking priority. Next in line are the close women of the primary rightsholder's clan born of the same mother but not the same father, then other women of his clan. Last in line to be allotted garden land are wives of the primary rightsholder's clansmen (Ogan 1971: 84). Subsidiary rights to land can be established on the death of the primary rightsholder, unless he had formally transferred his rights to his children (Ogan 1971: 85). To gain primary rights to the land, children provide a large feast to their father's close uterine kin and other clansmen either during their father's lifetime or in connection with his funeral (Ogan 1971: 85). This ensures they have full rights to the land—the same degree of rights as members of that clan. Finally, derivative rights are the claims to share in the produce of a tract of land and claims to primary or subsidiary rights in special circumstances. These rights can be obtained through affinal,[3] cognatic,[4] residential and other types of relationships (Ogan 1971: 85).

Observations made in the 2000s by both Bougainvilleans and non-Bougainvilleans indicate the matri-uxorilocal residence pattern among the Nasioi has facilitated economic growth and strengthened the matrilineal system. Women continue to work alongside their husbands in cultivating cocoa cash crops on land belonging to the matrilineage and are involved in the selling of cocoa to middlemen (Tavore 2008). Men continue to plant commercial cash crops on their wives' land, and these crops are inherited by their children, who are members of their wives' matrilineage. The children are members of the wife's matrilineage because descent is traced through the female line (their mother). This practice of the man cultivating cocoa cash crops on his wife's land does not pose any problems because the man has moved to his wife's clan land and the children are residing on their own matrilineal land.

Nagovisi

The Nagovisi language group borders the west of the Nasioi region and is north of the Siwai region. It is in west-central Bougainville in the Arawa LLG area. It has high population density and relatively high agricultural productivity.

Nagovisi society is divided into exogamous moieties. A moiety is one of two units into which a tribe or community is divided based on unilineal descent (where one's descent is traced exclusively through either the male or the female line). Within each moiety, there are usually named clans. Exogamous means to marry outside of one's own group and, in the case of the Nagovisi, outside one's moiety. For the Nagovisi, the two moieties are the Komo ('Hornbill') and Manka ('Eagle') (Nash 1974: 21). Each moiety has territorially based named matri-clans. Each clan has up to a dozen named lineages and each lineage is further divided into smaller groups called minimal lineages (Mitchell 1976: 9). There are various ways land can be transferred between individuals and groups among the Nagovisi.

---

3   Rights to customary land gained through marriage.
4   Rights to customary land gained through the individual's mother and father.

Although the most common way is from the oldest mother to the oldest daughter, property can also be transferred between two lineages in a clan, between clans or to other clans (Mitchell 1976).

Postmarital residence within the Nagovisi is matri-uxorilocal: women remain in their villages and husbands move to their wives' villages at marriage (Mitchell 1976: 10). Cocoa and subsistence crops are grown on the woman's matrilineal land and the couple works together on her land as an economic unit to support their children. Men continue to have obligations to their clan, although once they are married, they do not engage in any productive or economic activities with their matrilineal kinsmen. Men are also unable to profit materially from their matrilineal land (Nash 1974: 29). Obligations to their own clan include protecting clan land in land disputes and educating younger generations about clan matters. In terms of land-related tasks, men are responsible for clearing the bush and women for subsistence gardening.

In the Nagovisi region, commercial cash cropping of cocoa intensified in the 1950s, which affected the way people used land and placed pressure on the existing matrilineal system. Before this, the predominant use of land was temporary rather than permanent (tree crops and habitation), and there were few land disputes. From the 1950s, rapid population growth and the desire for increased income exacerbated land-related issues. Cocoa was planted in food gardens, which became permanent tree-crop plantings (Mitchell 1982: 62). The normal fallow cycle was disrupted as hundreds of hectares of cocoa were planted and soil was often exhausted. Monetary benefits from cash crops were unevenly distributed and one of the reasons for this was that social groups had unequal access to land (Mitchell 1982: 58).

Having initially conducted research in the Nagovisi region in the 1970s, American anthropologist Jill Nash returned for the first time in 2000, after the official end of the civil war in 1998. She observed several major changes: the rate of population growth had been maintained, birth intervals had decreased and the rate of unemployment had increased (Nash 2005). All these factors had led to people concentrating on subsistence agriculture and commercial cash crops and, as a result, virgin forest was being cut down to make room for more cocoa cash cropping. Nash also noticed that women continued to control the land and shell valuables, with both assets being passed from the senior female in the lineage to her eldest daughter (Nash 2005). Nagovisi women continue to play a significant role in fulfilling funeral obligations and initiation ceremonies (Nash 1977: 121).

Bougainville faces some challenges, including rapid population growth and land shortages in some areas (particularly in the small islands and atolls). However, it seems to be the view of various women, Bougainvillean and non-Bougainvillean, that in this post-crisis period, the strength of matriliny had in fact increased (Nash 2005; Saovana-Spriggs 2007). In addition, the Nagovisi continue to favour female babies, as they are considered vital to the survival and continuity of the clan and matriliny in general (Nash 2005: 408).

Final reflections

Modernisation theory describes the transition from a traditional rural, agrarian society to a secular, urban, industrialised, modern society and the entire process of change that occurs in that transition (Naidu 2010: 7). Modernisation also implies changes in social and cultural structures, increased access to education and the adoption of new technologies. The transition to modernisation assumes that not only will traditional societies 'develop' as they adopt more modern practices, but also traditional beliefs and cultural traits will become less important (Germond-Duret 2016: 1540–41; Peet and Hartwick 2015: 138–39). For developing countries, modernisation does not necessarily afford equal access to its economic benefits. There is evidence to suggest that while the transition to modernisation for developing countries can result in economic growth, it does not necessarily lead to economic development as the increases in income can go to relatively few people (Peet and Hartwick 2015: 2).

Developing countries transitioning to a modernised economy often face the challenges of political instability, rapid urbanisation and a lack of economic diversification. Bougainville faces some of these, as well as a heavy reliance on agriculture—in particular, cocoa cash cropping. This reliance on a single crop can pose economic risks due to fluctuations in global market prices, agricultural pests as well as natural disasters. Crop diversification within smallholder agriculture has been offered as a way to reduce these risks, as well as a strategy for poverty alleviation as it is considered ecologically feasible and cost-effective, especially among small-scale farmers (Feliciano 2019: 795).

Since the intensification of cash cropping in the 1960s, Bougainville's cocoa production has been consistent. From 1979 to 1989, before the civil war, Bougainville had the highest annual average rate of cocoa production in Papua New Guinea, of 15,600 tonnes (Scales et al. 2008: 23–25). During the civil war, cocoa production fell to a low of about 3,000 tonnes, in 1990–91 (Lummani 2005: 246). After the war ended in 1998, cocoa production steadily increased to 15,670 tonnes in 2004–05 (Scales et al. 2008: 23–25). When considering the significant disruption caused by the civil war, the fact that Bougainville's cocoa production returned to pre-crisis levels is a remarkable outcome. A few years after this recovery, the cocoa industry across Papua New Guinea suffered a major setback with infestation of the cocoa pod borer from 2008 to 2012, which caused production to fall (Xinhua 2019). While Bougainville is still affected by cocoa pod borer, cocoa-producing provinces across the country are continuing to see improvements in cocoa production levels. Bougainville's cocoa production figures in 2017 had recovered to approximately 11,150 tonnes (Cocoa Board of Papua New Guinea 2018).

While the cocoa cash cropping industry in Bougainville has consistently contributed to the economy, the variation in production levels highlights the need for crop diversification to strengthen the agricultural sector. Bougainville's economy relies on small-scale goldmining, subsistence agriculture, cocoa and copra cash cropping and some marine products (ABG 2018: 32). Since the early 2000s, cash cropping of vanilla beans has re-emerged as an export commodity in Papua New Guinea (Allen et al. 2009: 374) and there are some indications of its introduction in Bougainville (Makis 2019). Beyond agriculture, other opportunities for economic development have been identified, such as ecotourism and further exploration of fishing licence fees from Papua New Guinea's National Fisheries Authority (ABG 2018: 35). Relevant to the discussion of ecotourism is research that has shown that, in Fiji, customary land tenure has provided a platform for Fijians to engage in tourism and gain social and economic benefits, with state institutions in place to support community-based development (Scheyvens and Russell 2012: 21).

The issue of customary land tenure and economic development continues to elicit strong voices on both sides of the debate. There are still no guarantees that freehold or registration of individual or group customary land titles has produced the benefits promised by neoliberalism (Mugambwa 2007: 55). Given the high level of functionality in matrilineal descent systems—systems that provide people with a social safety net, food and housing—it would make little sense for a transition to individualised property rights in Papua New Guinea.

Despite the significant challenges Bougainville has faced, matriliny continues to provide a consistent foundation at both regional and community levels. Customary land tenure systems are important because landowners make decisions about land use for economic development as well as the wellbeing of their local community (Scheyvens and Russell 2012: 2). These systems can provide a stable platform for commercial industries and for new opportunities in business development, while helping Bougainville keep its valuable social systems intact.

This chapter has demonstrated that the matrilineal descent group ownership system in Bougainville is not only resilient, but also fluid and adaptable. Despite considerable pressures on these systems, they remain intact. Some Pacific Island scholars extend that argument further, proposing that modern 'events' can result in unprecedented changes that act as a catalyst to strengthen and reinforce Indigenous systems (Saovana-Spriggs 2007: 5–6). Further to this argument, Melchior Togolo (2005) has discussed the many foreign influences on his own language group, the matrilineal Torau of central Bougainville, over the past 130 years. These influences include the German colonial administration in the 1880s, Christian missionaries in the early 1900s and the Australian military administration in 1914 during World War I, followed by the Australian civil administration of Bougainville and Papua New Guinea. In addition, there were Chinese traders, merchants and planters, followed by the overwhelming assault on Bougainville by Japanese soldiers and Allied forces during World War II and subsequently the civil war. Togolo explains:

> [I]t can be argued that communities that have coped with the impact of all of these external or internal, social and economic pressures, are inherently strong, quite coherent, very resilient, and not prone to disintegration. The long process of adaption have [sic] given the Torau the social tools to manage such immense changes. (Togolo 2005: 289)

Despite enormous challenges, the matrilineal systems in Bougainville have endured because of their adaptability. This adaptability is central to the resilient nature of Indigenous land tenure systems, such as matriliny, and there is every reason to believe these systems will continue to adapt and provide a strong foundation for the modernisation of Bougainville's economy.

15

Collective Action for Sustainable Development: A case study of a Tayal Indigenous community in Taiwan

Ai-Ching Yen and Yin-An Chen[1]

Collective action by people with shared goals and a willingness to achieve them is an important driving force of communal self-governance and can facilitate exceptional results. In Taiwan, a group of Tayal Indigenous people organised the Makauy Business Group of community elites, which has achieved several important goals for the advancement of communal sustainable development. First, Tayal people have abandoned conventional farming and gradually adopted organic farming. Second, Tayal people have reconnected with their history of millennia of agroforestry practices to better organise natural resources for modern cultivation. Tayal people have adapted this ancestral Indigenous knowledge to their modern cultivation methods. Third, Tayal people developed 'Cinsbu learning' for tourists who visit the Cinsbu community, comprising multiple traditional methods that fit with sustainable development. This learning includes Tayal cultural

1   This research was supported by the Taiwanese Ministry of Science and Technology (the former National Science Council, NSC), which subsidised the following projects: 1) 'The Distress and Chance on Indigenous Reserved Land, Sustainable Agriculture, Land Use Control and Indigenous Community Development—A Case of Tayal Indigenes in Jianshih Township, Hsinchu County' (No. NSC 102-2420-H-004-002), project duration, 1/1/2013 to 31/12/2013; 2) 'Study on Agroforestry and Multifunctionality in Indigenous Areas—A Case of Tayal Indigenes in Jianshih Township, Hsinchu County' (NSC 103-2420-H-004-007-MY3), project duration, 1/1/2014 to 31/12/2016.

skills such as weaving and wooden handicrafts and knowledge of customs, taboos and ancestral oral instruction. Such knowledge is deeply held and revered by Tayal people, and they like to share this with tourists. Moreover, it is a great way to preserve Tayal culture for younger generations. In this study, we outline this move to a modern sustainable economic base through a literature review, in-depth interviews and participatory observation in the Tayal Indigenous community. We argue that the collective efforts by the Makauy Business Group and other Cinsbu residents have created a strong foundation for self-governing maintenance of a sustainable future.

Introduction

According to a census in June 2022, the population of Indigenous peoples in high mountain areas of Taiwan was 309,789,[2] representing 53.26 per cent of Taiwan's Indigenous peoples. For those living in these areas, agriculture is an essential economic activity. For most of their long history in this environment, these Indigenous peoples have practised self-sufficient cultivation using the slash-and-burn method that has little environmental impact. In recent decades, many Indigenes have converted forests into cultivated farmland and have applied chemical fertilisers and pesticides (so-called conventional agriculture) to increase productivity. Although this method raises agricultural yields and incomes, it has also caused a deterioration in farmers' health, barren and eroding soil, a decline in farmland fertility, water pollution and environmental degradation.

Forestry, rivers and farmland are the main elements of the landscape in many Indigenous high-mountain communities in Taiwan, such as the focus of this chapter, the Cinsbu community.[3] Cinsbu is a Tayal Indigenous community in Hbun Tunan Village,[4] Jienshih Township, Hsinchu County. This is a geographically remote area within the Mknazi Watershed. It is also within the catchment of Shihmen Reservoir. The community belongs to

---

2   The total number of Indigenous people was 581,694 in June 2022. For detailed census data, please refer to CIP (2022). According to the 2022 census, the total population of Taiwan was 23,186,278 (see Ministry of the Interior 2022).

3   In the Japanese colonial era, all the residents of Cinsbu and Smangus were originally from Cinsbu. Due to an increase in population, some people moved out and found a place named 'Smangus'. Nowadays, people usually call the two communities the 'Smangus–Cinsbu community'. In this study, we use 'Cinsbu community' to represent these two communities in their entirety.

4   Hbun Tunan is the name of the Tayal community at the intersection of the river. The Chinese name of Hbun Tunan is Xiuluan Village, which includes the eighth neighbourhood (Smangus) and ninth neighbourhood (Cinsbu).

the Mknazi Group, Sqlyk, of the Tayal people. As the landscape degraded rapidly and traditional culture began to fade away, the Indigenes in Cinsbu began to rethink their approach and consider how to revitalise the land's environmental vitality. Based on previous cooperation, some Tayal people took collective action and attempted to use environmentally friendly organic farming to alleviate harm to people and the land caused by the application of chemical fertilisers and pesticides. They set up an organisation to develop agroforestry, ecotourism and cultural revitalisation through collective action.

In recent years, most of the farming households in the community have begun adopting organic farming methods, surrounding their crops with trees to protect both water and soil. Such cases can be a model for other Indigenous communities. However, this transformation has not always proceeded smoothly in Cinsbu. The community recently began to work with the central government to formulate a regional plan for Indigenous peoples to solve issues of sustainable development. We adopt a literature review, in-depth interviews and participant observation in Indigenous communities to explore how collective action helps promote organic farming and landscape protection, and discuss ongoing challenges.

Theoretical and methodological review

As indicated by the World Commission on Environment and Development, sustainable development is meeting 'the needs of the present without compromising the ability of future generations to meet their own needs' (WCED 1987: 43). Sustainable development requires community collective action, which can be defined as voluntary action taken by a group to achieve common interests. Members can act directly on their own or through an organisation (Meinzen-Dick and Di Gregorio 2004: 4). As Putnam (1993) indicates, members of small businesses seek cooperation with one another to cope with external risks and improve the business environment. Social capital is necessary to mobilise collective action and existing social networks promote this evolution (Bianchi 2001: 117–18; Koutsou and Vounouki 2012: 88).

According to Putnam (1993: 167), social capital contains 'features of social organisations, such as trust, norms and networks that can improve the efficiency of society by facilitating coordinated actions'. The World Bank indicates a narrow view of social capital as a set of horizontal associations between people, consisting of social networks and associated norms that have an effect on community productivity and wellbeing. Information about technology and rural practices can be acquired through social networks formed by producers, which are fundamental in making cooperation between small farms viable (Rodríguez-Entrena et al. 2014: 72; Dias and Franco 2018: 37–38). Social capital facilitates coordination by underpinning trust and a spirit of cooperation (Bianchi 2001: 117–18).

In general, pre-existing social and economic networks seem to facilitate the emergence of new synergies (Brunori and Rossi 2000: 410) because of the existing trust relations. In some Indigenous communities in Taiwan, shared cultures and beliefs and pre-existing agricultural organisation that facilitates the development of social networks in rural areas through accepted norms of cooperation have facilitated the acceptance of network organisation (Rosenfeld 2001: 105). Such communities seem well adapted to undertaking new roles and helping farmers deal with contemporary risks. Collective action enables farmers to confront the outside world, especially in the form of the market economy, which requires developing relations with other farmers and local or national institutions to reduce the cost of production and increase the adoption of innovation and the dissemination of knowledge (Koutsou and Vounouki 2012: 86). However, studies have noted that high levels of social capital must still be activated through leadership for successful adaptation (Suharti et al. 2016: 693; Crona et al. 2017: 71) or through interactions with political power or financial capital in response to development opportunities or disturbances to produce effective community actions and outcomes (Harrison et al. 2016: 528; Yoder 2018: 355).

The Cinsbu community has been able to maintain much of their traditional cultivation style due to recent discoveries about the economic viability of cypress forestry. However, they have also developed tourism as a new opportunity. Because of the increasing number of tourists, the bed and breakfast (B&B) business has thrived to the point that tourism ranks second behind agriculture in the community's economic base. While tourism brings in customers, it also alters the environment, lifestyle and traditional culture of communities. To avoid these pitfalls and create sustainable development based on the experience of cooperative forestry production, community members continue to collect local information, learn their traditional knowledge and implement the Indigenous regional plan through collective action.

Collective action in Cinsbu community

Gaga, the starting point

The Tayal concept of gaga is the starting point for understanding Tayal people's views on the governance of collective action. A traditional Tayal community usually has three different organisations: the qutux gaga (group of co-worshiping ancestors), qutux mlata or qutux phaban (group of co-hunting, co-working and sharing) and gaga relative group (group following the same gaga and regulations). In the Tayal language, *alang* or *qalang* represents community, settlement and village, which are the basis of Tayal social structure. In the past, community structure was based on consanguinity, to constitute a political unit that had its own sovereignty and territory. Each community has the above three organisations to run its social functions. Gaga has multiple meanings; the most common interpretations are 'ancestors' words' or 'the words, regulations or taboos told by the elderly'. Different Tayal communities may have different gaga, but within each community, the people respect the same gaga and always follow the same regulations in a group to jointly work, hunt, share and burden themselves with sin and responsibility (Kojima 1984).

There is no obvious class concept in traditional Tayal society. The leader of the community is not hereditary but based on personal ability. Any internal constraint among group members derives from the belief in utux (ancestors' souls or ghosts). People believe that if one violates common values and ancestors' regulations, disaster will befall not only the violator, but also other gaga members. Traditional Tayal productive activity relies heavily on natural resources. If each person does not constrain their own behaviour, it will impact other community members' harvests. Therefore, Tayal people establish cooperative regulation to decrease possible conflicts over resource use. Moreover, Tayal people's productive activity relies primarily on the community labour force whereby they act collectively to create greater benefits than would accrue through the sum of individual efforts (Yen and Kuan 2004: 31).

History of business development in Cinsbu

The territories of the Cinsbu and Smangus communities are in Hbun-Tunan Village, Jianshih Township, Hsinchu County (Map 15.1). Cinsbu, in Tayal language, refers to 'the place where sunshine first comes at dawn', which derives from the fact that it is in a relatively high mountain area. Local people call their community 'the closest community to the God'.

Cinsbu is also the earliest known community in Hbun-Tunan. Traditions relate how Tayal ancestors migrated north from Ren-ai Township, Nantou County. They went through Sihyuan Wind Gap, the Ridge of Dabajian Mountain, Sinaji Mountain, Hbun-Tunan and finally arrived in Cinsbu.

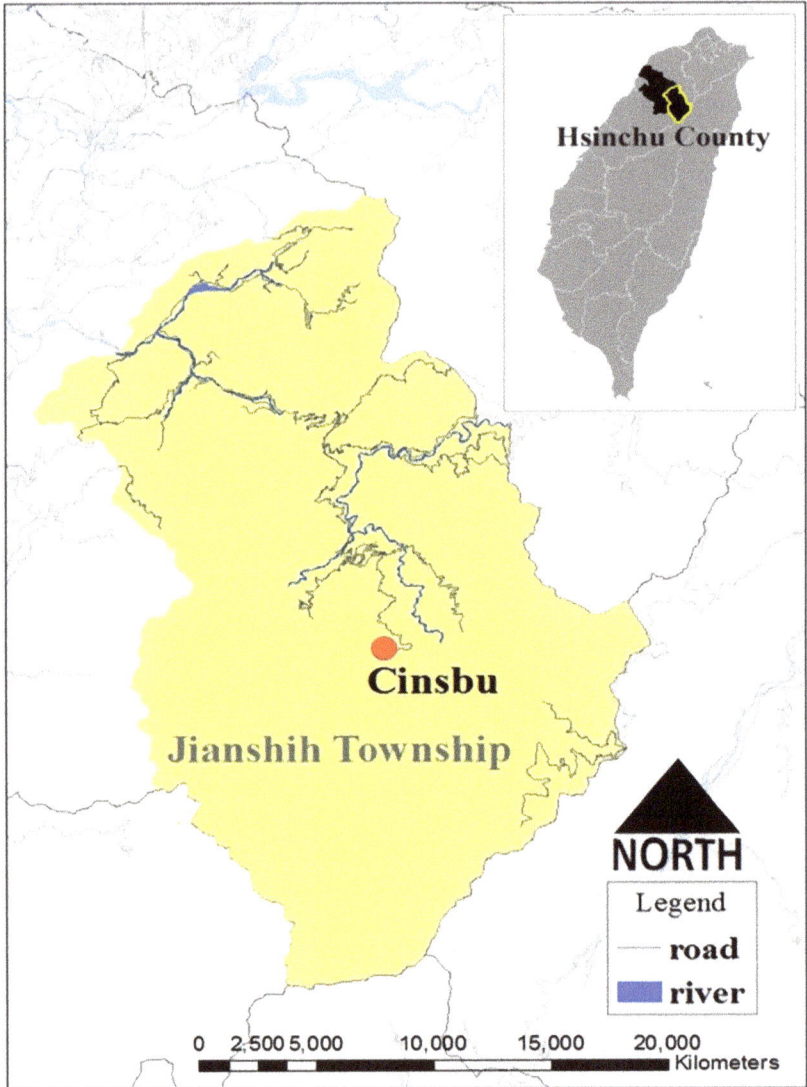

Map 15.1: Map showing Cinsbu within Jianshih Township, Hsinchu County.
Source: Courtesy of Da-Wei Kuan, 2008.[5]

---

5   The authors commissioned Professor Da-Wei Kuan to make the map of Cinsbu. We hereby express our thanks.

The Cinsbu community's traditional agricultural output includes cereal and root tubers. Millet is the most important crop because of its multiple functions for eating, brewing wine and ritual use. Other crops include beans (excluding pigeon pea), squash, vegetables and ramie. Cash crops include Japanese pear, peach, high-mountain vegetables, bell peppers, mushrooms and tomato. Japanese pear and peach contribute the largest quantity of seasonal fruit sales. Due to the influence of the mountain climate, community farmers' income is unstable, so that most farmers (most of whom are male) take temporary jobs outside or within the community to increase family income (Yen et al. 2007: 74).

Development of ecotourism

Cinsbu's tourism development originated in the development of primary cypress forestry. Taiwan's modern five-day working week created demand for outdoor activities for people to enjoy on their days off. Cinsbu had the natural and cultural resources to meet this need, which provided new business opportunities. The increase in tourist numbers also stimulated an increase in the number of local B&B ventures. However, because most tourists visit Cinsbu only on weekends, the revenue from a B&B can be high but uneven and unstable. Therefore, B&B owners continue to grow crops or fruit for a more stable baseline income. Community, organisation and town officeholders organise activities in different months to promote sales of peaches and Japanese pears to help income flow. For instance, there are peach festivals in March, June and July and a Japanese pear festival in September, during which thousands of tourists come to taste the area's popular fruits and other food and take in the beautiful natural scenery. These events also raise the occupancy rate of each B&B, further boosting the local economy (Yen et al. 2007: 74).

The establishment of self-governing collective organisations

Tayal Community Sustainable Development Association and Mknazi Tourism Association

Before the establishment of the Makauy Business Group, the Cinsbu community's efficient tourism development and other economic achievements saw many outside planning groups contacting them and offering to help submit proposals to the central government for funding subsidies. At the same time, community members were aware that development using their own resources had its limits and they would need government resources to take things further. After a series of community meetings and discussions, they agreed to establish an association to nurture communal talent and create more employment opportunities (Huang 2001: 3). The result was the Tayal Community Sustainable Development Association, which was formed in 1999. It not only undertook communal work, but also progressed spatial planning, communal arts, cultural business development and the nurturing of tourism. It was the base for agricultural transformation, the conservation of natural resources and the development of ecotourism and B&B accommodation (Hsiao 2005: 83–84).

After a year, however, association members had different opinions on how to operate. Some members left and established the Mknazi Tourism Association, in 2002, to market farm products. They promoted the community's cultural characteristics so customers could experience Tayal culture and food, and changed B&B operation methods from individual operation to co-management. The association instituted communal marketing mechanisms for the sale of farm products to achieve economies of scale (Hsiao 2004: 86).

The Makauy Business Group

In 2005, members of the Tayal Community Sustainable Development Association established the Makauy Business Group with help from the Taiwan Indigenous Community Empowerment Association. Makauy derives from the name maqaw, a kind of mountain pepper, which grows in low to middle altitudes (500–1,800 metres). For the Tayal, it is an important spice used as a seasoning and to relieve one's thirst. Makauy has a specific meaning of shared harmonising with others. This group's purpose was based on a key Tayal cultural value of maintaining the community's environment for sustainable development. Therefore, it strongly opposed giving territory to outside corporations to prevent Tayal culture being disrupted or displaced by outside interests. Informants A1, A2, A9, A11 and A12 said of their mission:

> The government claims that conservation is a precondition for
> development, but it is the perspective of outsiders, which does not
> meet the local need to promote development, and often results in
> many unforeseen problems. For Tayal people, forestry is the fountain
> of life; if forestry is destroyed, the growth of various crops will get

worse. We operate business with local experience and ecological wisdom. We will not destroy the surrounding natural environment. Ecological conservation can be achieved not only by Tayal traditional masonry methods, but also through the reconstruction of traditional ecological value … In addition, Tayal people know the nature of the forest deeply; the external government does not know the Indigenous culture and often frames the policy by imagination.

As to cultural inheritance, the Makauy Business Group often holds traditional rituals to consolidate community members' identity. Informant A1 said:

The preservation of Tayal culture is passed down through dictation and ceremony … In recent years, we have held the qo'tas ceremony … [W]e believe that Tayal culture is gifted to Cinsbu community by the God.

Although the Makauy Business Group is not registered in accordance with Taiwanese law, it helps B&B operators and other community members cooperate with one another and provides mechanisms for financial support to encourage the economy and cultural inheritance. For instance, it established internet marketing of farm products to enlarge their sales channels, held camping activities, led ecotourism and attracted tourists to visit to learn about Tayal culture (Hsiao 2004: 86–88). Peach growers in Cinsbu mainly rely on the Makauy Business Group to promote community production and marketing. Through communal cooperation, they can decrease the impact of wholesalers' prices and reduce their marketing costs, guaranteeing farmers a stable income. Informant A2, who is a member of this group, describes the work the group does to assist farmers:

To gain reasonable income, Makauy Business Group gathers the fruit farmers in several nearby communities to sell self-grown products, which has helped eight disadvantaged single-parent families and prevented their exploitation by brokers or even by farmers' associations.

Makauy Business Group's collective action

The above statement indicates how the mission of the Makauy Business Group differs from that of the Tayal Community Sustainable Development Association and Mknazi Tourism Association. Makauy's mission is to develop the community economy through tourism, but it emphasises that economic development must first ensure the health of the community's natural resources and Tayal traditional culture—that is, they must first achieve sustainability of their natural environment and culture to enable them to secure their economic future. Therefore, every business should operate under mutual consensus. Informant A3 said:

> Due to the limited land area, the community should develop various businesses and make strategic alliances ... to develop leisure, agriculture, together with tourism, B&B, cultural businesses, etcetera. It is essential and the future direction for Indigenous communities.

According to the purposes of establishment mentioned above, the Makauy Business Group's members devote themselves to protecting communal natural resources.

Learning organic agriculture

The Tayal people traditionally practised slash-and-burn cultivation, which is also called swidden agriculture. Forest is cleared and burned and crops are then grown in the fertile ash without the use of artificial fertilisers. People cultivate using implements rather than animals and cultivation occurs over short-term cycles in one location, with the land given a long fallow period to regenerate (Yen and Yang 2004: 398). Because of changes in social status and government control over sloping land, the community's farmland area has greatly declined and is now insufficient for meeting its subsistence needs. To satisfy basic life demands, farmers try to increase the yield per unit area of farmland. Although Cinsbu residents started to increase cultivation 20 years ago, this was primarily through conventional farming methods using chemical fertilisers. Some community members gained organic certification in 1998, but organic farming was not promoted.

In recent years, community residents have come to realise that tourism and chemical use in farming could risk resource degradation. Thus, residents—mainly driven by the Makauy Business Group—began to practise organic farming. Moreover, other Tayal communities in Jianshih Township also started to promote chemical-free natural farming[6] and achieve great results.

---

6   Broadly defined, in this study, 'natural farming' was introduced from Korea, which uses han-fang for cultivation without pesticide sprays. It is a low-cost, environmentally friendly way of producing safe food and, in its aims, is no different to 'organic farming'. However, natural farming in this study represents cultivation techniques, but also refers to communities that are progressing traditional ecological knowledge and communal interpersonal relationship rebuilding, beyond the current concept of organic farming. Furthermore, organic farming certification is very strict and expensive, so many Indigenous communal farmers cannot afford the fees. Thus, to distinguish methods of cultivation, this study adopts the term 'natural farming'.

The pioneering informants A4 and A10 talked about the limitations of tourism in advancing community interests and their experience of promoting organic farming:

> During the New Year holiday, the B&Bs in Cinsbu are all booked out, the income is around $500,000 [US$16,700], but the income will decrease 50 per cent in rainy seasons, and visitors shall come once in a while on weekends … Therefore, we have to make a living by farming. Decades ago, I promoted organic farming in the village and church, but villagers did not believe in me, and even teased me. In recent years, the villagers have come to me to learn organic farming after realising the merit and future of it.

When the group learned the Quri community had received assistance and subsidies from the government to run workshops on natural farming, they eagerly participated. Since most Cinsbu farmers were eager to make this agricultural transformation, they were keen to learn natural farming. Informants A5 and A11 said: 'The aged people in the community welcome and expect to have workshops for learning the skill of organic farming and exchange relevant information to increase the sense of place.'

To understand farmers' demands and teach new agricultural techniques, two Tayal instructors were invited to the workshops. The instructors were farmers who had successfully run natural farming or gained organic certification in other Indigenous communities. Because of their Tayal cultural background, language and production environment, these instructors could easily understand the local situation and teach in an appropriate way. Such workshops, in which farmers learn from farmers, have strengthened farmers' confidence in organic cultivation. Because all the attendees were relatives, friends or seniors from the same ethnic group, they did not feel hesitant or shy during the workshops and gained lots of natural farming knowledge from the instructors. As a result, more and more people started to cultivate organically. Informants A6 and A12 said:

> If there is no certain source of income, the young men will leave the community, so we spend lots of time learning how to conduct organic farming. About 15 years ago, only one family practised organic farming. But the family's practice and promotion led to not only the local residents (about 70 per cent) starting to apply organic farming methods, but also community members (about 30 per cent and usually the young) who had travelled and worked in cities to then come back to their home communities and begin organic farming.

Certainly, transformation is not without its obstacles. Informants A6 and A7 recalled the difficulties they encountered:

> Before we joined the organic farming, we had difficulties affording the production cost, paying the organic certification fee and finding sales channels. In the beginning, we had to invest around $300,000 [US$10,000] to build ... [a] simplified greenhouse and plant factory, then to pay the certification fee to verify the quality of farm products ... If farmers do not know the verification procedure, they will panic.

> In the beginning [about five years ago], we had to invest a large amount of money and gained a little bit of profit only after receiving the organic certification. During the transition, we had to shore up the unprofitable business at first and find other ways such as learning farming skills from an [agricultural] workshop to increase productivity and hopefully to gain income.

Agricultural transformation imposed a huge economic burden on community residents because of the unstable income during the transition period, but most considered it was worth the sacrifice for such an important reason. Informant A6 said:

> Conventional farming destroys land and human health due to chemical fertiliser and pesticide. Even if the seeds are good quality, unhealthy land still cannot grow good crops and gain profits in the long term. People don't have the foresight. The land needs to be used in sustainable ways for the welfare of our future generations. If the land is damaged, people will leave eventually. So, we have to tell our children that the land is the traditional territory given by the ancestors. We should maintain its integrity.

By 2015, more than half of the community's farming households had converted to chemical-free or organic agriculture and 22 had obtained certification for their organic products. The area with organic certification is 32.82 hectares, accounting for 21.5 per cent of the total farmland area of 152.5 hectares (MOI and COIP 2019: 34).

Cultivation in agroforestry: Harmonising production and environmental protection

Agroforestry is a business that combines agriculture and forestry. Spurgeon (1980) indicates that the development of agroforestry was a result of forest destruction by logging and degradation of soil fertility from the resulting intensification of slash-and-burn activities and reduced fallow periods due to land pressure. Through the application of scientific techniques, forest degradation can be gradually repaired and residents' subsistence needs satisfied. Therefore, it is necessary to promote agroforestry for conserving biomass and avoiding deforestation. In 1992, Agenda 21, set at the UN Earth Summit in Rio de Janeiro, promoted agroforestry as a sustainable land use (UNCED 1992: 82). King (1987) also indicates that agroforestry is a sustainable land management system, and it is compatible with local cultures and customs. Adoption of agroforestry can appropriately protect water and soil on sloping land, decrease flooding and landslides, increase humus levels and maintain soil moisture (Smith 2010: 12–14). As mentioned earlier, the traditional Tayal cultivation technique was slash and burn on temporarily cleared ground within an old-growth forest that was used and then allowed to regrow and replenish. However, with the great loss of old-growth forest, this type of cultivation has disappeared. Informants A8, A9, A10 and A12 told us that the Tayal ecological knowledge of citimene incorporated many techniques that are today labelled as agroforestry:

> We do not cut the trees on farmland, so tree roots can seize the soil to slow the erosion of topsoil, and the branches of the trees can be cut to provide sunlight for growing crops … We grow mountain fig beside the farmland because it grows quickly to maintain topsoil. If the land is cultivated for a long time, we grow Formosan alder to restore soil fertility. A long time ago, our ancestors grew crops on at least five plots for shifting cultivation. For example, the first plot was cultivated for four years, then Indigenous farmers moved to another plot … [T]hey learned that each abandoned patch normally had to be left fallow for at least 20 years before the soil became fertile enough to grow again. If there were Formosan alder on the farmland, farmers would not grow crops as the land fertility was not [high] enough.

The Cinsbu community is high in the mountains with much steeply sloping land that is easily eroded. To prevent erosion, farmers in the Makauy Business Group practise agroforestry, growing plenty of trees such as alder and cedar. These trees shelter crops, consolidate slopes, retain water and soil, and fertilise soil by defoliation (Plates 15.1 and 15.2). According to Smith (2010: 13), relatively few of the 650 woody species that can fix atmospheric nitrogen occur in temperate regions; of these, black locust (*Robinia pseudoacacia*), mesquites (Prosopis), alder (Alnus) and oleaster (Elaeagnus) have been investigated for their nitrogen-fixing potential (Smith 2010: 16). Significant transfers of fixed nitrogen to crops have been observed in a study that showed that 32–58 per cent of the total nitrogen in alley-cropped maize came from nitrogen fixed by the adjacent red alder (*Alnus rubra*).

Interestingly, farmers do not clear all weeds to decrease crop loss and they control pests and diseases by biological methods, such as pheromone traps or by co-planting celery, green onion, peppers or other bitter-tasting plants. Informants A1 and A12 told us how these practices prevent pests:

> If [all] the weeds were cut off, the insects would eat all the vegetables … [I]f the weeds were left without pesticides for the insects, the loss of the vegetables would decrease to 50 per cent … We grow cabbage, celery and green onion, which are bitter-tasting plants, so the insects will not come.

Plate 15.1: The agroforestry in Cinsbu community is combined with multiple crops growing in rotation and Taiwan fir at the lower end of the farmland.
Photo: Ai-Ching Yen.

Plate 15.2: Formosan alder grows at the upper end of the farmland.
Photo: Syax Tali.

Farmers also attempt as much as possible to use recyclable materials. For example, farmers used to cover each plot with plastic sheeting to stifle weeds. However, this led to soil salinisation and hardening that obstructed nutrition absorption and, because the plastic sheeting would break but did not degrade rapidly, polluted the land. Moreover, the sheets had to be changed every year, which was not environmentally friendly (Plate 15.3). Now, instead of plastic sheets, farmers apply plug seedlings, which also obstruct weeds, are convenient to use, durable and can be used for many years (Plate 15.4). Informants A1 and A12 explained the aim of switching to plug seedlings:

> The original function of plastic sheets is to suppress weeds, but once it is covered the soil respiration cannot be continued; it will accumulate salt ... If we use plug seedlings, the concentration of soil salinity is reduced by rainfall due to the soil being exposed in the air ... [I]f we use plastic sheets, people are more likely to enter and step on the field and the soil gets harder and harder ... [This] can be avoided with plug seedlings. A set of plug seedlings contains around 30 holes so that we can nurse seeds directly in the plant pot and place the plug seedling into the soil directly. The bottom of the plate hole touches the soil, so roots can grow deep into the soil. We pull up the entire plug seedling while harvesting. It is a labour-saving instrument. The cost of plug seedlings might be higher in the short term, but it can be reused for more than 10 years, and plastic sheeting has to be replaced every year, so that in the long term, the cost of plug seedlings will be lower than plastic sheets.

Plate 15.3: Crops are often covered with plastic sheeting to suppress the growth of weeds, but it damages quickly and the small pieces can pollute farmland.

Photo: Ai-Ching Yen.

Plate 15.4: Sets of plug seedlings can suppress weeds and be reused for several years, reducing pollution.

Photo: Ai-Ching Yen.

Informant A6 also told us that elders had passed down knowledge about the use of stones:

> Stone is fertiliser! The field without stones will accumulate water during rainy days, and the plant roots will go wrong from staying for more than four hours in the water. So, we will keep them as long as they do not affect the field cultivation. Stones have drainage functions and leave room for the soil to breathe. While millet is growing, the sun shines on the stone, which heats, accelerating the growth of crops.

Tayal agroforestry thus benefits from the wisdom of local farmers' experience. Through agroforestry, people can harmonise production, protect the environment and maintain local biodiversity. It establishes the basis for sustainable operations in agriculture and tourism.

Teaching tourists about Tayal Indigenous culture: 'Cinsbu learning'

Increasing numbers of tourists and the associated pollution and damage to the local ecosystem carry implications for the Cinsbu community's quality of life. Reducing the negative externalities of tourism is part of effective self-governance alongside ensuring economic viability. Furthermore, the community's elders deem it important that they follow their gaga to eat together, share traditional life experiences and maintain coexistent relationships with their mountains and forests. In recent years, Western positivism and contemporary pragmatism have increased while traditional Tayal cultural values have flowed away. For this reason, the Makauy Business Group put a lot of effort into maintaining Tayal culture and promoting it to outsiders.

To this end, the group developed 'Cinsbu learning', which offers a great amount of Tayal knowledge and includes courses on the following: 'mother tongue', 'eating, living and folk songs', 'traditional territory mapping' and 'weaving' (see Plates 15.5–15.7). The raw material for Tayal traditional weaving was ramie fibre, although this is now also mixed with other materials. In Tayal tradition, only women who were good at weaving were qualified to receive a facial tattoo. Group members construct natural community classrooms in which to provide instruction on humanity, education, business and ecology. They instruct tourists about forestry, experiencing the beauty of the mountains and traditional culture. 'Cinsbu learning' follows the principle of 'doing by learning and learning by doing' in instructing tourists and other customers. Informants A1 and A10 explained the aim of 'Cinsbu learning':

> The 30 members of the Makauy Business Group developed 'Cinsbu learning'. This learning park has been established for three years. We think the classroom is a concept of non-spatial limitation. For example, while we are working on the farm, the farm is the classroom; while we are working in the forest, the forest is the classroom. We cooperate with elementary, junior high and high schools to develop outdoor learning. Because many tourists just come to the tribal community to take a look, eat, sleep and learn nothing, we created 'Cinsbu learning' to share the elders' wisdom and have experiences in local agriculture, living and culture.

Plate 15.5: The Indigenous group's traditional territory is shown on a community topographical map.

Photo: Ai-Ching Yen.

Plate 15.6: Phytoncides, antimicrobial organic compounds, fill the air of the forest classroom.

Photo: Ai-Ching Yen.

Plate 15.7: An Indigenous woman demonstrates how to weave ramie.
Photo: Ai-Ching Yen.

'Cinsbu learning' is an important part of tourism, with tours arranged for schools and other organisations. The instructional and other work involved is allocated according to group members' professions and divided into activities, contact, traffic control, lecturing, cooking and other jobs. Every group member participates in each tour to provide good service for customers and tourists and to practise ancient 'working together' and 'sharing together' gaga regulation.

The synergy of initiation: The Specific Regional Plan for Indigenous Peoples

The Indigenous people of Cinsbu community follow the spirit of the gaga and protect their farmland, forest and watershed. However, the current land use regulations do not consider Indigenous history, culture and farming practices or residents' needs. This has resulted in illegal land use. To resolve these problems, the central government deliberated with the Cinsbu community to set up the Specific Regional Plan for Indigenous Peoples (SRPIP). To comply with the core value of taking care of the land ('mlahang'), the whole area covered by the SRPIP is delineated into watershed protection zones, potential disaster management zones, growth management zones, living and farming zones and ecological development zones, which were announced on 29 March 2019 (MOI and COIP 2019: 53). The government requires even stricter regulation to protect the watershed and forest for water and forestry conservation purposes in the water protection area and asked farmers to relocate and cultivate in the growth management area. As for cultivated land, the SRPIP allows only organic farming or traditional agroforestry with water and soil conservation. Through self-governance, the Cinsbu community can use the plan to further their sustainable land use objectives more efficiently.

Social capital influencing collective action

Social capital is a 'societal resource' that connects actors and permits them to jointly pursue common goals (Stolle 2003: 19; Jackman and Miller 1998). Although social capital has been defined in a variety of ways (cf. Coleman 1988; Putnam 1993; Temkin and Rohe 1998), there is a common emphasis on the aspects of social structure (trust, norms and social networks) that facilitate collective action. As Bourdieu (1980: 2; 1986a: 248) points out,

> Social capital is the whole of actual or potential resources which are linked to the possession of a durable network of, more or less institutionalized, relationships of inter-knowledge and inter-recognition.

In other words, social networks created and maintained through participation in groups have become instruments and assets for individuals to increase their economic capital—that is, accruing benefits (Portes 1998: 3).

The Makauy Business Group is a small organisation; nevertheless, its members have gradually created consensus and trust by overcoming conflict. According to our observations, several factors have influenced the business group members' behaviour.

Traditional gaga-based values

Tayal's traditional beliefs reflect the concept of gaga—the ancient regulations and taboos. If people disobey the values and regulations of gaga, disasters occur not only for the violator, but also for other members of the same gaga.

In our observations, with its religious and moral implications, the constraints of traditional internal regulation still affect community residents, even though capitalism has become the prevalent mainstream organising principle of Taiwanese society. To the Cinsbu community, nature is the daily provider of life and activities are regulated by the principle of 'sharing together'.

Sharing is the norm not only for this generation, but also for its offspring, so a cross-generational norm is the basis of sustainable development. The Makauy Business Group's purpose is to build the base of Tayal culture, sustain the community and the environment and emphasise that the use of agricultural land should be based on Tayal culture, including the protection of natural resources. These ideas are completely in keeping with Tayal gaga and the value of 'sharing together'.

Indigenous peoples–based resource governance

Government policies towards Indigenous farmland have often been criticised as elitist and dominating, emphasising government-based management modes. Without considering multiple values and viewpoints and without local consultation, the government can hardly resolve problems. The percentage of Taiwanese Indigenous peoples who live in mountainous areas is 30.82 per cent. Indigenous peoples' livelihoods greatly depend on natural resources. Once the government controls resources, Indigenous peoples' livelihoods are impacted. In addition, the Western scientific administration applied by the government differs from communities' traditional resource governance. As Tayal elders told us, there is no concept of 'management' in the Tayal language; such activities fall under the idea of 'care' and demonstrating consideration for the land. Community residents therefore do not agree with the government's singular policy approach that excludes community residents from decision-making processes.

In contrast, the Makauy Business Group's governance acknowledges that ancient, inherited wisdom can be used to constrain group members to work and share together. Residents recognise the logic of this type of Indigenous cultural governance.

Legislating fair and transparent regulation

Some self-governing organisations practising collective action create institutions and management systems for the fair distribution of long-term benefits and put in place positive incentives for sustainability. The abundance of natural resources in Cinsbu presents opportunities for community businesses; however, tourists bring negative externalities that are starting to impact the local ecology and people's communal lifestyles. To solve these problems, self-governance organisations have been formed to regulate community security conventions (see Table 15.1). Most members of the Makauy Business Group are also members of the Tayal Community Sustainable Development Association. Experience reveals that conflicts among members usually involve the distribution of benefits or free-rider problems. Therefore, this group has established a fairness institute for community business cooperation. To prevent undisclosed costs and benefits causing distrust among residents, they are transparent about all revenue and expenditure to ensure every member shares each dollar they earn and to avoid conflict.

Conclusion: The inspiration of collective action from the Makauy Business Group

The Makauy Business Group was aware the community was only paying attention to tourism and its abundant revenue and not the maintenance of local resources. They also realised that if people continued this way, community development would fade due to the degradation of the very resources that attracted tourists. They wanted to promote collective action in which people focused on events they were willing to complete with consensus. However, if any of the members selfishly focus simply on earning their own living, collective action will soon collapse, degrading social capital.

The Makauy Business Group plays an important leadership role in conserving local resources and Tayal culture. Both its members and other community residents realise that maintaining balance in the natural environment is essential for all the businesses they would like to retain. Their unique 'Cinsbu learning' is truly based on local resources. The Makauy Business Group members have been taking customers and tourists to their community to introduce them to true Tayal culture, including the knowledge of how forestry preserves, protects and provides Tayal people with healthy land, lives and food. 'Cinsbu learning' uses traditional gaga regulation, which is not only a transparent institution established to avoid conflict, but also a mode of self-governance free of governmental elitist policy. Moreover, gaga regulation indicates that Cinsbu learning is the best form of local resource governance. Collective action is based on experience, especially cooperative experience. People trust each other due to these past experiences, which allows them to act together towards the same goal. Also, collective action accumulates social capital. Therefore, when Cinsbu's internal (group members and community residents) and external (tourists) conditions have been satisfied, social capital will be accumulated progressively and help the growth of collective action.

Currently, many Indigenous communities in Taiwan are accumulating social capital to confront great change. Although the Indigenous communities in Cinsbu have not earned high revenue yet, collective action has enabled them to adjust their business goals while ensuring a sustainable resource base for the future. Recently, increasing numbers of tourists have come to the community to learn traditional Cinsbu knowledge. In addition, the Makauy Business Group members and Cinsbu's residents have taken the chance to make friends with tourists to accumulate social capital. As a result, Cinsbu learning has put the Tayal community on the path to a sustainable future.

Table 15.1: List of interviewees

Code	Community	Gender	Date of interview	Location of interview
A1	Cinsbu	M	6/3/2006 10/5/2012 9/3/2013	Cinsbu Church Own B&B
A2	Cinsbu	F	6/3/2006	Cinsbu church
A3	Cinsbu	M	17/5/2007 22/3/2010 10/3/2013	Own house
A4	Smangus	M	3/5/2011 19/5/2012	Own house
A5	Smangus	F	3/5/2011	Own organic farm
A6	Smangus	M	19/5/2012 9/3/2013	Own organic farm
A7	Smangus	F	8/9/2011 9/3/2013	Megalan Common organic farm
A8	Cinsbu	M	19/5/2012	Own house
A9	Cinsbu	M	10–11/5/2014	Cinsbu church
A10	Cinsbu	M	10–11/5/2014	Cinsbu church Own organic farm
A11	Smangus	M	10–11/5/2014	Cinsbu church
A12	Cinsbu	M	10–11/5/2014	Own organic farm

16

Māori and Pacific Islander Cultural, Educational and Economic Exchanges with the Mapuche of Southern Chile

Roannie Ng Shiu and Paul D'Arcy

Introduction

Over the past decade, the Indigenous Mapuche peoples of southern Chile have reached out to Indigenous peoples in the Pacific to investigate the efficacy of their Indigenous development models for their own needs. The Chilean Government and the Mapuche peoples, who make up about 10 per cent of Chile's population, have expressed a keen interest in drawing on the success of Māori and other Polynesian models of economic empowerment and cultural development to resolve mounting tensions between them over land alienation and socioeconomic marginalisation. These links are based on more than shared experiences of colonialism.

The Mapuche peoples in the history of Chile

The Mapuche peoples of Chile have a long history of resisting Spanish and Chilean attempts to subjugate and integrate them into the respective empire and nation-state. The Mapuche have also been referred to as the Reche, Aucas and Araucanians at different times (Dillehay and Rothhammer 2013: 150). Historians have generally argued that the Mapuche arose from various local hunter-gatherer peoples within the Araucanía region and only evolved into the Mapuche culture the Spanish first encountered relatively late in their pre-Hispanic history. While they may have experienced occasional infusions from Indigenous migrants from as far afield as Amazonia, the Mapuche are from and of Araucanía (Dillehay and Rothhammer 2013: 150–53). Recent advances in genetics have added precision to the rather limited oral, material and documentary evidence from before the arrival of the Spanish in the sixteenth century—most notably, in advancing strong evidence of a Polynesian connection not found in neighbouring peoples. At Spanish contact, the Mapuche as constituted today comprised five linguistic families of which Mapuche was one (Dillehay and Rothhammer 2013: 154).

The Mapuche offered some of the fiercest resistance the Spanish encountered on the entire continent, with the beginning of the Spanish invasion of their lands in 1541 serving to consolidate and unify local peoples in their resistance. Indeed, many historians argue today's Mapuche, as Chile's largest Indigenous group, have their origins in this early Spanish era by force of necessity (Dillehay and Rothhammer 2013: 151). This, however, underplays the paucity of evidence from before the Spanish as a barrier to identifying distinct ethnic groups and cultural patterns. This is also a politically charged subject in the modern era in a nation seeking to forge a unified identity based on citizenship while its largest constituent group, the Mapuche, asserts their distinct rights as original inhabitants with an unbroken bond to their customary territory and all the legal rights this might entail.

Elements of Mapuche culture have remained relatively consistent from the sixteenth century until now, despite their political minority status and disruption and adaptation in the face of European political domination and cultural intolerance. For example, from the sixteenth century, Mapuche settlements became larger and were increasingly located in areas away from zones of conflict and European activity. These allowed the concentration of warriors for defence and served as refuges for many other Indigenous peoples fleeing Chilean Government aggression (Dillehay and Rothhammer 2013: 155). While their lands encompassed a variety of ecosystems from the Pacific coast to the eastern foothills of the Andes, most Mapuche lived in small rural communities practising a mixed economy of horticulture, fishing and hunter-gathering depending on local resources. They were organised along patrilineal, patrilocal and bilateral lines and into autonomous chiefdoms of various sizes that might temporarily combine to resist Spanish and Chilean government invasions (Dillehay and Rothhammer 2013: 152–54).

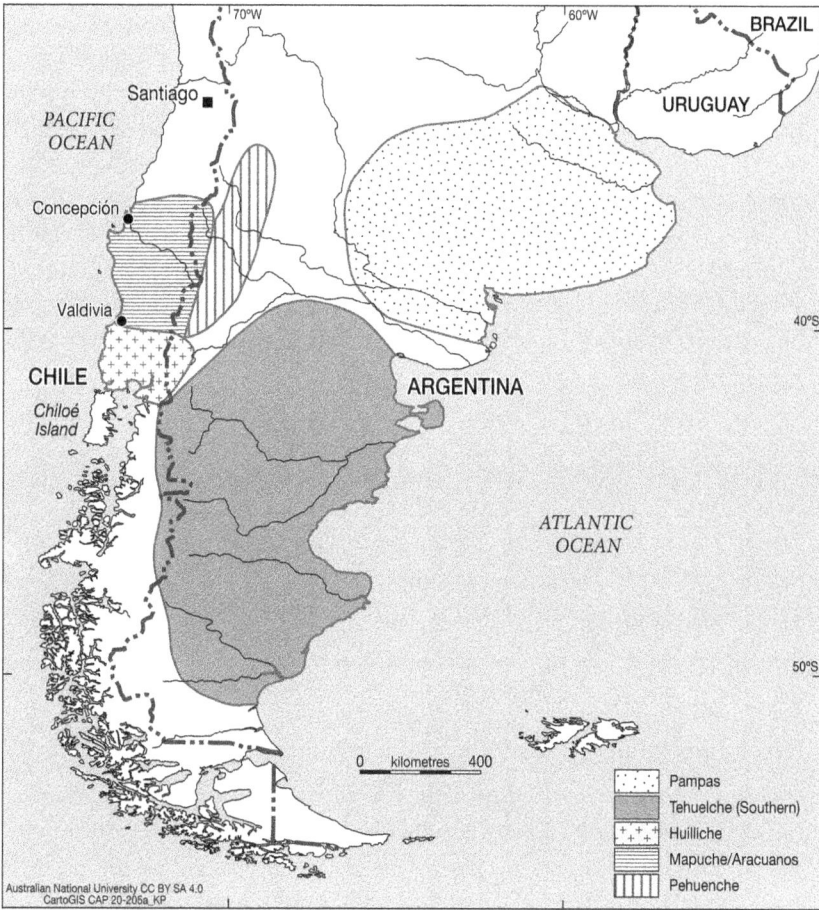

Map 16.1: Map showing distribution of the main Indigenous peoples of southern South America.

Source: Map by CartoGIS, The Australian National University.

The Mapuche were accomplished warriors who fiercely resisted Spanish and Chilean conquest and remained independent until a brutal campaign of pacification in 1883 (Funk 2012: 128; Carter, D. 2010: 62). This campaign led to their confinement on state-defined Indigenous lands, where they have endured marginalisation of their social, cultural and religious beliefs and attacks on their resource rights and control of land. The Mapuche's core homeland after 1883 has centred on the Araucanía region between the cities of Concepción and Valdivia. Approximately 10 million hectares were taken by the government and transferred to European settlers (Milesi 2018). The remaining homelands became the centre of modern Indigenous resistance to ongoing land takeovers by state and private interests (Dillehay and Rothhammer 2013: 152–53; Haughney 2006). While Mapuche lands originally embraced all ecosystems from the Pacific coast to the alpine Andes, since 1883, government actions mean Mapuche-controlled lands are confined solely to areas of temperate rainforest and mountainous terrain (Dillehay and Rothhammer 2013: 154; López Vergara and Lucero 2018: 649; The Guardian 2018). However, these homelands have allowed the Mapuche to retain their cultural identity far more successfully than the remainder of Chile's Indigenous peoples, who were largely relegated to urban slums or government-defined lands (Dillehay and Rothhammer 2013: 154).

Historical links between Chile and Polynesia

In 1888, just a few years after moving in force against the Mapuche, the Government of Chile annexed the closest Polynesian island to Chile, Rapa Nui (Easter Island). Rapa Nui society had been decimated in the 1860s after many people were recruited on false promises or by outright kidnapping by labour recruiters for the guano and plantation labour needs of Chile and Peru. Harsh working conditions and European diseases decimated this Pacific Island workforce, 93 per cent of whom died in service. Population loss among the Rapa Nui population was especially profound, decimating their society and weakening their ability to resist annexation by Chile. Some 1,407 Rapa Nui were among the 3,634 Pacific Islanders taken to South America as effective slaves in 1862 and 1863 before the French and British navies ended these hunts for human cargo. Only 148 of the 3,634 taken were repatriated (Crocombe 1991: 121; Maude 1981).

The island's bleak, treeless environment and relative isolation made it relatively worthless to most potential colonisers for anything but sheep and cattle farming (McCall 1995; Rauen 2019; López 1998). Chile even sought to sell the island to Japanese interests in the 1930s (McCall 1995). However, its true wealth lay hidden from view on the seabed in the form of minerals. Today, Chile has the largest EEZ in the eastern Pacific and is rich in both coastal zone fisheries and deep-sea seabed minerals. The crucial role Rapa Nui plays in defining and massively extending Chile's EEZ and the wealth of fishery and mineral deposits within it, plus the likely placement of large fishing and/or mineral processing stations on Rapa Nui in the future, mean Rapa Nui calls for greater autonomy have been resisted by the Chilean

Government. Rapa Nui are a small population on a barren island, which makes their control much easier for authorities than for the larger Mapuche population in forested terrain in Araucanía (Rauen 2019).

Polynesian peoples seem to have colonised Rapa Nui around 1200 CE. Palm trees (*Paschalococos disperta*) covered the landscape, and sea turtles and land birds were plentiful. Rapa Nui was colder than these people's tropical homelands, rainfall less regular and cold winds more frequent. However, a number of the colonisers' tropical crops such as sweet potato, taro, yams and bananas were successfully introduced and intensively cultivated.

The successful colonisation of Rapa Nui was subsequently undermined by climatic changes and Polynesian rat (*Rattus exulans*) stowaways on the colonisers' canoes. Climate changes after settlement altered rainfall, while the rat population exploded in the absence of local predators and feasted on palm seeds, adding to the demise of the palm already under way through agricultural clearance and the transport of stone monuments. Intense intercommunity competition to build heavy moai (stone statues) led to the felling of many palm trees to act as rollers to relocate moai from inland quarries to coastal sites. The loss of forest increased wind erosion, reduced soil fertility and removed the option of canoe construction to extend the resource base to neighbouring islands and offshore fisheries. Deforestation was nearly complete by the time the first European explorers arrived in the late eighteenth century. The introduction of diseases in the late 1700s and early 1800s from European naval and trade vessels set the population into a steep decline, to just 3,000 people in 1862, when the slave vessels arrived (Hunt 2007; Hunt and Lipo 2011; Prebble et al. 2012: 195; DiNapoli et al. 2021).

Advocates of Polynesian links for the Mapuche note features of specific coastal Mapuche groups' language, items and behaviour that are similar to those found in certain parts of eastern Polynesia, including Aotearoa New Zealand, which were not found among other Indigenous groups. These elements are seacraft, loanwords, especially relating to chiefs and warriors, and cultural concepts relating to the afterlife and chiefly protocols. Coastal Mapuche were observed to be notably taller than other Mapuche to Spanish eyes, although the evidence that this might relate to Polynesian genetic material remains disputed (Ramírez Aliaga 2010, 2011; Jones et al. 2011). Eastern Polynesians are among the tallest peoples in the world, with notably high average muscle mass, which some scientists attribute to their oceanic environment, as muscle mass is a good insulator (Houghton 1996). Two of the most compelling pieces of evidence for this contact are Polynesian chicken mitochondrial (mtDNA) material in local Araucanian chicken bones and the dating of this material to a period of active Polynesian exploration and geographical expansion in far eastern Polynesia. Human skeletal material from the island of Mocha, offshore from Mapuche lands, remains contested, but adds to the weight of evidence for Polynesian contact and has moved debate more to the nature and extent of contact than whether contact occurred (Matisoo-Smith and Ramírez-Aliaga 2010). While Dillehay and Rothhammer (2013: 156) continue to dismiss the evidence for significant contact between the Mapuche and Polynesians as flimsy and based largely on stylistic similarities between certain artefacts, words and cultural symbols, they do admit the possibility of limited and most likely unsustained contact between Polynesian voyagers and Mapuche on the basis of the mtDNA elements of Polynesian chickens in Araucanian chickens. They also point out that Gongora et al. (2008) challenged this assertion by noting that this mtDNA was more likely the result of European contact. They also placed Mapuche genetic origins firmly among Andean populations (Dillehay and Rothhammer 2013: 156–58).

The Mapuche in modern Chile

While the Communist Party of Chile supported the return of Indigenous lands to customary owners in the 1930s, Mapuche political and cultural advocates have found it difficult to have their beliefs incorporated into national agendas. This was the case even during the ascendancy in the 1960s and 1970s of pre-Pinochet leftist-leaning governments and the social movements of Eduardo Frei Montalva's government (1964–70) and socialist Salvador Allende's Unidad Popular alliance (1970–73) because of dominant class-based analysis and solutions (López Vergara and Lucero 2018: 650; Crow 2013: 77, 105, 139). The 1973 military coup to overthrow Allende ushered in two decades of repression and a dramatic shift to the right in national economic policy.

Modern Chile continues to live with the legacy of Augusto Pinochet's dictatorship (1973–90), when the economy was transformed along lines recommended by the neoliberal Chicago School. Chile gained entry to the Organisation for Economic Co-operation and Development (OECD) in 2010 as its overall national income rose, thanks in part to a booming minerals sector, while at the same time Chile registered the greatest income disparity between rich and poor in the OECD (Funk 2012: 126). Unlike its northern neighbours, but like Argentina and Uruguay, Chile has a largely urban population with distinct middle and working-class affiliations rather than predominantly ethnic affiliations (Funk 2012: 129–30; Drake and Hershberg 2006: 9–10). Indeed, as part of its nation-building and national re-envisaging campaign, the Pinochet regime consistently maintained there were no Indigenous peoples in Chile and distributed government funds based on social and economic criteria (Funk 2012: 130).

Chile's Indigenous peoples are disproportionately represented among its poorest citizens, with Araucanía, the home region of the Mapuche in south-central Chile, producing the worst socioeconomic indicators in the country. As previously noted, Chilean politics is dominated by a wealthy white-mestizo elite who have benefited from the alienation of Indigenous lands to control the resource sector of Chile's largely primary export–based economy. The national narrative pursued by the government was of a diverse but unified nation whose commonalities outweighed ethnic and regional identities and whose economic prosperity had helped avoid the cultural and ethnic fragmentation of its neighbours Peru and Bolivia (Funk 2012: 128; Richards 2010: 63; Carter, D. 2010: 59).

The Mapuche are the largest and most prominent Indigenous group in Chile. Most Mapuche peoples inhabited territory extending from the modern national capital, Santiago, down to the city of Valdivia in the south and across the modern border into western Argentina. However, the official Mapuche category incorporates a myriad of smaller Indigenous groups and makes up 90 per cent of Chile's Indigenous population. It is difficult to ascertain the percentage of Chile's population that identifies as Indigenous. Census data from the past 20 years places this at about 4 per cent, yet in 1992, this figure was 9.6 per cent, which may be in part due to changes in the wording of the 2002 census and the stigma of identifying as Indigenous or mestizo (Funk 2012: 128). In 2013, the Mapuche population was estimated to be about 1.7 million, or 10 per cent of Chile's total population, with the latest census data suggesting about 40 per cent of the total population is mixed with other Indigenous influences (RNZ 2013a). The number of Chileans identifying as Indigenous had changed dramatically by the 2017 census. On the 2017 census date, Chile had a population of 17.5 million, with 12.8 per cent identifying as Indigenous. The Mapuche people accounted for 9.9 per cent of the population, which equates to 1,745,147 people. In terms of numbers identifying as Indigenous, they are followed by the Aymara, Diaguita, Quechua, Rapa Nui and Lican Antai peoples (Milesi 2018).

However, the generally accepted government figure for Mapuche in Chile is between 600,000 and 700,000 of a current total national population of approximately 19.1 million (Dillehay and Rothhammer 2013: 152).

The Mapuche are not alone in opposing policies of the Chilean state in the post-Pinochet era, as the gap between rich and poor has not closed significantly in the face of the only slightly modified neoliberal policy framework. Even the presidency of Michelle Bachelet (2006–2010), with its relatively critical assessment of neoliberal economics, witnessed major street riots against lack of government investment in various sectors or groups— most notably, tertiary education (Funk 2012: 132). The nation's cities have been paralysed on several occasions since 2010 by massive street protests against the policies of President Sebastián Piñera (2010–2014, 2018–2022). The period since 2010 has also seen the first significant coalescence of Indigenous and larger urban protest objectives in opposition to government proposals for a series of large hydroelectric dams in the country's south, against the wishes of the Indigenous peoples living in these areas (Funk 2012: 132), as well as ongoing concern over a general lack of investment in health and education among the general population and Indigenous groups. The common link has been the issue of placing private sector interests ahead of those of the general population. The main developer of the dams is Endesa, a former state-owned enterprise that was privatised under Pinochet and has since been granted what some estimate to be up to 90 per cent of total water rights in Chile. While construction is already under way, the legal quandary of private sector–owned water on land communally owned by a different group remains unresolved and untested in the courts.

Many of the proposed dams are on Mapuche lands, as are many large commercial forestry operations. All are opposed by the more than 500 Mapuche communities affected, whose collective ownership and localised sustainable development beliefs run counter to the national-scale, private sector–led development supported by the government proposals (Funk 2012: 133; Richards 2010: 66; Carter, D. 2010: 71–72; Haughney 2006). The forestry projects involve clear felling of pristine temperate rainforest and its replacement with monoculture pine or eucalyptus plantations, which are not ecologically beneficial to soils and also dramatically reduce flora and fauna diversity (López Vergara and Lucero 2018: 652–53; Klubock 2014). These forestry operations have been under way for 50 years and much of the pristine temperate forests in the west of Araucanía are now lost to exotic forestry plantations. Most of these exotics, such as eucalyptus, require far more water than native plants, which has depleted watertables and created water shortages for locals, especially in the Biobío Region. Mapuche anger and frustration are mounting as this exploitation spreads across the region despite their protests. In 2017, 43 attacks were registered against local businesses. Most involved arson directed against logging operations. In 2018, Mapuche resistance escalated to commercial forestry operations that continued unabated despite increasingly vocal opposition. In April of that year, commercial pine plantations around the town of Lumaco were burnt by Mapuche protestors to deter further encroachment into pristine forests. In the same month, commercial crops were burned, roads blocked and forestry vehicles set ablaze. Hector Llaitul, a spokesman for the anti-capitalist, direct-action group Coordinadora Arauco-Malleco articulated the Mapuche sentiment behind these actions when he noted:

> We burned these forests as an act of legitimate resistance against the extractive industries that have oppressed the Mapuche people. If we make their business unprofitable they move on, allowing us to recover our devastated lands and rebuild our world. (Youkee 2018)

In the past decade, the government has made a major commitment to improve the circumstances and resource base of the Mapuche and other Indigenous peoples, while at the same time labelling any Mapuche resistance to ongoing alienation of their lands as criminal rather than political. Several Mapuche activists have been killed while defending their lands by Chilean law enforcement authorities on the grounds they were the initiators of violence (Funk 2012: 136; Planas 2011; Richards 2010). Given this response, Mapuche activists have reached out for support to international Indigenous organisations and their own Mapuche diaspora in North America and Europe (Funk 2012: 137). The Inter-American Court of Human Rights operated by the Organization of American States ruled Chile had violated international law by trying Mapuche activists under an Anti-Terrorism Law drafted under Pinochet (Planas 2011; Funk 2012: 136).

Confrontations between estate owners and Mapuche activists continued with no resolution, however, causing several deaths and much destruction of property on top of ongoing environmental degradation from estate farming and forestry. Human rights advocates, including the former UN special rapporteur on the rights of Indigenous peoples, James Anaya, verified numerous Mapuche complaints about police violence, while Chilean judges ordered police to 'stop using teargas against women and children while raiding Mapuche communities in search for suspects' (AP 2013). This continuing conflict prompted Pope Francis to visit Araucanía on

18 January 2018 to denounce violence as a political tool. Just hours before he gave mass, presumed Mapuche protestors burnt a church and three helicopters, while the previous year had seen churches, schools and forestry operations targeted in arson attacks. There was considerable irony in Pope Francis celebrating mass at Maquehue Air Base in Temuco to a largely Mapuche crowd. Maquehue was a former military base and Pinochet-era detention centre at the heart of the state activities against which Mapuche were protesting (López Vergara and Lucero 2018; The Guardian 2018).

Mapuche leaders and scholars have striven to maintain and record their cultural identity and knowledge. Organisations such as the Comunidad de Historia Mapuche have recorded a large body of cultural knowledge on a diverse range of topics such as concepts of social space and women's stories of everyday life and the physical and structural violence they have suffered under state colonialism since 1885. There has been mounting interest in language preservation as a core necessity for a vibrant culture through radio shows and publications in Mapuche (López Vergara and Lucero 2018: 651–52). For Mapuche displaced to urban centres in search of livelihoods by land alienation, forestry company harassment or the environmental degradation of their homelands from deforestation, this desire for cultural preservation is especially valued. By the 2017 census, 35 per cent of Mapuche lived in Santiago and only 18 per cent in Araucanía. The municipality of La Pintana on the southern outskirts of Santiago serves as a place for Mapuche living in the metropolitan area to hold cultural ceremonies and meetings (Milesi 2018). The key priorities of Mapuche leaders across Chile are the rights to land, water and multicultural education.

There has also been an acknowledgement of the necessity and importance of engaging with the Chilean state to preserve their rights and access to state resources to accomplish their objectives, such as ensuring a place for Mapuche culture in national education and health plans (López Vergara and Lucero 2018: 649–50). Since the 1990s, there has been a national move towards more holistic models of health service delivery that combine both traditional and modern medicine. Through the Special Program of Health and Indigenous Peoples, traditional medicine is now mainstreamed. In 2013, the first hospital offering Mapuche traditional medicine opened in Cañete's Intercultural Hospital Kallvu Llanka. Similarly, many state officials realise the necessity of engaging more with Mapuche on their own terms to improve their conditions for the benefit of both Mapuche and the nation. In 2019, the Piñera administration announced its intention to introduce a new subject on the cultures and languages of Indigenous peoples, which students will take for their first six years of schooling, up to 11 years of age. The government's stated aim is to 'rescue, revitalise and strengthen Indigenous languages and cultures and develop intercultural skills among students'. Indigenous consultation was promised during this process, although the level of decision-making powers on curricular form and content to be vested in Indigenous peoples remains unclear. The plan seems to stop short of the Aotearoa New Zealand model of education on cultural awareness of Indigenous peoples for the entire student body. Instead, the government's stated aim for the subject is 'to design common learning processes for bilingual intercultural education for the nine Indigenous peoples legally recognised in Chile: Aymara, Quechua, Licanantai, Colla, Diaguita, Kawesqar, Yagán, Mapuche and Rapa Nui' (Milesi 2018).

In June 2019, President Piñera announced the government was preparing a plan to boost local economic development in the Araucanía region with an emphasis on education, security, tourism, Indigenous development, infrastructure and rural connectivity. However, ongoing support for private corporate projects and suppression of Mapuche community protests have raised doubts about the government's sincerity. As one local mayor noted, Piñera had also made grand promises during his first term, between 2010 and 2014, 'but not much ever materialised' (Milesi 2018). This dialogue has, however, also prompted the engagement of Mapuche and Chilean Government officials with Indigenous peoples and governments elsewhere in the Pacific on policies and practices that have demonstrated tangible benefits in Indigenous sociocultural coherence and economic, health, educational and political advancement. It is to these recent engagements that we now turn.

Mapuche–Polynesian engagement since 2000

In 2013, the Chilean ambassador to Aotearoa New Zealand, Isauro Torres, expressed his government's keen interest to learn from New Zealand's successful race relations conciliation strategies and noted how overwhelmed a recent Mapuche visiting delegation had been with the estimated NZD35 billion Māori economy. Ambassador Torres invited Māori Affairs Minister Pita Sharples to discuss Māori business practices within Aotearoa New Zealand and abroad. The Chilean Government had also been impressed with the observations of Traci Houpapa, from the Federation of Māori

Authorities, about Māori economic development in relation to different sectors in Chile when she visited there in 2013 as part of Prime Minister John Key's tour of Latin American countries. A visit to Chile by Ngāi Tahu–owned Whale Watch Kaikoura followed in late 2013 to advise the government and the Mapuche people on how to boost the poorly developed Indigenous tourism sector, which constituted only about 1 per cent of Chile's tourism revenue (RNZ 2013a; de la Maza 2018). Regular exchanges between Mapuche and Māori have since taken place. By 2019, these exchanges were increasingly focused on Māori cultural and language revitalisation, Indigenous education, arts and tourism, especially the use of technology to enhance tourism experiences. Te Puni Kōkiri's Chile mission lead Ben Matthews noted Māori were primarily concerned with building enduring Indigenous to Indigenous relationships, raising the profile of Māori in Chile, strengthening business and trade links and creating more opportunities for future cooperation (Te Puni Kōkiri 2019; Latin America CAPE 2018, 2019; MAPLE Microdevelopment–Chile 2016).

Several New Zealand companies have significant commercial interests in Chile, including in Araucanía. For example, dairy company Fonterra is the primary owner of Soprole, a Chilean company making dairy products, while New Zealand electricity generator and distributor Mighty River Power is the primary owner of MRP Geotermia Chile (Muru-Lanning 2015). MRP Geotermia Chile is one of the largest companies in Chile in the field of geothermal power generation. It is also involved in other types of electricity production, but it is perhaps best known for having the most advanced geothermal projects in central-southern Chile on its exploitation concession at the Tolhuaca Volcano (Guía Chile Energía n.d.). In 2015, Marama Muru-Lanning, a Māori scholar of Waikato and Ngāti Maniapoto descent and an academic authority on Māori relations with rivers, worked on a fellowship in Araucanía on the impacts of privatised hydro and geothermal power schemes on Mapuche peoples.

In 2018, Roannie Ng Shiu from The Australian National University (ANU) and Nigel Vagana, the Pacific wellbeing and education manager from the Australian National Rugby League (NRL), were invited on a tour of Chile to explore intercultural sports education based on the success of the partnership between The Australian National University and the NRL's Pacific Wellbeing Program. They were hosted by the Universidad Católica de la Santísima Concepción (UCSC), led by the director of institutional and international affairs, Steve Baeza Abadie. The main aim of the tour was to strengthen links between Australasia, the Pacific and Chile in the priority areas of education and cultural promotion focused on sports. The ANU–NRL partnership offers local Chilean educational and sports organisations better ways of understanding the cultural complexities facing elite athletes and their transition into life after sport. In addition, the ANU–NRL partnership provides an innovative lens on sports development with a focus on cultural and educational empowerment and community engagement.

The tour involved two main sites, in Santiago and Concepción. At the outset, the program was designed to focus on intercultural sports development at the macro, meso and micro levels. The initial discussions were focused on higher education and professional athlete systems at the macro level that allow national athletes to pursue careers outside sport while maintaining high performance at an elite level for their chosen sport. This interest led to meetings with the Chilean Ministry of Sport, the National Institute of Sport and the National Football Program, which is the equivalent of the NRL in Chile but focused on football (soccer) rather than rugby league. The National Institute of Sport particularly focused on national athletes representing Chile at international events including the Olympic Games.

The visiting delegation travelled to Concepción, the capital of Biobío Region, which sits on traditional Mapuche land. Discussions were held with the minister of sport for Biobío Region, Juan Pablo Spoerer, who is a former international representative for the Chilean rugby team. The national rugby team infrastructure included pathways by which professional athletes could continue their higher education while pursuing their professional career. The Chileans were particularly interested in the Australian program under the Elite Athlete University network in which higher education providers endorsed by the Australian Institute of Sport provide additional support to ensure professional athletes can pursue both sporting and higher education careers concurrently. The Biobío Region was particularly interested in how national sports can partner with local universities such as UCSC given it currently hosts the national rowing headquarters and has ambitions to host several other high-performance sports facilities. In terms of Indigenous empowerment, the local technical college of UCSC is in Cañete, a town one hour from Concepción with a large Mapuche population.

The visiting delegation's ANU–NRL presentations highlighted the ongoing partnership focused on cultural empowerment of professional Pacific athletes in the NRL. The presentations provided much interest, particularly in Concepción, given the relationship between the region and the Mapuche. They highlighted the positive role of Indigenous elite athletes in community cultural empowerment to correct the common misperception of sport being isolated in a vacuum rather than a social and cultural practice deeply embedded in Indigenous communities from which elite athletes can draw strength as well as acting as role-models.

Both community members and academics were surprised by the cultural pride Pacific and Indigenous Australian NRL athletes demonstrated in various ethnic-specific programs that cut across all aspects of professional sport—for example, the All Stars game, which is an elite exhibition match in which the top Indigenous Australian athletes compete against the top non-Indigenous NRL athletes as a precursor to the formal competition season. The Pacific and Indigenous Australian cultural camps were another successful approach outlined; they began in 2012 and focus on sports development for professional athletes to provide specific cultural empowerment at an individual level to assist with wellbeing. The presentations emphasised community outreach programs and cultural programs such as the 2010 *Body Pacifica* photo exhibition, in which Pacific NRL athletes participated and were pictured adorned in traditional body costumes from their respective countries. This exhibition was curated by the Casula Powerhouse, a cultural facility in Australia, and photographed by Greg Semu, an internationally renowned Samoan photographer and creative artist. The *Body Pacifica* exhibition won the Museums & Galleries of NSW IMAGinE Award for public engagement, but for the athletes who participated, it was a reminder, as delegation member Nigel Vagana stated, 'for Pacific communities particularly in Australia, that we hadn't forgotten about them'—forgotten in the sense that, despite all their onfield success, Pacific athletes acknowledge this would not be possible without the ongoing support of Pacific families and communities. The suite of cultural programs across the whole NRL provided much promise and potential for the audience who identified as Mapuche and those who work with Mapuche.

It was clear from audience engagement and subsequent discussions with academics from UCSC in both Concepción and later Cañete that Mapuche young people face significant issues in terms of cultural pride and engagement. The delegation was asked on several occasions how they were able to get athletes to openly acknowledge their cultural heritage and participate and engage in public community events to demonstrate cultural pride. These questions were often followed by intense discussions on the impact these elite-athlete cultural programs had on Indigenous youth in Australasia and across the Pacific. For many in the audience, the programs the delegation shared were eye-opening; however, doubts about their local applicability were also raised. Many commented that this was great for Pacific and Indigenous Australian athletes and communities but, for Mapuche, they were unrelatable given many felt the need to hide their Indigenous cultural heritage. Some clues and context for this outlook came the following day as the delegation travelled to Cañete.

As the delegation headed out of Concepción, their hosts directed their attention to significant landmarks and rivers where Mapuche successfully immobilised Spanish troops and prevented further invasion of the South American continent. As they neared Cañete, their hosts then pointed to empty toll booths that had been vandalised and remnants of burnt materials on the side of the highway torched by local Mapuche communities in response to the massive exotic forestry enterprises that covered their land. They related the fact that Mapuche traditional landownership was ignored and their pleas to both the government and business to cease operations due to water shortages were also ignored. The vandalism of the toll booths and blockades of highways were a way to gain national attention to highlight the social injustices and inequities in natural resource management and resource use between local Indigenous residents and commercial interests, both at home and abroad. However, rather than acknowledging the social injustices, the government used these events to support its narrative of Mapuche as 'domestic terrorists' in its effort to quell support for local Indigenous communities' increasing political activism and cultural revitalisation.

On arrival in Cañete, Mapuche symbolism across the town is evident. At the Technical College of UCSC, the visiting Pacific delegation was greeted with a traditional welcoming ceremony that involved honouring the environment for providing sustenance and life. The audience this time were Mapuche high school students. As the visitors spoke of Pacific athletes using their platform to advocate for Pacific communities as cultural warriors, one young person commented that they found it difficult to be openly proud of their culture let alone become a cultural warrior. This is of great concern given that, throughout the trip, Chileans, both Indigenous and non-Indigenous, constantly reminded us how Mapuche were legendary for effectively halting the Spanish invasion. If this history does not instil a sense of 'warrior' pride for Mapuche, it is difficult to fathom what will. Mapuche sense of self and identity have come a long way, in a process Crow (2013) aptly describes as ranging 'from Araucanian warriors to Mapuche terrorists'.

The potential empowering benefits of elite sportspeople expressing pride in their culture are immense given the current prominence and popularity of sport as entertainment. Sports, culture and politics have intersected in a way the world has never seen before, as highlighted by the Black Lives Matter movement from the United States. However, this can only occur if Indigenous sporting champions are willing to become public cultural warriors. Mapuche young people need to reconnect with their history in a way that the tales and legends of their ancestors are not just stories of the past but become an inspiration today and invoke a renewed sense of pride, cultural revitalisation and warrior spirit. Exchanges like those outlined above with Māori and Samoans expose Mapuche and other community leaders, athletes and young people to processes already well under way across the vast Pacific, where young people are recognising with pride the massive achievements of their wayfarer ancestors. The rising tide of exchanges with other Indigenous peoples across the Pacific can only benefit the Mapuche, by providing both inspiration and practical templates for successful Indigenous initiatives in designing educational curriculums, creating appropriate educational institutions and developing sustainable, locally controlled enterprises.

This transformation is already under way. Biobío is one of the two leading regions for rugby league in Chile and a disproportionate number of players with openly acknowledged Indigenous heritage featured in the 2021 national rugby league squad at the World Cup 2021 qualifiers. Chile fielded several players with Polynesian and Melanesian heritage, including Iziah Esera Catrileo, Patrick Caamano, Mana Castillo-Sioni, Christian Sandoval and Jaden Laing. Former Chilean player Carlos Astorga Gonzalez was born on Rapa Nui, while in Australia, Canterbury Bulldogs player Marcelo Montoya is of mixed Fijian and Chilean heritage (APRLC 2020). Perhaps more significantly, the mood of the Chilean electorate is changing, as witnessed by the overwhelming result of a plebiscite on 20 October 2020, in which 79 per cent voted in favour of rewriting the national constitution to emphasise inclusive social justice, more diverse representation among elected members of parliament and officials, and sustainable development (Mojica 2020). The vast potential of Chile's extensive EEZ has made it keen to engage with other Pacific maritime nations on matters of sustainable harvests and countering illegal fishing by distant-water fishing nations. The Mapuche and other Indigenous groups have much to gain from but also much to offer in this new phase of Chilean history.

17

Sumak Kawsay and Biodiversity Conflicts in the Galápagos Islands: A case study of the relationship between local fisherfolk, sea lions and state environmental discourses

José Guerrero Vela

Sumak Kawsay (SK), the development model incorporated in the 2008 Ecuadorian Constitution, is based on the Kichwa Indigenous cosmovision and can be translated as 'good living' (Gudynas 2011: 442). Sumak Kawsay integrates social and environmental wellbeing as interdependent processes and provides constitutional legal rights to Pachamama (the Andean Earth Goddess or 'Mother Earth'). However, the application of such constitutional innovations is facing multiple challenges, one of which is dealing with biodiversity conflicts involving non-Indigenous communities.

Sumak Kawsay[1] in Ecuador is presented as a model that provides an alternative to traditional development visions and constitutes 'the foundation of a new social pact of coexistence' (Ramírez 2010: 61). Ecuador's new constitution has been defined as radical because it represents possibly the first 'eco-centric' (Stober 2010: 230) constitution or 'eco-constitution', giving priority to the

---

1   Sumak Kawsay and SK are used interchangeably in this chapter. Generally, the full term is used in relation to Indigenous cosmology and contexts while SK is used for legal and wider community contexts.

Indigenous vision of Sumak Kawsay and the Pachamama as deserving of a complete chapter of this document (Smith 2009: 15). This concept is generally translated as 'good living' (Radcliffe 2012: 240; Gudynas 2011: 442) from the Indigenous Kichwa language spoken in the Ecuadorian Andes as well as in Peru and Bolivia. The complexity of the term Sumak Kawsay is difficult to decode into English because, while it includes the view that wellbeing is possible only within a community, the idea of community in SK is expanded to include nature (Gudynas 2011: 441). Given this integration of community and nature, SK proposes a wider notion of wellbeing that integrates society and nature as interdependent components.

Critics of the Sumak Kawsay concept have asked whether it is a discursive tool that functions in the state's interests or is contributing to a deeper 'intercultural, inter-epistemic and pluri-national transformation' (Walsh 2010: 20). Drawing on the narratives of Galápagos fisherfolk about sea lions (*Zalophus wollebaeki*), this chapter assesses the tensions and synergies of such discourses in the national legal framework based on the Indigenous concept described above. Drawing on a case of biodiversity conflict, I argue that despite Sumak Kawsay having not yet produced deeper changes in society–environment relations, its conceptual parameters, inspired by an Indigenous cosmovision, propose a more integral understanding of environmental management, science and social justice. Such parameters could be the potential standpoint from which to transform local communities' perceptions, by integrating notions of social justice and nature rights into social and environmental interventions.

Sumak Kawsay, social justice and social policies

For René Ramírez, an economist specialising in development issues and former national secretary of planning and development in Ecuador, the country's new constitution demonstrates a political shift in understanding social justice, from a utilitarian model to a new concept based on what people consider is a good living beyond economic measures (Ramírez 2009: 8). Ramírez played a key role in the elaboration of the National Plan for Good Living, in which the definition of SK or good living is proposed as:

> A wager for change from the demands for equality and social justice;
> from the recognition, validation, and dialogue of peoples and their
> cultures, knowledges, and modes of life. Good living seeks to achieve

the satisfaction of necessities, the attainment of the quality of life and a dignified death, to love and be loved, the healthy flourishing of all, in peace and harmony with nature and the indefinite prolongation of human cultures. (SENPLADES 2009, in Walsh 2010: 19)

Ramírez (2010: 59) acknowledged the influence of the ideas of important theorists such as Amartya Sen in establishing a new conception of social justice embodied in the new constitution. Indeed, SK has incorporated Sen's views, which hold that the freedoms, opportunities, capabilities and real potentialities of individuals and collectives flourish when people are enabled to achieve what they value (Ramírez 2010: 61). A set of rights like those found in Western approaches is included in SK, but in a different framework that includes health, shelter, education, food and the environment (Gudynas 2011: 443).

Drawing on this political dimension of the Sumak Kawsay approach to social justice, these political changes have encouraged discursive and institutional changes in the way the state perceives justice and social wellbeing. With this vision of social justice, rather than representing a return to a mystical Indigenous past with no practical strategy, as some critics have suggested, SK presents specific proposals and strategies to achieve such notions of justice. In the social justice field, an important discursive transformation can be observed in the history of social policy, comparing the approaches within different moments of advancement in Ecuador. An article written by Jeannette Sánchez, former minister of economic and social inclusion, discusses the history of social policy approaches and identifies three moments of social policy in Ecuador that followed a regional and global trend (Sanchez 2012: 344). The first was the postwar creation of a welfare state; in the Ecuadorian case, global influences promoted the first attempts at providing universal education and health care. The second moment is described as a neoliberal period that encouraged market-managed social services and a minimal role for the state; at the national level, this was the stage when unconditional cash transfer mechanisms were introduced as an isolated, short-term policy focused on providing wellbeing to the poor. Social programs during this period had no connection with the entire body of policies and, as a result, had very little impact on improving social inclusion and social mobility (Sánchez 2012: 345). During this second phase, the concept of wellbeing as a measure of social programs assumed a market-centred logic in which social justice was seen as dependent on economic growth and increased income.

The third period was when the government implemented SK, in which the concept of 'wellbeing' was replaced with the broader concept of Sumak Kawsay. In an attempt to translate the SK view of wellbeing, the national secretary of planning and development proposed a change from 'wellbeing' to 'happiness' as a measure of SK, as happiness is the ultimate goal of human activity and is itself sufficient and free from any ulterior purpose (Ramírez 2009: 49). The implication of this conceptual approach is that the means of measuring social policy has also changed. As Ramírez (2009: 8) explains, previous discussions about wellbeing addressed poverty or levels of consumption or, in the best case, 'analysis which had simply incorporated the problem of inequality'. As an alternative, the conceptual transformation is justified by arguing that the concept of wellbeing lacks significance because of its limited capacity to measure happiness.

In his research, Ramírez (2009: 8) has used econometrical methodologies to demonstrate that the average person's happiness does not increase with the growth in national wealth—a phenomenon known as the Easterlin Paradox. Based on a national survey and a bibliographical review, Ramírez found the principal domains that produced happiness in Ecuador were those related to social and family life, as well as the availability of free time and fewer working hours. Ramírez's research also proposes that one's financial situation and livelihood are the domains that produce little satisfaction among Ecuadorians. Although Ramírez (2009: 50) recognises that income and growth are still important, his arguments have shaped several social programs that have been applied in ways that suggest there is a prioritisation of interventions that encourage social life and communitarian relations instead of livelihood or financial interventions (p. 51). An example of a policy focused on promoting social and community cohesion is the recently created Institute of Popular and Solidarity Economics whose objective is to promote associative and solidarity forms of organisation (Radcliffe 2012: 241). As a result, the discursive emphasis placed on communitarian activities reflects the kind of social policies incorporating Indigenous communitarian values in national planning strategies that aim to encourage social life and family cohesion and bring happiness to Ecuadorians proposed in Ramírez's research. The further question for Sumak Kawsay, then, is how this notion of social justice can be integrated with the nature rights provided by Sumak Kawsay.

Sumak Kawsay and nature rights

The main innovation of SK in relation to classical development models is the 'rupture of the ideology about progress' (Gudynas 2011: 446). Gudynas clarifies that if Sumak Kawsay aims to stand as a real alternative to development, the role the environment plays is crucial (2011). To understand this role, it is important to consider the concept of Pachamama (Mother Earth), in which 'life is reproduced and fulfilled (carried out), has the right to complete respect of its existence and the maintenance and regeneration of its vital cycles, structures, functions and evolutionary processes' (*Constitution of the Republic of Ecuador* 2008, cited in Stober 2010: 229).

Based on the Ecuadorian constitutional mandates, this author elaborates on the attributes of good living in relation to nature. First, nature has intrinsic values and the constitution recognises that rather than an object, it is a subject of rights—that is, ecosystems and landscapes, plants and animals have rights independent of what human goals might be (Gudynas 2011: 443). Therefore, the integration of human rights and the rights of nature 'requires that individuals, communities, peoples and nations … exercise their responsibilities in the context of interculturalism, respect for diversity and of harmonious coexistence with nature' (Article 274, in Kauffman 2014: 43).

This brings us to the second attribute of nature within the SK framework, which entails a dissolution of the society–nature duality, proposing instead a relationship between people and the environment based on diverse historical, cultural and environmental contexts, where people see themselves from their specific ecological circumstances (Gudynas 2011: 442). In particular, the Indigenous vision of Sumak Kawsay prioritises the communitarian space where harmonic coexistence with Pachamama and ecosystem conservation are parts of a lifestyle (Ringhofer et al. 2013: 3). These specific cultural values propose a new ethic that integrates society and nature. In that sense, economic activity must be at the service of happiness and quality of life to fulfill the harmonic relation with nature, where people take only what is needed to satisfy their food, health and habitat requirements (Quirola 2009, cited in Houtard 2014: 9). Here, we find a connection with the notion of happiness mentioned in the previous section, but with the additional consideration that happiness is related not merely to economic indicators, but also to a balanced relationship with nature.

The third attribute refers to SK's particular cultural origin, which must be acknowledged. Its Indigenous background means the construction of SK must be elaborated within an intercultural approach, considering its origins in ancient cosmologies in which the concept of economic development did not exist (Viteri Gualinga 2004, cited in Walsh 2010: 19). With this in mind, an unprecedented process of interculturalisation occurs in the inclusion of SK as a central framework in the Ecuadorian Constitution (Walsh 2010: 19). Again, we can see a discursive innovation in the way of thinking about relations between society and the environment. These new discourses assume a series of Indigenous cultural values, and therefore the challenge remains for the multiple non-Indigenous social groups in Ecuador to negotiate and incorporate such cultural values with their own historical, environmental and political backgrounds.

Sumak Kawsay and scientific legitimacy

Ramírez (2010) links SK and scientific research, explaining that the distributional pattern of science should be democratic and aim to contribute to good living. To achieve this democratic distribution, knowledge generation must include the notion of distributive justice that respects an 'ecology of knowledges'. This means different knowledges must engage in dialogue, and the results should be socially accurate and useful to satisfy the needs of society, with the final goal of an emancipatory transformation (Ramírez 2010: 56). The process of knowledge generation under the SK framework should also consider the articulation of environmental conservation elements in research, science, technology, ancestral knowledge and the sustainable use of environmental goods and services (Quirola 2009: 205).

Here, the Indigenous values of diversity and inclusion are also translated as an alternative framework to reorient science towards an emancipatory transformation of Ecuadorian society. Vanhulst and Beling (2013: 11) go beyond this proposal, arguing that the success of Sumak Kawsay is conditional on the consolidation of collective learning processes, which requires cultural and knowledge decentralisation as well as the development of social competences that enable harmonic relations between plural societies and between those societies and nature. Such a conjunction of Indigenous values and modern scientific knowledge demands a participatory approach to science.

This approach is based on the idea of distributive justice under the Sumak Kawsay concept and involves a similar approach to Durant's democratic model of society's participation in science. Durant (1999: 314) proposes two models to explain how this relationship has developed: deficit and democracy. The deficit model's principal assumption is that the public should have greater knowledge about science, engineering and technology (Durant 1999). This vision has been critiqued for operating with a basic view of science that does not recognise the informal but valuable knowledge held by laypeople. Within environmental resource management, deficit-oriented approaches have proved ineffective in establishing science as a basis for justifiable and reliable decision-making (Barker and Peter 1993, cited in Fischer 2003: 94). In contrast, the democratic model prioritises the participation of diverse social groups. By emphasising dialogue, the democratic model refers to new forms of public engagement with science and scientists through participatory processes (Durant 1999: 318). Such democratic approaches have also been incorporated within environmental management. Brewer (2013: 322) cites several authors who agree that public engagement with environmental management 'can enable dialogue, trust, reflection, deliberative analysis, and merging of experiential and scientific knowledge'.

It can be argued, therefore, that the SK view of science falls under a democratic model, opening the door for a participatory approach to science that could enhance the legitimacy of science and, consequently, compliance with environmental regulations. Many authors agree that one of the main elements determining compliance with environmental regulations is their level of legitimacy (Brewer 2013: 322; Eggert and Lokina 2010: 213; Viteri and Chávez 2007: 271; Nielsen and Mathiesen 2003: 412; Hatcher et. al. 2000: 449). In the context of fisheries regulations, legitimacy refers to the individual's feelings towards authority and its entitlement to dictate behaviour (Eggert and Lokina 2010: 213). Such feelings are based on individual experiences with authorities and personal and social views of whether a regulation is fair and is being applied in a fair manner (Eggert and Lokina 2010). If the engagement process occurs through isolated actions and is designed and facilitated by government staff or external facilitators with the only goal being to meet government agendas, the rationality of government will prevail (King 2012: 26). Sumak Kawsay, at a legal, discursive level, is intended to transform the way science operates, by inserting the notion of distributive justice, which can enhance the perceived legitimacy of science and scientific discourse among local actors.

The Galápagos Islands: Scientific legitimacy and social justice

As a resident of the Galápagos Islands who has studied abroad, I am frequently confronted, whenever I talk about the place I call home, with a reaction along the lines of: 'Oh, really! Do people live in the Galápagos? What is it like?' I am usually tempted to answer using the lines proposed by Henessy and McCleary (2011: 131): if there is one place that could be home to both pristine nature and a rapidly growing society, that is the Galápagos Islands. The pressures of access to and the use of marine resources (Castrejón and Charles 2012: 237), population and infrastructure growth (Quiroga 2013), alien species (Gardener et al. 2013: 349) and social inequality (Henessy 2011: 132), among many other processes, are part of the complex net of issues with which communities and institutions in the Galápagos Islands must deal. While the previously reviewed Ecuadorian national framework—based on harmonic relations with nature, inspired by an Indigenous cosmology—provides a discourse to manage society–environment relations, the case of Galápagos fisherfolk and their relations with sea lions highlights the gaps, tensions and synergies that have emerged under this framework.

Relations between sea lions and humans on San Cristóbal Island have been studied by Denkinger et al. (2014), who presented quantitative data about different stakeholders' perceptions of sea lions. Their study determined that fishers are the group with the most negative perception of sea lions compared with other groups such as those in the tourism sector and local businesses (Denkinger et al. 2014: 291). These authors argue that, despite the general agreement on protecting this endangered species (IUCN Category A2a) (Aurioles and Trillmich 2008, in Denkinger et al. 2014: 286), fishers do not share such a vision due to economic and political factors that influence their position (p. 284). While agreeing with this argument, I will provide a complementary approach to address this complex relationship by integrating qualitative information and assessing it using the previously presented SK framework.

The qualitative material presented here is based on a meeting in 2012 between fishers, local authorities and scientists at which I had the opportunity to undertake participant observation. The meeting was organised by the Galápagos National Park and a local university to present updated sea lion population data to organised groups of fishers and to discuss conservation measures to protect the species. Despite this stated objective, fishers also put on the table various other concerns about the non-legitimacy of scientific discourses and practices:

> [After a scientist presented data]
>
> Fisherman A: You are talking a lot about sea lions, aren't you? Okay, it seems to me that you have not really lived here in the Galápagos, you have not experienced the reality, what you are doing is just theory. Do you really know how many sea lions do live in this island? Not just in the town, but around the entire island, do you really know?
>
> Scientist A: Yes, between 500 and 700.
>
> Public: Never! That's a lie.
>
> Fisherman A: 500 sea lions? That's a lie [the public react negatively to the scientist]. One of these nights, I invite you to the beach near the pier, just in the town beach, there are more than 800 sea lions. Can you imagine how many are all around the island? You don't know! Here you are trying to earn more funds, which usually are only for some institutions! [Laughs, male voices agree]. Here in the Galápagos, first you have to count the sea lions in the whole island, not only in town, and you will see that there are too many sea lions! And then, you can come and invite us to a workshop based on the reality. This is a hoax that you are doing, you should talk based on the reality.
>
> Environmental official: Indeed, we have made global surveys—one was done in 2001 and another that was about 40 years ago, so we compare. We did the last census of this year in the whole island, with a methodology that is supported and proven worldwide.
>
> Fisherman B: But you did not even live here in those years? How do you know? [Laughter]

In this discussion, fishers' narratives were built on two broad elements: scientific legitimacy and social justice. Their view of the former shows they do not recognise the data offered by scientists and, in contrast, propose more valid information about the sea lion population based on their day-to-day experiences navigating around the island. Here, it can be argued that because of a 'deficit approach' (Durant 1999), in which government officials and scientists have not included fishers in the research process, the legitimacy of this process has decreased because the engagement occurred as a 'pseudo-participation' mechanism, in which people were consulted but their voices were constrained. Pseudo-participation has also occurred in other participatory processes involving fishers in the Galápagos Marine Reserve. Hearn (2008: 571) and Jones (2013: 5) agree that those processes failed because fishers believed the tourism sector received the main benefits from conservation and participatory management, which undermined scientific legitimacy in their eyes.

This sense of unfairness links with the notion of social justice that appears when one of the fishers doubts the destination of the economic resources considered by the research activities. The fishers' narrative in this regard expresses their perception of an unfair distribution of resources in the name of conservation initiatives. The concern about the scientists' agenda of receiving more funding illustrates the mistrust produced by a deficit approach to communication.

The social context of inequality can be defined as one of the principal reasons for this mistrust and negative perceptions of scientific information. Given that the benefits generated by the tourist industry are distributed in an unequal manner (Henessy and McCleary 2011: 147), the inequality experienced by the fishing sector has created conflict and tensions among local people, resulting in a lack of confidence in the whole system and a perception of unfairness with the participatory management process (Quiroga et al. 2009, cited in Henessy and McCleary 2011: 147). Therefore, as Denkinger et al. (2014) acknowledge, socioeconomic activities influenced the negative perception fishers have towards sea lions. However, a point that might be overlooked is how fishers perceive inequality. In the following excerpt from the meeting, fishers raise concerns about human health and the presence of sea lions:

> Fishermen C: There is something that worries us a lot. I would like that in this meeting there would be a health doctor, or the provincial director of health, because although they say that the sea lion does not have conjunctivitis and flu, when you go out for a walk with your kids to the beach, sea lions have conjunctivitis and that is contagious.

> Scientist B: No, that is another type of illness and is not contagious for humans. Indeed, there are lots of diseases that are transmitted from pets to sea lions, and we are doing research about it.

> Fisherman C: But the sea lion is always sick with flu and conjunctivitis. We see them on the beaches, as we live here, and that's contagious for people, it can become an epidemic for the people who are here in

the Galápagos. That would be because of the sea lions that live here. So, couldn't the sea lion be eradicated … If we move the sea lions far to the other side of the island [where there is no human settlement], there will be more job opportunities for the local people as tourists will contract [hire] us to take them there to see the sea lions; there would be more jobs for the local transport sector.

These health concerns can be understood as a manifestation of the general feeling of inequality that has already been observed. The concern about health is not superficial. Despite receiving thousands of tourists every year, the health system in the Galápagos is weak (Page et al. 2013) and problems of food security and quality have a 'direct health impact upon the residents of the islands'. Even though sea lions might have no direct impact on human health (Judith Denkinger, Pers. comm., 2012), fishers use this argument as a justification to remove the animals from the areas near the town to another part of the island, which would also increase job opportunities. It can be argued, then, that such negative perceptions among fishers are the effect of the unequal conditions this social group experience, which are manifested in realities such as the islands' weak health system. While these complex interactions between human health, social inequality, biodiversity conflicts and scientific endeavours are not easy to address, we argue that SK could provide conceptual elements to achieve greater balance. In this regard, we must next elevate the issue of the synergies and gaps between fishers' narratives about social justice, nature and science and the discourse of Sumak Kawsay and its renovated conceptual tools.

Sumak Kawsay and fisherfolk in the Galápagos: Synergies and challenges

The three parameters proposed by the SK framework for understanding social justice, nature and science can be applied to assess both the gaps and the meeting points between fisherfolk's narratives and SK. SK requires that social justice is constructed based on what people consider to be 'good living'. In the case of the fishers, good living obviously depends, among many other elements, on the improvement of health and equal access to the economic resources generated by tourism and conservation dynamics. However, the social policy transformations under SK focus not only on financial interventions or livelihoods, but also on the importance of encouraging communitarian relations and social life. The best way to achieve this could be integrated efforts at planning by the institutions responsible for social policy implementation and environmental agencies towards reaching the ideal of social justice proposed by the SK model.

Therefore, to apply the SK framework, conservation stakeholders and decision-makers in the islands should include the perspective of social justice in any policy intervention, especially in the environmental field, which is the main driver of interest in these famous islands. In the case of sea lions, environmental agencies' efforts to conserve this species could develop participatory strategies in which fishers' groups can contribute within a democratic, scientific framework. Additionally, dialogue between social policymakers and environmental agencies should find synergic interventions that facilitate not only fisherfolk but also all elements of local communities seeing economic benefits from environmental interventions. This could help to strengthen communitarian spaces, which as we saw previously, would contribute to the ultimate goal of happiness. Such inclusive activities are not a new idea and many have already taken place—for instance, projects that have hired fishers to remove waste from underwater and coastlines (Quiroga et al. 2011: 105, 204) have generated alternative economic benefits to compensate for fishing prohibitions. Also, technical skills training for fishers and their spouses and technology to commercialise their products have provided economical and organisational benefits. Additionally, it has been demonstrated that the marine recreational fishery can provide an alternative income source and ensure their wellbeing (Engio and Quiroga 2011: 204). All these alternatives could improve the conservation approach by including the notion of social justice established in the SK framework. While these alternatives have already been implemented over the short term, the national framework provided by SK could integrate them and support a long-term and more holistic and strategic application of social justice principles.

Following the social justice parameters of SK to address this biodiversity conflict should also incorporate a democratic approach to science. Instead of wasting resources on isolated meetings, workshops and so on, a democratic model of science in the Galápagos would include fishers and local communities in a collective learning process in which their knowledge is actively valued and incorporated into research processes and management decisions. As the SK framework recommends, it would be necessary to develop social competencies among fishers and local communities that enable harmonious relations between all social groups and this unique environment.

Distributive justice in knowledge generation entails a transformation in the way science is understood. Again, fishers have demonstrated interest in participating more actively in research and science (Usseglio et al. 2014: 194) and many initiatives have already taken place in the context of co-management (p. 187). Nonetheless, as was observed in their comments at the meeting, fishers perceive science as illegitimate—in this case, showing mistrust about the population data on sea lions. Such attitudes extended to fisheries regulations, associating science with fisheries closures that did not offer alternative sources of income (Usseglio et al. 2013: 189). In this context, the transformation in the way science operates offered by SK could increase the legitimacy of scientific discourses among local actors. A democratic approach should include fishers in the whole research process. In the case of sea lions, based on recommendations posed by Usseglio (2013: 198), fishers could be involved either in a direct way—by formulating research questions, choosing methodologies, generating hypotheses, registering sea lion population data, analysing such data and actively disseminating that information—or in an indirect way, by involving their children and others in research, education and scientific endeavours related to biodiversity.

Having assessed the potential SK offers for the integration of social justice and a democratic model of science, the final challenge is to accomplish the rights of nature. In this case, sea lions should be considered subject to such rights, which would entail respect for their habitat. To achieve a real implementation of nature rights and elimination of the duality of society and nature are not straightforward and should be approached as a long-term process that must start by acknowledging the historical inequality that groups such as fishers perceive in management systems. The new ethic proposed by SK requires economic activities to be at the service of happiness and quality of life—something the integration of social justice and democratic science would encourage. Nonetheless, it is important to acknowledge that all these cultural values have their origin in an Indigenous framework that is culturally different from that of the population of the Galápagos Islands. Given most people in the Galápagos identify as mestizo (a hybrid cultural background that integrates Indigenous and Spanish origins), the adaptation of a set of Indigenous cultural values to their relationship with nature could occur as part of a long-term intercultural dialogue and negotiation between the local Galápagos communities and the fisherfolk, within their specific historical, environmental and political contexts.

18

The Ocean in the Anthropocene: Pacific perspectives

Melody Tay

Introduction

In the 77 years since the end of World War II in 1945, the pursuit of military security and economic prosperity has inadvertently given humans the ability to make the Earth uninhabitable. The postwar proliferation of nuclear weapons, despite treaties to reduce their numbers, means there are still far more nuclear warheads than required to wipe out humanity through nuclear contamination and nuclear winters leading to crop failure. The growth of global manufacturing and trade on the back of the burning of fossil fuels has led to the second concern: pollution-induced global warming. The Intergovernmental Panel on Climate Change (IPCC) and other international scientific bodies consider a 3.7–4.0ºC increase in global temperatures as the tipping point for irreversible global environmental damage. The general failure to date of most nations to achieve the carbon emission reduction targets necessary to avoid this tipping point has serious implications for all life on Earth.

The challenge I pose in this chapter is this: to create a truly cohesive and sustainable world, nature herself must have a seat at the table. After outlining the recent framing of debates over climate change and economic progress, I focus on the ocean as the part of nature most central to my life and outline how vital it is to ensuring climate change mitigation, before discussing ways in which oceans and sustainable ecosystems in general can be better protected. I conclude by arguing that initiatives pushed by Indigenous peoples in the Pacific region to preserve nature are not only vital but also hold great lessons for the rest of the world. They also have much in common with the values and sentiments expressed by many young people around the globe increasingly frustrated by the inaction of the generations currently in power in the light of what is increasingly recognised as an existential threat to humankind (Shukman 2021).

As an increasingly urbanised species reliant on food grown beyond our immediate locality, we sometimes forget just how embedded, intertwined and dependent our lives are on more-than-human lives and ecological systems. Here, 'more-than-human' refers to the collective of other living beings like animals and plants and extends to the ocean, the stars, the Moon and the Sun. Instead of using the term 'non-human', I use 'more-than-human' because it is less anthropocentric and more evocative of the sublime. It is a term that reminds us we are part of a much larger web of long, deep and intricate connections between all things, most of which are largely unseen and unknown to us in our daily lives. We are disconnected from the more-than-human world, obsessed instead with the eternal growth of our economies, the digital worlds we have created and with running in the relentless hamster wheel of consumerism. Rivers are daily polluted by businesses, forests are burning because of our warming world and the integrity of whole ecological systems is being compromised by collective anthropocentric, human-driven activities. Plate 18.1 symbolises the underlying embedded reality of the human and more-than-human realms as argued in this chapter.

Yet, more-than-human beings have no way to defend themselves. They are unrecognised for the most part in our justice systems, with no legal standing or rights. More often than not, the damage done to them becomes just another number on a budget sheet, invisible except for the cost it took to destroy them. So, they are endlessly exploited.

Yet, within a few short months of the beginning of the worldwide shutdown due to Covid-19, the skies and waters began to clear. There were countless viral social media posts (many of them fabricated) about wildlife returning—testament to the deep desire of people to believe in the regenerative power of nature. But this period was far from enough to bring our world back into balance. The forced closure of global trade in 2020 did, however, open a window of possibility for real change.

Plate 18.1: *Embedded No.1,* **2019.**
Photo: Melody Tay.

The Anthropo-Scene: Concept, conceptualisation and challenge

'Anthropocene' is, at first glance, a most arrogant term: meaning 'the age of the human'. Since it first appeared in the field of earth system science (Crutzen and Stoermer 2000), it has been used 'promiscuously' in many other academic fields (Lorimer 2017). It has catalysed an outpouring of academic research with 'far-reaching ontological, epistemic, political and aesthetic consequences' (Lorimer 2017: 117). As a result, it is confusing as to what the 'Anthropocene' is really referring. By referring to two academic reviews of 'Anthropo-scene' literature (Lorimer 2017; Toivanen et al. 2017) as a guide, I will come to a definition of the term and show how it challenges the 'established boundaries' (Hamilton et al. 2015) of modern times and offers a foundation for giving rights to the ocean.

The established boundaries between nature and culture, climate and politics, natural sciences and social sciences and the humanities, as Hamilton et al. (2015: 6) understand them, can best be described in their own words, which I take as a description and definition of these boundaries:

> Nature is defined as 'external to society and governed by slow and steady laws, but free of any telos in its history.' Culture, or Society is 'teleologically oriented by progress towards a freedom understood as humankind wrenching itself out of any natural determination and limit.'

Correspondingly, on one side were the 'in-human' natural sciences and on the other were the 'anti-natural' social sciences and humanities (Hamilton et al. 2015). Natural sciences are concerned primarily with 'empiricism and verifiability', while the social sciences and the humanities 'build their body of knowledge through interpretative and critical modes of inspection' (Toivanen et al. 2017: 193). Something to note is that the separation of nature and culture is intrinsically tied to the divisions between these disciplines.

Political theory has traditionally looked at political regimes as purely intrahuman contracts and struggles and does not include the climate or the earth system at large. Climate studies also rarely include politics.

The Anthropocene challenges these established boundaries in several ways. First, the Anthropocene refers to the claim that we are facing an unprecedented epoch in which humans have become a geological force, altering the earth system as much as tectonics or volcanism (Hamilton et al. 2015). This is what Toivanen et al. (2017) refer to as the geological Anthropocene. It is also an ongoing scientific question (Lorimer 2017), mostly regarding start dates, which is being investigated in stratigraphy and earth system science by the Anthropocene Working Group. The Anthropocene, then, is an event in geological time in which human impact has tipped the scales and ushered us into an unknown and unpredictable earth system.

In response to this first concept of the Anthropocene, most research has reflected on how we arrived at this point, speculation about the future and calls for how we should respond. Through this, the concept of the Anthropocene comes to challenge (but sometimes deepen) established boundaries between nature and culture, science and politics, natural sciences, social sciences and the humanities. In trying to understand the causes of the Anthropocene are Toivanen et al.'s (2017) biological and social Anthropocenes: a biophysical and socio-environmental understanding of human–nature interactions through time. Here, we see a challenging of the nature/culture and climate/politics divide, for it is not just social and ideological structures (for example, colonialism, capitalism and globalisation), but also biophysical availabilities, that have led to the Anthropocene. As Chakrabarty (2009: 208) elegantly notes: 'The mansion of modern freedoms stands on an ever-expanding base of fossil fuel use.' But more importantly, it is the realisation that, in the pursuit of 'progress' and modern 'development', we have disturbed the very systems needed for our survival (Chakrabarty 2009). Governments can also thus no longer ignore climate change because it is only going to worsen poverty, hunger, social inequality and other welfare concerns (Agyeman et al. 2016). Nature can no longer be seen as a passive backdrop to human culture and political drama (Hamilton et al. 2015) because social structures operate within biophysical ones.

Furthermore, the 'rupture' of the Anthropocene (Hamilton 2016) and the uncertainty it entails have sparked many speculations about the future—most prominently through the medium of science fiction. Science fiction is being written by natural scientists, social scientists and humanists alike (Lorimer 2017)—a mixing of different disciplines. Natural scientists and social scientists are turning to the future instead of just studying the past and its trends. Natural scientists are more open to speculation and open-ended criticism, while social scientists and humanists are grounding their writings and art in scientific knowledge (Lorimer 2017). The established boundaries of the past are being unwritten by imagining the future. This chapter and, indeed, this entire collection argue that Indigenous remnants of past practices in our region offer viable and vital ways of mitigating the unfolding ecological disaster facing the planet due to powerful elements of humanity's obsession with human progress and economic futures.

Finally, in answering the question of how we should respond, there is a generation of new ontologies that emphasise the central role of human dominion and control but also question the 'anthropocentric accounts of agency' inherent in modern ontologies of the environment (Lorimer 2017). This also encompasses what Toivanen et al. (2017: 187) refer to as the 'cultural Anthropocene', where the concept functions as a 'tool for philosophical reflection on humanity and human–more-than-human relations'.

On the one hand, there is a move towards 'enlightened anthropocentricism' (Keulartz 2012), where humans can become better planetary managers and stewards through technological advances, bringing us into the 'good Anthropocene' (Lorimer 2017). These researchers argue for the 'decoupling' (Asafu-Adjaye et al. 2015) of human and natural systems, suggesting the possibility of economic growth without environmental impact. This concept of the Anthropocene is clearly a deepening of the separation between nature/culture and natural sciences/social sciences and humanities. To save nature, we need to be separated from it and manage it using human ingenuity. Other social sciences and humanities like sociology, history and art are not part of this Anthropocene. However, there is a definite trend towards including climate in politics: if the future is dependent on good governance of the planet, politics must consider the Earth's ecosystems.

In contrast, there is a move towards a more eco-centric ethic where humans are removed from their customary place 'above' nature and placed in a world made up of an 'interconnected web of relations in which there are no dividing lines between the living and non-living, or the human and more-than-human' (Eckersly 1990: 749, cited in Lövbrand et al. 2009: 12). This is an acknowledgement that the future of life on Earth depends on ecological integrity (Kotzé 2014) and a criticism of the anthropocentricism in Cartesian ontologies of the environment. This is where the context of my case for giving rights to the ocean lies.

These various concepts of the Anthropocene overwhelmingly challenge the 'established boundaries' of the modern world. It is not just the concepts of the Anthropocene, but also the very process of its conceptualisation in the academic discourse that are tearing down these boundaries. If the Earth is one complex system, then nature, culture, climate and politics are interconnected and overlapping, and the idea that only humans deserve legal and political rights cannot hold. The arrival of the Anthropocene is a recognition that we are in a different time—one that requires a reckoning. This new time is not necessarily populated with new ideas, but, rather, as we shall see in the case of the Pacific, it is populated with locally enduring but globally marginalised ideas adapted for evolving circumstances.

The oceans and the Anthropocene

No more-than-human entity is as exploited or as invisible as the ocean herself. Despite covering most of the Earth's surface, the ocean is largely ignored and unseen by humans. This is why vast floating islands of plastic and other rubbish can form in her waters without anyone making a fuss; the reaction would be very different if we dumped all that trash on to another country's land. And yet, the ocean is doing the most work in absorbing the tonnes of carbon dioxide we have pumped into the atmosphere. She is the source of most of the oxygen in the world and the source of life for so much of humankind.

The ocean plays a central role in regulating the Earth's climate. The IPCC's Fifth Assessment Report published in 2013 revealed the ocean has absorbed 93 per cent of the extra energy from the enhanced greenhouse effect, with warming now being observed at depths of 1,000 metres. This has led to increased ocean stratification (prevention of water mixing due to different properties of water masses), changes in ocean currents and expansion of depleted-oxygen zones. Changes in the geographical ranges of marine species and shifts in growing seasons, as well as in the diversity and abundance of species communities, are now being observed. At the same time, weather patterns are changing, with extreme events increasing in frequency (Doney et al. 2020; Union of Concerned Scientists 2019; NOAA 2020).

Carbon dioxide emissions are also making the ocean more acidic, increasing the vulnerability of many marine species and ecosystems. Ocean acidification reduces the ability of marine organisms such as corals, plankton and shellfish to build their shells and skeletal structures. It also exacerbates existing physiological stresses such as impeded respiration and reproduction and reduces growth and survival rates during the early life stages of some species (Doney et al. 2020; NOAA 2020).

The ocean and the climate are inextricably linked. The ocean plays a fundamental role in mitigating climate change by serving as a major heat and carbon sink. The ocean covers 71 per cent of the planet and provides many services to human communities, from mitigating weather extremes to generating the oxygen we breathe, and from producing the food we eat to storing the excess carbon dioxide we generate. However, the effects of increasing greenhouse gas emissions threaten coastal and marine ecosystems through changes in ocean temperatures and melting of ice, which in turn affect ocean currents, weather patterns and sea level. And, because the carbon sink capacity of the ocean has been exceeded, we are also seeing the ocean's chemistry change because of our carbon emissions. In fact, humankind has increased the acidity of our oceans by 30 per cent over the past two centuries (Doney et al. 2020; NOAA 2020).

The ocean also bears the brunt of climate change, as evidenced by changes in temperature, currents and sea-level rise—all of which affect the health of marine species and nearshore and deep-ocean ecosystems. As concerns about climate change increase, the interrelationship between the ocean and climate change must be recognised, understood and incorporated into government policymaking. Since the Industrial Revolution, the amount of carbon dioxide in our atmosphere has increased by more than 35 per cent, primarily from the burning of fossil fuels. Ocean waters, animals and habitats all help the ocean absorb a significant portion of the carbon dioxide emissions from human activities. Ocean acidification levels in the Pacific are already 52 parts per thousand beyond the maximum safe limit of 350 parts per million, while Pacific fisheries are shifting in response to changes in water temperature. Warmer temperatures are also affecting food and water security on land because of variable rainfall and the intensification of natural hazards (Bigg et al. 2003; Doney et al. 2020; NOAA 2020). The dramatic improvement in air quality and ocean health resulting from the reduction in global trade, industrial fishing and vehicle traffic volumes during Covid-19 reinforced the impact of economic policies and lifestyle choices on global warming (Duarte et al. 2020). However, the fact this reprieve was seen by many governments as a temporary glitch rather than cause for a major rethink of sustainable development leaves major concerns in the minds of many.

Raising awareness of the ocean

Despite the data outlined in the previous section on the vital role oceans play in the Earth's climate, most who see climate change as an immediate and serious threat to future life on Earth still look at the ocean and see just a flat expanse of empty space. To those who know her intimately, however, who know her swells and waves, she is alive and in a league of her own. The ancestors of Pacific Islanders knew this intimately. They knew her so well they could name currents and find their way to islands they had never visited but only heard of. The ocean was a wonder to be revered and was deeply embedded in their history, world view and sense of identity (Hau`ofa 1994; D'Arcy 2006).

The UN Convention on the Law of the Sea divided the oceans into human spaces that bore little relation to their various ecosystems and lacked the intimate associations of Indigenous sea peoples like Pacific Islanders, as outlined in Sections Two and Three of this collection. Forms of sovereignty are given to coastal nation-states extending out from the shoreline into EEZs, while the high seas are deemed a commons, open to all, but beyond the national jurisdictions of all and therefore also beyond their legal right to police and protect (UN 1982). But as the ocean has no rights of her own, there is nothing, in the legal and global senses, to defend. It is only in disputes over territorial waters that nations bother to defend the ocean, but then only the small part they deem their own—as though the ocean can be owned by anyone. This is just another symptom of the disconnect between human civilisation and more-than-human beings in today's world.

Before turning to the conveyance of legal and political standing on the ocean, let me briefly outline my own evolving relationship with the ocean and my fascination with her. It is a tale of learned intimacy evolving out of a society in many ways shaped by the ocean but unaware of the extent of her place in its past and future success. As a qualified diver, marine conservationist and performance artist now working for environmental NGOs, I have grown to understand the vital need to combine effective marine conservation with vastly enhanced global public awareness and empathy for ensuring healthy oceans for human and planetary survival in the Anthropocene.

I live in Singapore, a tiny island-state at the tip of the Malayan Peninsula. We call ourselves an island, but we rarely think of ourselves as island people. Sometimes we go to the beach, but otherwise, the ocean rarely enters even the fringes of our consciousness—odd for a nation that so heavily relies on international shipping and trade to survive. How is it that, on a tiny island, we can be so oblivious to the ocean that surrounds us? How is it that we live as though only the land on which we walk exists? The human body is adapted to the water—our hearts slow automatically on entering it—and our tears and sweat are as salty as the sea.

I remember the first time I went diving. It was painful, frankly, because I was not accustomed to going deep in the water and my ears had a lot of problems adjusting to the pressure. But it was wondrous to be able to swim all the way down, down, down. To feel the shift from the warmth in the top layer of water to the delicious coolness below. A refreshing underwater breeze.

I was always a little disappointed to see that the corals were not as colourful as the ones I saw in Finding Nemo. *Later, I found out that was because of the way the light filtered down—which is why underwater photographers often use red-light filters to colour-correct their photographs. This did not matter after a while, though, because the underwater world was fascinating. It was very quiet, aside from the bubbles, and, swimming past the reef, I had the sense that it was the closest to flying I would ever get, feeling the reef drop away, away, away from me, until it disappeared, and I was left hanging in the deep blue. I felt infinitely small and absolutely alive.*

In most of my diving experiences, the marks of human-caused destruction were everywhere. I doubt I have seen an undisturbed reef anywhere. In Lombok, Indonesia, the reefs were marked where fishers had used explosives. I saw the second-largest shark-fin market in Indonesia—legal, but selling illegal catches of species such as hammerhead sharks. I saw damaged, bleached coral.

I had dreamed of diving on the Great Barrier Reef, imagining a pristine reef full of life. But, of course, as we now know, this once-great reef, despite its size, is not immune to the warming waters of human-caused climate change. And in all my dives, I always saw life: sea-snakes, turtles, fish, crustaceans, octopus, sea cucumber … It was a wonder on my first big diving trip to the Gili Islands, also in Indonesia, to see the flourishing 'Biorock' reefs: human-made shapes, filled to the brim with corals able to withstand higher levels of stress, and schools of fish—human technology working not just as a technofix, but also as something that regenerates life.

Diving in Singapore, meanwhile, reveals how bad things can get. Diving there is no joke; it demands a lot of the diver—not because it is technical, like cave diving, but because the waters are so full of sediment from erosion, construction and land reclamation that it is easy to lose sight of your diving buddies. This is not to say there is no life; life is abundant even in such circumstances. But it is a rather sad—and very muddy—sight to behold.

In all my diving adventures, at the back of my mind, I was also distinctly aware that my travelling and diving were probably also adding to the damage. I had helped on some reef surveys, but I do not know whether that justified anything. The irony of today's nature-seekers is that we often end up adding to the harm. It is a paradox and a contradiction into which we have been thrown. There is nothing we can do today that is not hypocritical. Such is the Anthropocene.

How, then, should we approach this? One way is through stories and art, through recollection and memory. In earlier work partly produced below, I combined academic and artistic research to create an installation-performance titled *Sanctuary: Entanglements with the More-Than-Human*. Through this work, I coaxed people into telling their stories and sharing their memories of the more-than-human (in this project, it was about the Sun, Moon and stars) and reawakening their dormant connections to the world around them. Another way of achieving this objective is to claim a place for the more-than-human in legal and political spaces and to say that, yes, trees—and the ocean—*should* have legal standing.

Plate 18.2: *Hold Me*, **2019.**
Photo: Melody Tay.

For the remainder of this chapter, I wish to make a case for the ocean—that she should have rights of her own that can be defended and fought for. To make this case, I will draw on the great body of work on ecological justice, on case studies and on the world views, stories and knowledge of Indigenous peoples—in particular, those whose shores touch the Pacific Ocean.

Nature's standing in the Anthropo-scene: Lessons from the Pacific

You may think giving rights to more-than-human beings is far-fetched. However, two very real instances are the ratifying of the rights of nature in the Ecuadorian Constitution of 2008 and the recognition of the Whanganui River as a legal person in Aotearoa New Zealand. In the tropical Pacific, similar discussions are taking place about conveying legal rights on the ocean. Before going into detail, let us first situate the theories of ecological justice and the rights of nature in the Anthropocene.

The idea of giving nature legal standing and rights can be traced back to Stone's influential 1972 work *Should Trees Have Standing?*, which offered a 're-envisioned possibility for rights … to extend their application to nonhuman living entities' (Kotzé and Villavicencio Calzadilla 2017). When Stone introduced this concept, the term Anthropocene had not yet come into being. However, as Lorimer (2017) points out, the Anthropocene has resulted in a reinvigoration of fields like environmental humanities and a revisiting of various ontologies. There is much literature on environmental justice and the rights of nature that has referred back directly to Stone's idea and arguments (Kotzé 2014; Hutchison 2014; Kotzé and Villavicencio Calzadilla 2017). This idea has since been expanded by various scholars (Cullinan 2008; Kotzé 2014; Schlosberg 2014; Tanasescu 2014) and can be situated in Toivanen et al.'s (2017) biological, social and cultural approaches to the Anthropocene. It sits in Lorimer's (2017) 'new ontologies' category discussed earlier—specifically, in the eco-centric narrative. Within this narrative is the field of environmental law and within that is literature concerned with the rights of nature. This literature is critical of the anthropocentricism present in environmental law that has informed 'the way modern law constructs, categorizes and orders nature, [and] the manner in which law protects nature' (De Lucia 2015: 95, cited in Kotzé and Villavicencio Calzadilla 2017: 403)—mainly for the benefit of people and not for nature itself. It thus advocates for nature to have legal standing and rights.

Another field of relevance is that of ecological justice. In this area, Indigenous peoples and governments of the Pacific Ocean have been to the fore, especially in Ecuador, Aotearoa New Zealand and the nations of the Pacific Islands Forum, initially led by Cook Islands.

In September 2008, Ecuador ratified a new constitution with a section recognising that nature 'has the right to exist, persist, maintain and regenerate its vital cycles, structure, functions and its processes in evolution' (Republic of Ecuador 2008). It is the first of its kind and stems from the theoretical notion of the rights of nature (Stone 1972; Cullinan 2008) and Indigenous 'cosmovisions' (Kotzé and Villavicencio Calzadilla 2017), which acknowledge the inextricable links between nature and humans.

In a similar spirit, the expression 'Te Awa Tupua' is the Māori conception of the Whanganui River as an 'indivisible and living whole … incorporating its tributaries and all its physical and metaphysical elements' (Whanganui Iwi and the Crown 2012), and it was granted legal personhood in Aotearoa New Zealand in 2017. This relationship is expressed by local Māori as: 'Ko au te Awa, ko te Awa ko au [I am the River and the River is Me].'

This means the river has inherent rights to wellbeing and also that the river can enforce these rights against other legal persons. Two guardians, one from the Whanganui iwi (tribe), and one from the Crown, were appointed to act and speak on behalf of Te Awa Tupua (Whanganui Iwi and the Crown 2012).

Both the Ecuadorian Constitution and Te Awa Tupua were deeply influenced by Indigenous Andean and Māori world views, values and cultures, respectively. The notion of Sumak Kawsay means 'living well' in the Indigenous Andean Kichwa language and is deeply embedded in Andean thought and the decolonisation paradigm and seeks to 'dissolve the Western neoliberal human–nature binary' (Kotzé and Villavicencio Calzadilla 2017)—a direct challenge to the nature–culture boundary. The Ecuadorian Constitution states that 'the good way of living' requires people to live 'within the framework of … harmonious coexistence with nature' (Kotzé and Villavicencio Calzadilla 2017). In the case of Te Awa Tupua, the Whanganui iwi see the river not just as living, but also as an ancestor (Magallanes 2015), and this belief stems from the Māori cosmological vision that all things are alive and related through whakapapa (genealogy) (Waitangi Tribunal 2011). In other words, living and dead, inanimate and animate things are all considered alive and connected. In the final signed agreement on Te Awa Tupua, it is explicitly stated that the river is being granted legal personhood because it reflects 'the Whanganui iwi view' that the river is a 'living entity in its own right' and is 'incapable of being "owned" in an absolute sense' (Whanganui Iwi and the Crown 2012).

Ecuador's Constitution and Te Awa Tupua are not just theoretical speculations or philosophical meanderings. They are concrete manifestations of underlying world views and the idea of nature's rights in the legal sphere. They are policies dealing not just with intrahuman issues, but also with an integrated, interrelated natural and cultural world. As Kotzé and Villavicencio Calzadilla (2017: 401) state, the Ecuadorian Constitution announces 'a transition from a juridical anthropocentric orientation to an ecocentric position'. Nature's rights have been acted on successfully in the Ecuadorian Constitution and Te Awa Tupua is recognised as an innovative legal arrangement between Māori and Pākehā (non-Māori) and between an Indigenous people and its government.

However, there are criticisms that the rights discourse is 'all rhetoric and exhortation' (Henkin 1990) and there are concerns that these two cases are simply window-dressing to placate rising concerns about sustainable development. In 2012, the Ecuadorian Government allowed the building of a $1.77 billion open-pit copper mine in one of the most biodiverse areas in South America (Tegel 2012; BankTrack 2016). Furthermore, the value of the mining industry in Ecuador was projected to increase eightfold by 2021 (Jamasmie 2017). Such contradictory actions do not mean the eco-centric Ecuadorian Constitution challenges Hamilton et al.'s (2015) boundaries any less. Hiding behind the constitution, the ideology of progress and modern development seems to remain dominant; nature is still effectively treated as subservient to the economic priorities of society as defined by those in decision-making roles.

However, instead of giving into cynicism, we must understand that change comes slowly, particularly when it involves a multitude of actors, institutions, ideologies, values and narratives, as aptly demonstrated in the previous chapter on the application of these principles in the Galápagos Islands of Ecuador. There have been several cases filed on behalf of nature under the Ecuadorian Constitution and a few have been successful. A prominent case is that of the Vilcabamba River, where a couple living along the river sued a construction company for dumping large amounts of extracted material into it. In fact, more transdisciplinary, boundary-breaking research is needed to produce more effective policy that reflects eco-centric values and alternative paths of 'development'. In this way, these two case studies elicit the hidden complexities in the relationships between theory, values, knowledge and the 'real world'.

Momentum is building in the Pacific. Pacific Island peoples have been increasingly asserting their special relationship with the Pacific Ocean. In contrast to the earlier two examples, however, the Pacific Ocean is the largest geographical feature on Earth, forming an almost exclusively blue hemisphere when viewed from space. In 2012, Prime Minister of the Cook Islands Henry Puna reminded the non-Pacific world that his nation and its neighbours were not microstates confined to a few small islands, but rather, Large Ocean States that controlled vast expanses of the Earth's ocean surface. He noted that, collectively, 'the sum of our ocean territory is nearly two times the size of Russia' (Puna 2012). Pacific Islanders' increasing assertiveness in global forums of their unique relationship with the Pacific Ocean was prompted in part by one of the alternative paths of development advocated in the previous paragraph. In 1994, the late Tongan scholar Epeli Hau`ofa published an article entitled 'Our Sea of Islands' in which he noted that Pacific Island national boundaries were colonial constructs that disrupted millennia of wide-ranging interactions that extended resource bases and social relations along maritime highways. Hau`ofa (1994) argued that Pacific peoples must throw off the categorisations of them as microstate basket cases, reconnect with Indigenous traditions and repopulate their seas with the intimate detail of ancestral memories, tradition and recited navigation chants combining memory markers to connect them to the vast sea of endless opportunities and historical intimacy their ancestors once envisaged (Howe 2006).

In 2013, Puna made a call to confer legal protections and rights on the great ocean. He was not alone. The following year, President of Palau Tommy Remengesau Jr, called for collective consciousness and action when he received the Champion of the Earth award from the UN Environment Programme. In 2011, Dame Meg Taylor, the secretary-general of the PIFS, was appointed as the world's first ocean advocate by Pacific Forum members. Dame Meg's role as Pacific Ocean commissioner was to ensure 'the Pacific region had a champion to provide the necessary high level representation and commitment urgently required for dedicated advocacy and attention to Pacific Ocean priorities, decisions and processes at national, regional and international levels' (OPOC 2019). This position is well resourced and part of a wider regional commitment to protect the ocean and create a healthy and sustainable blue economy.

In summary, these three case studies challenge established boundaries on an ideological and a policy level. As the protections are relatively new, it remains to be seen how the rights of each more-than-human entity will be exercised.

The rights of nature in the Anthropocene and the global sustainability movement

The Anthropocene with its slow-moving indications has finally interrupted our present, appearing in our midst, glaring and impossible to ignore. It has seeped into everything we read and do. The #FridaysforFuture school-strike movement led by Greta Thunberg, with its mass demonstrations in March and September 2019, before the Covid-19 lockdowns, demanded adults take action to protect the future for their children and their children's children. Extinction Rebellion popped up in every other city across the world, disrupting the daily violence of shareholder capitalism, demanding change from governments and companies and providing a voice for those without one. Some business and world leaders such as former US president Donald Trump continued to deny climate change, highlighting an intergenerational rift and the burning anger of a generation at the inaction and irresponsibility of previous generations.

As if to prove the point of the countless climate protest movements across the globe, fires and floods erupted everywhere in 2020 as Covid-19 also created chaos—from the forest fires in the Amazon, followed by fires in Sumatra and devastating floods in Jakarta that displaced tens of thousands of people, to the unquenchable monster flames in Australia that claimed perhaps more than a billion more-than-human lives.

Our house is burning as we speak.

But there is always hope. A rising generation is taking up the mantle of leadership, holding on to the heavy responsibility of bringing us into an unknown future. Instead of short-termism and profit-driven growth, these leaders understand that the impact of one's actions goes beyond cost-benefit analysis. They understand that their responsibility extends far beyond shareholder dollars to workers, communities and the global commons.

At the biggest global conference for business and political leaders, held by the World Economic Forum, in Davos, Switzerland, in January 2020, the focus was overwhelmingly on the climate and the huge risks and opportunities climate change poses for businesses, governments and communities. 'Stakeholders for a Cohesive and Sustainable World' was the theme—one that finally gave marginalised youth and Indigenous peoples a seat at the decision-making table (Cann 2019). This was a major shift of emphasis—but is it enough? Pacific Indigenous peoples have led the way in conferring legal and political rights on elements of the more-than-human world. Enhancing awareness and alliances between such Indigenous peoples and youth movements seeking sustainable futures offers a promising way forward with practical examples to pressure leaders to commit to rapidly enacting the climate change mitigation measures these movements and most of the world's scientists believe are vital. Just over a year after Davos, the new US president, Joe Biden, held another global forum, in April 2021, which set far more ambitious climate mitigation targets, and the first Indigenous person occupied the role of US secretary of the interior, Deb Haaland of the Pueblo peoples. It remains to be seen whether these promises are matched by the necessary action desired and required.

Conclusion: Redefining progress in the Anthropocene— Pacific trajectories for global alternatives

Daya Dakasi Da-Wei Kuan and Paul D'Arcy

This collection has argued that solutions to issues of Indigenous political empowerment and economic viability will only be economically, socially and ecologically sustainable if they take account of distinct local contexts and cultures. Local communities must live with the consequences of environmental mismanagement and overexploitation while rarely benefiting from the short-term economic profits such actions may generate within the global system. National or international political, conservation and sustainable development policy frameworks ultimately rely on local community assent and compliance because of the limited resources provided to national and regional compliance monitors and implementation staff. Multiple generations of colonial indirect rule and the postcolonial, modern equivalent of consultation without representation or effective decision-making power have alienated local communities across our region. Without effective local participation and partnership, these externally imposed frameworks have rarely delivered viable, sustained, local environmental, cultural and economic benefits, nor have they fully benefited from millennia of local observation and understanding.

Long associations with specific ecosystems and localities provide insights into environmental management and social support that most chapters demonstrate survive in memory. These often need to be relearned by current generations because of external authorities' discouragement and stifling or less-healthy imported alternatives—be it education textbooks of the former colonial power written for students in temperate or continental environments or imported fatty meat offcuts and rice from Pacific Rim nations. Pacific Indigenous governments and communities actively participate in international deliberations that consistently fall well short of recommended targets and rarely deliver tangible environmental and economic benefits to poorer nations. However, they also act locally to preserve, enhance and climate-proof the lands and seas of their ancestors by drawing on the lessons of collective memories to replant with appropriate species and modify the land to enhance water conservation, and act collectively to restrain and modify their own use of local resources for sustained harvests and revived ecosystems. In so doing, they continue in the ways Papa Mape and many others have advocated and practised for generations.

This volume arose from frustration that awareness of our regional knowledge remains highly localised and largely marginalised or exoticised in dominant educational and media sources. This collection demonstrates that numerous local Indigenous systems are not only increasingly self-sustaining, but also much more productive than is usually claimed by advocates of industrial monocropping using added fertilisers for global supply. These local forms are also much less expensive to implement and far less dependent on imported elements subject to price fluctuations and competition from far larger and more profitable continental markets, or disruptions to supply chains caused by geopolitical rivalries, global economic shocks or pandemics. In addition, Pacific peoples' increasing interweaving of social, economic and environmental objectives fills a need that extends well beyond our region and into increasingly crowded urban habitats across the globe. For many urban dwellers, shopping for packaged or frozen food has become the only interaction with nature and a major form of social interaction.

In this regard, our Pacific Indigenous case studies offer 'Islands of Hope' for all communities marginalised by increasingly intrusive, rapid technological change and global dietary, economic, political and military forces with whom they have no direct contact or influence over. What unifies this collection are concepts of community identity based on a sense of being part of a long line of temporary guardians of local environments achieved through solidarity of action after consensus-based decision-making. This environmental guardianship requires acknowledging and following previous generations in identifying with, observing and nurturing the environment in specific locations. This knowledge has always had to be adaptable to meet variable climatic conditions. Such guardianship also requires social inclusiveness in not only leaving a sustainable legacy for the next generation but also respecting past and contemporary knowledge acquired through lifetimes of guardianship by people like Papa Mape, and collectively supporting all members who identify with a shared locality. For many Pacific communities, economic opportunities are often created by those with a shared sense of identity based on a specific locality forming a diasporic community, marrying and settling elsewhere. Today this often means residing in large Pacific Rim cities alongside many individuals and non-Indigenous groups. For such groups, our case studies' sense of local environmental purpose through ongoing connection, identity, collective support and empowerment has much to offer.

Islands of Hope has suggested three avenues of environmental protection and community re-empowerment in the wake of colonial disruption and global economic marginalisation. They offer lessons for the global community as a whole and the next generation, who will not have the option of enjoying the excessive overconsumption of global resources of the higher-income segments of the past two generations of humanity in developed nations. These avenues are: greater emphasis on locally controlled food production; countering ecosystem damage and promoting rehabilitation through daily action and increased awareness of local processes and local solutions producing solutions elsewhere; and promoting collective, consensus-based decision-making and action at local, national and international levels.

The first option—of enhanced local food production based on growing a variety of nutritional ground crops among tree crops, supplemented by harvesting forest foods—can create more income for local communities than the sale of logging rights and converting forest to palm-oil plantations, including by generating carbon credits for preserved forests. As demonstrated in Section One, this diversity of production and preserved species increases communities' climate change resilience as well as enhancing and restoring water tables and cooling ground temperatures. It allows communities the choice of devoting a smaller percentage of their lands to cash crops or logging in response to fluctuating global market demands if the opportunity arises (La Franchi and Greenpeace Pacific 1999; Madeley 2002, 2003; Bell et al. 2016; Suzuki and Hanington 2017: 152–61; Brown et al. 2018; Liu et al. 2019). Greater use of agroforestry also significantly increases the land's carbon sequestration potential. Agroforestry is probably the world's most efficient, productive and sustainable crop production method currently in use (Glaser and Birk 2012; Bezerra et al. 2016; Suzuki and Hanington 2017: 154–57).

Global food production and transport are ecologically damaging and incredibly wasteful. The Food and Agriculture Organization (FAO) of the United Nations estimates that one-third of all food grown for global markets either spoils before reaching its market or is thrown out or used as livestock feed because of the overstocking of wealthy markets and the limited purchasing power of most of the world's population. Price surges and food shortages in the past decade have also shown the system to be more fragile than usually advocated, while full-cost accounting of environmental rehabilitation and transport and energy costs has challenged the claimed profitability of many enterprises (Madeley 2002, 2003; Gustavsson et al. 2011; Fraser and Fraser 2014). This is not an argument to opt out of the global system, but rather that local patterns of consumption primarily for local and proximate markets with a surplus for export are important complementary alternatives to develop, especially in the era of climate change and fiscal instability and debt. Even those living in high-density urban apartments can show their support through the power of their democratic vote, creating local urban communities to foster green urban spaces and community gardens for social interaction as much as nutritional benefit, and directly connecting and sharing information with and about other urban and Pacific Indigenous communities.

The second option—of local conservation and rehabilitation—is also best done at a local level and, in this, sufficiently empowered Indigenous and other local communities have a major role and a positive impact that are underrepresented in the literature. The ecosystem benefits of diverse food forests noted above also rapidly and significantly alter local carbon footprints to create greater carbon sequestration and much fewer carbon emissions in our energy profiles. The creation and maintenance of local land-based carbon-sequestering ecologies are dwarfed by local attention to marine ecosystem health. The Pacific Ocean encompasses one-third of the Earth's surface and is a vital carbon sink to reduce global warming for planetary health. The key elements in ocean absorption rates are ocean biota in marine ecosystems currently under threat from overfishing by foreign fishing fleets and the discharge of land-based pollution. Section Two demonstrated how locally empowered Indigenous communities can preserve and restore these marine ecosystems and their biota through protecting fisheries and creating healthy terrestrial food production systems that not only sequester carbon, but also build up soil fertility naturally rather than depending on more and more fertiliser at the expense of toxic runoff into waterways, reefs and oceans. Section Three reiterated the importance of local Indigenous attitudes in creating sustainable and viable human–environment interactions to mitigate current environmental challenges, as well as the longer-term legacy of fluidity and flexibility to changing climatic and environmental conditions on which such approaches are built.

The third avenue is emphasising local empowerment over global forces, and greater social justice for all. Local solutions tailored to local circumstances create diverse solutions. That diversity enhances the chances of finding the range of innovative solutions needed to overcome the existential threat of climate change. This threat is already manifesting itself in a multiplicity of local contexts among populations who often have a long heritage of planning for climatic instability. Empowering the many requires an optimistic view of how individuals will act towards one another and their habitats once empowered. Restricting decision-making and enforcing compliance are premised on a more negative view of humanity that fears the consequences of individual empowerment, which is simply not borne out by our case studies. Optimism about the consequences of broadening empowerment is borne out by results outlined in this collection from the more inclusive allocation of resources and decision-making noted in the working principles of the Vanuatu Government and Te Puni Kōkiri to the rapid rehabilitation and restoration of local ecosystem resilience under local community management across our region. The concept of Oceanian sovereignty also offers exciting possibilities for local empowerment by placing local communities alongside governments and regional and international experts as complementary decision-making pathways. Oceanian pathways require such partnerships to be reinforced and maintained through ongoing action and dialogue rather than merely residing in a legally designated officeholder for the duration of their tenure.

The current impacts of the serious environmental and economic challenges facing humanity vary dramatically across individual, community and ecological circumstances and therefore require detailed observation and analysis at all levels to redefine progress for the benefit for human communities. While we should read and listen to currently dominant economic and scientific expert voices on the world stage to understand the global economy in the Anthropocene, focusing on the local makes us cautious about generalisations. All community knowledge-holders, including scientists and economists, must move between the local and the global in their observations. Understanding the global context helps us better recognise local distinctiveness in reactions to common experiences. One of the main purposes of this collection is to make Asia-Pacific

Indigenous communities more aware of the relevance and efficacy of other community responses to issues they also face. Section Four, in particular, has demonstrated the potential of locally engaged and culturally informed economic and scientific policies, as well as the applicability and relevance of locally devised models for other Asia-Pacific contexts. Ultimately, to endure and prosper, our successful responses to any challenge require cooperation, open dialogue, empathy, tolerance and understanding of our fellow humans and the wider webs of life of which we are part and on which we build our lives.

Bibliography

ABC News (2019). Why are Native Hawaiians protesting against construction of a giant telescope on Mauna Kea? *ABC News*, 25 July. Available from: www. abc.net.au/news/2019-07-25/native-hawaiians-protesting-against-mauna-kea-telescope/11345574.

Acciaioli, G., H. Brunt and J. Clifton (2017). Foreigners everywhere, nationals nowhere: Exclusion, irregularity, and invisibility of stateless Bajau Laut in Eastern Sabah, Malaysia. *Journal of Immigrant & Refugee Studies* 15(3): 232–249. doi.org/10.1080/15562948.2017.1319526.

Adam, T.C., R.J. Schmitt, S.J. Holbrook, A.J. Brooks, P.J. Edmunds, R.C. Carpenter and G. Bernardi (2011). Herbivory, connectivity, and ecosystem resilience: Response of a coral reef to a large-scale perturbation. *PLoS ONE* 6(8): e23717. doi.org/10.1371/journal.pone.0023717.

Agrawal, A. (1995). Dismantling the divide between Indigenous and scientific knowledge. *Development and Change* 26: 413–439. doi.org/10.1111/j.1467-7660.1995.tb00560.x.

Aguilar, G.D. (2004). Present and future role of the College of Fisheries and Ocean Sciences in fisheries and coastal resource management. In L.V. Villareal, V. Kelleher and U. Tietze (eds), *Guidelines on the collection of demographic and socio-economic information on fishing communities for use in coastal and aquatic resources management*. FAO Fisheries Technical Paper No. 439, Part 2, Annex 3, Paper 1. Rome: Food and Agriculture Organization. Available from: www.fao.org/3/y5055e/y5055e0k.htm.

Agyeman, J., D. Schlosberg, L. Craven and C. Matthews (2016). Trends and directions in environmental justice: From inequity to everyday life, community, and just sustainabilities. *Annual Review of Environment and Resources* 41(1): 321–340. doi.org/10.1146/annurev-environ-110615-090052.

Akkerman, S.F. and A. Bakker (2011). Boundary crossing and boundary objects. *Review of Education Research* 81(2): 132–69. doi.org/10.3102/0034654311404435.

Alava, J.J. and F. Paladines (2017). Illegal fishing on the Galápagos high seas. *Letters, Science* 357(6358): 1362. doi.org/10.1126/science.aap7832.

Ali, S.H. (2016). The new rise of Nauru: Can the island bounce back from its mining boom and bust? *The Conversation*, 15 July. Available from: theconversation.com/the-new-rise-of-nauru-can-the-island-bounce-back-from-its-mining-boom-and-bust-62419.

Alkire, W. (1965). *Lamotrek Atoll and Inter Island Socio-Economic Ties.* Urbana, IL: University of Illinois Press.

Allen, M. (2008). *Land reform in Melanesia.* State, Society and Governance in Melanesia Briefing Note No. 6. Canberra: The Australian National University.

Alliance of Small Island States (AOSIS) (2015). Statement by Republic of Maldives on behalf of the Alliance of Small Island States at the high-level event on climate change. News release, 29 June. New York, NY: Permanent Mission of the Republic of Maldives to the United Nations. Available from: maldivesmission. com/statements/statement_by_the_maldives_on_behalf_of_the_alliance_of_small_island_states_aosis_high_level_event_on_climate_change.

Altman, J.C., G.J. Buchanan and L. Larsen (2007). *The environmental significance of the Indigenous estate: Natural resource management as economic development in remote Australia.* CAEPR Discussion Paper No. 286/2007. Canberra: Centre for Aboriginal Economic Policy Research, The Australian National University. Available from: caepr.cass.anu.edu.au/sites/default/files/docs/2007_DP286_0.pdf.

Altman, J.C. and P.J. Whitehead (2003). *Caring for country and sustainable Indigenous development: Opportunities, constraints and innovation.* CAEPR Working Paper No. 20. Canberra: Centre for Aboriginal Economic Policy Research, The Australian National University. Available from: caepr.cass.anu. edu.au/sites/default/files/docs/CAEPRWP20_0.pdf.

Andersen, E., B. Elbersen, F. Godeschalk and D. Verhoog (2007). Farm management indicators and farm typologies as a basis for assessments in a changing policy environment. *Journal of Environmental Management* 82: 353–362. doi.org/10.1016/j.jenvman.2006.04.021.

Anderson, T. (2010). Land registration, land markets and livelihoods in Papua New Guinea. In T. Anderson & G. Lee (eds), *In Defence of Melanesian Customary Land*, pp. 11–20. Sydney: Aid/Watch.

Aqorau, T. (2016). How tuna is shaping regional diplomacy. In G. Fry and S. Tarte (eds), *The New Pacific Diplomacy*, pp. 223–236. Canberra: ANU Press. doi.org/10.22459/NPD.12.2015.18.

Aqorau, T. and E. Papastavridis (2015). The interception of vessels on the high seas: Contemporary challenges to the legal order of the oceans. In A. Chircop, S. Coffen-Smout and M.L. McConnell (eds), *Ocean Yearbook 29*, pp. 493–497. Leiden, Netherlands: Brill Nijhoff.

Armitage, L.A. (2001). Customary land tenure in Papua New Guinea: Status and prospects. Paper presented to Inaugural Pacific Regional Meeting of the International Association for the Study of Common Property, Brisbane, September 2–4.

Asafu-Adjaye, J., L. Blomquist, S. Brand, B.W. Brook, R. DeFries, E. Ellis, C. Foreman, D. Keith, M. Lewis, M. Lynas, T. Nordhaus, R. Pielke, R. Pritzker, P. Ronald, J. Roy, M. Sagoff, M. Shellenberger, R. Stone and P. Teague (2015). *An Ecomodernist Manifesto*. [Online]. Available from: www.ecomodernism.org/manifesto-english/.

Asia Pacific Rugby League Confederation (APRLC) (2020). Linking Chile, Polynesia, and Billy Slater's hometown. *News*, 29 July. Auckland, NZ: APRLC. Available from: asiapacificrl.com/2020/07/29/linking-chile-polynesia-and-billy-slaters-hometown/.

Asian Development Bank (ADB) (2011). *Pacific Climate Change Program Information Update No. 1, January*. Manila: ADB. Available from: www.adb.org/sites/default/files/publication/29151/pccp-information-update-01.pdf.

Asian Development Bank (ADB) (2014). *Solid Waste Management in the Pacific: Kiribati country snapshot*. June. Manila: ADB. Available from: www.adb.org/sites/default/files/publication/42671/solid-waste-management-kiribati.pdf.

Associated Press (AP) (2013). Chilean couple die in arson attack after land dispute with Mapuche Indians. *The Guardian*, 5 January. Available from: www.theguardian.com/world/2013/jan/04/chilean-couple-arson-land-mapuche.

Attran, S. (1993). *Cognitive Foundations of Natural History: Towards an anthropology of science*. Cambridge, UK: Cambridge University Press.

Australian Government (2009). *East Marine Bioregional Plan: Bioregional profile*. Canberra: Department of Sustainability, Environment, Water, Population and Communities.

Australian Government (2012). *Marine Bioregional Plan for the Temperate East Marine Region*. Canberra: Department of Sustainability, Environment, Water, Population and Communities. Available from: www.dcceew.gov.au/sites/default/files/env/pages/1e59b6ec-8b7e-42a8-9619-b5d728f878b2/files/temperate-east-marine-plan.pdf.

Australian Government (2013). *Securing Food Resources in the Federated States of Micronesia. Case study*. Canberra: Pacific Adaptation Strategy Assistance Program. Available from: terranova.org.au/repository/paccsap-collection/securing-food-resources-in-the-federated-states-of-micronesia/case-studies-fsm-4pp.pdf.

Australian Government (2015). *Our North, Our Future: White Paper on developing northern Australia*. Canberra: Department of Industry, Innovation and Science.

Australian Institute of Aboriginal and Torres Strait Islander Studies (AIATSIS) (2014). Emerging Issues in Land and Sea Management: A workshop to map current and future research and resource needs. National Native Title Conference, Coffs Harbour, NSW, 4 June.

Australian Museum (2014). *Garrigarrang: Sea country*. Permanent exhibition, Australian Museum, Sydney. Available from: australian.museum/exhibition/garrigarrang-sea-country/.

Australian Museum (2019). *Garrigarrang: Sea country*. Secondary Education Kit. Sydney: Australian Museum. Available from: media.australian.museum/media/dd/documents/Garrigarrang_Secondary_Ed_Kit_20Mar2019.b740946.pdf.

Australian National Audit Office (ANAO) (2011). *Indigenous Protected Areas*. Audit Report No. 14 2011–12, Performance Audit. Canberra: ANAO.

Australian and New Zealand Environment and Conservation Council (ANZECC) (1998). *Guidelines for Establishing the National Representative System of Marine Protected Areas*. Canberra: ANZECC Task Force on Marine Protected Areas.

Australian and New Zealand Environment and Conservation Council (ANZECC) (1999). *Strategic Plan of Action for the National Representative System of Marine Protected Areas: A guide for action for Australian governments*. Canberra: ANZECC Task Force on Marine Protected Areas.

Autonomous Bougainville Government (ABG). (2018). *Bougainville Strategic Development Plan 2018–2022*. Arawa: Autonomous Bougainville Government.

Ayres, W.S. (1983). Archaeology at Nan Madol, Pohnpei. *Bulletin of the Indo-Pacific Prehistory Association* 4: 135–142.

Bahn, P. and J. Flenley (1992). *Earth Island, Easter Island*. London: Thames & Hudson.

Bale, J.S. and S.A.L. Hayward (2010). Insect overwintering in a changing climate. *Journal of Experimental Biology* 213: 980–994. doi.org/10.1242/jeb.037911.

Bambridge T. (2008–11). RĀHUI reports 1, 2, 3, 4, 5, 6, 7. Unpublished ms, Department of the Environment, Papeete, Tahiti.

Bambridge, T. (2009). *La terre dans l'archipel des îles Australes. Etude du pluralisme juridique et culturel en matière foncière* [*Land in the Austral Islands Archipelago: Study of legal and cultural pluralism in land matters*]. Institut de Recherche pour le Développement (IRD) [Research Institute for Development] et Aux Vents des îles.

Bambridge, T. (2013a). Le foncier terrestre et marin en Polynésie française. L'étude de cas de Teahupo'o [Terrestrial and marine land in French Polynesia: The Teahupo`o case study]. *Land Tenure Journal* 3: 119–143.

Bambridge, T. (2016). The law of *rahui* in the Society Islands. In T. Bambridge (ed.), *The Rahui: Legal pluralism in Polynesian traditional management of resources and territories*. Canberra: ANU Press. doi.org/10.22459/TR.03.2016.06.

Bambridge, T., F. Chlous, J. Claudet, P. D'Arcy, N. Pascal, S. Reynaud, R. Rodolfo-Metalpa, S. Tambutté, A. Thomassin and L. Recuero Virto (2019). Society-based solutions to coral reef threats in French Pacific territories. *Regional Studies in Marine Science* 29: 1–8. doi.org/10.1016/j.rsma.2019.100667.

Bambridge, T., P. D'Arcy and A. Mawyer (2021). Oceanian sovereignty: Rethinking conservation in a sea of islands. *Pacific Conservation Biology* 27(4): 345–353. doi.org/10.1071/PC20026.

Bambridge T. and J. Vernaudon (2013). Espace, histoire et territoire en Polynésie. Une appropriation foncière de l'espace terrestre et marin [Space, history and territory in Polynesia: Land appropriation of terrestrial and marine space]. In E. Le Roy (ed.), *La Terre et l'homme. Espaces et ressources convoités, entre le local et le global* [*Earth and Man: Coveted spaces and resources, between the local and the global*]. Paris: Editions Karthala.

Bank of Papua New Guinea (BPNG) (2019). *September 2019 Quarterly Economic Bulletin (QEB)*. Port Moresby: BPNG. Available from: www.bankpng.gov.pg/wp-content/uploads/2020/01/September-2019-Quarterly-Economic-Bulletin-QEB.pdf.

BankTrack (2016). *El Mirador Copper Mine Ecuador*. Nijmegan, Netherlands: BankTrack. Available from: www.banktrack.org/project/el_mirador_copper_mine.

Barber, M. and E. Woodward (2018). *Indigenous Water Values, Rights, Interests and Development Objectives in the Fitzroy Catchment*. A technical report to the Australian Government from the CSIRO Northern Australia Water Resource Assessment, part of the National Water Infrastructure Development Fund: Water Resource Assessments. Canberra: CSIRO.

Barraclough, T. (2013). How far can the Te Awa Tupua (Whanganui River) proposal be said to reflect the rights of nature in New Zealand? Hons dissertation, University of Otago, Dunedin, NZ.

Barrau, J. (1958). *Subsistence Agriculture in Melanesia*. Honolulu: Bernice P. Bishop Museum.

Barrière, O. (1996). Gestion des ressources naturelles renouvelables et conservation des écosystèmes au Sahel: le foncier-environnement [Management of renewable natural resources and conservation of ecosystems in the Sahel: Land-environment]. PhD thesis, University of Paris 1 Panthéon-Sorbonne.

Bartley Johns, M., P. Brenton, M. Cali, M. Hoppe and R. Piermartini (2015). *The Role of Trade in Ending Poverty*. 2 vols. Geneva: World Trade Organization. Available from: documents.worldbank.org/curated/en/726971467989468997/ The-role-of-trade-in-ending-poverty.

Bauman, T. and D. Smyth (2007). *Indigenous Partnerships in Protected Area Management in Australia: Three case studies*. Canberra and Melbourne: AIATSIS and The Australian Collaboration.

Bayliss-Smith, T. and E. Hviding (2012). Irrigated taro, malaria and the expansion of chiefdoms: Ruta in New Georgia, Solomon Islands. In M. Spriggs, D. Addison and P.J. Matthews (eds), *Irrigated Taro (Colocasia esculenta) in the Indo-Pacific: Biological, Social and Historical Perspectives*. Senri Ethnological Studies 78, pp. 219–254. Osaka, Japan: National Museum of Ethnology.

Beamer, K. (1972). *The Beauty of Mauna Kea: Hawaiian slack key guitar in the real old style*. [Music recording.] Honolulu: Music of Polynesia.

Beck, C. (2020). Geopolitics of the Pacific Islands. *Security Challenges* 16(1): 11–16.

Beckwith, M. (1970). *Hawaiian Mythology*. Honolulu: University of Hawai`i Press. doi.org/10.1515/9780824840716.

Bedford, S., P. Siméoni and V. Lebot (2018). Anthropogenic transformation of an island landscape: Evidence for agricultural development revealed by LiDAR on the island of Efate, Central Vanuatu, Southwest Pacific. *Archaeology in Oceania* 53(1): 1–14. doi.org/10.1002/arco.5137.

Bell, J., M. Taylor, M. Amos and N. Andrew (2016). *Climate Change and Pacific Island Food Systems: The future of food, farming and fishing in the Pacific Islands under a changing climate*. Wageningen, Netherlands: Research Program on Climate Change, Agriculture and Food Security. Available from: cgspace.cgiar. org/bitstream/handle/10568/75610/Pacific%20Booklet%20Final%20web.pdf? sequence=6.

Bergen, M. (2016). Illegal fishing persists in protected waters. Here's how we're fighting it. [Blog.] Available from: blog.conservation.org/2016/09/illegal-fishing-persists-in-protected-waters-heres-how-were-fighting-it/ [page discontinued].

Berkes, F. (1993). Traditional ecological knowledge in perspective. In J.T. Inglis (ed.), *Traditional Ecological Knowledge: Concepts and cases*, pp. 1–10. Ottawa: International Program on Traditional Ecological Knowledge and International Development Research Centre. Available from: library.um.edu.mo/ebooks/b10756577a.pdf.

Berkes, F., C. Folke and M. Gadgil (1995). Traditional ecological knowledge, biodiversity, resilience and sustainability. In C. Perrings, K.-G. Maler, C. Folke, C.S. Holling and B.O. Jansson (eds), *Biodiversity Conservation*, pp. 281–299. Dordrecht, Netherlands: Kluwer. doi.org/10.1007/978-94-011-0277-3_15.

Berkes, F. (2007). Community-based conservation in a globalized world. *Proceedings of the National Academy of Sciences* 104: 15188–15193. doi.org/10.1073/pnas.0702098104.

Berkes, F. (2009). Indigenous ways of knowing and the study of environmental change. *Journal of the Royal Society of New Zealand* 39(4): 151–156. doi.org/10.1080/03014220909510568.

Berkes, F. (2012). *Sacred Ecology*. 3rd edn. New York, NY: Routledge. doi.org/10.4324/9780203123843.

Berkes, F., J. Colding and C. Folke (2000). Rediscovery of traditional ecological knowledge as adaptive management. *Ecological Applications* 10(5): 1251–1262. doi.org/10.1890/1051-0761(2000)010[1251:ROTEKA]2.0.CO;2.

Bertram, G. (1999). The MIRAB model twelve years on. *The Contemporary Pacific* 11(1): 105–138.

Bertram, G. (2006). The MIRAB model in the twenty-first century. *Asia Pacific Viewpoint* 47(1): 1–10. doi.org/10.1111/j.1467-8373.2006.00296.x.

Best, E. (1982a). *Māori Religion and Mythology. Part 1*. [First published in 1924 as *Dominion Museum Bulletin* No. 10]. Wellington: Government Printer.

Best, E. (1982b). *Māori Religion and Mythology. Part II*. [First published in 1924 as *Dominion Museum Bulletin* No. 11]. Wellington: Government Printer.

Bestelmeyer, B.T. and D.D. Briske (2012). Grand challenges for resilience-based management of rangelands. *Rangeland Ecology & Management* 65: 654–663. doi.org/10.2111/REM-D-12-00072.1.

Betzold, C. (2010). 'Borrowing' power to influence international negotiations: AOSIS in the climate change regime, 1990–1997. *Politics* 30(3). doi.org/10.1111/j.1467-9256.2010.01377.x.

Bezerra, J., E. Turnhout, I. Melo Vasquez, T.F. Rittl, B. Arts and T.W. Kuyper (2016). The promises of the Amazonian soil: Shifts in discourses of Terra Preta and biochar. *Journal of Environmental Policy & Planning* 21(5): 623–635. doi.org/10.1080/1523908X.2016.1269644.

Bianchi, T. (2001). With and without co-operation: Two alternative strategies in the food-processing industry in the Italian south. *Entrepreneurship and Regional Development* 13: 117–145. doi.org/10.1080/089856201750203581.

Biello, D. (2014). Engineering the ocean. *Aeon*, 1 July. Available from: aeon.co/essays/can-tiny-plankton-help-reverse-climate-change.

Bigg, G.R., T.D. Jickells, P.S. Liss and T.J. Osborn (2003). Review: The role of the oceans in climate. *International Journal of Climatology* 23(10): 1127–1159. doi.org/10.1002/joc.926.

Birth, K.K. (2012). *Objects of Time: How things shape temporality*. Basingstoke, UK: Palgrave Macmillan. doi.org/10.1057/9781137017895.

Blakers, A. (2017). Sustainable energy options. In P. Van Ness and M. Gurtov (eds), *Learning from Fukushima: Nuclear power in East Asia*, pp. 319–347. Canberra: ANU Press. doi.org/10.22459/LF.09.2017.11.

Bland, A. (2017). As oceans warm, the world's kelp forests begin to disappear. *Yale Environment 360*, 20 November. Available from: e360.yale.edu/features/as-oceans-warm-the-worlds-giant-kelp-forests-begin-to-disappear.

Boast, R. (1999). *Māori Land Law*. Wellington: Butterworths.

Boege, V., A. Brown, K. Clements and A. Nolan (2008). On hybrid political orders and emerging states: State-formation in the context of 'fragility'. In *Berghof Handbook Dialogue No. 8*. Berlin: Berghof Research Center for Constructive Conflict Management. Available from: berghof-foundation.org/library/on-hybrid-political-orders-and-emerging-states-state-formation-in-the-context-of-fragility.

Bohensky, E.L. and Y. Maru (2011). Indigenous knowledge, science, and resilience: What have we learned from a decade of international literature on 'integration'? *Ecology and Society* 16(4): 6. doi.org/10.5751/ES-04342-160406.

Borrini-Feyerabend, G., N. Dudley, B. Lassen, N. Pathak and T. Sandwith (2012). *Governance of Protected Areas: From understanding to action*. Gland, Switzerland: IUCN, GIZ and ICCA Consortium.

Botha, N. and K. Atkins (2005). An assessment of five different theoretical frameworks to study the uptake of innovations. Paper presented to 2005 New Zealand Agricultural and Resource Economics Society Conference, Nelson, New Zealand, 26–27 August.

Bottignolo, B. (1995). *Celebrations with the Sun: An overview of religious phenomena among the Badjaos.* Manila: Ateneo University Press.

Bourdieu, P. (1980). Le capital social [Social capital]. *Actes de la Recherche en Sciences Sociales [Acts of Research in Social Sciences]* 31: 2–3.

Bourdieu, P. (1986a). The forms of capital. In J.G. Richardson (ed.), *Handbook of Theory and Research for the Sociology of Education*, pp. 241–258. New York, NY: Greenwood Press.

Bourdieu, P. (1986b). Habitus, code et codification [Habits, code and codification]. *Actes de la Recherche en Sciences Sociales [Acts of Research in Social Sciences]* 64: 40–44. doi.org/10.3406/arss.1986.2335.

Bourke, R.M. and T. Harwood (eds) (2009). *Food and Agriculture in Papua New Guinea.* Canberra: ANU Press. doi.org/10.22459/FAPNG.08.2009.

Bracamonte, N.L. (2005). Evolving a development framework for the Sama Dilaut in an urban centre in the southern Philippines. *Borneo Research Bulletin* 36: 185–200.

Breeze, N. (2019). Climate restoration. *The Ecologist*, 17 June. Available from: theecologist.org/2019/jun/17/climate-restoration.

Bregman, R. (2017). *Utopia for Realists: And how we can get there.* London: Bloomsbury.

Brewer, J.F. (2013). From experiential knowledge to public participation: Social learning at the Community Fisheries Action Roundtable. *Environmental Management* 52(2): 321–334. Available from: www.springerprofessional.de/en/from-experiential-knowledge-to-public-participation-social-learn/5190780.

Brown, P. and A. Ploeg (1997). Introduction: Change and conflict in Papua New Guinea land and resource rights. *Anthropological Forum* 7(4): 507–527.

Brown, S.E., D.C. Miller, P.J. Ordonez and K. Baylis (2018). Evidence for the impacts of agroforestry on agricultural productivity, ecosystem services, and human well-being in high-income countries: A systematic map protocol. *Environmental Evidence* 7(24). doi.org/10.1186/s13750-018-0136-0.

Brownlee, G. (2015). Te Ture Whenua Māori Bill: Member's Bill. Draft for Consultation, June. Wellington: New Zealand Parliament. Available from: www.parliament.nz/media/7910/te-ture-whenua-m%C4%81ori-bill.pdf.

Brunori, G. and A. Rossi (2000). Synergies and coherence through collective action: Some insights from wine routes in Tuscany. *Sociologia Ruralis* 40(4): 409–423. doi.org/10.1111/1467-9523.00157.

Bryant-Tokalau, J. (2011). Artificial and recycled islands in the Pacific: Myths and mythology of 'plastic fantastic'. *The Journal of the Polynesian Society* 120(1): 71–86.

Bryant-Tokalau, J. (2018). *Indigenous Pacific Approaches to Climate Change: Pacific Island countries*. Palgrave Studies in Disaster Anthropology. Cham, Switzerland: Springer.

Buck, P. (1975 [1954]). *Vikings of the Sunrise*. Reprint. Christchurch, NZ: Whitcomb & Tombs Limited.

Buck, P. (1987 [1949]). *The Coming of the Māori*. Wellington: Whitcoulls.

Burgess, C.P., F.H. Johnston, H. Berry, J. McDonnell, D. Yibarbuk, C. Gunabarra, A. Mileran and R. Bailie (2009). Healthy country, healthy people: The relationship between Indigenous health status and 'Caring for Country'. *The Medical Journal of Australia* 190: 567–572. doi.org/10.5694/j.1326-5377.2009.tb02566.x.

Calamia, M.A. (1999). A methodology for incorporating traditional ecological knowledge with geographic information systems for marine resource management in the Pacific. *SPC Traditional Marine Resource Management and Knowledge Information Bulletin* 10: 2–12.

Cambers, G. and P.S. Diamond (2011). *Sandwatch: Adapting to climate change and educating for sustainable development*. Rev. edn. Paris: UNESCO.

Campaner, A. (2010). Essai d'aide à la gestion intégrée des littoraux récifaux dans la zone insulaire du Pacifique sud. Application à la presqu'île de Tahiti [Trial to support the integrated management of reef coastlines in the insular zone of the South Pacific: Application to the Tahiti peninsula]. Master's thesis in Environmental Geography. Faculty of Geography and Planning, University of Strasbourg, France.

Campion, N. (2017). The importance of cosmology in culture: Contexts and consequences. In A. Capistrano (ed.), *Trends in Modern Cosmology*. London: IntechOpen Limited. doi.org/10.5772/67976.

Cann, O. (2019). Davos 2020: World Economic Forum announces the theme. *News*, 17 October. Cologny, Switzerland: World Economic Forum. Available from: www.weforum.org/agenda/2019/10/davos-2020-wef-world-economic-forum-theme/.

Caritas (2014). *Small Yet Strong: Voices from Oceania on the environment*. Wellington: Caritas.

Carpenter, K.E., M. Abrar, G. Aeby, R.B. Aronson, S. Banks, A. Bruckner, A. Chiriboga, J. Cortés, J.C. Delbeek, L. Devantier, G.J. Edgar, A.J. Edwards, D. Fenner, H.M. Guzmán, B.W. Hoeksema, G. Hodgson, O. Johan, W.Y. Licuanan, S.R. Livingstone, E.R. Lovell, J.A. Moore, D.O. Obura, D. Ochavillo, B.A. Polidoro, W.F. Precht, M.C. Quibilan, C. Reboton, Z.T. Richards, A.D. Rogers, J. Sanciangco, A. Sheppard, C. Sheppard, J. Smith, S. Stuart, E. Turak, J.E.N. Veron, C. Wallace, E. Weil and E. Wood (2008). One-third of reef-building corals face elevated extinction risk from climate change and local impacts. *Science* 321(5888): 560–563. doi.org/10.1126/science.1159196.

Carter, D. (2010). Chile's other history: Allende, Pinochet, and redemocratisation in Mapuche perspective. *Studies in Ethnicity and Nationalism* 10(1): 59–75. doi.org/10.1111/j.1754-9469.2010.01070.x.

Carter, G. (2016). Establishing a Pacific voice in the climate negotiations. In G. Fry and S. Tarte (eds), *The New Pacific Diplomacy*, pp. 205–220. Canberra: ANU Press. doi.org/10.22459/NPD.12.2015.17.

Carter, L. (2010). Travelling landscapes: Ngai Tahu rock art and Ngai Tahu identity. In J. Stephenson, M. Abbott and J. Ruru (eds), *Beyond the Scene: Landscape and identity in Aotearoa New Zealand*, pp. 167–180. Dunedin, NZ: Otago University Press.

Carter, L. (2014). Criss-crossing highways: Pacific travelling and dwelling in times of global warming. *Journal of New Zealand and Pacific Studies* 2(1): 57–68. doi.org/10.1386/nzps.2.1.57_1.

Castrejón, M. and A. Charles (2012). Improving fisheries co-management through ecosystem-based spatial management: The Galapagos Marine Reserve. *Marine Policy* 38: 235–245. doi.org/10.1016/j.marpol.2012.05.040.

Cazalet, B. (2008). Droit des lagons en Polynésie française [Law of the lagoons in French Polynesia]. *Revue Juridique de l'Environnement* [*Environmental Legal Review*] 4: 391–407. doi.org/10.3406/rjenv.2008.4777.

Chakrabarty, D. (2009). The climate of history: Four theses. *Critical Inquiry* 35(2): 197–222.

Chan, T.U., B.T. Hart, M.J. Kennard, B.J. Pusey, W. Shenton, M.M. Douglas, E. Valentine and S. Patel (2012). Bayesian network models for environmental flow decision making in the Daly River, Northern Territory, Australia. *River Research and Applications* 28: 283–301. doi.org/10.1002/rra.1456.

Chapin, M., Z. Lamb and B. Threlkeld (2005). Mapping Indigenous lands. *Annual Review of Anthropology* 34: 619–638. doi.org/10.1146/annurev.anthro. 34.081804.120429.

Chappell, D. (1995). Active agents versus passive victims: Decolonized historiography or problematic paradigm? *The Contemporary Pacific* 7(2): 303–326. Available from: www.jstor.org/stable/23706930.

Chappell, D. (2015 [1997]). *Double Ghosts: Oceanic voyagers on Euroamerican ships*. Reprint. London: Routledge. doi.org/10.4324/9781315479132.

Chasek, P.S. (2005). Margins of power: Coalition building and coalition maintenance of the South Pacific Island States and the Alliance of Small Island States. *Review of European Community & International Environmental Law* 14(2): 125–137. doi.org/10.1111/j.1467-9388.2005.00433.x.

Chatwin. B. (1987). *The Songlines*. London: Franklin Press.

Chen, W.T. (1989). The study and meaning of age organization of the 'Amis of Tanman. *Bulletin of the Institute of Ethnology Academia Sinica* 68: 105–144.

Chiba, M. (1998). Droit non-occidental [Non-Western law]. In W. Capeller and T. Kitamura (eds), *Une introduction aux cultures juridiques non occidentales. Autour de Masaji Chiba [An Introduction to Non-Western Legal Cultures]*, pp. 37–44. Académie Européenne de Théorie du Droit de Bruxelles [European Academy of Theory of Law of Brussels]. Brussels: Editions Bruylant.

Cho, J.J., R.A. Yamakawa and J. Hollyer (2007). Hawaiian kalo, past and future. *Sustainable Agriculture*, February, SA-1. Honolulu: Cooperative Extension Service, University of Hawai`i at Mānoa. Available from: www.ctahr.hawaii. edu/oc/freepubs/pdf/SA-1.pdf.

Chou, C. (2003). *Indonesian Sea Nomads: Money, magic and fear of the Orang Suku Laut*. London: Routledge. doi.org/10.4324/9780203988718.

Chuuk Advisory Group on Education Reform (2013). *Report on the First Quarterly Meeting of the Chuuk Advisory Group on Education Reform: Findings and Recommendations*. Weno: Chuuk Advisory Group on Education Reform.

Chuuk Department of Education (n.d.). *Chuuk State Strategic Plan for Education 2007–2012*. Weno: Chuuk Department of Education. Available from: www. paddle.usp.ac.fj/cgi-bin/paddle?e=d-010off-paddle--00-1--0---0-10-TX--6-------0-11l--11-en-50---20-png---10-3-1-000--0-0-11-0utfZz-8-00&a=file&d= chu001.

Clarke, P.A. (2009). Australian Aboriginal ethnometeorology and seasonal calendars. *History and Anthropology* 20: 79–106. doi.org/10.1080/02757200902867677.

Clarkson, C., Z. Jacobs, B. Marwick, R. Fullagar, L. Wallis, M. Smith, R.G. Roberts, E. Hayes, K. Lowe, X. Carah, S.A. Florin, J. McNeil, D. Cox, L.J. Arnold, Q. Hua, J. Huntley, H.E.A. Brand, T. Manne, A. Fairbairn, J. Shulmeister, L. Lyle, M. Salinas, M. Page, K. Connell, G. Park, K. Norman, T. Murphy and C. Pardoe (2017). Human occupation of northern Australia by 65,000 years ago. *Nature* 547(7663): 306–310. doi.org/10.1038/nature22968.

Clifton, J. and C. Majors (2012). Culture, conservation, and conflict: Perspectives on marine protection among the Bajau of Southeast Asia. *Society & Natural Resources* 25(7): 716–725. doi.org/10.1080/08941920.2011.618487.

Climate Analytics (2013–15). *HLSM High-Level Support Mechanism for LDC and SIDS on Climate Change*. Berlin: Climate Analytics.

Climate Change Commission (2022). *Progress Towards Agricultural Emissions Pricing*. June. Wellington: New Zealand Government. Available from: www. climatecommission.govt.nz/our-work/advice-to-government-topic/agricultural-emissions/agricultural-progress-assessment/full-report-agricultural-progress-assessment/.

Climate Investment Funds (CIF) (2016). *Pilot Program for Climate Resilience*. Washington, DC: Climate Investment Funds. Available from: climate investmentfunds.org/sites/default/files/knowledge-documents/ppcr_fact_sheet_november_2016.pdf.

Cochrane, L. (2015). Pacific Islands Forum: Kiribati urges Australia, NZ to be 'real friends' on climate change. *ABC News*, 7 September, [Updated 8 September]. Available from: www.abc.net.au/news/2015-09-07/kiribati-urges-australia-nz-to-be-real-friends-on-climate-change/6755794.

Cocoa Board of Papua New Guinea (2018). *Cocoa Production by Sector & Province by Calendar Year, 2013–2017*. Kokopo, PNG: Cocoa Board of Papua New Guinea.

Coffin, A.N. and T.P. Kawe (2011). *Matakana Island Planning: An assessment of cultural values and identification of potential effects of urbanisation and land-use change on Maori communities of Makatana and Rangiwaea islands*. Tauranga, NZ: Tauwhao Te Ngare Trust.

Coleman, J.S. (1988). Social capital in the creation of human capital. *American Journal of Sociology* 94: S95–S120. Available from: www.jstor.org/stable/2780243. doi.org/10.1086/228943.

Colin, J.P. (2008). Disentangling intra-kinship property rights in land: A contribution of economic ethnography to land economics in Africa. *Journal of Institutional Economics* 4(2): 231–254. doi.org/10.1017/S1744137408000970.

Commoner, B. (2020). *The Closing Circle: Nature, man, and technology*. Mineola, NY: Courier Dover Publications.

Commonwealth of Australia (1999). *Environment Protection and Biodiversity Conservation Act 1999*. Canberra: Environment Australia.

Congress of the Federated States of Micronesia (FSM) (1983). *Public Law No. 3-12, First Regular Session 1983*. Palikir: Congress of the FSM.

Congress of the Federated States of Micronesia (FSM) (2013). *Public Law No. 18-34, Second Regular Session 2013*. Palikir: Congress of the FSM.

Connell, J. (2005). Bougainville: The future of an island microstate. *The Journal of Pacific Studies* 28(2): 192–217.

Conway, E. (2014). Just 5 questions: Hacking the planet. *News*, 14 April. La Cañada Flintridge, CA: NASA Jet Propulsion Laboratory. Available from: climate.nasa.gov/news/1066/just-5-questions-hacking-the-planet/.

Cordell, J. (1991). *Managing Sea Country: Tenure and sustainability of Aboriginal and Torres Strait Islander marine resources*. Canberra: Consultancy report for the Ecologically Sustainable Development Fisheries Working Group.

Cordell, J. (2007). *A Sea of Dreams: Valuing culture in marine conservation*. Berkeley, CA: The Ethnographic Institute.

Coulter, L., Z. Abebe, S. Kebede, E. Ludi and B. Zeleke (2012). Water-bound geographies of seasonality: Investigating seasonality, water and wealth in Ethiopia through the Water Economy for Livelihoods (WELS) approach. In S. Devereux, R. Sabates-Wheeler and R. Longhurst (eds), *Seasonality, Rural Livelihoods and Development*. London: Routledge.

Council of Indigenous Peoples (CIP) (2022). *Indigenous People Population Statistics in June*. New Taipei City: CIP. Available from: www.cip.gov.tw/zh-tw/news/data-list/940F9579765AC6A0/2276C0E026A831376F51CB2375B3D43B-info.html.

Craney, A. and D. Hudson (2020). Navigating the dilemmas of politically smart, locally led development: The Pacific-based Green Growth Leaders' Coalition. *Third World Quarterly* 41(10): 1653–1669. doi.org/10.1080/01436597.2020. 1773256.

Crawford, J. (2006). *The Creation of States in International Law*. Oxford, UK: Oxford University Press.

Crocombe, R. (ed.) (1971). *Land Tenure in the Pacific*. Melbourne: Oxford University Press.

Crocombe, R. (1991). Latin America and the Pacific Islands. *The Contemporary Pacific* 3(1): 115–144.

Crocombe, R. and M. Meleisea (1994). *Land Issues in the Pacific*. Suva: Institute for Pacific Studies, University of the South Pacific.

Crona, B., S. Gelcich and O. Bodin (2017). The importance of interplay between leadership and social capital in shaping outcomes of rights-based fisheries governance. *World Development* 91: 70–83. doi.org/10.1016/j.worlddev.2016. 10.006.

Crow, J. (2013). *The Mapuche in Modern Chile: A cultural history*. Gainesville, FL: University Press of Florida. doi.org/10.5744/florida/9780813044286.001.0001.

Crutzen, P.J. and E.F. Stoermer (2000). The 'Anthropocene'. *Global Change Newsletter* 41: 17–18.

Cullinan, C. (2008). If nature had rights. *Orion Magazine*. Available from: orion magazine.org/article/if-nature-had-rights/.

Culture Is Life (2014). *The Elders' Report into Preventing Indigenous Self-Harm & Youth Suicide*. Produced by People Culture Environment in partnership with Our Generation Media. Available from: apo.org.au/sites/default/files/resource-files/2014-04/apo-nid40060.pdf.

Curtin, T. (2003). Scarcity amidst plenty: The economics of land tenure in Papua New Guinea. In P. Larmour (ed.), *Land registration in Papua New Guinea: Competing perspectives*. State, Society and Governance in Melanesia Discussion Paper 2003/1, pp. 6–17. Canberra: The Australian National University.

Curtin, T. and D. Lea (2006). Land titling and socioeconomic development in the South Pacific. *Pacific Economic Bulletin* 21(1): 153–180.

Dacks, R., T. Ticktin, A. Mawyer, S. Caillon, J. Claudet, P. Fabre, S.D. Jupiter, J. McCarter, M. Mejia, P.A. Pascua and E. Sterling (2019). Developing biocultural indicators for resource management. *Conservation Science and Practice* 1(6): e38. doi.org/10.1111/csp2.38.

D'Arcy, P. (2006). *The People of the Sea: Environment, identity, and history in Oceania.* Honolulu: University of Hawai`i Press. doi.org/10.1515/9780824846381.

D'Arcy, P. (2009). Variable rights and diminishing control: The evolution of Indigenous maritime sovereignty in Oceania. In D. Ghosh, H. Goodall and S.H. Donald (eds), *Water, Sovereignty and Borders in Asia and Oceania*, pp. 20–38. London: Routledge.

D'Arcy, P. (2012). Oceania: The environmental history of one-third of the globe. In J.R. McNeill, E.S. Mauldin and S. Wongbusarakum (eds), *A Companion to Global Environmental History*, pp. 196–221. Oxford, UK: Wiley Blackwell. doi.org/10.1002/9781118279519.ch12.

D'Arcy, P. (2014a). Report on the 2012 International Austronesian Conference, Weaving Waves' Writings: Memories, stories and spiritual resonance in Oceania, Taipei, Taiwan, 27–28 November, 2012. *Outrigger: Blog of the Pacific Institute.* Canberra: The Australian National University. Available from: pacificinstitute. anu.edu.au/outrigger/page/17/?eo_month=2014-09.

D'Arcy, P. (2014b). The lawless sea? Policy options for voluntary compliance regimes in offshore resource zones in the Pacific. *Asia and the Pacific Policy Studies* 1(2): 297–311. doi.org/10.1002/app5.28.

Davidson-Hunt, I.J. (2006). Adaptive learning networks: Developing resource management knowledge through social learning forums. *Human Ecology* 34: 593–614. doi.org/10.1007/s10745-006-9009-1.

Davidson-Hunt, I.J., C.J. Idrobo, R.D. Pengelly and O. Sylvester (2013). Anishinaabe adaptation to environmental change in northwestern Ontario: A case study in knowledge coproduction for nontimber forest products. *Ecology and Society* 18(4): 44. doi.org/10.5751/ES-06001-180444.

Davis, A. and J.R. Wagner (2003). *Who* knows? On the importance of identifying 'experts' when researching local ecological knowledge. *Human Ecology* 31: 463–489. doi.org/10.1023/A:1025075923297.

Davis, J., M. Street, H. Malo, I. Cherel and E. Woodward (2011). *Mingayooroo— Manyi Waranggiri Yarrangi: Gooniyandi seasons (calendar), Margaret River, Fitzroy Valley, Western Australia.* Darwin: CSIRO.

Day, J., N. Dudley, M. Hockings, G. Holmes, D. Laffoley, S. Stolton and S. Wells (2012). *Guidelines for Applying the IUCN Protected Area Management Categories to Marine Protected Areas*. Gland, Switzerland: International Union for Conservation of Nature.

de Hutorowicz, H. (1911). Maps of primitive peoples. *Bulletin of the American Geographic Society* 43(9): 669–679. doi.org/10.2307/199915.

de la Maza, F. (2018). Tourism in Chile's Indigenous territories: The impact of public policies and tourism value of Indigenous culture. *Latin American and Caribbean Studies* 13(1): 94–111. doi.org/10.1080/17442222.2018.1416894.

De Lucia, V. (2015). Competing narratives and complex genealogies: The ecosystem approach in international environmental law. *Journal of Environmental Law* 27(1): 91–117.

Denkinger, J., D. Quiroga and J.C. Murillo (2014). Assessing human–wildlife conflicts and benefits of Galápagos sea lions on San Cristobal Island, Galápagos. In J. Denkinger and L. Vinueza (eds), *The Galapagos Marine Reserve: A dynamic social-ecological system*, pp. 285–305. New York, NY: Springer. doi.org/10.1007/978-3-319-02769-2_13.

Department of Agriculture and Livestock (2019). Cocoa. *Commodities*. Port Moresby: Government of Papua New Guinea.

Department of the Environment (n.d.). *Green Island Desalination Plant*. Canberra: Australian Government.

Department of the Environment and Heritage (2006). *A Guide to the Integrated Marine and Coastal Regionalisation of Australia. IMCRA version 4.0*. June. Canberra: Australian Government.

Department of Environment and Resource Management (n.d.). *Green Island National Park*. Brisbane: Queensland Government.

Department of Household Registration (2022). *Household Registration Statistics Data Analysis in June 2022*. Taipei: Ministry of the Interior, Republic of China. Available from: www.ris.gov.tw/app/portal/346.

Department of Primary Industries (DPI) (2017). *Yaegl native title and fishing*. Primefact No. 1592, Recreational & Indigenous Fisheries, September. Sydney: NSW Government. Available from: www.dpi.nsw.gov.au/__data/assets/pdf_file/0007/735640/Yaegl-Native-Title-and-Fishing.pdf.

Deroche, F. (2008). *Les peuples autochtones et leur relation originale à la terre* [*Indigenous Peoples and their Original Relationship to the Land*]. Paris: L'Harmattan.

Devatine, F. (1989). La notion du Tapu et du Rāhui [The notion of tapu and rāhui]. Premières journées de la recherche [First research days]. Unpublished ms, Papeete.

Dhimurru (2008). *Dhimurru IPA Plan of Management 2008 to 2015.* Prepared by Dhimurru Aboriginal Corporation, Wearne Advisors and S. Muller. Nhulunbuy, NT. Available from: www.dhimurru.com.au/uploads/8/9/3/6/8936577/dhimurru_pom_2008_to_2015_081221_l_res.pdf.

Diamond, J. (2005). *Collapse: How societies choose to fail or succeed.* New York, NY: Viking.

Dias, C. and M. Franco (2018). Cooperation in tradition or tradition in cooperation? Networks of agricultural entrepreneurs. *Land Use Policy* 71: 36–48. doi.org/10.1016/j.landusepol.2017.11.041.

Dibley, B. (2012). 'The shape of things to come': Seven theses on the Anthropocene and attachment. *Australian Humanities Review* 52: 139–153. doi.org/10.22459/AHR.52.2012.10.

Dillehay, T.D. and F. Rothhammer (2013). Quest for the origins and implications for social rights of the Mapuche in the Southern Cone of Latin America. *Latin American Antiquity* 24(2): 149–163. doi.org/10.7183/1045-6635.24.2.149.

Director of National Parks (2013). *Draft Temperate East Commonwealth Marine Reserves Network Management Plan 2014–24.* Canberra: Director of National Parks.

Dixon, R.B. (1916). *Oceanic Mythology.* Boston, MA: Marshall Jones Company.

Dixon, R.M.W. (1996). Origin legends and linguistic relationships. *Oceania* 67(2): 127–139. doi.org/10.1002/j.1834-4461.1996.tb02587.x.

Doney, S.C., D.S. Busch, S.R. Cooley and K.J. Kroeker (2020). The impacts of ocean acidification on marine ecosystems and reliant human communities. *Annual Review of Environment and Resources* 45(1): 83–112. doi.org/10.1146/annurev-environ-012320-083019.

Douglas, M. (1969). Is matriliny doomed in Africa? In M. Douglas and P.M. Kaberry (eds), *Man in Africa*, pp. 121–135. London: Tavistock.

Dove, M. (2002). Hybrid histories and Indigenous knowledge among Asian rubber smallholders. *International Social Science Journal* 54(173): 349–359. doi.org/10.1111/1468-2451.00387.

Drake, P.W. and E. Hershberg (eds) (2006). *State and Society in Conflict: Comparative perspectives on Andean crises.* Pittsburgh, PA: University of Pittsburgh Press. doi.org/10.2307/j.ctt9qh6wf.

Duarte, C.M., S. Agusti, E. Barbier, G.L. Britten, J.C. Castilla, J.-P. Gattuso, R.W. Fulweiler, T.P. Hughes, N. Knowlton, C.E. Lovelock, H.K. Lotze, M. Predragovic, E. Poloczanska, C. Roberts and B. Worm (2020). Rebuilding marine life. *Nature* 580: 39–51. doi.org/10.1038/s41586-020-2146-7.

Dudley, N. (ed.) (2008). *Guidelines for Applying Protected Area Management Categories*. Gland, Switzerland: International Union for Conservation of Nature. doi.org/10.2305/IUCN.CH.2008.PAPS.2.en.

Dumat-ol Daleno, G. (2007). High seas flood tiny Lekinioch, Chuuk. *Pacific Daily News*, [Guam], 3 May.

Durant, J. (1999). Participatory technology assessment and the democratic model of the public understanding of science. *Science and Public Policy* 26(5): 313–319. doi.org/10.3152/147154399781782329.

Eder, J.F. (2005). Coastal resource management and social differences in Philippine fishing communities. *Human Ecology* 33(2): 147–169. doi.org/10.1007/s10745-005-2430-Z.

Edwards, E. and A. Edwards (2010). *Rapanui Archaeoastronomy and Ethnoastronomy*. FLAG #83 Expedition Report, February–June. New York, NY: The Explorers Club.

Edwards, E. and A. Edwards (2013). *When the Universe was an Island: Exploring the cultural and spiritual cosmos of the ancient Rapa Nui*. Easter Island: Hangaroa Press.

Eggert, H. and R.B. Lokina (2010). Regulatory compliance in Lake Victoria fisheries. *Environment and Development Economics* 15(2): 197–217.

Eichenseher, T. (2011). Bridging Western science and Polynesian tradition: Elders start to work with scientists on preserving the biodiversity of Mo'orea. *National Geographic News*, 25 February. Available from: www.nationalgeographic.com/science/article/110223-biodiversity-cultural-tradition-moorea-indigenous-knowledge.

Elbert, S. and N. Māhoe (1978). *Nā Mele o Hawai`i Nei, 101 Hawaiian Songs*. Honolulu: University of Hawai`i Press.

Ellen, R. and H. Harris (2000). Introduction. In R. Ellen, P. Parkes and A. Bicker (eds), *Indigenous Environmental Knowledge and its Transformations: Critical anthropological perspectives*, pp. 1–33. Singapore: Harwood Academic Publishers.

Ellis, W. (1972 [1829]). *A la recherche de la Polynésie d'autrefois [In Search of the Polynesia of Yesteryear]*. Publication of the Society of Oceanists 25, vols 1–2. Paris: Musée de l'Homme.

Emberson-Bain, A. (1994). *Sustainable Development or Malignant Growth? Perspectives of Pacific Island women.* Suva: Marama Publications.

Engie, K. and D. Quiroga (2014). The emergence of recreational fishing in the Galapagos Marine Reserve: Adaptation and complexities. In J. Denkinger and L. Vinueza (eds), *The Galapagos Marine Reserve: A dynamic social–ecological system,* pp. 203–226. New York, NY: Springer Science and Business Media.

Ens, E.J., M. Finlayson, K. Preuss, S. Jackson and S. Holcombe (2012). Australian approaches for managing 'country' using Indigenous and non-Indigenous knowledge. *Ecological Management & Restoration* 13(1): 100–107. doi.org/ 10.1111/j.1442-8903.2011.00634.x.

Ens, E.J., P.L. Pert, P.A. Clarke, M. Budden, L. Clubb, B. Doran, C. Douras, J. Gaikwad, B. Gott, S. Leonard, J. Locke, J. Packer, G. Turpin and S. Wason (2015). Indigenous biocultural knowledge in ecosystem science and management: Review and insight from Australia. *Biological Conservation* 181: 133–149. doi. org/10.1016/j.biocon.2014.11.008.

Epstein, A.L. (1969). *Matupit: Land, politics, and change among the Tolai of New Britain.* Canberra: ANU Press. doi.org/10.1525/9780520324312.

Epstein, T.S. (1968). *Capitalism, Primitive and Modern: Some aspects of Tolai economic growth.* Canberra: ANU Press. Available from: hdl.handle.net/1885/114857.

Eriksen, M., L.C.M. Lebreton, H.S. Carson, M. Thiel, C.J. Moore, J.C. Borerro, F. Galgani, P.G. Ryan and J. Resser (2014). Plastic pollution in the world's oceans: More than 5 trillion plastic pieces weighing over 250,000 tons afloat at sea. *PLoS ONE* 9(12): e111913. doi.org/10.1371/journal.pone.0111913.

Erikson, S.H. and P.M. Kelly (2007). Developing credible vulnerability indicators for climate adaptation policy assessment. *Mitigation and Adaptation Strategies for Global Change* 12: 495–524. doi.org/10.1007/s11027-006-3460-6.

Escobar, A. (1995). Introduction: Development and the anthropology of modernity. In A. Escobar (ed.), *Encountering Development: The making and unmaking of the Third World.* Princeton, NJ: Princeton University Press.

Escobar, A. (2007). Worlds and knowledges otherwise: The Latin American modernity/coloniality research program. *Cultural Studies* 21(2–3): 179–210. doi.org/10.1080/09502380601162506.

Fabinyi, M. (2011). *Fishing for Fairness: Poverty, morality and marine resource regulation in the Philippines.* Canberra: ANU Press. doi.org/10.22459/FF.01.2012.

Fabre, P. (2021). Hybrid governance of rāhui at Taiarapu (Tahiti Peninsula): So what for coral reef conservation public policies? Doctoral thesis, PSL University, École Pratique des Hautes Études, Paris.

Fabre, P., T. Bambridge, J. Claudet, E. Sterling and A. Mawyer (2021). Contemporary Rāhui: Placing Indigenous, conservation, and sustainability sciences in community-led conservation. *Pacific Conservation Biology* 27(4): 451–463. doi.org/10.1071/PC20087.

Farrelly, E. (2003). *Dadiri: The spring within—The spiritual art of the Aboriginal people of Australia's Daly River region*. Darwin: Terry Knight & Associates.

Farrier, D. and M. Adams (2011). Indigenous–government co-management of protected areas: Booderee National Park and the national framework in Australia. In B. Lausche (ed.), *Guidelines for Protected Area Legislation: Special protected area types*, pp. 1–40. Gland, Switzerland: International Union for Conservation of Nature.

Federated States of Micronesia (FSM) Development Partners Forum (2012). *Federated States of Micronesia Development Framework: Looking to the future. A foundation for discussion at the FSM Development Partners Forum*. Kolonia, Pohnpei: FSM Development Partners Forum.

Federated States of Micronesia (FSM) Government (1979). *The Constitution of the FSM*. Palikir: FSM Government.

Federated States of Micronesia (FSM) Government (2009). *The FSM Climate Change Policy*. Palikir: FSM Government.

Federated States of Micronesia (FSM) Government (2010). *The Millennium Development Goals and Status Report 2010*. Palikir: FSM Government.

Feeny, S. (ed.) (2014). *Household Vulnerability and Resilience to Economic Shocks: Findings from Melanesia*. London: Routledge.

Feliciano, D. (2019). A review on the contribution of crop diversification to Sustainable Development Goal 1 'No Poverty' in different world regions. *Sustainable Development* 27: 795–808.

Ferrer, E.M. and C.M. Nozawa (1997). *Community-based coastal resources management in the Philippines: Key concepts, methods and lessons learned*. IDRC Research Results Working Paper. Ottawa: International Development Research Centre. Available from: idl-bnc-idrc.dspacedirect.org/handle/10625/37805?show=full.

Filer, C. (2019). The circularity of land reform in Papua New Guinea. *DevPolicy Blog*, 16 December. Canberra: Development Policy Centre, The Australian National University. Available from: devpolicy.org/the-circularity-of-land-reform-in-papua-new-guinea-20191216/.

Fingleton, J.S. (2005). *Privatising land in the Pacific: A defence of customary tenures.* Discussion Paper 80. Canberra: The Australia Institute.

Fingleton, J.S. and O. ToLopa (2008). Land registration among the Tolai people: Waiting 50 years for titles. In Australian Agency for International Development (AusAID), *Making Land Work. Volume Two: Case studies on customary land and development in the Pacific*, pp. 65–84. Canberra: AusAID.

Finney, B.R. (1973). *Big-Men and Business: Entrepreneurship and economic growth in the New Guinea Highlands.* Honolulu: University of Hawai`i Press.

Firth, S. (1989). Sovereignty and independence in the contemporary Pacific. *The Contemporary Pacific* 1(1–2): 75–96.

Firth, S. (2000). The Pacific Islands and the globalization agenda. *The Contemporary Pacific* 12(1): 178–192. doi.org/10.1353/cp.2000.0009.

Firth, S. (ed.) (2006). *Globalisation and Governance in the Pacific Islands: State, Society and Governance in Melanesia.* Canberra: ANU Press. doi.org/10.22459/GGPI.12.2006.

Firth, S. (2013). New developments in the international relations of the Pacific Islands. *The Journal of Pacific History* 48(3): 286–293. doi.org/10.1080/00223344.2013.812545.

Fischer, F. (2003). *Reframing Public Policy: Discursive politics and deliberative practices.* New York, NY: Oxford University Press. doi.org/10.1093/019924264X.001.0001.

Fisher, B., K.R. Turner and P. Morling (2009). Defining and classifying ecosystem services for decision making. *Ecological Economics* 68(3): 643–653. doi.org/10.1016/j.ecolecon.2008.09.014.

Flannery, T. (2017). *Sunlight and Seaweed: An argument for how to feed, power and clean up the world.* Melbourne: Text Publishing.

Fletcher, C.H. and B.M. Richmond (2010). *Climate Change in the Federated States of Micronesia: Food and water security, climate risk management, and adaptive strategies.* Honolulu: Center for Island Climate Adaptation and Policy.

Flood, J. (1999). *Archaeology of the Dreamtime: The story of prehistoric Australia and its people.* Sydney: Angus & Robertson.

Flores, E. (1994). Community-based coastal fishery management in the Philippines: A review of small island coral reef fishery management. In I. Ushijima and C.N. Zayas (eds), *Visayan Maritime Anthropological Studies I, 1991–93*, pp. 357–370. Quezon City, Philippines: CSSP Publications Office and University of the Philippines Press.

Folke, C. (2006). Resilience: The emergence of a perspective for social-ecological systems analyses. *Global Environmental Change* 16: 253–267. doi.org/10.1016/j.gloenvcha.2006.04.002.

Food and Agriculture Organization of the United Nations (FAO) (2016). *Illegal, Unreported and Unregulated Fishing*. Rome: FAO. Available from: www.fao.org/3/a-i6069e.pdf.

Food and Agriculture Organization of the United Nations (FAO) (2019). *Country Gender Assessment of Agriculture and the Rural Sector in Papua New Guinea*. Rome: FAO.

Food and Agriculture Organization of the United Nations (FAO) Regional Office for Asia and the Pacific (2017). Pacific leaders alarmed over climate change's negative impact on food system and food security. *News*, 11 November. Rome: FAO. Available from: www.fao.org/asiapacific/news/detail-events/en/c/1062269/.

Fortes, M. (1950). Kinship and marriage among the Ashanti. In A.R. Radcliffe-Brown and D. Forde (eds), *African Systems of Kinship and Marriage*, pp. 252–284. London: Oxford University Press.

Foucault, M. (1980). *Power/Knowledge: Selected interviews and other writings, 1972–1977*. London: Vintage.

Foundation for Climate Restoration (2020). Website. Los Altos, CA: Foundation for Climate Restoration. Available from: foundationforclimaterestoration.org/.

Fraser, D.J., T. Coon, M.R. Prince, R. Dion and L. Bernatchez (2006). Integrating traditional and evolutionary knowledge in biodiversity conservation: A population level case study. *Ecology and Society* 11(2): 1–14. doi.org/10.5751/ES-01754-110204.

Fraser, E. and E. Fraser (2014). 10 things you need to know about the global food system. *The Guardian*, 1 May. Available from: www.theguardian.com/sustainable-business/food-blog/10-things-need-to-know-global-food-system.

Fry, G. (2015a). Pacific climate diplomacy and the future relevance of the Pacific Islands Forum. *DevPolicy Blog*, 4 September. Canberra: Development Policy Centre, The Australian National University. Available from: devpolicy.org/pacific-climate-diplomacy-and-the-future-relevance-of-the-pacific-islands-forum-20150904/.

Fry, G. (2015b). Pacific Islands Forum: Climate 'consensus' on the road to Paris. *The Strategist*, 21 September. Canberra: Australia Strategic Policy Institute.

Fry, G. and S. Tarte (eds) (2016). *The New Pacific Diplomacy*. Canberra: ANU Press. doi.org/10.22459/NPD.12.2015.

Funk, K. (2012). 'Today there are no Indigenous people' in Chile? Connecting the Mapuche struggle to anti-neoliberal mobilizations in South America. [Book review.] *Journal of Politics in Latin America* 4(2): 125–140. doi.org/10.1177/1866802X1200400205.

Gadgil, M., F. Berkes and C. Folke (1993). Indigenous knowledge for biodiversity conservation. *Ambio* 22(4): 151–156.

Gale, S.J. (2016). The mined-out phosphate lands of Nauru, equatorial western Pacific. *Australian Journal of Earth Sciences* 63(3): 333–347. doi.org/10.1080/08120099.2016.1206621.

Gallen, S.L. (2016). Micronesian sub-regional diplomacy. In G. Fry and S. Tarte (eds), *The New Pacific Diplomacy*, pp. 175–188. Canberra: ANU Press. doi.org/10.22459/NPD.12.2015.15.

Galluzzi, G., P. Eyzaguirre and V. Negri (2010). Home gardens: Neglected hotspots of agro-biodiversity and cultural diversity. *Biodiversity and Conservation* 19(13): 3635–3654. doi.org/10.1007/s10531-010-9919-5.

Garde, M., B.L. Nadjamerrek, M. Kolkiwarra, J. Kalarriya, J. Djandjomerr, B. Birriyabirriya, R. Bilindja, M. Kubarku and P. Biless (2009). The language of fire: Seasonality, resources and landscape burning on the Arnhem Land Plateau. In J. Russell-Smith, P.J. Whitehead and P. Cooke (eds), *Culture, Ecology and Economy of Fire Management in North Australian Savannas: Rekindling the Wurrk tradition*, pp. 85–164. Melbourne: CSIRO Publishing.

Gardener, M.R., M. Trueman, C. Buddenhagen, R. Heleno, H. Jäger, R. Atkinson and A. Tye (2013). A pragmatic approach to the management of plant invasions in Galapagos. In L.C. Foxcroft, P. Pyšek, D.M. Richardson and P. Genovesi (eds), *Plant Invasions in Protected Areas: Patterns, problems and challenges*, pp. 349–374. Dordrecht, Netherlands: Springer-Verlag.

Garnett, S.T., N.D. Burgess, J.E. Fa, A. Fernández-Llamazares, Z. Molnár, C.J. Robinson, J.E.M. Watson, K.K. Zander, B. Austin, E.S. Brondizio, N.F. Collier, T. Duncan, E. Ellis, H. Geyle, M.V. Jackson, H. Jonas, P. Malmer, B. McGowan, A. Sivongxay and I. Leiper (2018). A spatial overview of the global importance of Indigenous lands for conservation. *Nature Sustainability* 1: 369–374. doi.org/10.1038/s41893-018-0100-6.

Gattuso, J.P., O. Hoegh-Guldberg and H.O. Pörtner (2014). Cross-chapter box on coral reefs. In C.B. Field, V.R. Barros, D.J. Dokken, K.J. Mach, M.D. Mastrandrea, T.E. Bilir, M. Chatterjee, K.L. Ebi, Y.O. Estrada, R.C. Genova, B. Girma, E.S. Kissel, A.N. Levy, S. MacCracken, P.R. Mastrandrea and L.L. White (eds), *Climate Change 2014: Impacts, adaptation, and vulnerability. Part A: Global and Sectoral Aspects. Contribution of Working Group II to the Fifth Assessment Report of the Intergovernmental Panel on Climate Change*, pp. 97–100. New York, NY: Cambridge University Press. doi.org/10.1017/CBO9781107415379.005.

Gegeo, D.W. (2001). Cultural rupture and indigeneity: The challenge of (re)visioning 'place' in the Pacific. *The Contemporary Pacific* 13(2): 491–507. doi.org/10.1353/cp.2001.0052.

Gerber, F., P. Holland and P.N. Lal (2011). *Assessing the Social and Economic Value of Climate Change Adaptation in the Pacific Region—A case study on water quality, quantity and sanitation improvements as an adaptation to climate change, Tuvalu.* A background case study for IUCN's report *Climate Change Adaptation in the Pacific: Making informed choices*, prepared for the Australian Department of Climate Change and Energy Efficiency. Suva: International Union for Conservation of Nature. Available from: gsd.spc.int/sopac/docs/nre/Water%20security%20Final.pdf.

Germond-Duret, C. (2016). Tradition and modernity: An obsolete dichotomy? Binary thinking, indigenous peoples and normalisation. *Third World Quarterly* 37(9): 1537–1558.

Ghasarian, C. (2016). Protection of natural resources through a sacred prohibition: The *rahui* in Rapa Iti. In T. Bambridge (ed.), *The Rahui: Legal pluralism in Polynesian traditional management of resources and territories*, pp. 139–153. Canberra: ANU Press. doi.org/10.22459/TR.03.2016.07.

Gibson, S., J. Wichep and M. Silbanuz (2009). *Preliminary Damage Assessment (PDA) Report.* Agricultural Damage Report. Palikir: Federated States of Micronesia Government.

Gidarjil Development Corporation (2021). Website. Bundaberg, Qld: Gidarjil Development Corporation. Available from: www.gidarjil.com.au/.

Gladwin, T. (1970). *East is a Big Bird: Navigation and logic on Puluwat Atoll.* Cambridge, MA: Harvard University Press. doi.org/10.4159/9780674037625.

Glaser, B. and J.J. Birk (2012). State of the scientific knowledge of the properties and genesis of Anthropogenic dark earths in Central Amazonia. *Geochimica et Cosmochimica Acta* 82: 39–51. doi.org/10.1016/j.gca.2010.11.029.

Global Environment Facility (GEF) (2012). *Pacific Adaptation to Climate Change Project (PACC).* GEF Project No. 3101. Washington, DC: Global Environment Facility. Available from: www.thegef.org/project/pacific-adaptation-climate-change-project-pacc.

Global Environment Facility (GEF) (2022). Micronesia. *Country-At-A-Glance.* Washington, DC: Global Environment Facility. Available from: www.thegef. org/projects-operations/country-profiles/micronesia.

Global Strategy for Plant Conservation (GSPC) (2002). *Report on the Liaison Group Meeting on the Global Strategy for Plant Conservation.* Convention on Biological Diversity. Geneva: United Nations Environment Programme. Available from: www.cbd.int/doc/meetings/pc/pclggs-01/official/pclggs-01-02-en.pdf.

Gongora, J., N.J. Rawlence, V.A. Mobegi, H. Jianlin, J.A. Alcalde, J.T. Matus, O. Hanotte, C. Moran, J.J. Austin, S. Ulm, A.J. Anderson, G. Larson and A. Cooper (2008). Indo-European and Asian origins for Chilean and Pacific chickens revealed by mtDNA. *Proceedings of the National Academy of Sciences* 105(30): 10308–10313. doi.org/10.1073/pnas.0801991105.

Gonschor, L. (2019). *A Power in the World: The Hawaiian Kingdom in Oceania.* Honolulu: University of Hawai`i Press. doi.org/10.1515/9780824880187.

Goodall, H. (2008). Riding the tide: Indigenous knowledge, history and water in a changing Australia. *Environment and History* 14(3): 355–384. doi.org/10.3197/096734008X333563.

Goodenough, W.H. (1951). *Property, Kin and Community on Truk.* Yale University Publications in Anthropology 46. New Haven, CT: Yale University Press.

Goodenough, W.H. (1986). Sky world and this world: The place of Kachaw in Micronesian cosmology. *American Anthropologist* [NS] 88(3): 551–568. doi.org/10.1525/aa.1986.88.3.02a00010.

Goodyear-Ka'ōpua, N., I. Hussey and E. Kahunawaika`ala Wright (eds) (2013). *A Nation Rising: Hawaiian movements for life, land and sovereignty.* Durham, NC: Duke University Press. doi.org/10.2307/j.ctv11cw7h9.

Gorman, J. and S. Vemuri (2012). Social implications of bridging the gap through 'caring for country' in remote Indigenous communities of the Northern Territory, Australia. *The Rangeland Journal* 34(1): 63–73. doi.org/10.1071/RJ11037.

Gosarevski, S., H. Hughes and S. Windybank (2004). Is Papua New Guinea viable? *Pacific Economic Bulletin* 19(1): 134–148.

Gough, K. (1961). Part 2: Variation in matrilineal systems. In D.G. Schneider (ed.), *Matrilineal Kinship*, pp. 445–652. Berkeley, CA: University of California Press.

Govan, H. (2008). Overview: Reclaiming protected areas as a livelihood tool for Pacific Island people. In P. Cohen, A.D. Valemei and H. Govan (eds), *Annotated Bibliography on Socio-Economic and Ecological Impacts of Marine Protected Areas in Pacific Island Countries*. World Fish Bibliography No. 1870. Penang, Malaysia: The World Fish Center.

Govan, H., A. Tawake, K. Tabunakawai, A.P. Jenkins, A. Lasgorceix, E. Techera, H. Tafea, J. Kinch, J. Feehely, P. Ifopo, R. Hills, S. Alefaio, S. Meo, S. Troniak, S. Malimali, S. George, T. Tauaefa and T. Obed (2009). *Community Conserved Areas: A review of status & needs in Melanesia and Polynesia*. CENESTA/TILCEPA/TGER/IUCN/GEF-SGP. Gland, Switzerland: International Union for Conservation of Nature. Available from: www.iucn.org/about/union/commissions/ceesp/topics/governance/icca/regional_reviews/.

Grear, A. (2015). Deconstructing *Anthropos*: A critical legal reflection on 'anthropocentric' law and Anthropocene 'humanity'. *Law and Critique* 26(3): 225–249. doi.org/10.1007/s10978-015-9161-0.

Great Barrier Reef Marine Park Authority (GBRMPA) (2020). *Traditional Use of Marine Resource Agreements*. Townsville, Qld: GBRMPA. Available from: www.gbrmpa.gov.au/our-partners/traditional-owners/traditional-use-of-marine-resources-agreements.

Green Climate Fund (GCF) (2022). *Federated States of Micronesia*. Incheon, Republic of Korea: GCF. Available from: www.greenclimate.fund/countries/micronesia.

Green Island Resort (2022). *Eco Sustainability*. Green Island, Qld. Available from: www.greenislandresort.com.au/sustainable-tourism.

Greenough, P. and A.L. Tsing (2003). *Nature in the Global South: Environmental projects in South and Southeast Asia*. Durham, NC: Duke University Press. doi.org/10.1215/9780822385004.

Gregory, R., L. Failing and M. Harstone (2008). Meaningful resource consultations with First Peoples: Notes from British Columbia. *Environment* 50(1): 36–45. doi.org/10.3200/ENVT.50.1.34-45.

Griffiths, J. (1986). What is legal pluralism? *Journal of Legal Pluralism and Unofficial Law* 18(24): 1–53. doi.org/10.1080/07329113.1986.10756387.

Groube, L. (1975). Archaeological research in Aneityum. *South Pacific Bulletin* 25(3): 27–30.

The Guardian (2018). Pope wades into Indigenous conflict telling Chile's Mapuche to shun violence. *The Guardian*, 18 January. Available from: www.theguardian.com/world/2018/jan/17/pope-francis-chiles-indigenous-mapuche-unite-against-violence.

Gudynas, E. (2011). Buen Vivir: Today's tomorrow. *Development* 54(4): 441–447. doi.org/10.1057/dev.2011.86.

Guía Chile Energía (n.d.). Twitter account. [Chile Energy Guide.] Available from: twitter.com/chileenergia.

Guo, P.Y. (2001). Landscape, history and migration among the Langalanga, Solomon Islands. PhD dissertation in Anthropology, University of Pittsburgh, PA.

Gustavsson, J., C. Cederberg, U. Sonesson, R. van Otterdijk and A. Meybeck (2011). *Global Food Losses and Food Waste: Extent, causes and prevention.* Study conducted for the International Congress SAVE FOOD! at Interpack2011 Düsseldorf, Germany. Rome: FAO. Available from: www.fao.org/3/a-i2697e.pdf.

Haglelgam, J. (2011). Interview with Professor John Haglelgam, former president of FSM. College of Micronesia, National Campus, Palikir, 11 January 2011.

Halbrook, S., A. Rassweiler, M. Lauer and R. Schmitt (2013). Adaptive capacity, resilience and coral reef state shifts in coastal social-ecological systems in Moorea. Project submitted to the National Science Foundation, Alexandria, VA.

Hamilton, C. (2016). The Anthropocene as rupture. *The Anthropocene Review* 3(2): 93–106. doi.org/10.1177/2053019616634741.

Hamilton, C., F. Gemenne and C. Bonneuil (2015). *The Anthropocene and the Global Environmental Crisis: Rethinking modernity in a new epoch.* London: Routledge. doi.org/10.4324/9781315743424.

Handy, E.S.C. and E.G. Handy (1972). *Native Planters of Old Hawaii: Their life, lore, and environments.* Honolulu: Bernice P. Bishop Museum.

Harrison, J.L., C.A. Montgomery and J.C. Bliss (2016). Beyond the monolith: The role of bonding, bridging, and linking social capital in the cycle of adaptive capacity. *Society & Natural Resources* 29(5): 525–539.

Harvey, D. (2005). *A Brief History of Neoliberalism.* Oxford, UK: Oxford University Press.

Haughney, D. (2006). *Neoliberal Economics, Democratic Transition, and Mapuche Demands for Rights in Chile*. Gainesville, FL: University Press of Florida.

Hau`ofa, E. (1993). Our sea of islands. In E. Waddell, V. Naidu and E. Hau`ofa (eds), *A New Oceania: Rediscovering our sea of islands*, pp. 2–18. Suva: University of South Pacific School of Social and Economic Development in association with Beake House.

Hau`ofa, E. (1994). Our sea of islands. *The Contemporary Pacific* 6(1): 148–161. Available from: scholarspace.manoa.hawaii.edu/server/api/core/bitstreams/77265cd6-ddfd-469d-a96b-04ace31ea67c/content.

Hau`ofa, E. (2005). The ocean in us. In A. Hooper (ed.), *Culture and Sustainable Development in the Pacific*, pp. 32–43. Canberra: ANU Press. doi.org/10.22459/CSDP.04.2005.02.

Hawaii News Now (2020). Lawmakers back Native Hawaiian reconciliation commission after TMT protests. *Hawaii News*, 12 February. Available from: www.hawaiinewsnow.com/2020/02/11/lawmakers-back-native-hawaiian-reconciliation-commission-after-tmt-protests/.

Hearn, A. (2008). The rocky path to sustainable fisheries management and conservation in the Galapagos Marine Reserve. *Ocean & Coastal Management* 51(8): 567–574. doi.org/10.1016/j.ocecoaman.2008.06.009.

Henkin, L. (1990). *The Age of Rights*. New York, NY: Columbia University Press.

Hennessy, E. and A.L. McCleary (2011). Nature's eden? The production and effects of 'pristine' nature in the Galápagos Islands. *Island Studies Journal* 6(2): 131–156.

Henry, M. (2013). Gonzaga Puas interview with Marion Henry, FSM Secretary of Resources and Development. Palikir, Pohnpei, 5 and 18 July 2013.

Henry, R., W. Jeffery and C. Pam (2008). *Heritage and Climate Change in Micronesia: A report on a pilot study conducted on Moch Island, Mortlock Islands, Chuuk, Federated States of Micronesia*. Townsville, Qld: James Cook University.

Henry, T. (1968). *Tahiti aux temps anciens [Tahiti in Ancient Times]*. Publication of the Society of Oceanists 1. Paris: Musée de l'Homme.

Hermann, E. and W. Kempf (2017). Climate change and the imagining of migration: Emerging discourses on Kiribati's land purchase in Fiji. *The Contemporary Pacific* 29(2): 232–263.

Herzog, H.J. (2018). *Carbon Capture*. Cambridge, MA: The MIT Press. doi.org/10.7551/mitpress/11423.001.0001.

Heylings, P. and M. Bravo (2007). Evaluating governance: A process for understanding how co-management is functioning, and why, in the Galapagos Marine Reserve. *Ocean & Coastal Management* 50(3): 174–208. doi.org/10.1016/j.ocecoaman.2006.09.003.

Hezel, F.X. (2001). *The New Shape of Old Island Cultures: A half century of social change in Micronesia.* Honolulu: University of Hawai`i Press. doi.org/10.1515/9780824843762.

Hezel, F.X. (2013). *Micronesians on the Move: Eastward and upward bound.* Pacific Island Policy Issue, No. 9. Honolulu: East-West Center.

Hi`iaka Working Group (2011). Indigenous knowledges driving technological innovation. *AAPI Nexus* 9(1–2): 241–248. doi.org/10.36650/nexus9.1-2_241-248_HiiakaWorkingGroup.

Hill, R., P.L. Pert, J. Davies, C.J. Robinson, F. Walsh and F. Falco-Mammone (2013). *Indigenous Land Management in Australia: Extent, scope, diversity, barriers and success factors.* Cairns, Qld: CSIRO Ecosystem Sciences.

Hill, R., F. Walsh, J. Davies and M. Sandford (2011). *Our Country Our Way: Guidelines for Australian Indigenous protected area management plans.* Canberra: Department of Sustainability, Environment, Water, Population and Communities.

Hobart, M. (1993). Introduction: The growth of ignorance? In M. Hobart (ed.), *An Anthropological Critique of Development.* London: Routledge.

Holmes, M.C.C. and W. Jampijinpa (2013). Law for country: The structure of Warlpiri ecological knowledge and its application to natural resource management and ecosystem stewardship. *Ecology and Society* 18(3): 19. Available from: www.ecologyandsociety.org/vol18/iss3/art19/. doi.org/10.5751/ES-05537-180319.

Houde, N. (2007). The six faces of traditional ecological knowledge: Challenges and opportunities for Canadian co-management arrangements. *Ecology and Society* 12(2): 34. Available from: www.ecologyandsociety.org/vol12/iss2/art34/. doi.org/10.5751/ES-02270-120234.

Houghton, P. (1996). *People of the Great Ocean: Aspects of human biology of the early Pacific.* Cambridge, UK: Cambridge University Press. doi.org/10.1017/CBO9780511629112.

Houtard, F. (2014). El concepto de Sumak Kawsay (Buen Vivir) y su correspondencia con el bien común de la humanidad [The concept of Sumak Kawsay (Good Living) and its correspondence with the common good of humanity]. *Journal Ecuador Debate* (84)(December).

Howe, K.R. (ed.) (2006). *Vaka Moana: Voyages of the ancestors—The discovery and settlement of the Pacific*. Honolulu: University of Hawai`i Press.

Hsiao, Y.W. (2005). The transformation of economy and self-governing on tourism resources of aboriginal society: A case study on the development of B&B business in Smangus and Cinsbu tribe. Master's thesis, Department of National Ethnology, National Chengchi University, Taipei.

Huang, G.C. (2001). The destruction and re-creation of 'the holy': Religious change among the Cinsbu Atayal (in Taiwan). Master's thesis, Department of Anthropology, National Tsinghua University, Hsinchu, Taiwan.

Hunn, E.S. (1993). What is traditional ecological knowledge? In N. Williams and G. Baines (eds), *Traditional Ecological Knowledge: Wisdom for sustainable development*. Canberra: Centre for Resource and Environmental Studies, The Australian National University.

Hunt, T. (2007). Rethinking Easter Island's ecological catastrophe. *Journal of Archaeological Science* 34(3): 485–502. doi.org/10.1016/j.jas.2006.10.003.

Hunt, T. and C. Lipo (2011). Easter Island's complex history. *Nature* 479: 41. doi.org/10.1038/479041c.

Hunter, D., K. Pouono and S. Semisi (1998). The impact of taro leaf blight in the Pacific Islands with special reference to Sāmoa. *Journal of South Pacific Agriculture* 5(2): 44–56.

Huntington, H.P. (2000). Using traditional ecological knowledge in science: Methods and applications. *Ecological Applications* 10(5): 1270–1274. doi.org/10.1890/1051-0761(2000)010[1270:UTEKIS]2.0.CO;2.

Hutchison, A. (2014). The Whanganui River as a legal person. *Alternative Law Journal* 39(3): 179–182. doi.org/10.1177/1037969X1403900309.

Hviding, E. (1998). Contextual flexibility: Present status and future of customary marine tenure in Solomon Islands. *Ocean and Coastal Management* 40(2–3): 253–269. doi.org/10.1016/S0964-5691(98)00042-8.

Imada, A. (2012). *Aloha America: Hula circuits through the U.S. empire*. Durham, NC: Duke University Press. doi.org/10.1515/9780822395164.

Imada, A. (2013). 'Aloha `Oe': Settler-colonial nostalgia and the genealogy of a love song. *American Indian Culture and Research Journal* 37(2): 35–52. doi.org/10.17953/aicr.37.2.c4x497167lx48183.

Indab, J.D. and P.B. Suarez-Aspilla (2004). Community-based marine protected areas in the Bohol (Mindanao) Sea, Philippines NAGA. *World Fish Center Quarterly* 27(1–2): 4–8.

Institut de la statistique de la Polynésie française [Institute of Statistics of French Polynesia] (ISPF) (2007–17). Population. Papeete: ISPF. Available from: www. ispf.pf/chiffres?theme=Population.

Intergovernmental Panel on Climate Change (IPCC) (2014). *Summary for policy makers.* In C.B. Field, V.R. Barros, D.J. Dokken, K.J. Mach, M.D. Mastrandrea, T.E. Bilir, M. Chatterjee, K.L. Ebi, Y.O. Estrada, R.C. Genova, B. Girma, E.S. Kissel, A.N. Levy, S. MacCracken, P.R. Mastrandrea and L.L. White (eds), *Climate Change 2014: Impacts, adaptation, and vulnerability. Part A: Global and Sectoral Aspects. Contribution of Working Group II to the Fifth Assessment Report of the Intergovernmental Panel on Climate Change*, pp. 1–32. New York, NY: Cambridge University Press. Available from: www.ipcc.ch/site/assets/uploads/2018/02/ar5_ wgII_spm_en.pdf. doi.org/10.1017/CBO9781107415379.003.

International Union for Conservation of Nature (IUCN) (1986). *Tradition, Conservation and Development: Occasional Newsletter of the Commission on Ecology's Working Group on Traditional Ecological Knowledge*, No. 4. Gland, Switzerland: IUCN.

International Union for Conservation of Nature (IUCN) (2013). *Guidelines for Reintroductions and Other Conservation Translocations. Version 1.0.* Gland: IUCN Species Survival Commission.

International Union for Conservation of Nature (IUCN) (2017). *Ocean Acidification.* Issues Brief, November. Gland, Switzerland: IUCN.

Jackman, R.W. and R.A. Miller (1998). Social capital and politics. *Annual Review of Political Science* 1: 47–73. Available from: www.annualreviews.org/doi/pdf/ 10.1146/annurev.polisci.1.1.47.

Jackson, S. (2004). *Preliminary Report on Aboriginal Perspectives on Land-Use and Water Management in the Daly River Region, Northern Territory.* Report to the Northern Land Council. Darwin: CSIRO.

Jackson, S., M. Finn and P. Featherston (2012). Aquatic resource use by Indigenous Australians in two tropical river catchments: The Fitzroy River and Daly River. *Human Ecology* 40(6): 893–908. doi.org/10.1007/s10745-012-9518-z.

Jackson, S., M. Finn, E. Woodward and P. Featherston (2011). *Indigenous Socio-Economic Values and River Flows.* Darwin: Tropical Rivers and Coastal Knowledge and CSIRO.

Jacob, J.-P. and P.-Y. Le Meur (2010). Citoyenneté locale, foncier, appartenance et reconnaissance dans les sociétés du Sud [Local citizenship, land ownership, belonging and recognition in societies of the South]. In J.-P. Jacob and P-Y. Le Meur (eds), *Politique de la terre et de l'appartenance. Droits fonciers et citoyenneté locale dans les sociétés du Sud* [*Politics of Land and Belonging: Land rights and local citizenship in Southern societies*], pp. 5–57. Paris: Karthala.

Jamasmie, C. (2017). Ecuador mining industry to grow eightfold by 2021—report. *Mining.com*, 19 April. Available from: www.mining.com/ecuador-mining-industry-to-grown-eightfold-by-2021-report/.

Jardine, T.D., N.E. Pettit, D.M. Warfe, B.J. Pusey, D.P. Ward, M.M. Douglas, P.M. Davies and S.E. Bunn (2012). Consumer–resource coupling in wet–dry tropical rivers. *Journal of Animal Ecology* 81(2): 310–322. doi.org/10.1111/j.1365-2656.2011.01925.x.

Jaynes, B. (2010). Chuuk students marginalized by Chuuk Department of Education. *The Kaselehlie Press*, [Pohnpei], 17 March. Available from: www.fm/news/kp/2010/mar10_1.htm.

Johns, T. (1990). *The Origins of Human Diet and Medicine: Chemical Ecology.* Tucson, AZ: University of Arizona Press. doi.org/10.2307/j.ctv1qwwj2q.

Jolly, M. (2001). On the edge? Deserts, oceans, islands. *The Contemporary Pacific* 13(2): 417–466. doi.org/10.1353/cp.2001.0055.

Jonassen, J. (1999). Diplomacy and the politics of culture: The case of voyaging canoes. Paper presented at Victoria University of Wellington, 18 May.

Jones, K.R., O. Venter, R.A. Fuller, J.R. Allan, S.L. Maxwell, P.J. Negret and J.E.M. Watson (2018). One-third of global protected land is under intense human pressure. *Science* 360(6390): 788–791. doi.org/10.1126/science.aap9565.

Jones, L.T. and P.A. McGavin (2001). *Land Mobilisation in Papua New Guinea.* Canberra: Asia Pacific Press.

Jones, P.J.S. (2013). A governance analysis of the Galapagos Marine Reserve. *Marine Policy* 41: 65–71. doi.org/10.1016/j.marpol.2012.12.019.

Jones, T.L., A.A. Storey, E.A. Matisso-Smith and J.M. Ramírez-Aliaga (eds) (2011). *Polynesians in America: Pre-Columbian contacts with the New World.* Lanham, MD: AltaMira Press.

Journeaux, P. and T.T. Kingi (2020). *Farm Systems Modelling for GHG Reduction on Māori Farms: Achieving the zero-carbon targets.* Prepared for NZAGRC. Hamilton, NZ: AgFirst Waikato. Available from: www.agfirst.co.nz/projects/achieving-zero-carbon-act-reduction-targets-on-farm.

Kabutaulaka, T. (2021). Mapping the Blue Pacific in a changing regional order. In G. Smith and T. Wesley-Smith (eds), *The China Alternative: Changing regional order in the Pacific Islands*, pp. 41–69. Canberra: ANU Press. doi.org/10.22459/CA.2021.01.

Kardol, R. (1999). Proposed inhabited artificial islands in international waters: International law analysis in regards to resource use, law of the sea and norms of self-determination and state recognition. Master's thesis, University of Amsterdam.

Kawharu, I.H. (1977). *Māori Land Tenure: Studies of a changing institution*. Oxford, UK: Clarendon Press.

Keil, J. (2005). Buin social structure. In A. Regan and H.M. Griffin (eds), *Bougainville before the Conflict*, pp. 332–345. Canberra: Pandanus Books.

Keim, M.E. (2010). Sea level rise disaster in Micronesia: Sentinel event for climate change? *Disaster Medicine and Public Health Preparedness* 4(1): 81–87. doi.org/10.1017/s1935789300002469.

Kench, P.S., M.R. Ford and S.D. Owen (2018). Patterns of island change and persistence offer alternate adaptation pathways for atoll nations. *Nature Communications* 9: 605. doi.org/10.1038/s41467-018-02954-1.

Kennard, M.J., B.J. Pusey, J.D. Olden, S.J. Mackay, J.L. Stein and N. Marsh (2010). Classification of natural flow regimes in Australia to support environmental flow management. *Freshwater Biology* 55: 171–193. doi.org/10.1111/j.1365-2427.2009.02307.x.

Keohane, R.O. and D.G. Victor (2011). The regime complex for climate change. *Perspectives on Politics* 9(1): 7–23. doi.org/10.1017/S1537592710004068.

Keulartz, J. (2012). The emergence of enlightened anthropocentrism in ecological restoration. *Nature and Culture* 7(1): 48–71. doi.org/10.3167/nc.2012.070104.

Kim, M. (2011). *Into the Deep: Launching culture and policy in the Federated States of Micronesia*. Pohnpei: Secretariat of the Pacific Community and Federated States of Micronesia Office of National Archives, Culture and Historic Preservation.

King, C. & M. Cruickshank (2012). Building capacity to engage: Community engagement or government engagement? *Community Development Journal* 47(1): 5–28.

King, K.F.S. (1987). The history of agroforestry. In H.A. Steppler and P.K.R. Nair (eds), *Agroforestry: A decade of development*, pp. 1–11. Nairobi: ICRAF.

King, K.F.S. (1993). The history of agroforestry systems. In P.K.R. Nair (ed.), *Agroforestry Systems in the Tropics*. Dordrecht, Netherlands: Kluwer Academic Publishers, in cooperation with ICRAF.

Kingi, T.T. (2008). Māori land ownership and management. In Australian Agency for International Development (AusAID), *Making Land Work. Volume Two: Case studies on customary land and development in the Pacific*, pp. 129–151. Canberra: AusAID.

Kingi, T.T. (2009a). The future of the Māori agricultural sector. *The Journal of the NZ Institute of Primary Industry Management* 13(2): 23–26.

Kingi, T.T. (2009b). Māori land ownership and economic development. *The New Zealand Law Journal* (November): 396–400.

Kingi, T.T. (2013). Cultural bastions, farm optimisation and tribal agriculture in Aotearoa (New Zealand). In D.L. Michalk, G.D. Millar, W.B. Badgery and K.M. Broadfoot (eds), *Revitalising Grasslands to Sustain Our Communities: Proceedings, 22nd International Grassland Congress, 15–19 September, Sydney, Australia*, pp. 1898–1904. Orange, NSW: NSW Department of Primary Industry.

Kingi, T.T. (2014). Tribal partnerships and developing ancestral Māori land. In P. D'Arcy, P. Matbob and L. Crowl (eds), *Pacific–Asia Partnerships in Resource Development*, pp. 197–204. Madang, PNG: Divine Word University Press.

Kingi, T.T., S. Wakelin, P. Journeaux and G. West (2016). *Modelling Adaptation and Mitigation Strategies for Māori Livestock Farms in Aotearoa New Zealand. Proceedings of the 10th International Rangelands Congress*, pp. 927–929. Available from: www.irc2016canada.ca/ [page discontinued].

Kingi, T.T., M.E. Wedderburn and O. Montes de Oca (2013). Iwi futures: Integrating traditional knowledge systems and cultural values into land use planning. In R. Walker, D. Natcher and D. Jojola (eds), *Reclaiming Indigenous Planning*, pp. 339–356. Montreal: McGill-Queen's University Press.

Kirch, P.V. (2002). *On the Road of the Winds: An archaeological history of the Pacific Islands before European contact*. Berkeley, CA: University of California Press.

Kirch, P.V. and J.-L. Rallu (eds) (2007). *The Growth and Collapse of Pacific Island Societies: Archaeological and demographic perspectives*. Honolulu: University of Hawai`i Press. doi.org/10.1515/9780824864767.

Klein, N. (2007). *The Shock Doctrine: The rise of disaster capitalism*. New York, NY: Metropolitan Books/Henry Holt & Company.

Klein, N. (2014). *This Changes Everything: Capitalism vs the climate*. New York, NY: Simon & Schuster.

Klubock, T.M. (2014). *La Frontera: Forests and ecological conflict in Chile's frontier territory.* Durham, NC: Duke University Press. doi.org/10.2307/j.ctv1131c0z.

Knudtson, P. and D. Suzuki (1992). *Wisdom of the Elders.* Toronto: Stoddart.

Kojima, Y. (1984 [1915]). Investigation of the custom of the Aboriginal in Taiwan. Unpublished translation by W.X. Huang and W.J. Yu. Taipei: Institute of Ethnology, Academia Sinica.

Korauaba, T. (2012). Media and the politics of climate change in Kiribati: A case study on journalism in a 'disappearing nation'. MComm dissertation, Auckland University of Technology, NZ.

Kotzé, L. and P. Villavicencio Calzadilla (2017). Somewhere between rhetoric and reality: Environmental constitutionalism and the rights of nature in Ecuador. *Transnational Environmental Law* 6(3): 401–433. doi.org/10.1017/S2047102517000061.

Kotzé, L.J. (2014). Human rights and the environment in the Anthropocene. *The Anthropocene Review* 1(3): 252–275. doi.org/10.1177/2053019614547741.

Koutsou, S. and E. Vounouki (2012). Collective action and innovation in rural areas: An efficient dialogue. A case study of Greece. *Revista de Estudios sobre Despoblación y Desarrollo* [*Journal of Depopulation and Rural Development Studies*]: 85–106. Available from: www.ceddar.org/content/files/articulof_357_06_Ager-13,03-Koutsou-Vounouki.pdf [in Spanish].

Krupnik, I. and D. Jolly (2002). *The Earth is Faster Now: Indigenous observations of Arctic environmental change.* Fairbanks, AK: Arctic Research Consortium of the United States.

Kubiszewski, I., R. Costanza, C. Franco, P. Lawn, J. Talberth, T. Jackson and C. Aylmer (2013). Beyond GDP: Measuring and achieving global genuine progress. *Ecological Economics* 93: 57–68. doi.org/10.1016/j.ecolecon.2013.04.019.

Kusuma, P., N. Brucato, M.P. Cox, T. Letellier, A. Manan, C. Nuraini, P. Grangé, H. Sudoyo and F.-X. Ricaut (2017). The last sea nomads of the Indonesian archipelago: Genomic origins and dispersal. *European Journal of Human Genetics* 25(8): 1004–1010. doi.org/10.1038/ejhg.2017.88.

Ladefoged, T., M. McCoy, G. Asner, P. Kirch, C. Puleston, O. Chadwick and P. Vitousek (2011). Agricultural potential and actualized development in Hawai`i: An airborne LiDAR survey of the leeward Kohala field system (Hawai`i Island). *Journal of Archaeological Science* 38: 3605–3619. doi.org/10.1016/j.jas.2011.08.031.

La Franchi, C. and Greenpeace Pacific (1999). *Island Adrift: Comparing industrial and small-scale economic options for Marovo Lagoon region of the Solomon Islands.* Suva: Greenpeace Pacific.

Lakau, A.A.L. (1997). Customary land tenure, customary landowners and the proposals for customary land reform in Papua New Guinea. *Anthropological Forum* 7(4): 529–547.

Langdon, R. (1989). When the blue-egg chickens come home to roost: New thoughts on the prehistory of the domestic fowl in Asia, America, and the Pacific Islands. *The Journal of Pacific History* 24(2): 164–192. doi.org/10.1080/00223348908572613.

Larson, S., N. Stoeckl and B. Blanco-Martin (2013). On the use of socioeconomic typologies for improved integrated management of data-poor regions: Explorations from the Australian north. *Australasian Journal of Environmental Management* 20(4): 302–319. doi.org/10.1080/14486563.2012.763145.

Latin America Centre of Asia-Pacific Excellence (Latin America CAPE) (2018). Strengthening Māori business capability in Latin America. *Latin America CAPE News*, 27 November. Wellington: Latin America CAPE.

Latin America Centre of Asia-Pacific Excellence (Latin America CAPE) (2019). He Aputahi Taketake: Māori delegates to Chile. *Latin America CAPE News*, 9 July. Wellington: Latin America CAPE.

Lauer, M. (2017). Changing understandings of local knowledge in island environments. *Environmental Conservation* 44(4): 336–347. doi.org/10.1017/S0376892917000303.

Lauer, M. and S. Aswani (2008). Integrating indigenous ecological knowledge and multi-spectral image classification for marine habitat mapping in Oceania. *Ocean & Coastal Management* 51(6): 495–504. doi.org/10.1016/j.ocecoaman.2008.04.006.

Lavallee, L.F. (2009). Practical application of an Indigenous research framework and two qualitive Indigenous research methods: Sharing circles and Anishnaabe symbol-based reflection. *International Journal of Qualitative Methods* 8(1): 21–40. doi.org/10.1177/160940690900800103.

Lawson, B. (1984). *Aboriginal Fishing and Ownership of the Sea.* Canberra: Department of Primary Industry.

Lebot, V. (2013). Coping with insularity: The need for crop genetic improvement to strengthen adaptation to climatic change and food security in the Pacific. *Environment, Development and Sustainability* 15(6): 1405–1423. doi.org/10.1007/s10668-013-9445-1.

Lebot, V. and C. Sam (2019). Green desert or 'all you can eat'? How diverse and edible was the flora of Vanuatu before human introductions? In S. Bedford and M. Spriggs (eds), *Debating Lapita: Distribution, chronology, society and subsistence*, pp. 403–414. Terra Australis 52. Canberra: ANU Press. doi.org/10.22459/TA52.2019.19.

Lefale, P.F. (2010). *Ua `afa le Aso* stormy weather today: Traditional ecological knowledge of weather and climate—The Sāmoa experience. *Climatic Change* 100: 317–335. doi.org/10.1007/s10584-009-9722-z.

Le Meur, P.-Y., P. Sauboua, E. Poncet and M. Toussaint (2012). Les enjeux de la gouvernance locale des ressources marines en Nouvelle-Calédonie. Contribution à la réflexion sur le foncier maritime à partir de deux études de cas [The challenges of local governance of marine resources in New Caledonia: Contribution to the reflection on maritime land based on two case studies]. In D. Carine and N. Meyer (eds), *L'intégration de la coutume dans l'élaboration de la norme environnementale* [*The Integration of Custom in the Development of the Environmental Standard*], pp. 235–252. Brussels: Bruylant.

Le Roy, E. (2011). *La terre de l'autre, une anthropologie des régimes d'appropriation foncière* [*The Land of the Other: An anthropology of land appropriation regimes*]. Anthropology Series 441. Paris: LGDJ.

Le Roy, E. (2013). *La Terre et l'homme. Espaces et ressources convoités, entre le local et le global* [*Earth and Man: Coveted spaces and resources, between the local and the global*]. Paris: Editions Karthala.

Leslie, D. (2008). Interview with Dora Leslie, Canberra, 26 September.

Li, M. (2020). The Belt and Road Initiative: Geo-economics and Indo-Pacific security competition. *International Affairs* 96(1): 169–187. doi.org/10.1093/ia/iiz240.

Liao, S.C. (1984). Tayal culture: Indigenous migration and development. Master's thesis, Division of Tourism Promotion, College of World Journalism, Taipei.

Liedloff, A.C., E.L. Woodward, G.A. Harrington and S. Jackson (2013). Integrating Indigenous ecological and scientific hydro-geological knowledge using a Bayesian network in the context of water resource development. *Journal of Hydrology* 499: 177–187. doi.org/10.1016/j.jhydrol.2013.06.051.

Lightfoot, C. (2005). Does customary land make economic sense? In J. Fingleton (ed.), *Privatising land in the Pacific: A defence of customary tenure*. Discussion Paper 80, pp. 22–33. Canberra: The Australia Institute.

Liu, W., S. Yao, J. Wang and M. Liu (2019). Trends and features of agroforestry research based on bibliometric analysis. *Sustainability* 11(12): 3473. doi.org/10.3390/su11123473.

Lo, S.-M. (2005). Distinction of sex, hierarchy and society: The ritual cycle of the millet in the 'Amis of 'Tolan. *Taiwan Journal of Anthropology* 3(10): 143–183.

Lo, S.-M. (2010). Cultural identity, ecological conflict and ethnic relations: Discourse on the traditional territory by the 'Amis of 'Tolan. *Journal of Archaeology and Anthropology* 72: 1–34.

Lo, S.-M. (2015). The cultural politics of environmental and developmental alternatives: Social struggle on traditional territory in 'Tolan, 'Amis. *Taiwan: A Radical Quarterly of Social Studies* 98: 239–257.

Lockie, S., S. Rockloff and B. Muir (2003). *Indigenous Coastal and Waterways Resource Management: Current reflections and future directions*. Brisbane: Cooperative Research Centre for Coastal Zone, Estuary and Waterway Management.

López, C. (1998). How did Chile acquire Easter Island? *Rapa Nui Journal* 12(4): 118–122.

López Vergara, S. and J.A. Lucero (2018). Wallmapu rising: New paths in Mapuche studies. *Latin American Research Review* 53(3): 648–654. doi.org/10.25222/larr.298.

Lorimer, J. (2016). The Anthropo-scene: A guide for the perplexed. *Social Studies of Science* 47(1): 117–142. doi.org/10.1177/0306312716671039.

Lourandos, H. (1977). Aboriginal spatial organisation and population: South-western Victoria reconsidered. *Archaeology and Physical Anthropology in Oceania* 12(3): 202–225.

Lövbrand, E., J. Stripple and B. Wiman (2009). Earth System governmentality: Reflections on science in the Anthropocene. *Global Environmental Change* 19(1): 7–13. doi.org/10.1016/j.gloenvcha.2008.10.002.

Lowe, P. and P. Pike (2009). *You Call it Desert: We used to live there*. Broome, WA: Magabala Books.

Lu, C.-M. (2015). Eco-enhancing livelihood practices in Sa'owac Niyaro. *Taiwan: A Radical Quarterly of Social Studies* 98: 259–287.

Luckert, M.K., B.M. Campbell, J.T. Gorman and S.T. Garnett (2007). *Investing in Indigenous Natural Resource Management*. Darwin: Charles Darwin University Press.

Lummani, J. (2005). Post-1960s cocoa and copra production in Bougainville. In A. Regan & H.M. Griffin (eds), *Bougainville before the Conflict*, pp. 239–257. Canberra: Pandanus Books.

MacGregor, G. (1937). *Ethnology of Tokelau Islands*. Honolulu: Bernice P. Bishop Museum.

Maclean, K. and The Bana Yarralji Bubu Inc. (2015). Crossing cultural boundaries: Integrating Indigenous water knowledge into water governance through co-research in the Queensland wet tropics, Australia. *Geoforum* 59: 142–152. doi.org/10.1016/j.geoforum.2014.12.008.

Madeley, J. (2002). *Food for All: The need for a new agriculture*. London: Zed Books.

Madeley, J. (2003). *A People's World: Alternatives to economic globalisation*. London: Zed Books.

Magallanes, C.J.I. (2015). Reflecting on cosmology and environmental protection: Māori cultural rights in Aotearoa New Zealand. In A. Grear and L.J. Kotzé (eds), *Research Handbook on Human Rights and the Environment*, pp. 274–308. Cheltenham, UK: Edward Elgar Publishing. Available from: ideas.repec.org/h/elg/eechap/15280_14.html.

Mahuta, N. (2019). Indigenous development and the Māori experience. Speech by Hon. Nanaia Mahuta, Minister of Foreign Affairs of New Zealand, 26 March. New Zealand Government. Available from: www.beehive.govt.nz/speech/Indigenous-development-and-māori-experience.

Makis, P. (2019). Vanilla farming can economically empower B'villeans: Korokoro. *The Post Courier*, [Port Moresby], 22 May. Available from: postcourier.com.pg/vanilla-farming-can-economically-empower-bvilleans-korokoro-2/.

Māori Land Court (2022). *Your Māori Land*. Wellington: New Zealand Government. Available from: www.maorilandcourt.govt.nz/your-maori-land/.

MAPLE Microdevelopment–Chile (2016). *A First Step: The Mapuche of Chile and the Māori of New Zealand*. 9 February. Eugene, OR: MAPLE Microdevelopment. Available from: www.maplemicrodevelopment.org/blog/2016/2/9/a-first-step-the-mapuche-of-chile-and-the-maori-of-new-zealand.

Marchetti, R. (2013). Political agency in the age of globalisation. In B. Maiguashca and R. Marchetti (eds), *Contemporary Political Agency: Theory and practice*. London: Taylor & Francis.

Marrfurra McTaggart, P., M. Yawalminy, M. Wawul, K. Kamarrama, C. Bamulying Ariuu, T. Kumunerrin, M. Kanintyanyu, T. Waya, M. Kannyi, H. Adya, L. Tjifisha and G. Wightman (2014). *Ngan'gi Plants and Animals*. Darwin: Merrepen Arts, Culture and Language and Northern Territory Department of Land Resource Management.

Marsden, M. (1975). God, man and universe: A Māori view. In M. King (ed.), *Te Ao Hurihuri: The world moves on*, pp. 191–219. Auckland, NZ: Reed.

Marshall, M. (2004). *Namoluk beyond the Reef: The transformation of a Micronesian community*. Boulder, CO: Westview Press.

Martin, K. (2004). *Land, custom and conflict in East New Britain*. Resource Management in Asia-Pacific Working Paper No. 53. Canberra: The Australian National University.

Martin, K. (2007). Land, customary and non-customary, in East New Britain. In J. Weiner and K. Glaskin (eds), *Customary Land Tenure and Registration in Australia and Papua New Guinea: Anthropological perspectives*, pp. 39–56. Canberra: ANU Press. doi.org/10.22459/CLTRAPNG.06.2007.03.

Martyn, J. (1993). *The History of Green Island: The place of spirits*. Cairns, Qld: Bolton Imprint.

Mason, P. (2015). *Postcapitalism: A guide to our future*. London: Allen Lane.

Matisoo-Smith, L. and J.M. Ramírez-Aliaga (2010). Human skeletal evidence of Polynesian presence in South America? Metric analyses of six crania from Mocha Island, Chile. *Journal of Pacific Archaeology* 1(1): 76–88.

Matsuda, M.K. (2012). *Pacific Worlds: A history of seas, peoples, and cultures*. Cambridge, UK: Cambridge University Press. doi.org/10.1017/CBO9781139 034319.

Maude, H.E. (1981). *Slavers in Paradise: The Peruvian labour trade in Polynesia, 1862–1864*. Canberra: ANU Press. Available from: hdl.handle.net/1885/114682.

Mawyer, A. and J.K. Jacka (2018). Sovereignty, conservation and island ecological futures. *Environmental Conservation* 45(3): 238–251. doi.org/10.1017/S0376 89291800019X.

McAdam, J. (2010). *'Disappearing states', statelessness and the boundaries of international law*. UNSW Law Research Paper No. 2010-2. Sydney: University of New South Wales. Available from: papers.ssrn.com/sol3/papers.cfm?abstract_id=1539766.

McCall, G. (1995). Japan, Rapanui and Chile's uncertain sovereignty. *Rapa Nui Journal* 9(1): 1–7. Available from: islandheritage.org/wp-content/uploads/2010/06/RNJ_9_1_McCall.pdf.

McGuire, S., S. Posner and H. Haake (2012). Measuring prosperity: Maryland's Genuine Progress Indicator. *Solutions* 3(2): 50–58.

McTaggart, P., M. Yawulminy, C. Ariuu, D. Daning, K. Kamarrama, B. Ngulfundi, M. Warrumburr, M. Wawul and E. Woodward (2009). *Ngan'gi Seasons, Nauiyu—Daly River, Northern Territory, Australia*. Darwin: CSIRO Ecosystem Sciences.

Mead, H.M. and N. Grove (2001). *Ngā Pēpeha a Ngā Tīpuna* [*The Sayings of the Ancestors*]. Wellington: Victoria University Press.

Meinzen-Dick, R. and M. Di Gregorio (2004). Overview. In R.S. Meinzen-Dick and M. Di Gregorio (eds), *Collective Action and Property Rights for Sustainable Development*. 2020 Vision Focus. Washington, DC: International Food Policy Research Institute. Available from: ebrary.ifpri.org/utils/getfile/collection/p15738coll2/id/129299/filename/129510.pdf.

Micronesian and Australian Friends Association (MAFA) (2016). Kuchuwa Community Project: Indigenous youth responses to water and waste management in the Federated States of Micronesia. In F. Le Meur (ed.), *D5.2 Report on the Use of the Seed Funding*. Canberra: Pacific Europe Network for Science, Technology and Innovation. Available from: plus.pacenet.eu.s3-website-eu-west-1.amazonaws.com/system/files/documents/PNP_D5.2_Report%20on%20the%20use%20of%20the%20Seed%20funding_final_0.pdf.

Micronesian Presidents' Summit (MPS) (2015). *Boknake Haus Communiqué: 15th Micronesian Presidents' Summit, Majuro, Marshall Islands, July 14–15 2015*. Majuro: MPS.

Milesi, O. (2018). Land, water and education, priorities for Chile's Mapuche people. *Inter Press Service News*, [Rome], 30 August. Available from: www.ipsnews.net/2018/08/land-water-education-priorities-chiles-mapuche-people/.

Ministry of Agriculture and Forestry (2011). *Māori Agribusiness in New Zealand: A study of the Māori freehold land resource*. Wellington: New Zealand Government.

Ministry of Business, Innovation & Employment (MBIE) (2015). *Business Growth Agenda: Towards 2025*. Wellington: New Zealand Government. Available from: www.beehive.govt.nz/sites/default/files/Business%20Growth%20Agenda%20-%20Towards%202025.pdf.

Ministry for the Environment (MFE) (2014). *New Zealand's Greenhouse Gas Inventory 1990–2012*. Wellington: New Zealand Government.

Ministry for the Environment (MFE) (2020). *National Policy Statement for Freshwater Management 2020*. ME 1518, 1 August. Wellington: New Zealand Government.

Ministry of the Interior (MOI) (2022). *Population Data*. Taipei: Government of the Republic of China. Available from: www.ris.gov.tw/app/portal/346.

Ministry of the Interior (MOI) and Council of Indigenous Peoples (COIP), Executive Yuan (2019). *The Specific Regional Plan for Indigenous Peoples—The Tayal. Cinsbu Community and Smangus Community*. Taipei: Government of the Republic of China.

Ministry for Primary Industries (MPI) (2012). Northland Dairy: Key results from the Ministry for Primary Industries 2012 dairy monitoring programme. *Farm Monitoring 2012*. Wellington: Ministry of Primary Industries. Available from: www.mpi.govt.nz/dmsdocument/4193-Farm-Monitoring-Report-2012-Pastoral-Monitoring-Northland-Dairy.

Ministry for Primary Industries (MPI) (2013). *Growing the Productive Base of Māori Freehold Land*. Report prepared by PricewaterhouseCoopers. Wellington: New Zealand Government.

Mitchell, D.D. (1976). *Land and Agriculture in Nagovisi, Papua New Guinea*. Monograph 3. Port Moresby: Institute of Applied Social and Economic Research.

Mitchell, D.D. (1982). Frozen assets in Nagovisi. *Oceania* 53(1): 56–66.

Mojica, C. (2020). Constitutional plebiscite in Chile: A road to build a more inclusive and prosperous nation. [Blog post], 2 November, Regional Bureau for Latin America and the Caribbean. New York, NY: United Nations Development Programme. Available from: www.latinamerica.undp.org/content/rblac/en/home/blog/2020/constitutional-plebiscite-in-chile--a-road-to-build-a-more-inclu.html.

Morgan, D., M. Allen, P. Bedford and M. Horstman (2004). Fish fauna of the Fitzroy River in the Kimberley region of Western Australia—including the Bunuba, Gooniyandi, Ngarinyn, Nyikina and Walmajarri Aboriginal names. *Records of the Western Australian Museum* 22: 147–161. doi.org/10.18195/issn.0312-3162.22(2).2004.147-161.

Morgan, K.B. (2004). A Tangata Whenua perspective on sustainability using the Mauri model. Presentation to International Conference on Sustainability Engineering and Science, Auckland, New Zealand, 7–9 July.

Mori, E. (2008). Address by H.E. Emanuel Mori, president of the Federated States of Micronesia, before the 63rd United Nations General Assembly, New York, 25 September 2008. Available from: www.fsmgov.org/fsmun/ga63_main.htm.

Morley, J. (2017). '… Beggars sitting on a sack of gold': Oil exploration in the Ecuadorian Amazon as *buen vivir* and sustainable development. *The International Journal of Human Rights* 21(4): 405–441. doi.org/10.1080/13642987.2016.124 9140.

Morphy, H. (2010). *Population, people and place: The Fitzroy Valley Population Project.* CAEPR Working Paper, 70/2010. Canberra: Centre for Aboriginal Economic Policy Research, The Australian National University.

Morrison, J. (1966). *Le Journal de James Morrison, second maître à bord de la Bounty* [*The Diary of James Morrison, Mate aboard the Bounty*]. French translation by B. Jaunez. Paris: Musée de l'Homme. doi.org/10.4000/books.sdo.159.

Morton, K. (2011). Climate change and security at the third pole. *Survival* 53(1): 121–132. doi.org/10.1080/00396338.2011.555606.

Mou, F. (2015). SIS leaders demand 1.5 degree target. *Loop PNG*, 8 September. Available from: www.looppng.com/content/sis-leaders-demand-15-degree-target.

MRAG Asia Pacific (2016). *Towards the Quantification of Illegal, Unreported and Unregulated (IUU) Fishing in the Pacific Islands Region.* February. Brisbane: MRAG Asia Pacific. Available from: www.ffa.int/files/FFA%20Quantifying%20 IUU%20Report%20-%20Final.pdf.

Mugambwa, J. (2007). A comparative analysis of land tenure law reform in Uganda and Papua New Guinea. *Journal of South Pacific Law* 11(1): 39–55.

Mukherjee, N. (2002). *Participatory Learning and Action: With 100 field methods.* New Delhi: Concept Publishing Company.

Mulalap, C.Y. (2013). Islands in the stream: Addressing climate change from a small island developing state perspective. In R. Abate and E. Warner (eds), *Climate Change and Indigenous People: The search for legal remedies*, pp. 377–408. Cheltenham, UK: Edward Elgar Publishing. Available from: www.elgar online.com/view/9781781001790.00032.xml. doi.org/10.4337/9781781001 806.00032.

Muller, S. (2008). Indigenous payment for environmental service (PES) opportunities in the Northern Territory: Negotiating with customs. *Australian Geographer* 39(2): 149–170. doi.org/10.1080/00049180802056831.

Murdock, G.P. (1949). *Social Structure.* New York, NY: Macmillan.

Muru-Lanning, M. (2015). Thoughts on water. *Cultural Studies Review* 21(1): 304–309. doi.org/10.5130/csr.v21i1.4346.

Nagatsu, K. (2013). Spatial data on distribution of Sama-Bajau population in the southern Philippines. *Hakusan Review of Anthropology* 16: 139–147.

Naidu, V. (2010). Modernisation and development in the South Pacific. In A. Jowitt and T.N. Cain (eds), *Passage of Change: Law, society and governance in the Pacific*, pp. 7–32. Canberra: ANU Press. doi.org/10.22459/PC.11.2010.01.

Nakashima, D., K. Galloway McLean, H. Thulstrup, A. Ramos-Castillo and J. Rubis (2012). *Weathering Uncertainty: Traditional knowledge for climate change assessment and adaptation*. Paris and Darwin: UNESCO and United Nations University Traditional Knowledge Initiative.

Nakayama, M. (2009). Statement before the Committee of Religious NGOs and the United Nations, The Last Push Before Copenhagen: Defining Positions Strategies and Goals on Climate Change. New York, 10 November. Available from: www.fsmgov.org/~hxprzkmy/fsmun/ga64_chu.htm.

Nash, J. (1974). Matriliny and modernisation: The Nagovisi of south Bougainville. *New Guinea Research Bulletin*, No. 55. Canberra: The Australian National University.

Nash, J. (1977). Women and power in Nagovisi society. *Journal de la Societe des Oceanistes* 33: 119–126. doi.org/10.3406/jso.1978.2974.

Nash, J. (2005). Nagovisi then and now, 1963–2000. In A. Regan and H.M. Griffin (eds), *Bougainville before the Conflict*, pp. 400–409. Canberra: Pandanus Books.

National Museum of Australia (NMA) (2010). *Yiwarra Kuju: The Canning Stock Route*. Canberra: National Museum of Australia Press.

National Oceanic and Atmospheric Administration (NOAA) (2020). *Ocean Acidification*. Washington, DC: NOAA. Available from: www.noaa.gov/education/resource-collections/ocean-coasts/ocean-acidification.

National Oceans Office (2002). *Sea Country: An Indigenous perspective. The South-East Regional Marine Plan. Assessment reports*. Hobart: Australian Government. Available from: www.awe.gov.au/sites/default/files/documents/indigenous.pdf.

National Statistics Office (2003). Central Visayas: Three in every five households had electricity (Results from the 2000 Census of Population and Housing, NSO). Press release, 15 July. Manila: National Statistics Office. Available from: web.archive.org/web/20120221224038/http://www.census.gov.ph/data/pressrelease/2003/pr0302tx.html.

Natural Resource Management Ministerial Council (2010). *Australia's Biodiversity Conservation Strategy 2010–2030*. Canberra: Department of Sustainability, Environment, Water, Population and Communities.

The Nature Conservancy (2010–12). *Micronesia Challenge*. Arlington, VA: The Nature Conservancy. Available from: www.nature.org/en-us/about-us/where-we-work/asia-pacific/the-pacific-islands/stories-in-the-pacific-islands/micronesia-challenge/.

Nazarea, V.D. (2013). Temptation to hope: From the 'idea' to the milieu of biodiversity. In V.D. Nazarea, D. Virgina, R.E. Rhoades and J. Andrews-Swann (eds), *Seeds of Resistance, Seeds of Hope: Place and agency in the conservation of biodiversity*, pp. 19–41. Tucson, AZ: University of Arizona Press.

Nazarea, V.D. and R.E. Rhoades (2013). Conservation by design: An introduction. In V.D. Nazarea, D. Virgina, R.E. Rhoades and J. Andrews-Swann (eds), *Seeds of Resistance, Seeds of Hope: Place and agency in the conservation of biodiversity*, pp. 3–16. Tucson, AZ: University of Arizona Press.

Neate, G. (2002). Reconciliation on the ground: Meeting the challenges of native title mediation. Parts 1 & 2. *ADR Bulletin* 89: 6, 112.

Neue, H. (1993). Methane emission from rice fields: Wetland rice fields may make a major contribution to global warming. *BioScience* 43(7): 466–474. doi.org/10.2307/1311906.

Newbury, C. (1967). Aspects of cultural change in French Polynesia: The decline of the Ari`i. *Journal of the Polynesian Society* 76(1): 7–26.

New Zealand Government (1993). *Te Ture Whenua Māori Act 1993 (Māori Land Act 1993)*. Public Act 1993 No. 4, 21 March. Wellington: New Zealand Government. Available from: www.legislation.govt.nz/act/public/1993/0004/latest/DLM289882.html.

New Zealand Government (2021). *Te Ture Whenua Maori Act 1993. Maori Land Act 1993*. Amendment (October 2021). Wellington: Parliamentary Counsel Office. Available from: www.legislation.govt.nz/act/public/1993/0004/latest/DLM289882.html.

New Zealand Government (2022). *Wellbeing Budget 2022: A secure future*. 19 May. Wellington: New Zealand Government. Available from: www.budget.govt.nz/budget/pdfs/wellbeing-budget/b22-wellbeing-budget.pdf.

Nicholson, A. and S. Cane (1994). Pre-European coastal settlement and use of the sea. *Australian Archaeology* 39(1): 108–118. doi.org/10.1080/03122417.1994.11681535.

Nielsen, J.R. and C. Mathiesen (2003). Important factors influencing rule compliance in fisheries lessons from Denmark. *Marine Policy* 27(5): 409–416.

Nimea, F.S. (2006). *Federated States of Micronesia: National assessment report—Support to the formulation of National Sustainable Development Strategy in the Pacific Small Island Developing States*. Project INT/04/X70, June. Palikir: Division for Sustainable Development, United Nations Department of Economic and Social Affairs. Available from: www.un.org/esa/sustdev/natlinfo/nsds/pacific_sids/fsm_nar.pdf.

Nimmo, H.A. (2001). *Magosaha: An ethnography of the Tawi-Tawi Sama Dilaut*. Quezon City, Philippines: Ateneo de Manila University Press.

Nixon, C. (2003). *Ngai Tahu seafood: Case study in business development*. Working Paper 25. Wellington: NZ Trade Consortium.

North Australian Indigenous Land and Sea Management Alliance Ltd (NAILSMA) (2012). About us. Website. Darwin: NAILSMA. Available from: nailsma.org.au/.

Northern Land Council (NLC) (2022). *Sea Country Rights*. Darwin: NLC. Available from: www.nlc.org.au/our-land-sea/sea-country-rights

Northern Territory University (1993). *Turning the Tide: Conference on Indigenous peoples and sea rights, 14 July – 16 July 1993—Selected papers*. Darwin: Faculty of Law, Northern Territory University.

Nunn, P.D. (2003). Fished up or thrown down: The geography of Pacific Island origin myths. *Annals of the Association of American Geographers* 93(2): 350–364. doi.org/10.1111/1467-8306.9302006.

Nunn, P.D. (2009a). Responding to the challenges of climate change in the Pacific Islands: Management and technological imperatives. *Climate Research* 40: 211–231. doi.org/10.3354/cr00806.

Nunn, P.D. (2009b). *Vanished Islands and Hidden Continents of the Pacific*. Honolulu: University of Hawai`i Press. doi.org/10.21313/hawaii/9780824832193.001.0001.

Nunn, P.D. (2013). The end of the Pacific? Effects of sea level rise on Pacific Island livelihoods. *Singapore Journal of Tropical Geography* 34(2): 143–171. doi.org/10.1111/sjtg.12021.

Oceania 21 (2015). *Lifou Declaration: 'Paris 2015: Save Oceania!'* Third Oceania 21 Summit, Lifou, Loyalty Islands, New Caledonia, 30 April. Available from: www.sprep.org/attachments/VirLib/New_Caledonia/Lifou_Declaration_2015.pdf.

Office of the Auditor-General (2011). *Report of the Auditor-General: Performance audit report on access to safe drinking water*. Parliamentary Paper No. 2011, 24 October. Vaiaku, Funafuti: Tuvalu Government.

Office of the FSM National Public Auditor (FSMOPA) (2010). Audit of solid waste management of Pohnpei State released. Press release, 12 July. Palikir: Government of the Federated States of Micronesia. Available from: www.fsmgov.org/press/pr07121b.htm.

Office of the Pacific Ocean Commissioner (OPOC) (2019). *Pacific Ocean Commissioner*. OPOC website. Suva: Pacific Islands Forum Sectretariat. Available from: opocbluepacific.org/pacific-ocean-commissioner/.

Office of Statistics, Budget and Economic Management, Overseas Development Assistance and Compact Management (SBOC) (2010). *Millennium Development Goals and Status Report 2010: The Federated States of Micronesia*. 15 December. Palikir: Government of the Federated States of Micronesia.

Ogan, E. (1971). Nasioi land tenure: An extended case study. *Oceania* 42(2): 81–93.

Ogan, E. (1972). Business and cargo: Socio-economic change among the Nasioi of Bougainville. *New Guinea Research Bulletin*, No. 44. Canberra: The Australian National University.

Ogan, E. (2005). An introduction to Bougainville cultures. In A. Regan and H.M. Griffin (eds), *Bougainville before the Conflict*, pp. 47–56. Canberra: Pandanus Books.

Oliver, D. (1974). *Ancient Tahitian Society*. 3 vols. Honolulu: University of Hawai`i Press.

Oliver, J. and S. Tucker (2019). Geoengineering at sea: Ocean fertilization as a policy option. In P. Harris (ed.), *Climate Change and Ocean Governance: Politics and policy for threatened seas*, pp. 424–436. Cambridge, UK: Cambridge University Press. doi.org/10.1017/9781108502238.026.

Ortiz-Ospina, E., D. Beltekian and M. Roser (2014). Trade and globalization. *Our World in Data*. Available from: ourworldindata.org/trade-and-globalization.

Osorio, J.K. (1984). *Hawaiian Spirits Live Again*. [Music recording.] Recorded by R. and R. Cazimero. Honolulu: Hawaiian Hula Eyes, Mountain Apple Music.

Osorio, J.K. (2013). *Kahea i Ke Aloha `Āina [Call to the Patriot]*. [Song.]

Osorio, J.K. (2014). Hawaiian souls: The movement to stop the U.S. military bombing of Kaho`olawe. In N. Goodyear-Ka`ōpua, I. Hussey and E. Kahunawaika`ala Wright (eds), *A Nation Rising: Hawaiian movements for life, land, and sovereignty*, pp. 137–160. Durham, NC: Duke University Press. doi.org/10.2307/j.ctv11cw7h9.15.

Osorio, J.K. (2015). *Poliahu i ke Hau*. [Song.]

Osorio, J.K. and R. Borden (1979). *Hawaiian Soul Hawaiian Eyes*. [Music recording.] Honolulu: Starnight Records.

Ottino-Garanger, P., M.-N. Ottino-Garanger, B. Rigo and E. Tetahiotupa (2016). *Tapu* and *kahui* in the Marquesas. In T. Bambridge (ed.), *The Rahui: Legal pluralism in Polynesian traditional management of resources and territories*, pp. 43–78. Canberra: ANU Press. doi.org/10.22459/TR.03.2016.03.

Pacific Adaptation Strategy Assistance Program (PASAP) (2011). *Securing Food Resources in the Federated States of Micronesia*. Canberra: Australian Government. Available from: terranova.org.au/repository/paccsap-collection/securing-food-resources-in-the-federated-states-of-micronesia/case-studies-fsm-4pp.pdf.

Pacific Islands Development Forum (PIDF) (2015). *Suva Declaration on Climate Change*. Suva: Pacific Islands Development Forum.

Pacific Islands Forum (PIF) (n.d.). *Smaller Island States*. Suva: Pacific Islands Forum Secretariat. Available from: www.forumsec.org/pages.cfm/strategic-partnerships-coordination/smaller-island-states/?printerfriendly=true.

Pacific Islands Forum (PIF) (1988). *Forum Communiqué: Nineteenth South Pacific Forum, Nuku`alofa, Tonga, 20–21 September*. Nuku`alofa: Pacific Islands Forum Secretariat. Available from: www.forumsec.org/wp-content/uploads/Communiqu%C3%A9/1988%20Communiqu%C3%A9-Tonga%2020-2%20Sept.pdf.

Pacific Islands Forum (PIF) (1989). *Forum Communiqué: Twentieth South Pacific Forum, Tarawa, Kiribati, 10–11 July*. Tarawa: Pacific Islands Forum Secretariat. Available from: www.forumsec.org/wp-content/uploads/Communiqu%C3%A9/1989%20Communiqu%C3%A9-Kiribati%2010-11%20July.pdf.

Pacific Islands Forum (PIF) (2008). *The Niue Declaration on Climate Change*. Suva: Pacific Islands Forum Secretariat. Available from: www.forumsec.org/2008/02/21/the-niue-declaration-on-climate-change/.

Pacific Islands Forum (PIF) (2009). *Forum Communiqué: Fortieth Pacific Islands Forum, Cairns, Australia, 5–6 August*. Cairns, Qld: Pacific Islands Forum Secretariat. Available from: www.forumsec.org/wp-content/uploads/2017/11/2009-Forum-Communique_-Cairns_-Australia-5-6-Aug.pdf.

Pacific Islands Forum (PIF) (2013). *Majuro Declaration for Climate Leadership*. 5 September. Majuro: Pacific Islands Forum Secretariat. Available from: www.forumsec.org/wp-content/uploads/2017/11/2013-Majuro-Declaration-for-Climate-Leadership.pdf.

Pacific Islands Forum (PIF) (2015). *Smaller Island States Leaders' Port Moresby Declaration on Climate Change*. Suva: Pacific Islands Forum Secretariat. Available from: www.forumsec.org/2015/09/07/smaller-island-states-leaders-port-moresby-declaration-on-climate-change/.

Page, R., M. Bentley and J. Waldrop (2013). People live here: Maternal and child health on Isla Isabela, Galapagos. In S. Walsh and C. Mena (eds), *Science and Conservation in the Galapagos Islands*, pp. 141–153. New York, NY: Springer. doi.org/10.1007/978-1-4614-5794-7_8.

Pala, C. (2014a). Kiribati president purchases 'worthless' resettlement land as precaution against rising sea. *Inter Press Service News*, [Rome], 9 June. Available from: www.ipsnews.net/2014/06/kiribati-president-purchases-worthless-resettlement-land-as-precaution-against-rising-sea/.

Pala, C. (2014b). The nation that bought a back-up property. *The Atlantic*, [Washington, DC], 21 August.

Pallesen, A. (1985). *Culture Contact and Language Convergence*. Linguistic Society of the Philippines Monograph 24. Manila: SIL.

Palsson, G. (1998). Learning by fishing: Practical engagement and environmental concerns. In F. Berkes and C. Folke (eds), *Linking Social and Ecological Systems: Management practices and social mechanisms for building resilience*, pp. 48–66. Cambridge, UK: Cambridge University Press.

Pandey, D. and M. Agrawal (2014). Carbon footprint estimation in the agricultural sector. In S.S. Muthu (ed.), *Assessment of Carbon Footprint in Different Industrial Sectors. Volume 1*, pp. 25–47. Singapore: Springer. doi.org/10.1007/978-981-4560-41-2_2.

Parsonson, G. (1966). Artificial islands in Melanesia: The role of malaria in the settlement of the southwest Pacific. *New Zealand Geographer* 22(1): 1–21. doi.org/10.1111/j.1745-7939.1966.tb00001.x.

Peet, R. and E. Hartwick (2015). *Theories of Development: Contentions, arguments, alternatives*. New York, NY: Guilford Press.

Permanent Mission of the Federated States of Micronesia to the UN (FSM Permanent Mission) (2008). *Federated States of Micronesia: Views on the possible security implications of climate change to be included in the report of the Secretary-General to the 64th Session of the United Nations General Assembly*. Submitted pursuant to UN General Assembly Resolution A/RES/63/281. New York, NY: United Nations. Available from: www.un.org/esa/dsd/resources/res_pdfs/ga-64/cc-inputs/Micronesia_CCIS.pdf.

Petersen, N. and B. Rigsby (eds) (1998). *Customary Marine Tenure in Australia: Proceedings of a workshop convened by the Australian Anthropological Society in 1996*. Sydney: Oceania Publications, University of Sydney.

Pizzirani, S., S.J. McLaren and J.K. Seadon (2014). Is there a place for culture in life cycle sustainability assessment? *The International Journal of Life Cycle Assessment* 19(6): 1316–1330.

Planas, R. (2011). Chile's Mapuches call for regional autonomy. *North American Congress on Latin America,* 9 September. New York, NY: NACLA. Available from: nacla.org/news/chiles-mapuches-call-regional-autonomy.

Pollnac, R.B., B.R. Crawford and M.L. Gorospe (2001). Discovering factors that influence the success of community-based marine protected areas in the Visayas, Philippines. *Ocean & Coastal Management* 44(11–12): 683–710. doi.org/10.1016/S0964-5691(01)00075-8.

Polynesian Leaders Group (PLG) (2015). *The Polynesian P.A.C.T.: Polynesia Against Climate Threats. Taputapuātea Declaration on Climate Change*. 16 July. Papeete. Available from: www.samoagovt.ws/wp-content/uploads/2015/07/The-Polynesian-P.A.C.T.pdf.

Portes, A. (1998). Social capital: Its origins and applications in modern sociology. *Annual Review of Sociology* 24: 1–24. Available from: www.annualreviews.org/doi/abs/10.1146/annurev.soc.24.1.1.

Post, K. (2016). *Increasing the Resilience of Marine Ecosystems: Creating and managing marine protected areas in the Philippines*. Manila: Marine Conservation Philippines.

Prebble, M., A. Anderson and D.J. Kennett (2012). Forest clearance and agricultural expansion on Rapa, Austral Archipelago, French Polynesia. *The Holocene* 23(2): 179–196. doi.org/10.1177/0959683612455551.

Prober, S.M., M.H. O'Connor and F.J. Walsh (2011). Australian Aboriginal peoples' seasonal knowledge: A potential basis for shared understanding in environmental management. *Ecology and Society* 16(2): 12. doi.org/10.5751/ES-04023-160212.

Puapua, T. (2002). Speech by Sir Tomasi Puapua, Governor-General of Tuvalu. 57th Session of the United Nations General Assembly, New York, 14 September.

Puas, G. (2012). How could the agricultural sector become more conducive towards climate change mitigation and adaptation? Paper presented to CliMates International Student Organisation, Paris.

Puas, G. (2021). *Federated States of Micronesia's Engagement with the Outside World: Control, self-preservation and continuity.* Canberra: ANU Press. doi.org/10.22459/FSMEOW.2021.

Puas, G. and N. Halter (2015). Micronesia in focus. [Editors' introduction to special issue on Micronesia.] *Tamkang Journal of International Affairs* 19(2): 1–10.

Puna, H. (2012). Large ocean island states: The Pacific challenge. Speech by Prime Minister of the Cook Islands Henry Puna, 43rd Pacific Islands Forum, Rarotonga, 27 August. Available from: www.ciherald.co.ck/articles/h631a.htm.

Putnam, R.D. (1988). Diplomacy and domestic politics: The logic of two-level games. *International Organization* 42(3): 427–460. doi.org/10.1017/S0020818300027697.

Putnam, R.D., R. Leonardi and R.Y. Nanetti (1993). *Making Democracy Work: Civic traditions in modern Italy.* Princeton, NJ: Princeton University Press. doi.org/10.1515/9781400820740.

Putnis, A., P. Josif and E. Woodward (2008). *Healthy Country, Healthy People: Supporting Indigenous engagement in the sustainable management of Northern Territory land and seas.* Darwin: CSIRO Sustainable Ecosystems.

Quiroga, D. (2009). Crafting nature: The Galapagos and the making and unmaking of a 'natural laboratory'. *Journal of Political Ecology* 16(1): 123–140. doi.org/10.2458/v16i1.21695.

Quiroga, D. (2013). Changing views of the Galapagos. In S.J. Walsh and C.F. Mena (eds), *Science and Conservation in the Galapagos Islands*, pp. 23–48. New York, NY: Springer.

Quiroga, D., C. Mena, L. Karrer, H. Suzuki, A. Guevara and J.C. Murillo (2011). Dealing with climate change in the Galapagos: Adaptability of the tourism and fishing sectors. In I. Larrea and G. Di Carlo (eds), *Climate Change Vulnerability Assessment of the Galápagos Islands*, pp. 81–109. Quito: WWF and Conservation International.

Quirola Suárez, D. (2009). *Sumak Kaway. Hacia un nuevo pacto social en armonía con la naturaleza* [*Sumak Kaway: Towards a New Social Pact in Harmony with Nature*]. Quito: Editorial Abya-Yala.

Radcliffe, S. (2012). Development for postneoliberal era? *Sumak kawsay*, living well and the limits to decolonization in Ecuador. *Geoforum* 43(2): 240–249. doi.org/10.1016/j.geoforum.2011.09.003.

Radio New Zealand (RNZ) (2013a). Chile looks to Māori to empower its Indigenous people. *Radio New Zealand*, 28 June. Available from: www.rnz.co.nz/news/te-manu-korihi/138754/chile-looks-to-Māori-to-empower-its-Indigenous-people.

Radio New Zealand (RNZ) (2013b). Pacific leaders put out climate change declaration as summit ends. *Radio New Zealand*, 5 September. Available from: www.rnz.co.nz/international/pacific-news/220672/pacific-leaders-put-out-climate-change-declaration-as-summit-ends.

Radio New Zealand (RNZ) (2015). Officials visit cyclone-ravaged Tanna. *Radio New Zealand*, 18 March. Available from: www.rnz.co.nz/international/pacific-news/268792/officials-visit-cyclone-ravaged-tanna.

Ramírez, R. (2009). *Felicidad, desigualdad y pobreza en la Revolución Ciudadana* [*Happiness, inequality and poverty in the citizens' revolution*]. Working Paper No. 3. Quito: Ecuadoran Secretariat for Planning and Development.

Ramírez, R. (2010). Socialismo del sumak kawsay o biosocialismo republican [Sumak kawsay: Socialism or republican biosocialism]. In *Socialismo y Sumak Kawsay* [*Socialism and Sumak Kawsay*], pp. 55–77. Quito: Ecuadoran Secretariat for Planning and Development.

Ramírez-Aliaga, J.M. (2010). The Mapuche–Polynesian connection: Soft and hard evidence and new ideas. *Rapa Nui Journal* (24)1: 29–33.

Ramírez-Aliaga, J.M. (2011). The Mapuche connection. In T.L. Jones, A.A. Storey, E.A. Matisoo-Smith and J.M. Ramírez-Aliaga (eds), *Polynesians in America: Pre-Columbian contacts with the New World*, pp. 93–107. Lanham, MD: AltaMira Press.

Rauchholz, M. (2011). Notes on clan histories and migration in Micronesia. *Pacific Asia Inquiry* 2(1): 53–68.

Rauen, A. (2017). *Limiting Migration to Rapa Nui*. 23 May. Washington, DC: Council on Hemispheric Affairs. Available from: www.coha.org/tag/easter-island/.

Raynal, J.B. (2004). Le littoral en mutation de Taiarapu oust [The changing coastline of West Taiarapu]. MC.Geog. thesis, University of French Polynesia, Papeete.

Redman, C.L. and A.P. Kinzig (2003). Resilience of past landscapes: Resilience theory, society, and the longue durée. *Ecology and Society* 7(1): 14. doi.org/10.5751/ES-00510-070114.

Regan, A. and H.M. Griffin (eds) (2005). *Bougainville before the Conflict*. Canberra: Pandanus Books.

Regenvanu, R. (2009). *The Traditional Economy as Source of Resilience in Vanuatu*. Port Vila: Vanuatu Cultural Centre.

Republic of Ecuador (2008). *Constitution of the Republic of Ecuador*. National Assembly Legislative and Oversight Committee. Published in the Official Register, 20 October 2008. Available from: pdba.georgetown.edu/Constitutions/Ecuador/english08.html.

Republic of the Philippine Islands (1998). *Philippine Fisheries Code of 1998 (Republic Act No. 8550)*. Available from: www.ecolex.org/details/legislation/philippine-fisheries-code-of-1998-republic-act-no-8550-lex-faoc016098/.

Resource Assessment Commission (1993). *The Coastal Zone Inquiry Final Report*. Canberra: Commonwealth of Australia.

Reuters (2014). Kiribati president favors buying land elsewhere as islands are threatened by rising sea levels. *The Huffington Post*, 22 September. Available from: www.huffingtonpost.com/2014/09/22/kiribati-president-buying-land_n_5860064.html.

Richards, A. (1950). Some types of family structure amongst the Central Bantu. In A.R. Radcliffe-Brown and D. Forde (eds), *African Systems of Kinship and Marriage*, pp. 297–351. London: Oxford University Press.

Richards, P. (2010). Of Indians and terrorists: How the state and local elites construct the Mapuche in neoliberal multicultural Chile. *Journal of Latin American Studies* 42(1): 59–90. doi.org/10.1017/S0022216X10000052.

Rigo, B. (2004). *Altérité polynésienne et conscience occidentale* [*Polynesian Alterity and Western Consciousness*]. Paris: Edition du CNRS.

Ringhofer, L., S.J. Singh and B. Smetschka (2013). *Climate change mitigation in Latin America: A mapping of current policies, plans and programs*. Institute for Social Ecology Working Paper No. 143. Vienna: Faculty for Interdisciplinary Studies, Klagenfurt University.

Rist, L., A. Felton, M. Nyström, M. Troell, R.A. Sponseller, J. Bengtsson, H. Österblom, R. Lindborg, P. Tidåker, D.G. Angeler, R. Milestad and J. Moen (2014). Applying resilience thinking to production ecosystems. *Ecosphere* 5(6): 1–11. doi.org/10.1890/ES13-00330.1.

Roberts, M., F. Weko and L. Clarke (2006). *Maramataka: The Māori moon calendar*. Agribusiness and Economics Research Unit, Research Report No. 283. Lincoln, NZ: Lincoln University.

Robinson, C.J. and T.J. Wallington (2012). Boundary work: Engaging knowledge systems in co-management of feral animals on Indigenous lands. *Ecology and Society* 17(2): 16. Available from: www.ecologyandsociety.org/vol17/iss2/art16/. doi.org/10.5751/ES-04836-170216.

Rodriguez, M. (1995). *Les Espagnols à Tahiti* [*The Spaniards in Tahiti*] *(1772–76)*. Publications of the Society of Oceanists No. 45. Paris: Musée de l'Homme. doi.org/10.4000/books.sdo.476.

Rodríguez-Entrena, M., M. Arriaza and J.A. Gómez-Limón (2014). Determining economic and social factors in the adoption of cover crops under mower control in olive groves. *Agroecology Sustainable Food Systems* 38(1): 69–91. doi.org/10.1080/21683565.2013.819478.

Rogers, E.M. (2003). *Diffusion of Innovations*. 5th edn. New York, NY: Free Press.

Rohling, E.J. (2017). *The Oceans: A deep history*. Princeton, NJ: Princeton University Press. doi.org/10.2307/j.ctvc77hkh.

Rose, D.B. (1996). *Nourishing Terrains: Australian Aboriginal views of landscape and wilderness*. Canberra: Australian Heritage Commission.

Rose, D.B. (2000). *Dingo Makes Us Human: Life and land in an Australian Aboriginal culture*. Melbourne: Cambridge University Press.

Rosenfeld, S.A. (2001). Networks and clusters: The yin and yang of rural development. In *Exploring Policy Options for a New Rural America*, pp. 103–120. Kansas City: Economic Research Department, Federal Reserve Bank of Kansas City.

Rout, M., B. Lythberg, J.P. Mika, A. Gillies, H. Bodwitch, D. Hikuroa, S. Awatere, F. Wiremu, M. Rakena and J. Reid (2019a). *Kaitiaki-Centred Business Models: Case studies of Māori marine-based enterprises in Aotearoa New Zealand*. Wellington: Sustainable Seas National Science Challenge.

Rout, M., J. Reid, H. Bodwitch, A. Gillies, B. Lythberg, D. Hikuroa, L. Mackey, S. Awatere, J.P. Mika, F. Wiremu, M. Rakena and K. Davies (2019b). *Māori Marine Economy: A literature review*. Wellington: Sustainable Seas National Science Challenge.

Ruru, J. (2018). Te Tiriti me Ōna Whakatau: The Waitangi Tribunal and treaty settlements. In M. Reilly, S. Duncan, G. Leoni, L. Paterson, L. Carter, M. Rātima and P. Rewi (eds), *Te Kōparapara: An introduction to the Māori world*, pp. 288–303. Auckland, NZ: Auckland University Press.

Ruru, J., J. Stephenson and M. Abbott (eds) (2011). *Making our Place: Exploring land-use tensions in Aotearoa New Zealand*. Dunedin, NZ: Otago University Press.

Russell-Smith, J., P. Whitehead and P. Cooke (eds) (2009). *Culture, Ecology and Economy of Fire Management in North Australian Savannas: Rekindling the Wurrk tradition*. Melbourne: CSIRO Publishing. doi.org/10.1071/9780643098299.

Sahlins, M. (1981). *Historical Myths and Mythical Realities: Structure in the early history of the Sandwich Island Kingdom*. Ann Arbor, MI: University of Michigan Press. doi.org/10.3998/mpub.6773.

Sahlins, M. (1983). Other times, other customs: The anthropology of history. *American Anthropologist* 85(3): 517–543. doi.org/10.1525/aa.1983.85.3.02a00020.

Sahlins, M. (1985). *Islands of History*. Ann Arbor, MI: University of Michigan Press.

Sahlins, M. (2005). Structural work: How microhistories become macrohistories and vice versa. *Anthropological Theory* 5(1): 5–30. doi.org/10.1177/1463499605050866.

Salm, R.V., J.R. Clark and E. Siirila (2000). *Marine and Coastal Protected Areas: A guide for planners and managers*. Washington, DC: International Union for Conservation of Nature. doi.org/10.2305/IUCN.CH.2000.13.en.

SĀMOA Pathway (2015). SIDS Accelerated Modalities of Action outcome statement. Apia: Department of Economic and Social Affairs, United Nations.

Samonte-Tan, G.P., A.T. White, M.A. Tercero, J. Diviva, E. Tabara and C. Caballes (2007). Economic valuation of coastal and marine resources: Bohol Marine Triangle, Philippines. *Coastal Management* 35(2–3): 319–338. doi.org/10.1080/08920750601169634.

Sánchez, J. (2012). Equidad y políticas sociales: algunas reflexiones para el caso ecuatoriano [Equity and social policies: Some reflections for the Ecuadorian case]. In Alfredo Serrano Mancilla (Coordinator), *A redistribuir: Ecuador para todos* [*Let's Redistribute: Ecuador for all*], pp. 335–385. Quito: Ecuadoran Secretariat for Planning and Development.

Sand, C. (2012). Certainly the most technically complex pondfield irrigation within Melanesia: Wet taro field systems of New Caledonia. In M. Spriggs, D. Addison and P.J. Matthews (eds), *Irrigated Taro (Colocasia esculanta) in the Indo-Pacific*, pp. 167–188. Senri Ethnological Studies 78. Osaka, Japan: National Museum of Ethnology.

Saovana-Spriggs, R. (2007). Gender and Peace: Bougainvillean women, matriliny and the peace process. PhD thesis, The Australian National University, Canberra.

Sather, C. (1997). *The Bajau Laut: Adaptation, history, and fate in a maritime fishing society of south-eastern Sabah*. New York, NY: Oxford University Press.

Scales, I., R. Craemer and I. Thappa (2008). *Market Chain Development in Peace Building: Australia's roads, wharves and agriculture projects in post-conflict Bougainville.* Canberra: AusAID.

Scheyvens, R. and M. Russell (2012). Tourism, land tenure and poverty alleviation in Fiji. *Tourism Geographies* 14(1): 1–25.

Schlosberg, D. (2014). Ecological justice for the Anthropocene. In M. Wissenburg and D. Schlosberg (eds), *Political Animals and Animal Politics*, pp. 75–89. London: Palgrave Macmillan. doi.org/10.1007/978-1-349-68308-6_6.

Schneider, D.M. (1961). Introduction. In D.M. Schneider and K. Gough (eds), *Matrilineal Kinship*, pp. 1–29. Berkeley, CA: University of California Press.

Schult, J. and S. Townsend (2012). *River Health in the Daly Catchment: A report to the Daly River Management Advisory Committee.* Report 03/2012D. Darwin: Northern Territory Department of Natural Resources, Environment, The Arts and Sport.

Schulze, H. (2020). Māori economy 2020: Beyond the magic $42 billion Māori asset base. *Our Mahi*, 29 June. Wellington: Bureau of Economic Research Ltd. Available from: www.berl.co.nz/our-mahi/maori-economy-2020.

Schwimmer, B. (1995). Marriage systems: Cross-cousin marriage, bilateral forms. Anthropology course unit, University of Manitoba, Winnipeg.

Secretariat of the Pacific Community (SPC) (2011). *Food Security in the Pacific and East Timor and its Vulnerability to Climate Change.* Nouméa: SPC.

Secretariat of the Pacific Community (SPC) (2013). *Pocket Statistical Summary.* Nouméa: SPC.

Secretariat of the Pacific Community (SPC) (2015). *National Minimum Development Indicators.* Nouméa: SPC. Available from: www.spc.int/nmdi/mdireports.

Secretariat of the Pacific Regional Environment Programme (SPREP) (n.d.). *Improved Waste Management in Kiribati: A case study.* Apia: SPREP. Available from: sprep.org/attachments/CaseStudy/Case-Study-_improved_waste_management_in_Kiribati.pdf.

Secretariat of the Pacific Regional Environmental Programme (SPREP) (2006). *Pacific Islands Framework for Action on Climate Change 2006–2015.* Apia: SPREP.

Secretariat of the Pacific Regional Environment Programme (SPREP) (2017a). Adaptation Fund approves USD 9 million project for FSM. *News*, 28 March. Apia: SPREP. Available from: www.sprep.org/news/adaptation-fund-approves-usd-9-million-project-fsm.

Secretariat of the Pacific Regional Environmental Programme (SPREP) (2017b). Rights of the ocean need to be explored—Cook Islands Prime Minister. *News*, 8 June. Apia: SPREP. Available from: www.sprep.org/news/rights-ocean-need-be-explored-cook-islands-prime-minister.

Secretariat of the Pacific Regional Environmental Programme (SPREP) (2020). *Pacific Climate Change Portal*. Apia: SPREP. Available from: www.pacificclimate change.net/.

Sharma, K.L. (2007). Food security in the South Pacific Island countries with special reference to the Fiji Islands. In G.-K. Basudeb, S.A. Shabd and B. Davis (eds), *Food Insecurity, Vulnerability and Human Rights Failure*, pp. 35–57. Basingstoke, UK: Palgrave Macmillan. doi.org/10.1057/9780230589506_2.

Shiferaw, B., M. Smale, H.J. Braun, M. Reynolds and G. Murichio (2013). Crops that feed the world 10: Past successes and future challenges to the role played by wheat in global food security. *Food Security* 5(3): 291–317. doi.org/10.1007/s12571-013-0263-y.

Shukman, D. (2021). Climate change: Sir David Attenborough in 'act now' warning. *BBC News*, 26 October. Available from: www.bbc.com/news/science-environment-59039485.

Silva, B. (2019). Transnational astronomy: Science, technology and local agenda in Cold War Chile. In D. Pretel, I. Inkster and H. Wendt (eds), *History of Technology: Special Issue—History of Technology in Latin America* 34: 187–202. doi.org/10.5040/9781350085626.0012.

Simbizi, M.C.D., R.M. Bennett and J. Zevenbergen (2014). Land tenure security: Revisiting and refining the concept for sub-Saharan Africa's rural poor. *Land Use Policy* 36: 231–238. doi.org/10.1016/j.landusepol.2013.08.006.

Siméoni, P. (2009). *Atlas du Vanouatou [Atlas of Vanuatu]*. Port Vila: Editions Géo-consulte.

Siméoni, P. and V. Lebot (2012). Spatial representation of land use and population density: Integrated layers of data contribute to environmental planning in Vanuatu. *Human Ecology* 40: 541–555. doi.org/10.1007/s10745-012-9487-2.

Sitan, P. (2014). The development of the tuna fisheries in the Federated States of Micronesia. Delivered to Micronesia in Focus Symposium. The Australian National University, Canberra, 28 February.

Smallacombe, S., M. Davis and R. Quiggin (2006). *Scoping Project on Aboriginal Traditional Knowledge*. Alice Springs, NT: Desert Knowledge Cooperative Research Centre.

Smith, G. (2009). In Ecuador, trees now have rights. *Earth Island Journal* 23(4): 1–15.

Smith, G. and T. Wesley-Smith (eds) (2021). *The China Alternative: Changing regional order in the Pacific Islands.* Canberra: ANU Press. doi.org/10.22459/CA.2021.

Smith, J. (2010). *Agroforestry: Reconciling production with protection of the environment—A synopsis of research literature.* Hamstead Marshall, UK: The Organic Research Centre, Elm Farm.

Smith, L.T. and P. Reid (2000). *Māori Research Development: Kaupapa Māori principles and practices—A literature review.* Prepared for the Ministry of Māori Development by International Research Institute for Māori and Indigenous Education, University of Auckland, with Te Rōpū Rangahau Hauora a Eru Pōmare, Wellington School of Medicine, University of Otago.

Smyth, D.M. (1993). *A Voice in All Places: Aboriginal and Torres Strait Islander interests in Australia's coastal zone.* Consultancy report. Canberra: Resource Assessment Commission.

Smyth, D.M. (1994). *Understanding Country: The importance of land and sea in Aboriginal and Torres Strait Islander societies.* Council for Aboriginal Reconciliation. Canberra: AGPS.

Smyth, D.M. (1997). *Saltwater country.* Oceans Policy Issues Paper No. 6. Canberra: Commonwealth of Australia.

Smyth, D.M. (2001). Management of sea country: Indigenous people's use and management of marine environments. In R. Baker, J. Davies and E. Young (eds), *Working on Country: Contemporary Indigenous management of Australia's lands and coastal regions*, pp. 60–74. Melbourne: Oxford University Press.

Smyth, R.B. (1878). *The Aborigines of Victoria. Volume 1.* Melbourne: Government Printer.

Sopher, D.E. (1965). *The Sea Nomads: A study of the maritime boat people of Southeast Asia.* Singapore: National Museum.

Sopoaga, E. (2015). Tuvalu intervention, 46th Pacific Islands Forum Plenary Session, Port Moresby, 9 September.

Spriggs, M. (1981). Vegetable kingdoms: Taro irrigation and Pacific prehistory. PhD dissertation, The Australian National University, Canberra.

Spriggs, M. (2007). Population in a vegetable kingdom: Aneityum Island (Vanuatu) at European contact in 1830. In P.V. Kirch and J.-L. Rallu (eds), *The Growth and Collapse of Pacific Island Societies: Archaeological and demographic perspectives*, pp. 278–305. Honolulu: University of Hawai`i Press.

Spurgeon, D. (1980). Agroforestry: a promising system of improved land management for Latin America, *Interciencia* 5(3): 176–178.

Squires, D. (2014). Biodiversity conservation in Asia. *Asia & the Pacific Policy Studies* 1(1): 144–159. doi.org/10.1002/app5.13.

Stacey, N. (2007). *Boats to Burn: Bajo fishing activity in the Australian fishing zone.* Canberra: ANU Press. doi.org/10.22459/BB.06.2007.

Star, S.L. and J.R. Griesemer (1989). Institutional ecology, 'translations' and boundary objects: Amateurs and professionals in Berkeley's Museum of Vertebrate Zoology, 1907–39. *Social Studies of Science* 19(3): 387–420. doi.org/10.1177/030631289019003001.

Statistics New Zealand (Stats NZ) (2008). *Farm Types Used in Agricultural Production Statistics: A comparison between ANZSIC96 and ANZSIC06 classifications.* Wellington: Statistics New Zealand.

Sterling, E.J., P. Pascua, A. Sigouin, N. Gazit, L. Mandle, E. Betley, J. Aini, S. Albert, S. Caillon, J.E. Caselle, S.H. Cheng et al. (2020). Creating a space for place and multidimensional well-being: Lessons learned from localizing the SDGs. *Sustainability Science* 15(4): 1129–1147. doi.org/10.1007/s11625-020-00822-w.

Stewart, A. (2019). Tuvalu PM slams Kevin Rudd's proposal to offer Australian citizenship for Pacific resources as neo-colonialism. *ABC News*, 18 February. Available from: www.abc.net.au/news/2019-02-18/tuvalu-pm-slams-kevin-rudd-suggestion-as-neo-colonialism/10820176.

Stober, S. (2010). Ecuador: Mother Nature's utopia. *International Journal of Environmental, Cultural, Economic and Social Sustainability* 6(2): 229–239.

Stolle, D. (2003). The sources of social capital. In M. Hooghe and D. Stolle (eds), *Generating Social Capital: Civil society and institutions in comparative perspective*, pp. 19–42. Basingstoke, UK: Palgrave Macmillan. doi.org/10.1057/9781403979544_2.

Stone, C.D. (1972). *Should Trees Have Standing? Toward legal rights for natural objects.* Los Altos, CA: William Kaufmann.

Storrs, M. and P. Cooke (2001). Caring for country: The development of a formalised structure for land management on Aboriginal lands within the Northern Land Council region of the Northern Territory. *Ngoonjook* (December): 73–79.

Suharti, S., D. Darusman, B. Nugroho and L. Sundawati (2016). Strengthening social capital for propelling collective action in mangrove management. *Wetlands Ecology and Management* 24: 683–695. doi.org/10.1007/s11273-016-9496-9.

Susumu, G. (2013). Interview with Gibson Susumu, Palikir, 13 July.

Susumu, G. and M. Kostka (2010). *Federated States of Micronesia Food Security.* Palikir: Department of Resources and Development.

Susumu, G., J. Wichep and M. Silbanuz (2009). *Preliminary Damage Assessment (PDA) Report Federated States of Micronesia: Agricultural damage report.* December. Palikir: Department of Resources and Development.

Suzuki, D. and J. Hanington (2017). *Just Cool It! The climate crisis and what we can do—A post-Paris agreement.* Sydney: NewSouth Publishing.

Suzuki, D. and P. Knudtson (1997). *Wisdom of the Elders: Sacred native stories of nature.* Sydney: Allen & Unwin.

Suzuki, D. with A. McConnell and A. Mason (2007). *The Sacred Balance: Rediscovering our place in nature.* 2nd edn. Vancouver, BC: D&M Publishers Inc.

Sydney Morning Herald (SMH) (2004). Green Island. *Sydney Morning Herald,* 8 February. Available from: www.smh.com.au/lifestyle/green-island-20040208-gdkqe0.html.

Taaroa, M. (1971). *Mémoires de Marau Taaroa dernière reine de Tahiti—raduit par sa fille, la princesse Ariimanihinihi Takau Pomare* [Memoirs of Marau Taaroa Last Queen of Tahiti—Reduced by her daughter, Princess Ariimanihinihi Takau Pomare]. Translated by Ariimanihinihi Takau Pomare. Paris: Société des Océanistes. Available from: books.openedition.org/sdo/227?lang=en. doi.org/10.4000/books.sdo.227.

Tabani, M. (2014). Lorsque la kastom est mise au service de l'aliénation foncière à Vanuatu [When kastom is used for land alienation in Vanuatu]. In S. Blaise, C. David and V. David (eds), *Le développement durable en Océanie. Vers une éthique nouvelle?* [Sustainable Development in Oceania. Towards a new ethic?] Brussels: Editions Bruyland.

Tabe, T. (2014). The first encounter: Reconceptualizing the relocation of the Gilbertese settlers from atolls in Micronesia to high islands in Melanesia. Presentation to Pacific History Association 21st Biennial Conference 'Lalan Chalan Tala Ara'. Taipei and Taitung, Taiwan, 3–6 December.

Talagi, T. (2015). Niue intervention, 46th Pacific Islands Forum Plenary Session, Port Moresby, 9 September.

Tanasescu, M. (2014). The rights of nature: Theory and practice. In M. Wissenburg and D. Schlosberg (eds), *Political Animals and Animal Politics*, pp. 150–632. London: Palgrave Macmillan. doi.org/10.1007/978-1-349-68308-6_11.

Tavore, J. (2008). Personal Communication. Arawa, Autonomous Region of Bougainville. 22 September.

Taylor, M., A. McGregor and B. Dawson (eds) (2016). *Vulnerability of Pacific Island Agriculture and Forestry to Climate Change*. Nouméa: Secretariat of the Pacific Community.

Teaiwa, K.M. (2014). *Consuming Ocean Island: Stories of people and phosphate from Banaba*. Bloomington, IN: Indiana University Press.

Tegel, S. (2012). Ecuador's green president pushes massive Chinese mine. *The World*, [Boston], 30 March. Available from: www.pri.org/stories/2012-03-30/ecuador-s-green-president-pushes-massive-chinese-mine.

Temkin, K. and W. Rohe (1998). Social capital and neighborhood stability: An empirical investigation. *Housing Policy Debate* 9: 61–88. doi.org/10.1080/10511482.1998.9521286.

Tengö, M., M. Kvarnström, P. Malmer and M. Schultz (2011). *Potentials and Pitfalls in Exchange of Knowledge Systems in Cross-Scale Ecosystem Assessment*. Report from an Informal Expert Meeting with Representatives of the International Indigenous Forum on Biodiversity, EU Experts and Scientists Engaged in Traditional Knowledge and Intergovernmental Science-Policy Platform on Biodiversity and Ecosystem Services. Jokkmokk, Sweden, 21–22 June. doi.org/10.13140/RG.2.1.4468.0807.

Te Puni Kōkiri [Ministry of Māori Development] (n.d.). Website. Wellington: Te Puni Kōkiri. Available from: www.tpk.govt.nz/en.

Te Puni Kōkiri [Ministry of Māori Development] (2011). *Owner Aspirations Regarding the Utilisation of Māori Land (Kongatumanako o ngatangatawhai whenua Māori)*. Wellington: Te Puni Kōkiri.

Te Puni Kōkiri [Ministry of Māori Development] (2014). The actual utilisation and economic value of Māori land. Unpublished report. Wellington: Te Puni Kōkiri.

Te Puni Kōkiri [Ministry of Māori Development] (2019). Successful visit to Chile concludes. Media release, 27 March. Wellington: Te Puni Kōkiri. Available from: www.tpk.govt.nz/mi/mo-te-puni-kokiri/our-stories-and-media/successful-visit-to-chile-concludes.

Thead, E.A. (2016). *Oceans and sea level rise: Consequences of climate change on the oceans*. Paper, October. Washington DC: Climate Institute. Available from: www.climate.org/topics/sea-level.

Thorburn, D., D. Morgan, H. Gill, M. Johnson, H. Wallace-Smith, T. Vigilante, I. Croft and J. Fenton (2004). *Biological and Cultural Significance of the Freshwater Sawfish (*Pristis microdon*) in the Fitzroy River, Kimberley, Western Australia*. Perth: Threatened Species Network.

Thornton, A. (1992). *The Story of Maui by Te Rangikaheke*. Edited with translation and commentary by A. Thornton. Christchurch, NZ: Canterbury Māori Studies.

Tipa, G. and L. Teirney (2006). *A Cultural Health Index for Streams and Waterways: A tool for nationwide use*. Wellington: New Zealand Ministry for the Environment.

Togolo, A. (2008). Matriliny under siege? Economic growth and customary land tenure in Papua New Guinea. Honours thesis, The Australian National University, Canberra.

Togolo, M. (2005). Torau response to change. In A. Regan and H.M. Griffin (eds), *Bougainville before the Conflict*, pp. 274–290. Canberra: Pandanus Books.

Togolo, M. (2020). Interview with Melchior Togolo, 11 February.

Toivanen, T., K. Lummaa, A. Majava, P. Järvensivu, V. Lähde, T. Vaden and J.T. Eronen (2017). The many Anthropocenes: A transdisciplinary challenge for the Anthropocene research. *The Anthropocene Review* 4(3): 183–198. doi.org/10.1177/2053019617738099.

Tong, A. (2014). Statement by H.E. President Anote Tong. 69th United Nations General Assembly, New York, 26 September. Available from: www.un.org/en/ga/69/meetings/gadebate/pdf/KI_en.pdf.

Tonghe Township Office (2016). *History of Tonghe Township*. 2 vols. Tonghe, Taiwan: Tonghe Township Office, Taitung County.

Toussaint, S. (2008). Kimberley friction: Complex attachments to water-places in northern Australia. *Oceania* 78(1): 46–61. doi.org/10.1002/j.1834-4461.2008.tb00027.x.

Toussaint, S. (2014). Fishing for fish and for jaminyjarti in northern Aboriginal Australia. *Oceania* 84(1): 38–51. doi.org/10.1002/ocea.5034.

Toussaint, S., P. Sullivan, S. Yu and M. Mularty, jr (2001). *Fitzroy Valley Indigenous Cultural Values Study: A preliminary assessment*. Perth: Water and Rivers Commission.

Tregear, E.R. (1891). *Māori–Polynesian Comparative Dictionary*. Wellington: Lyon & Blair. Available from: nzetc.victoria.ac.nz/tm/scholarly/tei-TreMaor.html.

Tryon, D. (2005). The languages of Bougainville. In A. Regan and H.M. Griffin (eds), *Bougainville before the Conflict*, pp. 31–46. Canberra: Pandanus Books.

Tsing, A.L. (2011). *Friction: An ethnography of global connection*. Princeton, NJ: Princeton University Press.

Tukuitonga, C. (2015). SPC Director-General intervention, 46th Pacific Islands Forum Plenary Session, Port Moresby, 6 September.

Union of Concerned Scientists (2019). *CO2 and Ocean Acidification: Causes, impacts, solutions*. 30 January, [Updated 6 February]. Cambridge, MA: Union of Concerned Scientists. Available from: www.ucsusa.org/resources/co2-and-ocean-acidification.

United Nations (UN) (1982). *The United Nations Convention on the Law of the Sea*. New York, NY: United Nations. Available from: www.un.org/Depts/los/convention_agreements/texts/unclos/closindx.htm.

United Nations (UN) (1992). *Framework Convention on Climate Change*. Bonn: UNFCCC Secretariat. Available from unfccc.int/files/essential_background/background_publications_htmlpdf/application/pdf/conveng.pdf.

United Nations Conference on Environment and Development (UNCED) (1992). *Earth Summit: Agenda 21*. New York, NY: United Nations. Available from: sustainabledevelopment.un.org/outcomedocuments/agenda21.

United Nations Framework Convention on Climate Change (UNFCCC) (2011). *Report of the Conference of the Parties on its Seventeenth Session, Durban November 28 – December 17, 2011*. Geneva: UNFCCC Secretariat.

United Nations Framework Convention on Climate Change (UNFCCC) (2014). *Lima Call for Climate Action*. Decision 1/CP.20. Geneva: UNFCCC Secretariat.

United Nations Framework Convention on Climate Change (UNFCCC) (2021). *Adaptation Fund*. Geneva: UNFCCC Secretariat. Available from: www.adaptation-fund.org/.

University of the South Pacific (USP) (2012). *Pacific Adaptive Capacity Analysis Framework (PACAF): An assessment of the capacity of 12 local communities in the Pacific Islands to adapt to climate change*. 12 January. Suva: Australian Government Pacific Australia Climate Change Science and Adaptation Planning program. Available from: www.awe.gov.au/sites/default/files/documents/usp-pacific-adaptive-capacity-analysis-framework-12.pdf.

Usher, B. (2019). *Renewable Energy: A primer for the twenty-first century*. Earth Institute Sustainability Primers. New York, NY: Columbia University. doi.org/10.7312/ushe18784.

Usseglio, P., A. Schuhbauer and A. Friedlander (2014). Collaborative approach to fisheries management as a way to increase the effectiveness of future regulations in the Galapagos archipelago. In J. Denkinger and L. Vinueza (eds), *The Galapagos Marine Reserve: A dynamic social–ecological system*, pp. 187–202. New York, NY: Springer Science and Business Media.

VandenBroucke, H., P. Mournet, R. Malapa, J.C. Glaszmann, H. Chair, H. and V. Lebot (2015a). Comparative analysis of genetic variation in kava (*Piper methysticum*) assessed by SSR and DaRT reveals zygotic foundation and clonal diversification. *Genome* 58(1): 1–11. doi.org/10.1139/gen-2014-0166.

VandenBroucke, H., P. Mournet, H. Vignes, H. Chair, R. Malapa, M.F. Duval and V. Lebot (2015b). Somaclonal variants of taro (*Colocasia esculenta Schott*) and yam (*Dioscorea alata L.*) are incorporated into farmers' varietal portfolios in Vanuatu. *Genetic Resources and Crop Evolution* 63(3): 495–511. doi.org/10.1007/s10722-015-0267-x.

van Groeningen, K.J., C. van Kessel and V. Hungate (2012). Increased greenhouse-gas intensity of rice production under future atmospheric conditions. *Nature Climate Change Letters* 3(3): 288–291. doi.org/10.1038/nclimate1712.

Vanhulst, J. and A.E. Beling (2013). Buen vivir: la irrupción de América Latina en el campo gravitacional del desarrollo sostenible [Good living: The irruption of Latin America in the gravitational field of sustainable development]. Revibec: revista iberoamericana de economía ecológica [*Ibero-American Journal of Ecological Economics*] 21: 1–14.

Van Ness, P. and M. Gurtov (eds) (2017). *Learning from Fukushima: Nuclear power in East Asia*. Canberra: ANU Press. doi.org/10.22459/LF.09.2017.

Vanuatu National Statistics Office (VNSO) (2009). *National Census of Population and Housing. Summary release*. Port Vila: Ministry of Finance and Economic Management.

Vaughan, A. (2020). Antarctica's doomsday glacier is melting. Can we save it in time? *New Scientist*, 15 January. Available from: www.newscientist.com/article/mg24532650-900-antarcticas-doomsday-glacier-is-melting-can-we-save-it-in-time/.

Visser, M.E. and C. Both (2005). Shifts in phenology due to global climate change: The need for a yardstick. *Proceedings of the Royal Society B* 272(1581): 2561–2569. doi.org/10.1098/rspb.2005.3356.

Visser, M.E., C. Both and M.M. Lambrechts (2004). Global climate change leads to mistimed avian reproduction. *Advances in Ecological Research* 35: 89–110. doi.org/10.1016/S0065-2504(04)35005-1.

Viteri, C. and C. Chávez (2007). Legitimacy, local participation, and compliance in the Galapagos Marine Reserve. *Ocean & Coastal Management* 50(3): 253–274. doi.org/10.1016/j.ocecoaman.2006.05.002.

von Benda-Beckmann, F. and K. von Benda-Beckmann (2006). How communal is communal and whose communal is it? Lessons from Minangkabau. In F. von Benda-Beckmann, K. von Benda-Beckmann and M.G. Wiber (eds), *Changing Properties of Property*, pp. 194–217. Oxford, UK: Berghahn.

Waitangi Tribunal (2011). *Ko Aotearoa Tēnei: A report into claims concerning New Zealand law and policy affecting Māori culture and identity. Te Taumata Tuarua.* WAI 262, Vol. 1. Wellington: Ministry of Justice. Available from: forms. justice.govt.nz/search/Documents/WT/wt_DOC_68356054/KoAotearoa TeneiTT1W.pdf.

Walker, B.H., L.H. Gunderson, A.P. Kinzig, C. Folke, S.R. Carpenter and L. Schultz (2006). A handful of heuristics and some propositions for understanding resilience in social-ecological systems. *Ecology and Society* 11(1): 13. Available from: www. ecologyandsociety.org/vol11/iss1/art13/. doi.org/10.5751/ES-01530-110113.

Walker, R. (2004). *Ka Whawhai Tonu Matou: Struggle without end.* 2nd edn. Auckland, NZ: Penguin Books.

Walsh, C. (2010). Development as *buen vivir*: Institutional arrangements and (de)colonial entanglements. *Development* 53(1): 15–21. doi.org/10.1057/dev. 2009.93.

Walter, A. and V. Lebot (2007). *Gardens of Oceania.* ACIAR Monograph No. 122. Canberra: Australian Centre for International Agricultural Research.

Walter, R. and R. Hamilton (2014). A cultural landscape approach to community-based conservation in Solomon Islands. *Ecology and Society* 19(4): 41. doi.org/ 10.5751/ES-06646-190441.

Ward, A. (1999). *An Unsettled History: Treaty claims in New Zealand today.* Wellington: Bridget Williams Books. doi.org/10.7810/9780908912971.

Ward, G. and E. Kingdom (1995). *Land, Custom and Practice in the South Pacific.* Melbourne: Cambridge University Press. doi.org/10.1017/CBO97805115 97176.

Webb, A.P. and P.S. Kench (2010). The dynamic response of reef islands to sea-level rise: Evidence from multi-decadal analysis of island change in the central Pacific. *Global and Planetary Change* 72(3): 234–246. doi.org/10.1016/j.glo placha.2010.05.003.

Weightman, B. (1989). *Agriculture in Vanuatu. A historical review*. Portsmouth, UK: British Friends of Vanuatu.

Weiner, J. and K. Glaskin (2007). *Customary Land Tenure and Registration in Australia and Papua New Guinea: Anthropological perspectives*. Asia-Pacific Environment Monograph 3. Canberra: ANU Press. doi.org/10.22459/CLTRA PNG.06.2007.

West, P. (2006). *Conservation is Our Government Now: The politics of ecology in Papua New Guinea*. Durham, NC: Duke University Press. doi.org/10.2307/j.ctv1198x8f.

Westervelt, W.D. (2009). *Legends of Maui: A demi-god of Polynesia*. Honolulu: Evinity Publishing.

Whanganui Iwi and the Crown (2012). *Tūtohu Whakatupua*. Agreement between Whanganui Iwi and the Crown, 30 August 2012. Wellington: New Zealand Government. Available from: static1.squarespace.com/static/55914fd1e4b01 fb0b851a814/t/560842cbe4b017614f85bf30/1443381963419/Whanganui+ River+Agreement.pdf.

Wheen, N.R. and J. Hayward (2012). *Treaty of Waitangi Settlements*. Wellington: Bridget Williams Books. doi.org/10.7810/9781927131381.

Whitehead, P.J., D.M.J.S. Bowman, N. Preece, F. Fraser and P. Cooke (2003). Customary use of fire by Indigenous peoples in northern Australia: Its contemporary role in savanna management. *International Journal of Wildland Fire* 12: 415–425. doi.org/10.1071/WF03027.

Williams, C., K. Galloway McLean, G. Raygorodetsky, A. Ramos-Castillo and B. Barrett (2013). *Traditional Knowledge & Climate Science Toolkit*. Darwin: United Nations University. Available from: collections.unu.edu/view/UNU:1500.

Williams, H.W. (1975 [1844]). *A Dictionary of the Māori Language*. 7th edn. Wellington: A.R. Shearer, Government Printer NZ.

Williams, T.O. (1998). Multiple uses of common pool resources in semi-arid West Africa: A survey of existing practices and options for sustainable resource management. *ODI Natural Resource Perspectives* 38: 1–10. Available from: www.researchgate.net/publication/42765194_Multiple_Uses_of_Common_Pool_ Resources_in_Semi-Arid_West_Africa_A_Survey_of_Existing_Practices_and_ Options_for_Sustainable_Resources_Management.

Wisner, B. (2004). Assessments of capability and vulnerability. In G. Bankoff, G. Frerks and D. Hillhorst (eds), *Mapping Vulnerability: Disasters, development and people*, pp. 183–194. London: Earthscan.

Wohling, M. (2009). The problem of scale in Indigenous knowledge: A perspective from northern Australia. *Ecology and Society* 14(1): 1. Available from: www.ecologyandsociety.org/vol14/iss1/art1/. doi.org/10.5751/ES-02574-140101.

Wonder Badjao (2017). *Earth Day Diary: Badjao spearfishermen, spearfishing in Bohol, Philippines*. [Video]. 7 August. Available from: www.youtube.com/watch?v=D6ND6iEM4eY.

Wood, D. (1992). *The Power of Maps*. New York, NY: The Guilford Press.

Wood, L. (2016). *Tupunis Slow Food Festival, Lamenu Nakamal Lenakel, Tanna, Vanuatu*. Port Vila: Vanuatu Cultural Centre.

Woodward, E. (2008). Social networking for Aboriginal land management in remote northern Australia. *Australasian Journal of Environmental Management* 15: 241–252. doi.org/10.1080/14486563.2008.9725208.

Woodward, E. (2010). Creating the Ngan'gi seasons calendar: Reflections on engaging Indigenous knowledge authorities in research learning communities. *International Journal of Learning in Social Contexts* 2: 125–137.

Woodward, E., S. Jackson, M. Finn and P. Marrfurra McTaggart (2012). Utilising Indigenous seasonal knowledge to understand aquatic resource use and inform water resource management in northern Australia. *Ecological Management & Restoration* 13(1): 58–64. doi.org/10.1111/j.1442-8903.2011.00622.x.

Woodward, E. and P. Marrfurra McTaggart (2015). Transforming cross-cultural water research through trust, participation and place. *Geographical Research* 54(2): 129–142. doi.org/10.1111/1745-5871.12136.

Woodward, E. and P. Marrfurra McTaggart (2019). Co-developing Indigenous seasonal calendars to support 'healthy country, healthy people' outcomes. *Global Health Promotion* 26: 26–34. doi.org/10.1177/1757975919832241.

World Bank (2014a). *The Fruit of Her Labour: Promoting gender-equitable agribusiness in Papua New Guinea—Cocoa sector summary*. Washington, DC: The World Bank.

World Bank (2014b). *Hardship and Vulnerability in the Pacific Island Countries: A regional companion to the World Development Report 2014*. Washington, DC: The World Bank.

World Bank (2019). *Country Data: Papua New Guinea.* Washington, DC: The World Bank. Available from: data.worldbank.org/country/papua-new-guinea.

World Commission on Environment and Development (WCED) (1987). *Our Common Future.* New York, NY: Oxford University Press.

World Health Organization (WHO) (2010). Pacific Islands pay heavy price for abandoning traditional diet. *Bulletin of the World Health Organization* 88(7): 484–485.

Wright, G. (2001). *Aboriginal Use of the Sea in South-Western and South-Eastern Victoria.* Lakes Entrance, Vic.: Research Unit, National Native Tribunal.

Wright, R. (2004). *A Short History of Progress.* Cambridge, MA: Da Capo Press.

Wu, S.-Y. (2000). *The New Taiwan Wild Plants: World of the 'Amis wild plants.* Taipei: Big Trees Culture.

Wunambal Gaambera Aboriginal Corporation (2010). *Wunambal Gaambera Healthy Country Plan: Looking after Wunambal Gaambera Country 2010–2020.* Kalumburu, WA: Wunambal Gaambera Aboriginal Corporation.

Xinhua (2019). Cocoa production in PNG jumps in past decade. *Xinhuanet,* [Beijing], 4 January. Available from: www.xinhuanet.com/english/2019-01/04/c_137719323.htm.

Yen, A.C., T.Y. Chen and P.C. Liu (2007). Strategies on issues of ecotourism development in Indigenous areas: Case of Xinguang and Cinsbu communities, Hsinchu County. *Modern Land Affairs* 316: 72–84.

Yen, A.C. and D.W. Kuan (2004). Traditional institution and the institutional choice: Two CPR self-governing cases of Tayal tribe in Taiwan Indigenes. *Journal of Geographical Science* (37): 27–49.

Yen, A.C. and G.Z. Yang (2004). *Indigenous Land Institution and Economic Development.* Taipei: Dao Xiang Press.

Yoder, L. (2018). Tracing social capital: How stakeholder group interactions shape agricultural water quality restoration in the Florida Everglades. *Land Use Policy* 77: 354–361. doi.org/10.1016/j.landusepol.2018.05.038.

Youkee, M. (2018). Indigenous Chileans defend their land against loggers with radical tactics. *The Guardian,* 14 June. Available from: www.theguardian.com/world/2018/jun/14/chile-mapuche-indigenous-arson-radical-environmental-protest.

Yu, S. (2003). Ngapa kunangkul (living water): An Indigenous view of groundwater. In A. Gaynor, A. Haebich and M. Trinca (eds), *Country: Visions of land and people in Western Australia*, pp. 33–55. Perth: Western Australian Museum.

Ziembicki, M.R., J.C.Z. Woinarski and B. Mackey (2013). Evaluating the status of species using Indigenous knowledge: Novel evidence for major native mammal declines in northern Australia. *Biological Conservation* 157: 78–92. doi.org/10.1016/j.biocon.2012.07.004.

Zurba, M. and F. Berkes (2014). Caring for country through participatory art: Creating a boundary object for communicating Indigenous knowledge and values. *Local Environment: The International Journal of Justice and Sustainability* 19(8): 821–836. doi.org/10.1080/13549839.2013.792051.

www.ingramcontent.com/pod-product-compliance
Lightning Source LLC
Chambersburg PA
CBHW051440270326
41932CB00025B/3382